STEP
IT
DOWN

STEP
IT
DOWN

Games, Plays, Songs, and Stories from the

Afro-American Heritage

by *Bessie Jones* and *Bess Lomax Hawes*

HARPER & ROW, PUBLISHERS

New York   Evanston   San Francisco   London

1817

STANDARD BOOK NUMBER: 06-011783-4

LIBRARY OF CONGRESS CATALOG CARD NUMBER: 71-83598

Contents

4: Singing Plays   67

5: Ring Plays   87

6: Dances   123

7: House Plays and Home Amusements   149

8: Outdoor Games   171

9: Songs and Stories   189

Acknowledgments

I should first like to thank all my students who have so patiently listened while I developed and reformulated, in the guise of lectures, many of the ideas in this book.

My teaching colleagues—Edmund Carpenter, Ralph Heidsiek, Joan Rayfield, Councill Taylor, and Gregory Truex—read portions of the manuscript and were unfailingly helpful and stimulating in their comments. More distant associates—Roger Abrahams, Alan Dundes, and Brian Sutton-Smith—were kind enough to read the entire manuscript in its early stages and to cheer me on. I also owe appreciation to Mildred Johnson, Margot Slocum, Guy Carawan, Barbara LaPan, and Graham Wickham for editorial comments and assistance.

The workshop mentioned in the Introduction took place at the Idyllwild Arts Foundation, now a facility of the University of Southern California, under the direction of Max and Beatrice Krone; to them, my appreciation and thanks. Radio station KPFK and Ed Cray kindly allowed me to quote from a radio interview with Mrs. Jones.

Alan Lomax, who introduced me to Mrs. Jones, also read the manuscript, gave extensive editorial advice, and, most important, allowed me to quote from the many sensitive and skillful taped interviews he and his wife, Antoinette Marchand, had already held with Mrs. Jones.

Corey Hawes Denos, Naomi Hawes Bishop, and Nicholas Hawes typed manuscript, copied music, sang the harmony parts, tried out the directions, and took extensive field notes. I couldn't have done it without them. Baldwin Hawes not only tolerated his wife's being "with book" during an interminable period, he approved and encouraged the project in a hundred ways.

The Georgia Sea Island Singers—John Davis, Peter Davis, Mabel Hillary, Emma Ramsey, and Ed Young of Tennessee—helped both Mrs. Jones and me without stint during the entire workshop period. Their special and essential contributions are acknowledged throughout the pages that follow.

B.L.H.

Introduction

This book is really about one of the ways of growing up in the United States. In part, it is a memoir—the long rememberings of a Negro woman born in the Southern poverty belt around the turn of this century, a detailing of the mind and body and heart skills she learned in her "days coming up." As set down here, the games and dances that she remembers form a kind of double image, for throughout them moves a sense of the shape and thrust of the crowded, impoverished, life-demanding, life-loving complex of the Negro family of fifty years ago.

Mrs. Bessie Jones, one of the authors of this book, was born sixty-five years ago in Dawson, Georgia—a small black farming community—and grew up like thousands of other girls of her time in the rural South. She started to work when she was still a child, helping out her big family; she chopped cotton, planted potatoes, watched out for the littler children, took her schooling when her family could spare her and as it was offered. Her formal education ended when she was ten.

Balanced on the edge of real poverty almost all her life, she learned early how to amuse and entertain herself and others. Music—especially singing—is not only one of the least expensive art forms; it is also one in which you can participate while you are doing something else. There was a great deal of singing in Mrs. Jones's family; it didn't cost a cent or take any time away from the job to be done. Her maternal and paternal grandparents had sung while they worked in the fields during slavery times; some of the songs their little granddaughter learned from them were then well over a hundred years old. Mrs. Jones's mother was a fine singer and dancer; though her father never sang, "he could play any instrument you gave him."

Dawson itself must have been a musical community during Mrs. Jones's childhood. She speaks lovingly of the beautiful singing of the "old people" in the little community church on Sundays, of weekday mornings in the same small building, turned schoolhouse until the next Sunday, when the schoolteacher would lead the children in morning hymns and school songs. She tells of the long Southern twilights, when the grownups would be busy with their own affairs and the children would run outside to their games and mock dances.

I remember a hundred games, I suppose; I would say a hundred because there are so many of them. We had all kinds of plays; we had house plays, we had outdoor plays. Some of the plays have songs, some have just plays—you know, just acts or whatnot. . . . In my time coming up, the parents they would give quiltings and they would have songs they would sing while they were quilting and we would listen at those songs. And we would have egg crackings and taffy pullings and we would hear all those things—riddleses and stories and different things. That's why I'm so loaded. . . . And then I has a great remembrance of those things, that's another thing about it.

Bessie Jones, "loaded" as she was with games and songs and her own particular and irrepressible joy in living, got married and moved to her husband's home, St. Simons Island, one of the long string of coastal islands that edge the eastern shoreline of North America. There she met the Georgia Sea Island Singers, a Negro choral group whose early period has been described in a book by Mrs. Lydia Parrish (see Bibliography). The Singers, dedicated to the preservation of the old musical ways of their forebears, were so impressed with Mrs. Jones's buoyant personality, extensive repertoire, and experienced singing style that they invited her to join their group; she became one of the only mainlanders ever so honored. Mrs. Jones, in her turn, felt at home with the Singers' dignity and with their pride in their African and Afro-American heritage—the same kind of dignity and pride that had been so carefully taught her by her own parents and grandparents.

During the summer of 1964, Mrs. Jones and I met together in California to engage in a highly unusual educational experiment. Together with four other members of the Georgia Sea Islanders,* we presented a two-week workshop for Californians in which we attempted to teach some of the games, dances, and songs of the Negro South. The Singers—led by Mrs. Jones when we were dealing with children's activities—took on the somewhat unfamiliar formal responsibility of teachers; I functioned as organizer and interlocutor. The events of those crowded and productive weeks actually germinated this book.

We met from two to four hours every day with a shifting group of white Californians as students, perhaps twenty at a time: some teenagers, a few children, mothers, fathers, teachers, recreation specialists, dancers. Every day the same scene would be repeated. Mrs. Jones would urge everyone on their feet to play; the students, meanwhile, with pencils and notebooks ready, waited to be told *what* to play and *how* to play it. The white students, myself included, were desperately anxious to know what was going to happen, to understand the "rules"; then we could decide whether to play this particular game or not. After all, we might be asked to do something we didn't know how to do; we would perhaps be awkward, everyone would see our failure, we would "lose."

The impasse was finally resolved by having the Singers demonstrate first; they would play the game for us and we would then repeat it. The Islanders thought this was all rather silly, but for me, this arrangement provided a fascinating double perspective. As I watched first the Islanders and then the students, it seemed to me that the *game* was the same (we had learned the "rules") but the *play* was not (our emotional commitment and consequent emotional gratification was different). As the Singers, most of them grandparents, several in their sixties, danced their way through countless repetitions of "Little Johnny Brown" with fresh joy and humor each

---

* John Davis, Peter Davis, Emma Ramsey, and Mabel Hillary. Mr. Ed Young of Memphis, Tennessee, though not a regular member of the Singers, also joined us.

time, it seemed to me that I could never recall having played any game with that much involvement, that much gaiety, even as a child. Other white students confirmed my impression; we had all played games, but not quite that way, somehow.

Looking back on it now, the situation seems obvious: with all the mutual goodwill in the world, we did not really have the same thing in mind at all. Some of the conflicts were plain at the time; others became clearer in later reflection. To summarize them briefly, where the one group (white) anticipated competition, the other (black) expected cooperation and mutual support. Where one promoted individual skill and achievement, the other wanted general participation. Where one insisted on knowledge of and compliance with a set of rules, the other stressed dramatic interpretation and perceptiveness. Those of us who thought of games in terms of winning or losing were especially frustrated; there were no winners and few losers. I think most of the white students felt that we were not really playing games at all; we were doing something else, but what it was, we weren't sure.

A verbal cue from Mrs. Jones was, for me, the key to the problem. Folklorists have often reported the Negro use of the noun "play" where a non-Negro might say "game." This had never seemed especially significant to me; I assumed the terms were interchangeable. Then one day, referring to "Bob-a-Needle," Mrs. Jones remarked, "That's a game. Of course it's a play, too, but really it's a *game.*"

Checking back through my taped interviews, I discovered that Mrs. Jones did indeed use the nouns "play," "game," and "dance" to refer to different items in her repertoire, and in a logical and definable way. She referred to abstract (nonmimetic) movement patterns, especially when performed by couples, as "dances." (Rudimentary "dances," seeming to function largely as rhythm and motion practice for the very young, she called "jumps" or "skips.") The term "game" she reserved not exactly for competitive but rather for conditional sequences of actions. For example, in "Bob-a-Needle," *if* you are caught with the needle, you pay a forfeit; *if* you pass it on successfully, you do not.

By far the bulk of her repertoire, however, she called "plays." Suddenly it occurred to me that the noun "play" has more than one meaning; in addition to being, according to Webster's, "exercise or action for amusement or diversion," it can also be "a drama . . . a composition . . . portraying life or character by means of dialogue and action."

Using this second definition as a starting point, the special quality of fun the Sea Islanders were having became clearer. When they "played," they were constructing over and over again small life dramas; they were improvising on the central issues of their deepest concerns; they were taking on new personalities for identification or caricature; they were *acting*.

Over half the repertoire of amusements contained in this book, then, are "plays" and should be regarded as such. They are ceremonials, small testimonies to the ongoingness of life, not miniature battles. In order to be enjoyed properly, therefore, they must be done properly—that is, joyfully and humorously but with an underlying seriousness of intent to make it all come out right, to make, as Mrs. Jones says so often and so touchingly, "a beautiful play."

Even the "games" have their basis in dramatic action; the difference seems to be in the possibilities for variation in the outcome of the plot. Competition is present, but it is on an extremely simple and unelaborate level. (I found, for example, no specialized and exclusive name for "it." Mrs. Jones did not use the term at all; when there was such a player, he was referred to casually as "the one in the middle" or "the counter.")

Both games and plays, however, are full of dramatic confrontations and conflict, the games perhaps more openly. The world the Southern Negro child awakes to every morning is a complex and often brutal one. The openly dramatized content of his reflections upon this world is apt, therefore, to be very down-to-earth. Both games and plays deal with realistic situations: getting food, quarreling with your mother, finding a "partner," working. And though the action is, in a dramatic sense, "realistic" and emotionally satisfying, the comment of the accompanying songs is frequently ironic and detached.

Two further factors important to both games and plays should be mentioned. Almost all must be performed by a group; thus all dramatic conflict is worked through in public, so to speak. Secondly, almost all involve both music and dance, and thus nearly the whole range of expressive behavior available to human beings is called upon.

Most of the above ideas came through to me first while I was actually playing the games. Mrs. Jones was right; there is no play until play begins. Though I had "known" for a long time that gesture and motion are forms of communication, I had never *felt* before, for example, that when you turn your back on someone you truly reject him. And when each of us stepped out into the center of the ring while the group stood and clapped for us, I think all the white students felt a sudden panic. There was no one to compete with, no one to compare ourselves to, nothing in our cultural experience had prepared us for this moment when we must say by our actions what we were, ungraded and unranked. The Islanders knew that the clapping group was signaling their support; the white students clapped and watched to see if they couldn't do it better.

However, most important in explaining the meaning of these games to me—the why as well as the how—were the sensitive and accurate comments of Mrs. Jones. Most of the real ideas, as well as the repertoire of games, in this book are hers.

All her life she has taken care of children—her little brothers and sisters, neighbor children, her own babies and grandbabies, the sons and daughters of her white employers, for whom she was both house-keeper and nurse. She speaks of the games she knows and has taught children so many times with the expertise of an educator and the joy of a participant. She declares forthrightly that her games are "good for children" and she knows just how: which help develop rhythmic coordination or big muscle skills, which promote responsiveness or sharing. She has sifted out through her memories of her own child-hood the activities that meant—and still mean—most to her; she has added others to them from her more recent experience, "collecting," as do all the great folk singers, new games and plays that especially appealed to her. Today she is a carrier of the finest of that huge repertoire of children's games, family pastimes, and infant amuse-ments of the Southern Negro family of yesterday and today.

It is important to realize, however, that when Mrs. Jones and I were talking and singing and dancing together, she was intent on transferring to me—and through me, to a wider audience—the strength and the vitality of her childhood traditions. The shadowy hurts, the fights, the fears and betrayals, the deep and hidden wounds suffered by all children, and especially by those growing up in the black South, do not appear here except by implication. She was not *documenting* anything; she was *teaching*. And as a teacher, she was passing on that part of her knowledge she considered to be "good" for children.

She may have remembered some plays which, in her mind, were of dubious value. She did not tell me these, nor did I press her for them. These are her free offerings—the best she knew—to her own people and, in a larger sense, to all children.

Santa Monica, California   B.L.H.

Note to Parents and Teachers

Many participants in the California workshop asked me to make available or publish the games and songs they had been learning. Somehow the simple setting down of words and tunes and actions had lost its validity for me; perhaps I have absorbed too much of Mrs. Jones's point of view. The "how" had become more important than the "what" and the "why" most vital of all. So I have tried to write an instruction book which will give some clues to the understanding of all three, in the hope that parents and teachers who may use this book may come to have an appreciation for the totality of this tradition, and not just rifle it for its substance.

For this reason, I have organized the book in an unconventional way. In the first place, I have included what seemed to me relevant and useful historical data, and I have indicated where more could be found. I have also described some games as well as some adult musical activities which are obviously impractical for the average schoolyard or family; these were included for their own interest and for the insights they lend to the over-all subject. Lastly, I have grouped the games, not in over-all order of difficulty, but in the categories to which Mrs. Jones allotted them: "clapping plays," "jumps and skips," "ring plays" and so on. This will, I hope, make clear her developmental picture of how the child matures, socially and physically.

Each section is preceded by a general introduction in which the category is discussed, historical background provided, and any special techniques of dance or musicianship outlined. These section introductions also include some statements on the relative ease or difficulty of the specific games that follow. Generally, within each section, the games are arranged from "easy" to "hard."

Each game or play has its own double introduction: a brief explanatory statement attempting to set the game in historical or functional perspective;

and comments from Mrs. Jones (in italics) which pin down that quality which is so elusive, the emotional "feel" of the game.

The following statements are suggestions for teachers and parents on how to use this book. (See also directions for dance steps, pp. 44–46, and suggestions for ring play on pp. 90–91.

1. These games are an enormous amount of fun, but the real fun doesn't happen until the games are actually *played*. Leaf through the book and try different ones out, selecting, as Mrs. Jones does, those that especially appeal to you.

2. Learn the song, if it is a singing game, by singing it over and over until you have it by heart. Then change the order of the verses—or add new ones from your own imagination—as the spirit of the game *as it is being played* dictates. Once you have the pattern down, don't be afraid to change the words to fit the particular situation. One easy thing to do, for example, is to put the names of different children into such games as "Way Go, Lily."

3. The tunes of these songs are basically quite simple; some have only three or four notes. Like almost all black singers, Mrs. Jones likes to decorate her melodies with a variety of free vocal effects such as slides or scoops, some of which have been indicated by the grace notes used in the music notation. When first trying a song out, *ignore the grace notes until you have learned the basic tune* (shown in the standard sized notes). Then try adding one or two short slides up to or away from a note (as indicated by the grace notes) but do not try to emphasize them or give them a hard-and-fast fixed time value or make them into distinct, athletic vocal leaps. Their effect should be casual, like short, light *glissandi*. The great gospel singer Mahalia Jackson does a lot of this vocal ornamentation; she has been described as adding "flowers and feathers" to her songs. A "flower" or a "feather" here and there, you will find, adds greatly to the rhythmic swing and sparkle of Mrs. Jones's tunes.

4. Many of Mrs. Jones's plays are chanted rather than sung. Such chants have been written out on the music staff with "x" notes, in order to approximate the pitch pattern as well as the rhythm. When trying these, do *not* worry about absolute pitch; simply let your eye travel along the curve of the "melodic line" and follow it with your speaking voice. You will find the effect falls just halfway between speaking and singing.

5. Do *not* try to accompany the songs on the piano, or even on such portable "folk" instruments as the guitar or the auto-harp. All they need is a simple off-beat clap, as described in the introduction to "Clapping Plays." If you are playing the game yourself, as you should be, you won't have time to play an instrument anyway.

6. The singing games should be danced, not played in a "see who can get there first" spirit. The really important stylistic quality is *to move in time with the music;* the social value being expressed, I believe, is coordination of individual and group effort. This is helped enormously by the steady offbeat clapping and the rhythmic quality of the lead voice. It is much easier to sing rhythmically when you are yourself in motion; and this is why the teachers (or lead singers) should themselves be playing the game.

7. The lead singing part can be—and often is—changed "in mid-flight," while the game is going on. Children can frequently take over on the lead

once they know the song, and will do a good job of it. After all, it was their game first.

8. If there is a leading part in terms of the *action,* however, as there is in all the ring plays, be sure to give everybody a turn at it if you have to play the same game right through recess. The Islanders were always uncomfortable if we had to stop "in the middle"; it violated the basic democratic construction of the game itself.

9. Don't be afraid of what appear to be the "hard" games. A few minutes' quiet observation of children, both white and black, at work on their own tradition of singing games, jacks, jump rope, hop scotch and so on, will convince you that many adults seriously underestimate the motor capacities of children, not to mention their attention span and capacity for self-motivation.

10. Consider the possibility that some of the children, depending on their backgrounds, might already know these games or others like them. Perhaps they can teach the teacher.

11. Enjoy yourself. This is a beautiful and democratic tradition, full of joy and the juices of life. Don't be too solemn, or too organized; these are for *play.*

1:
Baby Games and Plays

If I rock this baby to sleep,
  Go to sleepy, little baby,
Someday he will remember me,
  Go to sleepy, little baby. . . .

Mrs. Jones and Miss Emma Ramsey and I sat one long morning around the kitchen table, drinking coffee and talking about babies.

Miss Ramsey didn't talk much. She kept saying in a mock-sad voice, "I had to go to work, when I was twelve—I never had time to learn any plays!" And then we would all laugh, because underneath the comedy was a real memory of a real little girl put to work too young, and what could you do about it now but laugh a little?

Mrs. Jones had never had much time to play with the babies herself, so the number of "infant amusements" the two ladies remembered that morning was not very large. But Mrs. Jones had thought about babies a great deal and about how to begin the long process of introducing them to the world. She had much counsel and advice for me on general matters of baby care, and as we settled down into a long, comfortable chat, she began with what was to prove her major theme: that a child's first need is to learn what it is to love and to be loved.

When you get a child or a job, [taking care of children] do like I used to do—don't _suffer_ the little childrens. Get them to sleep in a good peaceable way. Treat them like you wish to be treated.

I think babies should be rocked at times, of course. I don't think a baby ever should be throwed aside. It gives them—well, I don't know —I think you should rock him _some_ anyway, if you just shake him a little while. It does something for him. He's better—like he's nursed.

You can see sometimes when you carry him in the room and he just knows you're going to throw him away—carry him in a room and shut the door and stick a bottle or a pacifier in his mouth. And he'll just look at you, and it looks like he ain't not ready. He just know you're going to carry him in the room and throw him away, and he go to pulling to you and cleaving to you. Well, he _need_ that cleaving to you. He _need_ you to take a little more pains with him at that time. . . . He sure do. . . .

Like all country people, Mrs. Jones had little patience with new-fangled ways.

The poor little baby, they used to could get him to sleep. He would be normal and sleep normal, and he would have a good way of sleeping because they were normal babies. But now you don't know what he is yourself, and he don't know _himself_, because he drink all manners of kind of milk, you see. And the baby is supposed to be nursed off his mother's milk and none other milk _but_ that. But now you expect him to be quiet and laugh, and he got bull's milk in him, or goat milk, or something. He can't be so quiet with all that crazy kind of milk in him. . . .

As I listened, it seemed to me that the accuracy of Mrs. Jones's information was not nearly as important as the accuracy of her feelings. In the era of the plastic shell and the infant car seat, she still thought that all babies needed to know the warmth of a human lap, the touch of human hands. At one point, she confessed with a little embarrassment,

I stretch babies too. Sometimes I get with people nowadays, their babies ain't stretched out, and I'm sitting down looking at the baby, and I slip and play with him and stretch him. . . . Their backs need to be stretched like you stretch yourself, you know? Pull his arms, you know, and his leg, and sometimes hold him in the midst of his back and have his weight pull him. That keeps his back from being humped. . . . A lot of people don't think about stretching babies; all *they want to do is to lay 'em down. But he need exercise, just like your ownself. . . .*

Mrs. Jones, however, does not accept tradition uncritically. She looks at procedures with the thoughtful and analytical eye of an educator; she is concerned, ultimately, with results. For this reason, though she is a tradition carrier, she does not hesitate to say when she thinks the "old peoples" were wrong.

Some things way back there I kind of disapprove with now that I've brought up children myself . . . like you telling a baby, "Tee, tee?" when you're telling him, "See, see?" I think you should tell him directly what you're saying. You should tell him, "See that?" instead of "Tee dat?" because he hear you saying that and he'll come right up saying the same thing, and you're going to have to teach him over again. I think you should speak the words pronounced right. Long years ago, when I was coming up, they didn't do it; they talked baby talk to babies, you see. But I think it's right to speak plain, or after a while you got to straighten him over again. Because a baby want to learn how to talk. . . .

She commented dryly on the not infrequent exhaustion and boredom that the most devoted of mothers sometimes feels.

I sang to babies so much, just all church songs, you know, just sing and sing and sing, just anything I could think of. And at last one day, I jumped off on "Casey Jones." Mama come to the door, she say, "Well! I never heard nobody put no babies to sleep on 'Casey Jones'!" I had just sung on out . . . I had just sung and sung and sung, and he wouldn't go to sleep, so I got off on "Casey Jones"! I sing all manner of songs. . . . You sing some of those hymns, old draggy songs, you likely to go off to sleep with the baby. . . .

Throughout the morning, she interlarded her advice and general comments with the little plays and songs and rhymes in the section to follow. As I thought about the whole conversation later, it seemed to me that she was showing me the starting point of all the qualities she hoped to develop in children: strong, flexible, well-coordinated bodies, rhythmic sensitivity, and most important, a quality which I find hard to name. Perhaps the best word for it is "interplay": rapport with and concern for another person, a kind of responsiveness which can sustain you even when you are alone.

Sometimes I want to break 'em out of this rocking in my lap. . . . And you ease right on the bed with 'em and continue rocking or continue patting, and you hum sometimes, just a little hum to him, and he'll hum himself—some of them will. Some babies will get that little hum to themselves. Well, he know he needs that attention, that's why. That's a great little thing to think about, he need that attention. . . . He need that humming, and that be the only way he'll get it, humming himself.

> If I rock this baby to sleep,
>   Go to sleepy, little baby,
> Someday he will remember me,
>   Go to sleepy, little baby. . . .

Go to Sleepy, Little Baby

This is a lullaby, such as getting the babies to sleep, which I love.
I love so well getting the babies to sleep. . . .

This is Mrs. Jones's version of the classic Southern lullaby, sung throughout the South by white and black mothers alike. It is always sad; the poignant subcurrent of the great tragedy of slavery—the separation of mother and child—always runs through it, but Mrs. Jones's version is gentle rather than bitter.

	Tune phrases (see music)
Go to sleepy, little baby, Before the booger man catch you.	(1)
All them horses in that lot, Go to sleepy, little baby.	(2)
Go to sleep, go to sleep, Go to sleepy, little baby.	(3)
Mama went away and she told me to stay And take good care of this baby.	(4)
Go to sleep, go to sleep, Go to sleepy, little baby.	(3)
All them horses in that lot, Go to sleepy, little baby.	(2)
Can't you hear them horses trot? Go to sleepy, little baby.	(2)
Go to sleep, go to sleep, Go to sleepy, little baby.	(3)
If I rock this baby to sleep, Go to sleepy, little baby,	(2)
Someday he will remember me, Go to sleepy, little baby.	(2)
Go to sleep, go to sleep, Go to sleepy, little baby.	(3)

Go to Sleepy, Little Baby

(1) Rocking slowly ♩ = 96

Go to sleep-y, lit-tle ba-by,— Be-fore the boog-er man catch— you.

(2)

All them— hor-ses— in that lot,— Go to sleep-y, lit-tle ba-by.

(3)

Go to sleep,— Go to sleep, Go to sleep-y, lit-tle ba-by.

(4)

Ma-ma went a-way— and she told me to stay— and take good care of this ba-by.

New words and new music adaptation by Bessie Jones; collected and edited with additional new material by Alan Lomax. TRO—© copyright 1972 Ludlow Music, Inc., New York, N.Y. Used by permission.

This Little Piggy

You can do that with either fingers or toes; start with the thumb. The main reason for doing that when we come up was to pop them, that's stretching the joints and giving you good joints. That'll make you have good large strong limbs. . . .

Whether played as strenuously as Mrs. Jones describes it or more easily, this familiar "infant amusement" has been a staple baby game for more than a hundred years. It is played with the baby in your lap; the parent says the following rhyme and tugs or gently pinches the toes of the baby's foot—one toe for each "pig," starting with the big one.

Emma Ramsey remembered the accompanying rhyme in the way I have most often heard it:

This little piggy went to market,
This little piggy stayed home,
This little piggy had roast beef,
This little piggy had none,
This little piggy cried, "Wee, wee, wee!" all the way home!

Mrs. Jones commented, "I heard it the way Emma said it later on up when I got to be a big girl. This was really the slavery-time way of doing it."

This little piggy wants some corn.
This little piggy says, "Where you going to get it from?"
This little piggy says, "Out of Massa's barn."
This little pig says, "Run go tell!"
This little pig says, "Twee, twee, twee, I'll
    tell old Massa, tell old Massa!"

Mrs. Jones and Miss Ramsay laughed heartily over the betrayal by the last two little pigs. I have wondered since about that laughter—and wondered, too, if the situation satirized here might not be the same one that gave rise to the "hypocrite," the "back-biter," and the "so-called friend that's easy for to bend" of the spirituals and the blues. Actually, Mrs. Jones's version is older than she realized; her poem has been recorded in books of English nursery rhymes, and may have originated among the serfs of feudal England.

Jump That Jody

I'd bounce him on my lap, and he was so heavy and my arms would get so tired. And he'd say, "Jump for Jody, Mama; jump for Jody, Mama," and he'd be so heavy and just be jumping. . . .

Mrs. Jones made up this little tune for her own first-born, but it follows a traditional pattern of baby play. Stand the baby on your lap, holding his arms stretched over his head and "jump" him up and down.

Jump that Jody, jump it,
Jump that Jody, boy.
Jump that Jody, jump it,
Jump that Jody, boy.

That's for their knees, to get their knees stretched out for walking, to get their kneecaps slipped so they won't walk funny. . . . That's why we always jumped babies; the old folks would tell us to jump them so their legs wouldn't be bowlegged.

Jump That Jody

Ride, Charley, Ride

You mostly call your knee Charley, because it's [a horse] going to throw you. The baby sit on your knee and you're jumping it: "Ride, Charley, ride!" And sometimes a little child will get on your knee and say, "Ride, horsey!" because they know that's what you're going to do. And then you set him on astraddle if it's a boy, so he can learn to sit straddle and ride a horse that way. You set the girl on both knees or either set her sideways because you got to set her so it won't tickle and jar her stomach. You can ruin her stomach so quick inside. . . .

Throughout the Western world, "dandling" or bouncing a baby on the knee has been a favorite infant amusement. Mrs. Jones did not know the more elaborate "Ride a cock-horse to Banbury Cross" but sang her own, probably again made up for her own babies.

Ride, Charley, ride.
Ride that horsey, ride! (repeated ad lib)

Ride, Charley, Ride

With vigor ♩ = 152

Ride, Char - ley, ride.   Ride___ that hor - sey, ride!

New words and new music adaptation by Bessie Jones; collected and edited by Alan Lomax. TRO—© copyright 1972 Ludlow Music, Inc., New York, N.Y. Used by permission.

Finger Names

But in those days, they taught you things. . . .

Mrs. Jones is speaking here about her school years, a period which she remembers with affection and pride, even though, as she wrote me once, "I never has went to school a whole term and I didn't get past the fifth grade; every school day I had to keep other people's babies, and sometimes I had to work in the fields."

But Mrs. Jones's teacher, whom she often quotes, did indeed teach her many things, including such traditional lore as the names of the fingers. In older times each finger, like the thumb, had indeed a separate name: in England, the names are sometimes still given as thumb, toucher, longman, lecheman (for the doctor, who used that finger in tasting medicines or applying ointment), and finally, little-man.

Such names are often recited while tugging on the baby's fingers, in the same way that the toes are pulled while "This Little Piggy" is recited. Mrs. Jones, however, did not use these names for play purposes but as part of her vocabulary.

You call'em Tom Thumb, dog finger, middle finger, no finger, and little finger. We had a teacher taught us that back in Dawson, Georgia. He give us to understand that the no finger [ring finger] is called that because it isn't much help.

Your dog finger, that's your bad-luck finger. That dog finger causes bad luck to people, and today I don't put that finger on a sore because it's apt to cause a scar. I put salve or anything on with the middle finger. And you don't point it at people. If an old man or old lady point their dog finger at you, you know you're going to have bad luck. They'll put mouth on you with that finger—bad mouth on you. Some of those old people, when they'd point their dog finger at you, it was there—they meant that thing.

John Davis, coming in just then, told us the finger names he had learned when he was a boy on St. Simons Island: thumb, potlicker, longman, lingman, littleman. Everybody broke up over "potlicker."

Patty Cake

I think it's better to teach babies little games, to give them some consolation to be with you. As long as you're doing that [playing games], they're looking dead at you, they look straight at you. . . .

"Patty Cake" has been giving babies and their parents "consolation" for more than two centuries at least. The baby sits on your lap "looking dead at you," and the parent holds the baby's hands, clapping them together in rhythm during the first three lines of the poem to follow. During the fourth line, the baby's palms are rotated against each other, as though there were a ball of dough between them, and on the fifth line, both the baby's arms are swung to one side in a flinging motion. Then, of course, as the baby grows older, he can mirror your movements and both of you can play it independently, still face to face.

> Patty cake, patty cake, baker's man.
> Put it in the oven and spike it with tea,
> Save it for supper for baby and me.
> Roll 'em . . . roll 'em . . . roll 'em . . . roll 'em . . .
> Da-a-a-sh 'em in the oven!

British patty cakes are little teacakes usually containing raisins; in Georgia, however, they may be different.

That play tickles the baby. D-a-a-sh 'em in the oven! . . . You're making batter cakes and you have tea to drink with it, you see. Looks like they would say "beat it, beat it," but they wouldn't; it was "roll it, roll it." . . . It was patty cake, like you make up the hoecake bread, you know; you pat it out in your hands. That must be what it was. . . .

Tom, Tom, Greedy-Gut

I never believe in tickling babies, because it makes them stutter. The old peoples say it makes them stammer. You can show them how to clap hands, Greedy-Gut, and different things. . . . Learn them how to use their <u>hands</u>.

Though I have looked carefully, I have found no reference to this play in any other collection, except for the nursery rhyme:

> To bed, to bed, says Sleepyhead.
> Tarry a while, says Slow.
> Put on the pot, says Greedy-Gut,
> We'll sup before we go!

That rhyme, however, does not seem to have a game that goes with it. The Ewe people of Ghana, however, do a social dance that is accompanied partly by drumming and partly by a pattern of alternate hand-clapping and chest-slapping almost identical to the movements Mrs. Jones makes with this play. Perhaps "Tom Tom Greedy-Gut" is a real cultural amalgam, part West African, part old English.

"Greedy-Gut" is played to entertain a lap baby, sitting facing you, preferably one who is old enough to mirror the actions. The parent holds his own hands close to his chest, claps three times, slides the right hand back to slap the chest and follows this by slapping his chest with the left hand. These movements are expanded into the following sequence; the rhythm is indicated on the second line:

Clap	clap	clap	slap	slap;	clap	slap	slap,	clap	slap	slap
1 &	2 &	3	&	4 &	1	&	2 &	3	&	4 &

This exactly matches the spoken rhythm of the first line of the couplet that follows; the second line is spoken to a more syncopated rhythm, though the clap continues to repeat the above formula.

> Tom, Tom, Greedy-Gut, Greedy-Gut, Greedy-Gut.
> Eat all the meat up, meat up, meat up.

Tom, Tom, Greedy-Gut

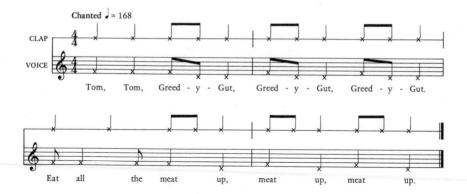

Written and adapted by Bessie Jones; collected and edited by Alan Lomax. TRO—© copyright 1972 Ludlow Music, Inc., New York, N.Y. Used by permission.

2:
Clapping Plays

If you know how to clap and what you're clapping for you can come out right with the song. . . . You're supposed to have your music come out even with your singing. . . .

In many parts of the South, the word "music" simply means any instrumental accompaniment for a song. Mrs. Jones says "music" whenever she is talking about the hand-clapping with which she and the other Islanders accompany almost every game or play or song. And their hand-clapping *is* music—in every sense of the word; it is varied and expressive and subtle, completely different from a routine beating out of the time.

Learning "how to clap" turns out to be a developmental process as Mrs. Jones describes it. It starts with the baby games, like "Patty Cake" or "Tom, Tom, Greedy-Gut," in which the child copies the parent's movements. Next, as will be seen later in this chapter, come the clapping games played with a partner, such as "Green Sally Up"; these require increased cooperation and produce more interesting tonal effects. Finally, the almost-grown child graduates to the sophistication of the elaborate solo rhythms involved in such plays as "Hambone" or "Juba."

The plays in the following section, then, deal with "how to clap"; they are little practice pieces through which the child learns and polishes his rhythmic skills. The group clapping—the real "music" that accompanies all the singing games—is a different matter. Here, as Mrs. Jones puts it, you have to know "what you're clapping *for*." And what you're clapping *for* seems to be, at least in part, the creation of a rhythmic bond, the fusion of the group into a single internally cooperative unit.

The only time I ever saw Mrs. Jones stop a game was during a practice of "Oh Green Fields, Roxie" when a player whose turn it was to take the center of the ring simply walked in at a normal pace. "You got to *dance* it, you got to play *on time*, you got to *be* on time, you got to do it *right!*" was Mrs. Jones's agonized comment. In all the singing and rhythm plays she taught, "being on time" was essentially equivalent to "doing it right."

Mrs. Jones's advice as to *how* to be on time was eminently practical. "Move your feet!" she would say to the students, and to the other Singers as well on the rare occasions when a song or a clap pattern was not developing as it should. Magically, the rhythm would steady; the group would come together. Mrs. Jones's foot "move," then, is worth some examination.

Basically, even when she was sitting down, it was a shift of weight, requiring two counts on each side. Sitting, she would place first her right foot out a bit in front, landing flat-footed, and then step with the same foot back in place, repeating the pattern with the left foot. Standing, she would step on her right foot, bring her left foot close to her right, and "step it down" *without a weight change*, repeating the pattern to the left. Though each movement was done flat-footed, as though stamping, she normally kept her footfalls quiet, except when she wanted an extra drumming effect.

As I watched, it seemed to me that this was basically a dance movement. Though restrained, it is strong; the body swings slightly with it. The movements are on the first and third beats of the measure, at the points where the dancer would probably take his strong steps.

To clap well, then, you must start with your feet, since the claps come *after* the weight changes (or "steps") and thus occur on the normally unaccented beats of the measure (the second and the fourth). The movement Mrs. Jones calls "stepping it down" (putting the foot down without changing weight) coincides with the claps.

one	two	three	four
R step	clap	L step	clap

L (step it down)   R (step it down)

Thus the performer finds that his feet and hands are holding a kind of conversation—feet stating, hands answering—in the classic antiphonal (or answering-back) structure that seems to underlie all American Negro music. The footfalls, however, are light; the claps are loud, so that the sounded emphasis falls on the "weak" beats, or offbeats, of the measure. Most of the time you cannot hear the "strong" beats at all, the feet step so quietly.

The basic accompaniment for all the songs in this book, with the exception of lullabies and those game-songs in which the players' hands are otherwise occupied, is the single offbeat hand-clap just described. Mrs. Jones always used it when she was singing by herself, occasionally varying it with a double offbeat clap pattern:

one	and	two	and	three	and	four	and
step		clap	clap	step		clap	clap

(Since this pattern *looks* more complicated, it may be worth pointing out that it is exactly like the single offbeat clap except that you clap twice each time instead of once.)

However, to the Sea Islanders, descendants of the great African polyrhythmic drum choirs, such patterns as the above are pretty simple stuff; they think of both the single and the double offbeat claps as only a kind of skeleton or framework for the rhythmic structures they like to build. Like Afro-American musicians throughout the country, the Sea Islanders further elaborate their rhythmic effects in two ways: varying the pitch of their percussive sounds and practicing polyrhythmic clapping (two or more rhythms being sounded out at the same time).

Pitch variation. All percussive sounds have pitch—that is, they sound "high" or "low"—but some musical systems have elaborated upon this and others have not. West Africa is one of the parts of the world where drums function almost as melodic instruments, their pitch variation is so complex. It is interesting that in West Africa, many of the native languages are "tonal"; in such languages the meaning of a word can be changed by the pitch at which it is spoken. The so-called talking drums are in part based on this quality; possibly the importance of pitch variation in the drumming style is a reflection of the importance of pitch variation in the language.

North American plantation owners during the era of slavery were well aware of the possibility that their slaves might be able to communicate from plantation to plantation by drumming and thus organize revolts. For this reason, and also because they feared that the use of drums might consolidate African religious practices and slow down the slaves' conversion to Protestantism, they made serious attempts to eliminate the playing of drums entirely. They were in part successful; the playing of real drums in the old African way almost completely died out in the United States. However, although the instruments were destroyed, the activity itself was not; Negroes did and do drum on anything available—pots and pans, the floor, their own bodies.

Body-slapping, which the old folks call "patting" and the young people call "hand jive," is especially interesting in its emphasis on pitch as well as rhythm. If you slap your thigh and then the back of your hand, you will notice that the second slap is higher in pitch than the first. Slap other parts of your body—chest, side, cheek, the top of your head—and you will discover a whole range of pitches can be sounded on your own anatomy. "Tom, Tom, Greedy-Gut" uses this principle for an infant play; a more complex development of the same idea may be seen in "Hambone" and "Juba" later in this chapter.

The Islanders carry this notion into their hand-clapping as well; they clap in three distinct pitch ranges; bass, baritone, and tenor. Anatomical structure and the hardness of the palms have something to do with each person's possible range; essentially, however, the pitch is determined by the position in which the hands are held.

To clap bass, cup your palms slightly and clap with your palms at right angles to one another; the fingers do not strike together at all, only the palms. The sound should be dull, not popping.

To clap baritone, the left palm is cupped and struck with the fingers, slightly cupped, of the right hand; again the clapping motion is crosswise, one hand at a right angle to the other. (Mrs. Jones described this position once: "Let your hand be just a little bit folded where the wind can catch them four fingers.") A strong baritone clap on a hard palm can sound like a pistol shot.

Tenor is clapped variously, depending on how high you want the sound; sometimes it is clapped like the baritone, except that the left palm and right fingers are *not* cupped. To get the highest pitch of all, strike the fingers of both hands together in a flattened-out but relaxed position.

This type of clapping is not a casual stunt. The Islanders hear these various pitches as parts of a percussion orchestra; they can be as pained by a feeble or uncertainly pitched clap as a symphonic musician would be by a badly tuned violin. Further, they feel that group clapping should be balanced; if there are too many people clapping in the baritone range, someone should change over and clap tenor or bass. But the various ranges of pitch are rarely clapped simultaneously; each part normally takes on its own rhythmic pattern, resulting in a demonstration of another essentially African musical principle: the sounding of several rhythms at the same time.

Polyrhythm. Each person in a group clapping "music"—that is, accompanying a song—may either duplicate, at his own pitch, a rhythm being taken by another person, or he may perform variations on his own; with experienced clappers, the latter is invariably the case. Essentially the Sea Islanders' clapping patterns seem to cluster around the following framework:

	one	and	two	and	three	and	four	and
Baritone			X				X	(X)
Bass	X				X		X	
Tenor		X	(X)	X	(X)	X	(X)	X

This should be thought of as the core pattern; each part may be (and is) varied extensively according to the following principles:

The baritone clap is invariably the lead clap as well as the solo clap; when in doubt, clap baritone. The baritone part is also the one most generally duplicated by other clappers; it should be the strongest and the loudest, since all the other rhythmic parts are established by the baritone beat (which is, of course, the single off-beat pattern previously discussed). The bass clap may be extended into a "shave and a hair cut; six bits" pattern and infinitely varied in other ways. However, in spite of the fact that the bass pattern generally starts on the count of "one," the baritone clap invariably precedes by a measure or two the start of the bass clap and sets the fundamental tempo. The tenor clap acts as punctuation in between the other two.

The Islanders, of course, don't count their rhythmic patterns out; they "feel" them and do them. Learners will likely have to count, but some of the "feeling" that makes this complex musical interplay possible may be made clearer by the following incident. Taping one day, I wanted to be sure I had captured each rhythmic part clearly and asked the Islanders to record for me, starting their clapping parts consecutively. I asked Mrs. Jones, who always clapped lead baritone, to begin and explained that I wanted Miss Emma Ramsey, the group's stellar tenor clapper, to come in next so, as I put it, "I can see how her clap rhythm works against yours." Mrs. Jones smiled gently. "Emma don't clap *against* me; she claps *with* me."

Suddenly the cultural gulf between us yawned very wide indeed. To me, as to all white Americans, I suspect, a person who is "with" me must do just what I am doing, must copy my movements (and my ideas and my speech and my dress and my clapping). "Clap with me, children," and all the little first-graders watch carefully to see when the teacher spanks her hands together so that they can do it then, too. To Mrs. Jones and the Sea Islanders, to be "with" somebody means to respond to them, to complement and support their silences, to fill in their statements (musical, physical, and verbal) with little showers of comment, to answer their remarks—to clap a *different* pattern.

But it is not only a different pattern, it is a sympathetic and supportive pattern, as it can be only when it is grounded in a basic shared impulse—in this situation, the foot move. This, then, is why Mrs. Jones became angry at dancers who were out of rhythm; *they* were indeed not "with" her. They had rejected the unifying principle that was holding the entire group together, and, in that rejection, they had denied the total social impulse of the music. To her they must have seemed aggressive and lonely figures. In any case, this was the only occasion on which I ever heard her imply that an individual variation was wrong.

If you know how *to clap and what you're clapping* for, *you can come out* right *with the song. . . .*

The next chapter shows the child at work, beginning to learn this complex musical tradition.

Green Sally Up

PETER DAVIS: *We always said, "Rabbit in the hatchet." When I could step it like a rabbit with a long-tailed coat and a beaver on, I could really dance it then. . . .*

As Peter Davis suggests, this rhyme could be used for dancing as well as a clapping rhythm. Mrs. Jones plays this like "Pease Porridge Hot"; children sit facing each other in pairs, alternately clapping their own and their partners' hands:

1. Each player claps his own hands.   (O)
2. Players clap right hands across.   (R)
3. Each player claps his own hands.   (O)
4. Players clap left hands across.   (L)

The above pattern may be repeated indefinitely. Significantly and characteristically, Mrs. Jones starts with step two; this brings the heavy accent (of the players' own hands being clapped together) on the offbeat, rather than on the downbeat, as white children usually play it.

  R O L O   R O L O
Green Sally up,   Green Sally down,

  R O L O R O L   O
Green Sally bake her possum brown.

Asked my mama for fifteen cents
To see that elephant jump the fence.

He jumped so high, he touched the sky,
He never got back till the fourth of July.

You see that house, on that hill,
That's where me and my baby live.

Oh, the rabbit in the hash come a-stepping in the dash,
With his long-tailed coat and his beaver on.

The last couplet, "Oh, the rabbit in the hash," may be repeated over and over, either at a steady tempo or speeded up as much as three times faster. The "Green Sally" couplet functions as a refrain, and may be put in anywhere you want it.

Green Sally Up

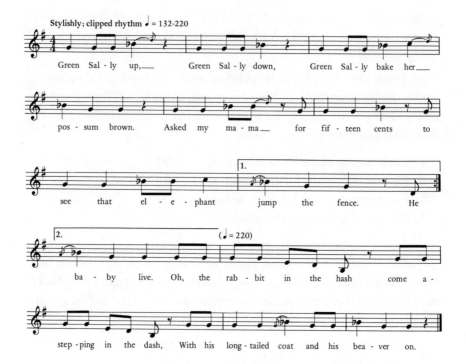

Green Sal - ly up,___ Green Sal - ly down, Green Sal - ly bake her___

pos - sum brown. Asked my ma - ma___ for fif - teen cents to

see that el - e - phant jump the fence.

He

ba - by live. Oh, the rab - bit in the hash come a -

step - ping in the dash, With his long - tailed coat and his bea - ver on.

New words and original music by Bessie Jones; collected and edited with additional new material by Alan Lomax. TRO—© copyright 1972 Ludlow Music, Inc., New York, N.Y. Used by permission.

One-ry, Two-ry

Hallibo, crackibo—that seem like driving a team. . . .

This rhyme may be clapped by two players sitting or standing face to face, alternately clapping their own and their partner's right or left hands, just as in "Green Sally Up." Or a larger group may play, standing in a circle. In this case, the children clap their neighbors' hands on either side at the same time and then their own in continuous alternation.

I have seen Los Angeles children playing this circle clap, though to different rhymes, in an even more difficult manner: clapping their neighbors' hands with right hand clapping up and left hand down; clapping their own hands together; clapping their neighbors' hands *left* hand up and *right* hand down; clapping their own hands, etc. Children can do this with enormous speed as early as the age of six. Interestingly, A. M. Jones describes just such clapping play in a child's game from West Africa.

Whether played by partners or a group, however, the clap rhythm is accented in the same manner as that of "Green Sally Up." The clap is also kept steady even through such syncopated lines as "twinkle, twankle, twenty-one."

      R   O   L   O   R   OL   O
One - ry, two -ry, dicker-y seven,

      R   O   L   O   ROL   O
Halli-bo, cracki-bo, ten e-leven.

      R O L O R   O   L   O
Pee, po, must be   done,

      R   O   L   O   R   O   L O
Twin-kle, twan-kle, — twen - ty one.

Mrs. Jones adds that this rhyme and the one that follows ("One Saw, Two Saw") may be used as counting-out rhymes to determine who is to be the "it" in such games as "Bob-a-Needle" or "Hide and Seek." Further, she sometimes uses this rhyme (or "One Saw, Two Saw") in place of the rhyme said in "Engine Rubber Number Nine." (See Outdoor Games.)

One-ry, Two-ry

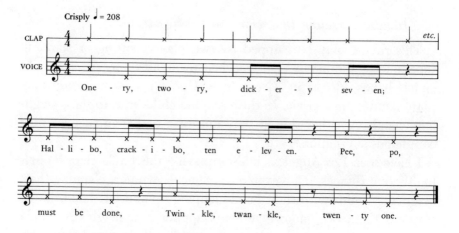

One - ry, two - ry, dick - er - y sev - en;

Hal - li - bo, crack - i - bo, ten e - lev - en. Pee, po,

must be done, Twin - kle, twan - kle, twen - ty one.

New words and new music adaptation by Bessie Jones. TRO—© copyright 1972 Ludlow Music, Inc., New York, N.Y. Used by permission.

One Saw, Two Saw

I don't know where Mary come in at, but she's there. . . .

Both "One Saw, Two Saw" and "One-ry, Two-ry" are ancient and extraordinarily widespread rhymes. Scholars have debated over their origin for a long time. One theory traces the "nonsense" syllables of these rhymes to a method of counting in ancient Celtic languages, practiced in Great Britain since before the Roman conquest and still persisting in remote areas of the British Isles. Another suggestion is that some of the words are street-boy parodies of Latin as spoken by the educated during the Middle Ages; this may explain the presence, which troubles Mrs. Jones, of the Virgin Mary in a child's rhyme. In any case, these verbal formulas are centuries old.

For the game, the clapping pattern is started off by slapping the partner's hands first, then your own, as in "Green Sally Up" and "One-ry Two-ry."

    R   O   L   O   R   O   L   O
One saw, two saw, ziggy zaw zow,

    R   O   L   O   R   O   L   O
Bob-tail domin-icker deedle dall dow.

    R   O   L   O   R   O   L O
Hail-em, scail-em, Vir-gin Ma-ry,

    R O   L   O   R   O   L   O
Ike to my link-tum Buck!

One Saw, Two Saw

♩ = 208

CLAP

VOICE

One saw, two saw, zig - gy zaw zow,

Bob - tail dom - i - nick - er deed - le dall dow. Hail - em, scail - em,

Vir - gin Ma - ry, Ike to my link - tum Buck!

Written and adapted by Bessie Jones; collected and edited by Alan Lomax. TRO—© copyright 1972 Ludlow Music, Inc., New York, N.Y. Used by permission.

Head and Shoulder, Baby

The children do it pretty because they're on time; they can do that knee and ankle and be right back there on time.

With its jazzy beat, "Head and Shoulder" appears to be a fairly modern game. Although, as Mrs. Jones points out, it requires good coordination, it has turned up in city schoolyards across the country, where it appears to be mostly performed by girls. Girls seem to prefer partner-style clapping games such as this one, while their brothers are working out with solo hand jive (see "Hambone").

FORM: Though this game can be (and probably should be) practiced alone, Mrs. Jones says it should be done by partners standing and facing each other. Both chant and sing the rhyme.

VOICES	ACTION
Head and shoulder, baby,	Players touch their own heads, shoulders, and heads again.
One, ——	Players clap right hands across and then their own hands.
Two, ——	Players clap left hands across and then their own hands.
Three.	Players clap right hands across.
Head and shoulder, baby,	Players touch their own heads, shoulders, and heads again
One, ——	Players clap right hands across and then their own hands.
Two, ——	Players clap left hands across and then their own hands.
Three.	Players clap right hands across.
Head and shoulder,	Players touch their own heads and shoulders.
Head and shoulder,	Repeat.
Head and shoulder, baby,	Players touch heads, shoulders, heads.
One, ——	Players clap left hands across and then their own hands.
Two, ——	Players clap right hands across and then their own hands.
Three.	Players clap right hands across.
Knee and ankle, baby, One, two, three.	As above except players touch their own knees, ankles, and knees again.

Knee and ankle, baby,
One, two, three.
Knee and ankle, knee and ankle,
Knee and ankle, baby,
One, two, three.

Milk the cow, baby,   As above except the players act out
One, two, three.   milking a cow, first with right hand,
Milk the cow, baby,   then left, and then right again.
One, two, three.
Milk the cow, milk the cow,
Milk the cow, baby,
One, two, three.

Throw the ball, baby,   As above except players act out
One, two, three.   throwing a ball.
Throw the ball, baby,
One, two, three.
Throw the ball, throw the ball,
Throw the ball, baby,
One, two, three.

I ain't been to Frisco,   No action; Mrs. Jones occasionally
And I ain't been to school;   "acted it out."
I ain't been to college
But I ain't no fool.

To the front,   Players jump toward each other (both
                                       feet).

To the back,   Players jump back from each other
                                       (both feet).

To the front,   Players jump toward each other.
To the back,   Players jump away from each other.
To the si- si- side,   Players jump (both feet) right, left,
                                       and right.

To the si- si- side!   Repeat; left, right, and left.

Head and Shoulder, Baby

Very syncopated ♩ = 96-116

Head and shoul - der, ba - by, one, two, three.
Knee and ank - le,
Milk the cow,____
Throw the ball,____

Head and shoul - der, ba - by, one, two, three.
Knee and an - kle,
Milk the cow,____
Throw the ball,____

Head and shoul - der, head and shoul - der, head and shoul - der, ba - by,
Knee and an - kle, knee and an - kle, knee and an - kle,
Milk the cow,____ milk the cow,____ milk the cow,____
Throw the ball,____ throw the ball,____ throw the ball,____

1.
one, two, three.
2.
three. I

ain't been to Fris - co, And I ain't been to school;

I ain't been to col - lege, but I ain't no fool.

To the front, to the back, to the front, to the back,

To the si - si - side,____ To the si - si - side!____

Words and music by Bessie Jones; collected and edited with new material by Alan Lomax. TRO—
© copyright 1972 Ludlow Music, Inc., New York, N.Y. Used by permission.

Hambone

You just say it, and then you say it with your hands.

"Hambone" probably refers to the part of the anatomy most involved in playing this hand jive game, though there is undoubtedly more to it than that. Most young black men, I find, know it in one version or another.

"Hambone" may be performed alone or with a group all jiving together. While the rhyme is being said, the players slap their thighs lightly on the offbeat. *After* each line of the poem, they "pat" in the following rhythm:

(The foregoing pattern is not exactly what you expect to hear; it is, however, what Mrs. Jones does.)

The "patting" may be done on one side of the body only, using the right hand and thigh; or on both sides at the same time in parallel motion. The triplet phrase is done as follows:

1. Slap the side of the thigh with the palm of the hand in an upward brushing motion.
2. Continuing the upward brushing; strike the side or the chest with the palm of the hand.
3. Strike the thigh downward with the back of the hand.

Do this series twice, then slap your thigh three times. The entire pattern is repeated after each line of the following rhyme, in which Mrs. Jones starts with the "Hambone" poem until she suddenly merges into a series of verses from the familiar "Frog Went A-Courting."

VOICE

Ham<u>bone</u>, Ham<u>bone</u>, pat him <u>on</u> the shoul<u>der</u>,
If you <u>get</u> a pretty <u>girl</u>, I'll show you <u>how</u> to hold <u>her</u>.
Hambone, Hambone, where have you been?
All 'round the world and back again.

ACTION

Pat thigh on the offbeat while the rhyme is being recited. (The first two lines have been underscored on the offbeat as an example.) At the end of each line of the rhyme, do the hambone "pat" as previously described.

Hambone, Hambone, what did
   you do?
I got a train and I fairly flew.
Hambone, Hambone, where did
   you go?
I hopped up to Miss Lucy's door.
I asked Miss Lucy would she
   marry me.
(in falsetto) "Well, I don't care if
   Papa don't care!"
First come in was Mister Snake,
He crawled all over that wedding
   cake.
Next walked in was Mister Tick,
He ate so much that it made him
   sick.
Next walked in was Mister Coon,
We asked him to sing us a wed-
   ding tune.
Now Ham- . . .
Now Ham- . . .

On one occasion, Mrs. Jones improvised a way of playing "Hambone" in which she tapped an answering rhythm with her feet instead of "patting."

The group followed her pattern, and soon things were going so
well that she superimposed the following clap:

"Oh, he's *hamming* it!" she said, in great satisfaction.

Hambone

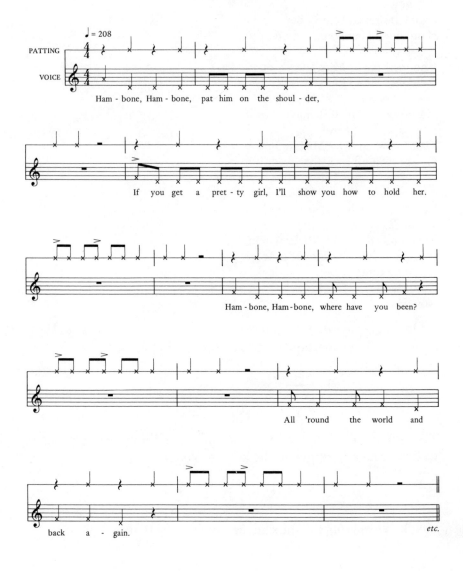

New words and new music adaptation by Bessie Jones; collected and edited with additional new material by Alan Lomax. TRO—© copyright 1972 Ludlow Music, Inc., New York, N.Y. Used by permission.

Juba

That's one of the oldest plays I think I can remember our grand-
father telling us about, because he was brought up in Virginia. He
used to tell us about how they used to eat ends of food; that's what
"juba" means. They said "jibba" when they meant "giblets"; we
know that's ends of food. They had to eat leftovers.

He used to say they would take mixed-up food and put it together,
that they had to eat out of those long troughs—mush, and cush, and
all that stuff put together and put plenty milk in it. But he live a
hundred and five years, so, I can't say that made him live but I
say it didn't kill him. And I'm up here a long time too; I never eat
like that, but yet and still he have taught us a many a time how he
did that. . . .

Mrs. Jones is right; this is one of her oldest rhymes. George Washington Cable saw African slaves doing a dance called "the Juba" in
New Orleans' Congo Square long before emancipation; today it may
be seen in some of the Caribbean Islands. In the United States, occasional mention of "juba" may be found in songs, generally associated with hand-clapping, but the dance itself appears to have been
lost.

The word "juba" is probably a variation of one of the West African day names, which were often used also for girls' given names.
In the United States, the original African meaning has long since
been forgotten; and, as Mrs. Jones ingeniously suggests, the word
may have become associated with the like-sounding English word
"giblets." Here is the Juba rhyme, with Mrs. Jones's explanation of
each line given in parentheses:

Juba this and Juba that	(That means a little of this and a little of that.)
And Juba killed a yellow cat	(That means mixed-up food might kill the white folks. And they didn't care if it did, I don't suppose.)
And get over double trouble, Juba.	(Someday they meant they would get over double trouble . . .)
You sift-a the meal, you give me the husk, You cook-a the bread, you give me the crust.	(You see, so that's what it mean— the mother would always be talking to them about she wished she could give them

You fry the meat, you give me the skin,
And that's where my mama's trouble begin.
And then you Juba,
You just Juba.

Juba up, Juba down,
Juba all around the town.
Juba for ma, Juba for pa,
Juba for your brother-in-law.

some of that good hot corn-bread or hot pies or hot what-not. But she couldn't. She had to wait and give that old stuff that was left over. And then they began to sing it and play it. . . .)
(That mean everywhere,)
(All around the whole country.)

(See, that meant everybody had juba. And they made a play out of it. So that's where this song come from; they would get all this kind of thing off their brains and minds. . . .)

"Juba" may be played alone. If there is a group present, normally one person acts as lead singer-clapper while the rest dance. During section A, all do the Juba "pat" (see page 22). During sections B and C, the lead singer may clap for the rest, who dance, either individually or in couples.

LEAD VOICE

A. Juba, Juba
   Juba this and Juba that
   And Juba killed a yellow cat
   And get over double trouble, Juba.
   You sift-a the meal,
   You give me the husk;
   You cook-a the bread,
   You give me the crust,
   You fry the meat,
   You give me the skin,
   And that is where my mama's trouble begin.
   And then you Juba,
   You just Juba.

B. (Lead singer starts single off-beat clap.)
   Say, Juba up, Juba down,
   Juba all around the town.
   Juba for ma, Juba for pa,

ACTION

All pat thighs alternately.
All do Juba pat, which continues to the end of this section.

Dancers "jump for joy" alone or with partner. (See p. 44.)

Juba for your brother-in-law.
You just Juba, Juba.

C. (Lead singer starts double off-beat clap)   Dancers continue jumping for joy.

Let's Juba this and Juba that,
And Juba killed a yellow cat;
You get over double trouble,
    Juba.
You sift-a the meal, you give me
    the husk
You cook-a the bread, you give
    me the crust,
You fry the meat, you give me
    the skin,
And that's where my mama's
    trouble begin,
And that's where my mama's
    trouble begin.

Juba pat: (L)   Slap left thigh with left hand.
          (LB) Slap back of left hand with right hand (left hand
                    should be raised from thigh).
          (L)   Slap left thigh with left hand.
       Repeat on other side:
          (R)   Slap right thigh with right hand.
          (RB) Slap back of right hand (raised) with left hand.
          (R)   Slap right thigh with right hand.

Continue, alternating from one side to the other. This pat, when
speeded up, has a kind of galloping triple-time "Hi-yo Silver" effect.
Since this essentially triple rhythm is carried evenly over a four-beat
rhyme, the effect is extremely syncopated.

```
L  LB  L   R  RB  R   L  LB  L  R   RB   R  L   LB  L
Ju ba this and Ju ba that and Ju ba killed a yel low cat

R   RB R  L  LB  L  R  RB  R  L  LB  L  R  RB  R  etc.
And get o ver doub  le troub le Ju  ba
```

*They be dancing, then, you see; the children be jumping—we call
it dancing, which it is. They be jumping. Nowadays I have the children do the Charleston with it, have the boys do their knees together
like they cutting scissors. I learned the Charleston, way back in
Miami time—nineteen and twenty-five. . . . I didn't never do it, but
I prayed for the rest of them that did.*

Juba

New words and new music adaptation by Bessie Jones; collected and edited with additional new material by Alan Lomax. TRO—© copyright 1972 Ludlow Music, Inc., New York, N.Y. Used by permission.

3:
Jumps and Skips

And use your feet. You hardly can clap without using your feet, not and stay on time. . . . That [clap] didn't go so good for me, because you've got to get it <u>all over</u>, and use your feet, see? . . .

The more I watched Mrs. Jones and the Islanders, the more convinced I became that *all* their music-making activities involved basic body movement, or what the white community would call "dance." The point is, as Mrs. Jones puts it, "you've got to get it all over." *All* singing was accompanied by swaying, weight shifts, and hand, head, and body movements of greater or less degree, all suggesting a dance that was not yet quite visible. Their "real" dances seemed, then, simply broader, more explicit statements of the dances they were already doing while they "stood still" to sing.

The Islanders' point of view toward their dance style, however, was considerably more sophisticated than mine. Dancing, to them, was a highly elaborated activity, organized into long series of "steps," each with its own descriptive name. This tradition is an old one; in the minstrel theater the white vaudevillians in blackface (who had learned their trade through careful observation of Negro dancers) were experts in the Pigeon Wing, the Double Shuffle, and the Turkey Trot as early as the 1840's.

I myself was able to learn only a few of the Islanders' steps—

those Mrs. Jones considered suitable for children's dance (and a few others that slipped by her). Most were dramatic or imitative in nature but highly formalized. Here it might be useful to point out that American Negroes, contrary to popular legend, are not "free" in their dancing. They do not fling themselves about; their bodies are under strict control at all times, like those of all good dancers.

The "rules" I was able to absorb are few but important. The foot keeps contact with the ground as much as possible, and full contact at that. All dancing is done flat-footed; this is extremely difficult for Euro-Americans, whose first approach to a dancing situation is to go up on their toes. (A clear mental picture of the difference in basic foot position might be gained if Bill Robinson's and Fred Astaire's tap dancing styles could be visualized.)

The foot is generally set down flat—all at once—neither toe-heel nor heel-toe; and foot swings, jumps, and kicks are kept "low and draggy." Most up-and-down motion is gotten by bending and straightening the knees. If you try walking with knee and foot action as described, you will find that the hips are forced out behind slightly and that the trunk movement will be a slight swing forward and back, *not* side to side. The Islanders regarded exaggerated hip swings or hip rotation as vulgar.

The upper part of the body is erect but supple; the body often bows forward slightly. The arms are loose but not flapping, the shoulders often revolving slightly. In many dances, the shoulder movement alternates, first right, then left; in the "buzzard lope" step, the shoulders move together like wings.

Overall, all movements are loose and supple; most whites dance far too tensely. All movement is restrained as well; though the sex of the dancers is obvious, the dancing is not elaborately "sexy."

The following is a cataloguing of the steps called for in this book, only a fraction of the Islanders' total repertoire.

JUMP FOR JOY. A strongly restrained Charleston step, with the high side kick eliminated; the feet should be kept as close to the ground as possible.

BALL THE JACK. Holding the legs together from foot to hip, rotate the knees in a circle; this obviously rotates the hips also. Mrs. Jones seemed to feel this was mildly improper for small

children—the sort of thing that you should tell them not to do,
but you know they are going to do it anyway.

SNAKE HIPS. This, on the other hand, is a little bit scandalous,
whether performed by child or adult. The movement is the
same, but the knees are not kept together and move forward
and back, first one knee, then the other. Mrs. Jones made a
strong distinction between balling the jack and doing snake
hips, both in the techniques—which she had verbalized—and in
their social propriety.

STEP IT DOWN. This term refers both to the side-to-side movement that Mrs. Jones always makes when she sings and claps,
as described in the introduction to Chapter 2 (p. 20), *and* to
a formal dance step. The *dancer* "steps it down" in a forward-
and-back motion: one—put the foot out in front as though
stepping on something but do not change weight; two—put the
same foot back in place and step on it, changing weight; repeat
with the other foot to a count of two on each side. Thus the
dancer, in contrast to the clapper, syncopates by weight
changes on the *second* and *fourth* beats.

ZUDIE-O. This is simply a two-step: step, slide, step, to a count of
one and two (rest), as in the fox trot. (See the dance by the
same name for a fuller description.)

RANKY TANK. Dance teachers would refer to this as a "buzz step";
the actual motion is rather like riding a scooter. The weight is
on the forward foot, and the back foot pushes the dancer along
the floor in a short shoving motion to a count of one, two.

BUZZARD LOPE. The Islanders knew a complex religious dance by
this name, a description of which is beyond the scope of this
book. They also use the term, however, to indicate a movement
that appears in children's (or nonreligious) dance. In this latter
context, the term means to turn the body at the waist so that
one shoulder is pointing forward, and revolve both shoulders in
parallel motion, forward to back. The arms are held loosely bent
at the elbows, and the shoulder movement then makes the
elbows stand out and flap slightly, like wings.

SHOUT. This term is also used in two different contexts: religious
and secular, in neither of which does it mean anything to do
with the voice. The word itself comes from an Arabic term

"saut," meaning, loosely, to dance. The nonreligious shout step appears in several traditional children's plays as follows: with weight on the active foot, give a little shove backward as though hopping without the foot leaving the floor; dancers sometimes call this movement a "chug." While "chugging" back on the right foot, swing the left foot forward. Step on the left foot and "chug" it backward while swinging the right foot forward. This is done to a count of two: step, chug. The ultimate result, by the way, is that you stay in the same place.

SANDY REE. An extension of the shout step to a count of four: step, step, step, chug. The positioning of the feet is also more elaborate; for a full description, see the dance by the same name.

POSSUM-LA. A shuffling jump, landing on both feet, almost like a two-footed "chug." The dancer lands heavily, at the same instant bending both knees sharply.

MAKE A MOTION. This is the moment of improvisation. Faint hearts simply perform a standard step they know; more experienced dancers make their own statement, depending on the way they are feeling at the moment. Since the call to "make a motion" (sometimes, "make *your* motion") often occurs in courtship plays, the opportunity for personal display of agility, coordination, and finesse of movement brings out the best in the dancers.

Some further discussion on the question of percussive dancing may be useful. On the whole, the Islanders all danced in a relatively soft-footed manner, with only occasional stomps and heel knocks. When these occurred, they seemed to serve the function of rhythmic accenting rather than to be actual parts of the dance *movement*. My whole impression was that their floor sounding—any kind of tapping or stamping—was actually a kind of *musical* accompaniment, was, indeed, a substitute for an absent drum.

Mrs. Jones definitely used her feet as instruments to accompany her singing. Her strong, simple foot movement when she sang standing up has already been described. When she was relaxed and sitting back in a chair, her foot-tapping became considerably more complex. Her usual rhythm was a rapid soft sounded double beat performed in one of two ways: tapping with the toe of one foot and the heel of the other simultaneously, and then reversing; or a steady double-timed soft stamp with the left foot, while the right foot tapped alternately with the heel and the toe. As we practiced this, she would laugh at me if I could not sound both my feet at *exactly* the same instant. Then, anxious like all great teachers to turn a failure into a positive experience, she would announce proudly that I had made "a double beat!"

This rapid, soft, steady tapping (normally eight counts to every four-four measure) could be varied at will by occasional rhythmic breaks, which she usually put in at the end of the poetic line of the song or during rests in the melody. Again, I felt that at these moments, the tapping feet were playing a responsive "tune" back to the voice, just as the blues picker's guitar answers the singer between vocal phrases. Further, in these breaks each foot took on its own role, and each responded to the other: the left foot (L) kept the basic rhythm, landing flat-footed and always on the counts of one and three, while the right foot handled the accents, sometimes flat-footed (R) and sometimes toe-heel (t-h) or heel-toe (h-t). Here are a few of the rhythms she showed me:

four	and	one	two	three;	four	and	one	two	three
t	h	L	R	L	t	h	L	R	L

four	and	one	and	two	three;	four	and	one	and	two	three
t	h	L	t	h	L	t	h	L	t	h	L

The two above combined, with the toe-heel sequence reversed:

four	and	one	two	three;	four	and	one	and	two	three
h	t	L	R	L	h	t	L	h	t	L

Another variation, with the heel leading:

four	and	one	two	and	three	and	four;	one	and	two	three
h	t	L	h	t	L	h	t	L	h	t	L

Her movements were small and discreet always; one could barely see her knees moving up and down under her dress skirts. The heel-toe movement was accompanied by a slight brushing forward of the foot; for the toe-heel, the foot brushed backward. Like any expert musician, she had no need to show off; she was too busy creating *music* with crisp even taps like an expert drummer's. Once she told me that she was making a "joyful noise."

In this context, one is tempted to see in the modern tap dancer a lonely figure, recreating for his own ears all the joyful noises that should be being sounded for him by hands, feet, sticks, and drum heads. And again one is puzzled by how hard it is to distinguish between *musical* values and *dance* values. Perhaps the only practical solution is the one suggested in Mrs. Jones's frequent remark, "You've got to get it *all over.*"

In the task of learning *how* to "get it all over" the jumps and skips in this chapter are again practice pieces, preparing the small child for the complications of later group play and dance. As Mrs. Jones used them, they seem to have been designed both to teach individual steps and to develop specific physical skills. Indeed, all the plays she included in this category, with the single exception of "Just from the Kitchen," can be done by a single dancer, though they are more pleasantly played by more.

Skip to the Barbershop

In a way, besides learning [at school] they got to get their exercise, too. This [play] is to keep their legs and all in good shape. . . .

Mrs. Jones speaks very affectionately about her few years of formal education in Dawson, Georgia, around the turn of the century, where school met in a one-room church house and the children spent Friday afternoons cleaning the building so that it would be ready for meeting on Sunday. Many of her plays and games she learned in school, and many of them she feels are truly educational in nature, preparing a child for later, more complex activity.

"Skip to the Barbershop" she classifies as

just a little skip, where you learn the children how to skip, because some children cannot skip. You get them in line and you can have something for them to pick up—go over to the other side of the room and pick it up and bring it back—and you tell them, "Skip to the barbershop." You can do it with untied feets or tied feets; untied feets are better. That way you see which one of the children can skip over and bring something back the fastest and the prettiest. . . .

> Skip, skip, to the barbershop,
> I left my hat at the barbershop
> And three sticks of candy.
> One for you, one for me,
> And one for sister Sally.
>
> Skip, skip, to the barbershop,
> I left my coat at the barbershop, etc.

The play can continue with various other articles of clothing substituted in the rhyme for "hat" and "coat" until all the players have a turn. Though the rhyme could be recited by all the players together, Mrs. Jones usually chanted it alone, accompanying herself with a single offbeat clap.

Skip to the Barbershop

Expressively ♩ = 192

Skip, skip, to the bar - ber - shop, I left my hat at the

bar - ber shop and three sticks of can - dy. One for you,

one for me, And one for sis - ter Sal - ly.

New words and new music adaptation by Bessie Jones; collected and edited with additional new material by Alan Lomax. TRO—© copyright 1972 Ludlow Music, Inc., New York, N.Y. Used by permission.

Just from the Kitchen

This is just a little skip. We'd do it in the yard or either in the house if it was raining. But it means this, you know, that the children would sometimes go to the kitchen and they'd give us some biscuits. At that time, some of the children they didn't have biscuits often. And when they'd get the biscuits, it was really fun. I think "shoo lie loo" means something like "I'm really glad!"

Though John Davis maintained that any play taking place in a circle is a "ring play," Mrs. Jones insisted on calling "Just from the Kitchen" a "skip," I suspect because it requires no center player. In this play, the lead singer, standing as part of the circle of players, calls out the "real" name of a different child in each verse; and the child whose name is sung then skips across the ring with his arms outstretched—"flying away over yonder."

Other kinds of food may be sung about, too; Mrs. Jones gave some of us handfuls of tomatoes, rabbit, meat skins, potatoes, and chitterlings as her imagination dictated. On one occasion she described this as an "after-slavery play":

He's so glad—he's free and got his own bread so he fly away over yonder. . . . He's so glad he got freedom food! . . .

F O R M : Circle of children standing and clapping.

LEAD VOICE	GROUP VOICE	ACTION
Just from the kitchen,		All stand and clap.
	Shoo lie loo,	
With a handful of biscuits,		
	Shoo lie loo,	
Oh (Miss Mary),		Child whose name is sung
	Shoo lie loo,	skips across ring with
Fly away over yonder		arms outstretched, flying. (Don't flap; sail.) At other side, turn (on word "away") and clap with the others.

Just from the Kitchen

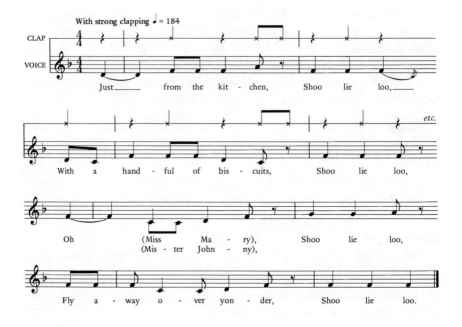

New words and new music adaptation by Bessie Jones; collected and edited with additional new material by Alan Lomax. TRO—© copyright 1972 Ludlow Music, Inc., New York, N.Y. Used by permission.

Shoo, Turkey

Well, that's a little jump. You squats and you jumps, you know, like that . . . and you do your hands this way, shooing the turkey each side. Oh, it's pretty. . . .

This "pretty little jump" begins with a stylized conversation between the leader and the group of children who stand in a line facing her. At the end of the conversation, the children turn and snake-dance through the yard, shooing the turkeys by waving their hands first to one side and then the other. The leader may dance with them but had probably better save her breath for the singing, as the dancers will get winded soon.

F O R M : Line of children facing the leader.

LEAD VOICE	GROUP VOICE	ACTION
Little girl, little boy?		None.
	Yes, ma'am.	
Well, did you go downtown?		
	Yes, ma'am.	
Well, did you get any eggs?		
	Yes, ma'am.	
Well, did you bring them home?		
	Yes, ma'am.	
Well, did you cook any bread?		
	Yes, ma'am.	
Well, did you save me mine?		
	Yes, ma'am.	

(Begin offbeat clap)
Well, shoo, shoo, shoo, turkey,
    Throw your feather way
        yonder.
Shoo, shoo, shoo, turkey,
    Throw your feather way
        yonder.

(Repeat above verse ad
    lib)

I'm going to buy me another
    turkey,

Each child makes a quarter turn to his right and follows the end player, who leads out on a winding course. The step used is a chug in a squatting position; the arms are thrown out to right and left alternatively on each chug keeping time to the downbeats of the song.

Throw your feather way
yonder.
I'm going to buy me another
turkey,
Throw your feather way
yonder.

(Repeat ad lib)

Shoo, Turkey

Written and adapted by Bessie Jones; collected and edited by Alan Lomax. TRO—© copyright 1972 Ludlow Music, Inc., New York, N.Y. Used by permission.

Knock Jim Crow

When I was a little girl, I thought Jim Crow might have been a bird, because it was "going down to the new ground," and they always shoot them birds out of the corn. "New ground" is ground where the trees have been cut off, but it's never been planted in. So that was what I understood at the time, that was my idea. But we don't know what the old folks meant, we sure don't.

JOHN DAVIS: *I don't believe the old folks knew what they were talking about their ownselves. Anyway, they didn't* tell *nobody. . . .*

Probably, to begin with, "Jim Crow" was a bird, as Mrs. Jones and Mr. Davis suggest, but during the late 1820's the name became attached to a young white actor, Thomas D. Rice, who had invented a stage characterization of the "jolly, carefree" plantation slave. In this role, which rapidly became a popular stereotype in the minstrel theater, the young vaudevillian, wearing blackface and in comical rags, did a little eccentric dance while singing:

I kneel to the buzzard,
I bow to the crow,
And eb'ry time I w'eel about
I jump jis' so.

W'eel about an' turn about an' do jis' so,
An' eb'ry time I w'eel about I jump Jim Crow.

Reportedly, he had heard this refrain from an old Negro man some years earlier.

"Jim Crow" thus developed from a dance imitating the motions of birds and hunters, and quite possibly magical in nature, into a commercial caricature. No wonder the term, when used in a political context, has a bitter taste today. The Islanders, however, clearly regard this as a pleasurable dance, probably about birds, and "knock Jim Crow" with enthusiasm and alacrity.

FORM: Indefinite; group of children standing in a line or ring. There may be a lead singer, or the children may all sing together.

LEAD AND GROUP VOICE	ACTION
Where you going, buzzard?	Step on right foot, raise left leg with
Where you going, crow?	knee straight (like a high goose
I'm going down to new ground	step) and clap hands together

To knock Jim Crow.

Up <u>to</u> my knee<u>cap</u>,

around it; repeat, raising alternate
legs until,

On "to" raise right knee (bent) and
slap it with right hand.

On "cap" raise left knee (bent) and
slap it with left hand.

Down <u>to</u> my toe,___

On "to" point down to ground with
right index finger.

On beat after "toe" point down to
ground with left index finger.

And every time I jump up,
I knock Jim Crow.
    (Speed increases)
I knock,
I knock Jim Crow.
I knock,
I knock Jim Crow.
I knock, I knock,
I knock Jim Crow.
    (repeat ad lib)

Resume raising alternate legs and
clapping around them as in first
step.

Dancers increase speed, continuing to
lift legs and clap while turning
round in place until exhaustion
sets in.

Be sure that the steps are on the downbeat, so that the claps can
come on the offbeat.

where you go - ing buz - zard, where you go - ing crow?
step   clap   step clap step   clap   step   clap

Knock Jim Crow

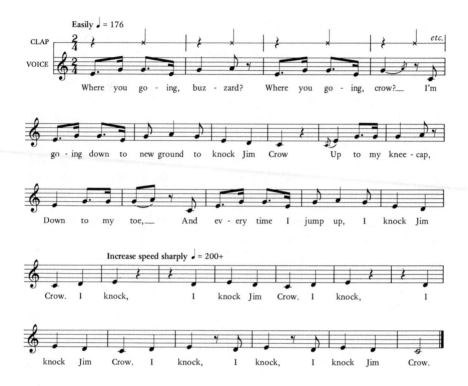

Josephine

This is a little play that the children all stand in a line [for]. And you stand facing them and when you call on one, it mean all, because they're all called on one name: Josephine. . . .

Like "Shoo, Turkey," "Josephine" begins with a formal conversation. This kind of prelude seems to be still another way of teaching the child responsiveness and giving him a preliminary taste of the pleasures of antiphonal singing.

At the end of the conversation, the leader sings and claps for the children, who "act out" the words with their hands while they dance the shout step (see page 45). As Mrs. Jones warns,

This is a jump . . . you got to do it to do it! But the children get tired, because it's a long shout. . . .

FORM: Line of children standing facing the lead singer.

LEAD VOICE (speaking)	GROUP VOICE (speaking)	ACTION None
Josephine?		
	Ma'am?	
You want to shout?		
	Yes, ma'am!	
When?		
	Right now!	
(Chanting and clapping) Shout, Josephine!		Line of dancers start
	Shout, shout!	shout step which
Shout, Josephine!		continues through-
	Shout, shout!	out without stop-
I've got a <u>ball</u> of cord,		ping until the last
	Shout, shout!	verse.
I've got a ball of cord,		Dancers place one
	Shout, shout!	hand at back of
I've got a <u>pain</u> in my head,		head, feeling an
	Shout, shout!	imaginary knot of
I've got a pain in my head,		hair.
	Shout, shout!	Dancers put one hand to forehead.

LEAD VOICE (Chanting and clapping)	GROUP VOICE	ACTION
I've got a finger ring,		Dancers put index fin-
	Shout, shout!	ger of one hand on
I've got a finger ring.		other index finger.

                        Shout, shout!
I've got a pain in my back,
                        Shout, shout!
I've got a pain in my back,   Dancers put one hand
                        Shout, shout!   to small of back.
I've got slipper shoes,
                        Shout, shout!
I've got slipper shoes,   Dancers point index
                        Shout, shout!   fingers down to-
I've got a pain in my knee,   ward their feet.
                        Shout, shout!   Dancers touch knee.
I've got a pain in my knee,
                        Shout, shout!
I'll shake the baby,   Dancers hold arms as
                        Shout, shout!   though cradling a
I'll shake the baby,   baby, swing them
                        Shout, shout!   from side to side.

(Singing and clapping)
Aunt Jenny's cornbread is sweet, sweet, sweet,   Dancers stop the shout
Take some and leave some, sweet, sweet, sweet,   step and all "jump
Aunt Jenny's cornbread is sweet, sweet, sweet,   for joy" (see page
Take some and leave some sweet, sweet,   44) until the end.
Take some and leave some sweet, sweet!

Josephine

Written and adapted by Bessie Jones; collected and edited by Alan Lomax. TRO—© copyright 1972 Ludlow Music, Inc., New York, N.Y. Used by permission.

Elephant Fair

This is just a jump; it's a play that we always played. Mama used to play it too. I have it now for the children; they stands in a line or either in a ring as they want to but they all jump, you know, dance this. It's a hard jump; it's good for you, makes you strong. I played it with the children this morning and one boy said, "Oh, tell me when to stop! Just stop me!" He was really doing it. . . .

When Mrs. Jones claps and chants this verse, accenting it strongly and expressively, the rhythm does start carrying you along and it's hard to know how to stop. The step is the "jump for joy" (described on page 44), done all the way through and speeded up on the last line for as many repetitions as your breath will allow you.

The first two lines of the verse are known all over the South; the rest is a combination of many traditional rhymes and songs. The content is rough and emotionally very satisfying, I suspect. Mrs. Jones started to laugh one day after she said the line, "Now you Alabama sucker, take your hand off of me," and remarked, "You know, we couldn't *use* words like that. We *liked* it!"

FORM: Line, circle, or other formation, if any at all. Lead singer and
    clapper is essential, as the dancers will be too out of breath shortly
    to be audible.

LEAD VOICE (chanting and clapping)   ACTION
I went down to the elephant fair,   Jump for joy.
And the birds and bees was there.
And they went all around by the Maypole stand
And drug their snout on the ground.
        It's the best old lady, it's the best old man;
        I like the pretty boy who totes the money.
        Old lady, old man; it's no wonder you can't
            stand.
Now you Alabama sucker, take your hand off
        of me,
Take your hand off of me.
You better not mess with Lula;
I'll tell you the reason why.
She'll cut out your heart with a razor,
And she'll cut out your insides too,
        And she'll cut out your insides too.
        She'll cut out your insides too (repeated   Jump for joy speeded up
            ad lib)   faster and faster.

Elephant Fair

Strongly accented ♩ = 168
Tempo increases slightly throughout.

I went down to the el-e-phant fair, And the birds and the bees was there. And they went all a-round by the May-pole stand and drug their snout on the ground. It's the best old la-dy, it's the best old man; I like the pret-ty boy who totes the mon-ey. Old la-dy, Old man;— It's no won-der you can't stand. Now you Al-a-ba-ma suck-er, take your hand off of me. take your hand off of me. You bet-ter not mess with Lu-la; I'll tell you the rea-son why.— She'll cut out your heart with a ra-zor, And she'll cut out your in-sides

Increase speed sharply ♩ = 208+   *(repeat ad lib.)*

too. She'll cut out your in-sides too, She'll cut out your in-sides too.

New words and new music adaptation by Bessie Jones; collected and edited with additional new material by Alan Lomax. TRO—© copyright 1972 Ludlow Music, Inc., New York, N.Y. Used by permission.

Pizza, Pizza, Mighty Moe

It really is pretty the way they carry it. . . . And they know it they own self, they like it, it's modern. And when they get on that thing, it's good! . . .

This fragmentary but gay curiosity is included for its own sake, as well as for what it can indicate about the current development of play. Since "Pizza, Pizza, Mighty Moe" is not an old play, the Islanders did not know how to do it, and therefore I have not seen their version performed. They did describe it, however, with considerable amusement and gusto.

Apparently they themselves saw "Pizza" at what must have been a remarkable play presented by the children of the Brunswick, Georgia, elementary school a few years ago. Both Evalina and Pizza were characters in this drama, and in one scene a chorus came out, dancing in line, one behind the other, to act out this rhyme. A generation maturing during the age of the Jerk and the Monkey would not need much instruction in how to dance to this chant; apparently, "Pizza" has caught on among the Island children as well as in Los Angeles, and, as Mrs. Jones says, "When they get on that thing, it's good!"

Evalina?
    Pizza, Pizza, Mighty Moe.
Well, have you seen her?
    Pizza, Pizza, Mighty Moe.
She's got a wooden leg.
    Pizza, Pizza, Mighty Moe.
But can she use it?
    Pizza, Pizza, Mighty Moe.
Oh yes, she use it.
    Pizza, Pizza, Mighty Moe.
Well, do she 'buse it?
    Pizza, Pizza, Mighty Moe.
I *know* she use it.
    Pizza, Pizza, Mighty Moe.
Well, can she ball it?
    Pizza, Pizza, Mighty Moe.
I say, *ball* it!
    Pizza, Pizza, Mighty Moe.

Pizza, Pizza, Mighty Moe

Stylishly ♩ = 144

Ev - a - li - na? (Piz - za, Piz - za, Might - y Moe) Well, have you seen her?

(Piz - za, Piz - za, Might - y Moe) She's got a wood - en leg.

(Piz - za, Piz - za, Might - y Moe) But can she use it? *etc.*

New words and new music adaptation by Bessie Jones; collected and edited with additional new material by Alan Lomax. TRO—© copyright 1972 Ludlow Music, Inc., New York, N.Y. Used by permission.

4:
Singing Plays

As Mrs. Jones says over and over in many different ways, children not only have to learn *how* to do something, they must also learn what they are doing it *for*. To her, the plays that teach individual skills—the claps, the jumps, and the skips—are only preparations for the moment when those developing skills are put to use within a larger context, within the group. Down from the mother's lap, away from the close one-to-one contact of the clapping plays, the growing child wanders into the larger complex whirl of the family, the play group, and the community.

The Afro-American child, both during the era of slavery and after, faced an especially difficult problem: the comprehension of an essentially bicultural world. To understand it, he had to look in two directions at the same time: to his own family and people, and to the dominant white community that surrounded him.

As he watched his white contemporaries, he confronted an example of one of the small wonders of history—the stability and perseverance of the traditions of childhood. Undisturbed by distance and political upheaval, the sons and daughters of Georgia and South Carolina planters went on playing the same games that their great-great-grandparents had played in the streets of London or Edinburgh. The black children from the "quarters" stood and watched, or perhaps they were allowed to play, too.

The group of games in this section, then, might be considered a kind of platform upon which Euro-American and Afro-American children met during our country's growing up. Originally I put them together simply because they did not seem to fit anywhere else, and I had titled this section "Miscellaneous" until I realized that the term is inaccurate. There is a logical relationship here; these are the singing games that hold closest to British origins. (Other singing games in other sections can be traced back to England, too, but through a more complicated path.)

Mrs. Jones, by the way, did not know what to call these particular games herself. She referred to various ones of them at various times as "plays," "singing plays," and "little what-nots." I have used the second of her titles, although the third reflects her point of view more accurately, I think.

Interestingly, these are always the favorite plays among white students I have taught; this is, I believe, because of their emphasis upon *form* rather than *style*. Mrs. Jones, too, appreciated this quality; the ceremonial tracing out of pattern which is so important in these games deeply appealed to her. She referred to them over and over as *"beautiful* plays" and, intuitively striking at the heart of the matter, would say

Oh, I like that. There's so much meaning *to it.* . . .

Green, Green, the Crab Apple Tree

It's a play . . . I'll tell you how it go. You stand in a ring and just go round and you call different ones' names, and they turn back, you know. . . . They're flowers, see? . . .

I first played this game with Mrs. Jones and the Sea Islanders on a bright morning in my living room, climbing over dogs and recording equipment to do so. It was a strange experience to "turn back my head" on the friendly clutter of my own life, while my friends and I moved through the ancient pattern, originally a child's re-enactment of a mourning rite. In most of the English-speaking world, "Green, Green, the Crab Apple Tree" is called "Green Gravel" or, sometimes, "Green Graves."

Actually it is a ceremonial dance, rather than a game; the pace should be moderate and the movements smooth. While I was learning the tune, Mrs. Hillary joined in with a "tenor" part of such brilliant and intense dissonance that I have transcribed it here. Though the game is always played quite cheerfully, when Mrs. Hillary's vocal part is added, this little fragment of man's remote past becomes solemn and mysterious.

FORM: A ring of children holding hands. All walk in a counterclockwise circle while all sing.

LEAD VOICE	GROUP VOICE	ACTION
	Green, green, the crab apple tree, Where the grass grows so deep.	Children, holding hands, circle in a walking step in time to the singing.
	Miss	
Emma,		
	Miss	
Emma,		
	Your true lover is dead. He wrote you a letter To <u>turn</u> back your head.	On "turn," child whose name has been sung drops hands, turns halfway around with back to the center of the ring, and joins hands again, and the circling movement continues until all the players have been called.

Green, Green, the Crab Apple Tree

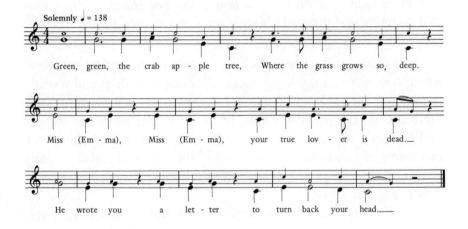

Solemnly ♩ = 138

Green, green, the crab ap - ple tree, Where the grass grows so, deep.

Miss (Em - ma), Miss (Em - ma), your true lov - er is dead.__

He wrote you a let - ter to turn back your head.__

Words and music by Bessie Jones; collected and edited with new material by Alan Lomax. TRO—
© copyright 1972 Ludlow Music, Inc., New York, N.Y. Used by permission.

Johnny Cuckoo

The children are in a line and one person walks up and he be's one Johnny Cuckoo. And he sings back and forth and takes one and takes him back with him. Then there's two Johnny Cuckoos. . . .

The ancient British game "Three Dukes A-Riding" is a courtship play in which an increasing number of "dukes" come to choose their brides from a line of young maidens, in what may be a reflection of marriage customs between clans in old Britain. Both British and American writers describe it as a line play, with the parallel lines of maidens and dukes advancing and retreating, looking "contemptuously and criticizingly" at each other as they sing "You are too black and blowsy" and "We are quite as good as you, sirs" before they finally join forces.

The Sea Islanders don't bother with "contemptuous and criticizing looks"; they simply turn their backs and "switch" their hips in their opponents' faces. (The hip-switching motion is achieved by standing with the legs together and bending one knee forward while the other goes back into a locked position; alternate knees for the other side.) Further, the plot of Mrs. Jones's version no longer concerns coquetry and courtship but the choosing of "soldiers"; the phrase "You are too black and dirty" is scarcely part of the language of love.

In play, however, this is an uproariously good-humored game and one of the favorites of both adults and children. Both sides get to dramatize hostility in a very down-to-earth fashion; and even though children are used to having rude remarks made about their personal appearance, the ones I have seen playing this game get absolutely enormous satisfaction out of being able to answer back, for once, "I am just as clean as you are!"

FORM: Line of children singing and clapping a single offbeat clap. One player (Johnny Cuckoo) faces the line.

ALL VOICES*	ACTION
Here comes one Johnny Cuckoo, Cuckoo, Cuckoo. Here comes one Johnny Cuckoo On a cold and stormy night.	Single player approaches line and walks back and forth inspecting the "troops."

What did you come for,
Come for, come for,
What did you come for
On a cold and stormy night?

I come for me (We come for us)
    a soldier,
Soldier, a soldier,
I come for me (We come for us)
    a soldier
On a cold and stormy night.

(Slight increase of speed, begin
    double offbeat clap)
You look too black and dirty,
Dirty, dirty,
You look too black and dirty
On a cold and stormy night.

All players in the line turn their backs on Johnny Cuckoo and switch their hips at him, turning to face him on the last word.

I am (We are) just as clean as
    you are,
You are, you are,
I am (We are) just as clean as
    you are
On a cold and stormy night.

Center player turns his back on the line and switches his hips at them, turning back and selecting another player on the last word.

Now here comes two Johnny
    Cuckoos, etc.

Game is repeated with two Johnny Cuckoos, at the end of which the original selects another player to repeat the play with three, and so on.

° Though this is a game in which the conversation switches back and forth from the line to Johnny Cuckoo, the Sea Islanders sing all the verses together all the way through. I suspect this is just because they enjoy singing the song in harmony.

Johnny Cuckoo

Here comes one John - ny Cuck - oo, Cuck - oo,— Cuck - oo.
What— did you— come for, come for,— come for.
come for us a— sol - dier, sol - dier,— sol - dier, We
(me) (I)

Here comes one John - ny Cuck - oo on a cold and storm - y night.
What— did you— come for on a cold and storm - y night? We
come for us a— sol - dier on a cold and storm - y (I)
(me)

night. You— look too black and dirt - y, dirt - y,
I am just as clean as you are, you are,
(We are)

dirt - y,— You look too black and dirt - y— on a cold and storm - y night.
you are, I am just as clean as you are— on a cold and storm - y night.

Written and adapted by Bessie Jones; collected and edited by Alan Lomax. TRO—© copyright
1972 Ludlow Music, Inc., New York, N.Y. Used by permission.

Oh Green Fields, Roxie

This play moves, *and just like you're hearing it go now, you move* with *it. . . . You got to move with it, so you can really be stirred*.

Mrs. Jones's passionate remark was caused by her catching sight of a player tramping casually, and out of rhythm, into the center of the ring. If you do "clap it right and play it *right*," as Mrs. Jones points out, this little play really *does* move.

It is also an excellent example of the Afro-American way with a British song. Its early ancestor was a delicate little verse to a skipping rhythm:

> Green grow the rushes, oh,
> Green grow the rushes, oh,
> He who will my true love be
> Come and sit by the side of me!

In Mrs. Jones's neighborhood, the breathy word "rushes" became the explosive and crackling "Roxie!"; the tempo changed from a skip to a strut. When accompanied by a solid offbeat clap, this can be one of the most jazzily rhythmic of all Mrs. Jones's plays.

FORM: Ring of children standing and clapping. In the middle of the ring is a chair with a player sitting in it. The "caller," who leads the singing, stands by the chair.

LEAD VOICE	GROUP VOICE	ACTION
Oh green fields,		All players clapping.
	Roxie,	
Oh green fields,		
	Roxie,	
Tell me who you love,		Caller leans over to player in
	Roxie,	the chair, who whispers the
Tell me who you love,		name of another player to the
	Roxie,	caller.
(Lead voice solo)		
Oh, Miss (Mabel) your name is called,		Caller sings the whispered name.
Come take a seat right side your love,		Player called struts to chair,
Shake his hand and let him go,		shakes hands with player in chair,

Don't let him sit in that chair
      no more.

and sits down. First player
dances back to the ring and
the game is repeated without
pause.

Oh Green Fields, Roxie

Written and adapted by Bessie Jones; collected and edited by Alan Lomax. TRO—© copyright
1972 Ludlow Music, Inc., New York, N.Y. Used by permission.

Go In and Out the Window ✳

This is another example of how fortunate Americans are to have British melody and African rhythm combining into their national musical language. To anyone who has doggedly skipped (or trudged when the teacher wasn't looking) through this play on a hot asphalt playground, the Sea Islanders' swing through this old chestnut will be a revelation. Be sure and give it a solid offbeat clap.

Mrs. Jones says that "to measure your love" you take a piece of paper (about the size of a small envelope), hold it by diagonal corners up to the breast of your partner, "measuring" by raising and lowering your hands in a seesawing motion, so that first one corner is up, then the other.

The refrain "As we have came today" is probably a variation of the line "As we have gained the day" from the widespread version which begins, "We're marching round the levee." Grammarians may make their own selection.

FORM: Children standing in a ring, holding hands with arms high to form arches. Drop hands and clap after first verse. One player in center, who has a piece of paper or handkerchief in hand (see above).

ALL VOICES EXCEPT
CENTER PLAYER

ACTION

Go in and out the window,
Go in and out the window,
Go in and out the window,
As we have came today.

Center player walks, to time, out of ring through one arch, back in through next, and so on.

I kneel because I love you,
I kneel because I love you,
I kneel because I love you
As we have came today.

Center player kneels before the player he has reached at beginning of verse; no choice allowed.

I measure my love to show you,
I measure my love to show you,
I measure my love to show you
As we have came today.

Center player "measures love" as described above; this action must be done to time.

Shake <u>hands</u> before I leave you,   Center player and partner shake
Shake hands before I leave you,   hands, also to time.
Shake hands before I leave you
As we have came today.   Center player and partner change
                                         places and play continues with new
                                         center player, who takes the "mea-
                                         sure" with him.

Go In and Out the Window

Written and adapted by Bessie Jones; collected and edited by Alan Lomax. TRO—© copyright
1972 Ludlow Music, Inc., New York, N.Y. Used by permission.

Draw Me a Bucket of Water

Back up to where I was brought up at, we had big huge wells with two buckets on it. You know how to draw up that way? Bring up one bucket and carry down another one, you know, so you won't lose no time. . . . And so anyway, the wells what we had, the top wouldn't be on it—you know, just an open well—and they made a song about that. The frog would get in our well, you see, because it didn't have no top on it. And snakes would get in our well, but we'd shake 'em out or fish 'em out or get 'em out because you sure couldn't dreen the well and wash 'em out. And we had to drink the water. . . .

Mrs. Jones's imaginative explanation accounts for the combination here of two traditional games of British origin ("Draw a Bucket of Water"and "Frog in the Middle"). Her version differs from other descriptions I have seen in the method of play and perhaps is closer to dance than game. It was a strong favorite with all students at the summer workshop.

The play is unique in Mrs. Jones's repertoire in that it requires an exact number of players. Two couples stand in the form of a square, holding hands with their opposite partners; each couple sways back and forth pulling their arms in a seesawing motion. At the phrase "Go under, sister Sally," the couple whose arms are on top of the cross raises arms to make an arch on one side only. The player on that side ducks under and thus is the "one in the bunch"; she does *not* drop her partner's hands.

The verse is repeated until the opposite partner of the "one in the bunch" ducks under the alternate raised arms to make "two in the bunch." On the third repetition, the inside couple raises their clasped hands to arch so that one of the outside couples can come under. After the fourth repetition, all players will find that they are standing with their arms twined around each other. They then dance around with a "buzz step" through the first singing of the "Frog in the Bucket" verse, and "step it down" the second time.

The major directions to remember here are neither to drop hands nor to twist or cross them; the pattern is extremely simple to execute (though difficult to describe). Emotionally, there is an enormous satisfaction in completing this lovely weaving figure.

FORM: Four children standing in a square; each holds hands with the opposite partner. (See diagram.) A's and B's arms are on top of the cross. Do *not* drop hands until last verse.

ALL VOICES
Draw me a bucket of water
For my oldest daughter.
We got none in the bunch,
We're all out the bunch.
You go <u>under</u>, sister Sally.

Draw me a bucket of water
For my oldest daughter.
We got one in the bunch
And three out the bunch.
You go <u>under</u>, sister Sally.

Draw me a bucket of water
For my oldest daughter.
We got two in the bunch
And two out the bunch.
You go <u>under</u>, sister Sally.

Draw me a bucket of water
For my oldest daughter.
We got three in the bunch
And one out the bunch.
You go <u>under</u>, sister Sally.

Frog in the bucket and I can't
   get him out. (Repeat four times.)

Frog in the bucket and I can't
   get him out. (Repeat four times.)

ACTION
Players sway forward and back in a seesawing motion.

Player D ducks under arch formed by right arm of player A and left arm of player B.
Swaying motion continues; players C and D do *not* drop hands; neither do A and B.

Player C ducks under arch made by left arm of player A and right arm of player B.
Swaying continues, though C and D, still holding hands, have to confine their motion.

Player A ducks under arch made by right arm of player C and left of player D.
Swaying continues, though space is highly constricted.

Player B ducks under arch made by raised left arm of player C and right of player D.

With arms entwined, still holding the original hands, players dance round in a circle, using the buzz step.

Players drop hands and rejoin them in a simple circle and "step it down."

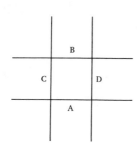

Draw Me a Bucket of Water

Smoothly ♩ = 112

Draw me a buck - et of wa - ter, For my old - est daught - er, We got
none in the bunch, We're all out the bunch, You go un - der, sis - ter Sal - ly

one   and three
two   and two
three   and one

Snappily ♩ = 208

Frog in the buck - et and I can't get him out, Frog in the buck - et and I can't get him out,

Frog in the buck - et and I can't get him out.

1. Frog in the buck - et and I

2. can't get him out. Frog in the buck - et and I can't get him out.

Written and adapted by Bessie Jones; collected and edited by Alan Lomax. TRO—© copyright 1972 Ludlow Music, Inc., New York, N.Y. Used by permission.

Nana, Thread Needle

This is a beautiful play. . . . This play shows you how people can borrow from you and never pay it back. And when they say, "I'm going to wind up this bunkum," it means, "I'm going to wind up this borrowing." I like this because there's so much <u>to</u> it, there's so much meaning in it. . . .

This is another combination of several British plays widespread, in various forms, through the Caribbean area as well as the Southern United States. It is one of the most satisfying of all Mrs. Jones's plays, but to really enjoy it remember that it is a *play*, a ceremonial tracing of pattern, not a *game*.

Mrs. Jones was quite firm about the phrase "thread needle." When players sang "thread *the* needle," she remarked, "We didn't know nothing about no thread *the* needle; it's *thread needle*." I do not know why this was so important to her.

To play, a group of children stand in line; they hold hands throughout the entire game. They should be arranged roughly by height, from the tallest to the shortest (here indicated from A to Z). The two players on the ends of the line hold a brief conversation:

A (tallest): Neighbor, neighbor, lend me your hatchet.
Z (shortest): Neighbor, neighbor, step and get it.

A then starts out at a steady walking pace and leads through the arch made by the hands of B and C. This forces B to turn under her own arm, a movement called in some games "wringing the dishrag." (If the players do not hold hands tightly but allow the turning player's hand to rotate naturally, she will revolve back to her original position without a sprained wrist.) Player A continues leading the marching line around and through the arch between players C and D, and so on through each pair of arms in a gradually enlarging concentric spiral, while singing:

LEAD VOICE (PLAYER A)	GROUP VOICE	ACTION
Nana,		(As described above)
	Thread needle.	
Nana,		
	Thread needle.	

I wants my needle.

> Thread needle.

I lost my needle.

> Thread needle.

My gold-eyed needle.

> Thread needle.

It's mama's needle.

> Thread needle.

The lead singer's lines are improvised, depending on choice and the length of the line; she may return to "nana," which Mrs. Jones says means "mama," whenever she likes.

When the space Y and Z has been "sewn" through and the line returned to its original form, there is another conversation.

> Z (shortest): Neighbor, neighbor, send me my hatchet.
> A (tallest): Neighbor, neighbor, I ain't got it.

Z then starts skipping out, leading her end of the line around A, who stands still. Z (who has to be in pretty good condition) continues skipping around and around until the whole line is wound up in a concentric spiral, like a tight watch spring, around A. The players do *not* drop hands, and must move with each other; there should be no pulling apart. While this circling movement is going on, all players sing, repeating over and over:

> Going to wind up-a this bunkum, bunkum,
> Wind up-a this bunkum.
> Wind up-a this bunkum, bunkum,
> Wind up-a this bunkum.

When this movement is finished, and you have, as Mrs. Jones puts it, "nothing but a big ball of children," all the players jump up and down together, singing:

> Going to shake down-a this bunkum, bunkum,
> Shake down-a this bunkum.
> Shake down-a this bunkum, bunkum,
> Shake down-a this bunkum.

After everyone is "shaken down" sufficiently (the verse may be repeated as often as desired), Z turns back and retraces her skip, leading the line back to the starting position, while singing:

Going to unwind-a this bunkum, bunkum,
Unwind-a this bunkum.
Unwind-a this bunkum, bunkum,
Unwind-a this bunkum. . . .

Nana, Thread Needle

Fast steady walking pace ♩ = 120

Na - na,___ Thread nee - dle. Na - na,___ Thread nee - dle. I

wants my nee - dle. Thread nee - dle. I lost my nee - dle. Thread nee - dle. My

Repeat ad lib until dance figure is complete.

gold - eyed nee - dle. Thread nee - dle. It's ma - ma's nee - dle. Thread nee - dle.

Briskly ♩ = 120

Going to wind up - a this bun - kum, bun - kum, Wind up - a this bun - kum.
shake down - a   Shake down - a
un - wind - a   Un - wind - a

Wind up - a this bun - kum, bun - kum, Wind up - a this bun - kum.
Shake down - a   Shake down - a
Un wind - a   Un wind - a

New words and new music adaptation by Bessie Jones; collected and edited by Alan Lomax. TRO—©
copyright 1972 Ludlow Music, Inc., New York, N.Y. Used by permission.

5:
Ring Plays

And the children all stand in a ring . . .

The notion of a ring has always had a quality of magic; during play it is, literally, a "charmed circle." It includes and excludes at the same time. It surrounds and enfolds while it walls off and repels. Inside a ring, within its bounds, you are safe from what is "outside"; you are in a special world in which you may be either king or prisoner. The ring is without gap or weakness—perhaps strength is its underlying symbolic quality.

The strength of a ring is in its construction. Since it has neither beginning nor end, there can be no ranking of its parts—no strong or weak, big or little. In the old fairy tales, the giving of a ring often is a token of union and a pledge of constancy, but sometimes the magical ring has another function: it makes the wearer invisible. And so with the individual. When you are part of a ring, you are just that—part of a ring. There are no head and foot couples, no captains, no opposing ranks. It is the signal form of democracy.

Given the basic construction of a ring, there are many ways in which dramatic or symbolic play can develop. Its strength can be attacked from the outside or from the inside. It may develop gaps which must be filled, as in the many forms of "Drop the Handkerchief." Gates may open to allow players to leave the circle and make a venture into the outside world, or it may expand concentrically into two circles. It can become a wheel, or two wheels, which can rotate together or in opposing motion.

Such basic circular play forms, as well as many others, have been the historic property of both children and adults in all times and all places. It seems likely, then, that the ring plays of black Americans are revisions and combinations of both European and African games and ceremonials.

But as I have already mentioned, there are lots of things that can happen inside and outside of a ring. In thinking about Mrs. Jones's repertoire of circle games, there is one set of actions so frequent that it seems, both to me and to Mrs. Jones, a special category. It is this particular set of actions which are referred to as "ring play" throughout this book.

The "ring play," as the term is used here, consists of a group standing in a circle, clapping, singing, and musically supporting a single central character who acts out his own brief drama on center stage, as it were, before he chooses another to take his place. Mrs. Jones puts it more succinctly:

One gets in the middle of the ring and they all clap and sing, you see. . . . And it go on until you get to each one. . . .

The center player in the ring play, then, stands alone to make his statement by dance or "acting," usually within the context of courtship play. But this is a different kind of courtship than that dramatized by British children, for instance, who choose partners and end by singing:

> Now, you are married, you must be good
> And make your husband chop the wood.

The ring player makes his statement of romantic availability all by himself; at the end of his turn, he picks out not so much a partner as a successor. There is little, if any, paired or coupled action.

The emotional climate of ring play is humorous, if not uproarious. The Islanders clearly thought the ring plays were the most fun of all. They provided an opportunity for the hottest dancing, the most ridiculous miming, the most exaggerated horseplay. As I watched, it seemed to me that the ring play was the moment of individuation—

for the child, the culmination of his learning skills, the announcement of his separation from the family.

For one thing, the usual family taboos and prohibitions are suspended. Black children are not encouraged in "real life" to "put on airs" or to flaunt themselves publicly. In the ring play, they may strut and tease, flirt and wiggle, while everybody claps for them. In Mrs. Jones's comment on "Soup, Soup" you can find her own recognition of the pleasure she found in being able to break the rules, to act out the forbidden.

But the separation is not complete. The ring player is not alone; he is accompanied by singing, and the singers make constant contact with him. "What can you do?" they ask him. "Show me your motion!" Usually, however, the group simply comments on the action, rather than directing it. "Way go, Lily!" they sing, as Lily flies across the ring. Or they make remarks about the player's person—"Oh, she's neat in the waist, and she's pretty in the face."

Adult Negroes in Southern rural churches will give just such vocal support as they respond to the prayers and testimonies of church members who feel the call to speak. To use their own lovely phrase, they will "bear up" their minister as he preaches, just as the trumpet and trombone fill in musically under the clarinet solo in the New Orleans jazz ensemble. In the ring play, a further extension of the principle of antiphony, or responsiveness, begins to be plain: the individual is always supported by a nondirective group and, just as important, he comes out of and eventually returns to that group.

The Islanders found it almost incomprehensible that I wanted an explanation of the ring plays before I would try them myself. "Come on, it's just a little play!" they would urge. The power of the ring, for them, was unbroken. They *knew* that the surrounding group would support the shy or the awkward just as strongly as it would the bold or the graceful, and that no dancer would get more or less time than any other. For them, the ring play seemed to be the ultimate opportunity for personal reassurance, for feeling the warmth and support of a tight-locked and indestructible circle within which they could act out all their feelings without any fear of rejection or shame. And so it must be, too, for the black child making his first steps into the larger world beyond the family.

For me, though—and, I suspect, for most of the other white

players—the taking of the center of the ring was a kind of horrible, publicly stated moment of truth. I didn't have many motions, to begin with, and those I had seemed all wrong. It is, perhaps, one of the finest ironies of the American dilemma that the isolated minority should be able to speak among its friends so much more freely than the dominant majority.

However, due to the patience and enthusiasm of the Islanders, I did eventually begin to get some of the feeling of ring play. Here are some of its working principles, many of which, because of the central importance of the form, are applicable to plays not included in this section.

1. There may be almost any number of players, odd or even, though it is difficult to work with less than six or more than ten or twelve. On one occasion when we had thirty players, I suggested to Mrs. Jones that we use two central figures, moving in different parts of the ring. Though she agreed and I felt the arrangement worked out well, it was obviously not a normal or comfortable procedure for Mrs. Jones. There should be only *one* player in the ring; her solution, as I realized later, would have been to divide into two separate groups.

2. The circle players always sing, clap, and usually "step it down" a little as well, shifting their weight from side to side in the foot move described at the beginning of Chapter 2: Clapping Plays (p. 20). This is *not* the dance step also known as "stepping it down" but the ordinary physical accompaniment to *clapping* that serves, here, both to keep the rhythm solid and to keep each player physically tensed and ready to take his turn. Since each center player chooses the one to follow him, the other players' turns may come at the end of any run-through.

3. These are *plays*, not games. The center player is an actor and should "act out" each phrase of the song that describes him. For instance, in "East Coast Line" the center player may strut or dance inside the circle through the first five lines of the song, but should act out the lines "she's neat in the waist and she's pretty in the face" even if, as Mrs. Jones remarked, "she's got a big old whomper like me."

4. The center player is also a *dancer*, and walks (dances) to time from the moment he comes out of the surrounding ring until he returns to it. When he chooses the next dancer, the choice must al-

ways "come out right with the music." If he misjudges, he must choose the player he can reach on time.

5. Play is continuous. While the moment when an action should *begin* is indicated by underlining the appropriate word in the song text, the action should be carried on until the next direction is given. And at the end of one round of play, when a new center player takes over, play continues without pause until everyone has had a turn.

6. "Lead singer" and "center player" are, of course, different roles. The lead singer may be *any* player with a strong voice and some extra energy; when the time comes for the singer to take a turn as center player, another voice will often take over the lead role. Thus the center player position changes with each run-through of the play, while the lead singer may continue through the entire play session, or, as her voice grows tired, a fresher voice may spontaneously take over.

7. Some of the plays included in this section could have been placed elsewhere; actually, Mrs. Jones called some of them different things at different times. Man and his works are simply too diverse to be neat. However, to the player, the problem of categorization doesn't matter much, except in the subtle area of how a game "feels." Most of the workshop students, probably for emotional reasons, seemed to find the "pure" ring plays, such as "Soup, Soup" or "East Coast Line," the most difficult; they tended to prefer (find easier) those plays which are closer to dance, such as "Way Down Yonder in the Brickyard" or "Steal Up, Young Lady." All the plays, however, call on basically the same *physical* skills, though "Way Go, Lily" has the simplest movement pattern and "Uncle Jessie" the most complicated. Because of this cultural complication, I have made no effort to arrange the items in this section according to difficulty, and players will simply have to decide for themselves which are "hard" and which are "easy."

Little Johnny Brown

You got to time it right to play it right. . . .

This seems to me to be a very old play; I have not found it reported anywhere else. The specific nature of the early part of the action makes it very popular with children, though the later (and more characteristic) part is more difficult.

Mrs. Jones's concern with timing showed here with her insistence, during play, that the "comfort" (comforter) be spread down on the fourth line of the verse, so that there would be no awkward time gap to be filled in by the center player. The folding of the comfort (usually represented by a bandanna or man's large handkerchief) is ceremonial: one corner is folded to the center, then the opposite corner, then the side corners in turn, leaving a much reduced square of cloth. The player walks around to a different corner of the handkerchief and stoops down each time he makes a fold.

FORM: Ring of players standing and clapping; one player in the center.

GROUP AND LEAD VOICES TOGETHER		ACTION
Little Johnny Brown,		Center player walks around in
Spread your comfort down.		middle of the ring.
Little Johnny Brown,		Center player spreads hand-
Spread your comfort down.		kerchief out in middle of the floor.

LEAD VOICE	GROUP VOICE	
Fold one corner,		Center player folds one corner
	Johnny Brown.	of handkerchief to middle.
Fold another corner,		Center player folds opposite
	Johnny Brown.	corner as above.
Fold another corner,		Center player folds side corner.
	Johnny Brown.	
Fold another corner,		Center player folds last corner.
	Johnny Brown.	
Take it to your lover,		Center player dances over to
	Johnny Brown.	player in ring. He must face
Take it to your lover,		partner by the last "lover."
	Johnny Brown.	
Show her your motion,		Center player "makes his mo-
	Johnny Brown.	tion" (see p. 46).

Show her your motion,

    Johnny Brown.

Lope like a buzzard,

    Johnny Brown.

Lope like a buzzard,

    Johnny Brown.

Give it to your lover,

    Johnny Brown.

Give it to your lover,

    Johnny Brown.

Give it to your lover,

    Johnny Brown.

Center player does "buzzard lope" (see p. 45).

Center player hands folded handkerchief to his partner, who then goes to center ring and play begins over without pause.

Little Johnny Brown

Smoothly ♩ = 176

Lit - tle John - ny Brown, Spread your com - fort down. Lit - tle John - ny Brown,

Spread your com - fort down. Fold___ one cor - ner, John - ny Brown.

Faster; with vigor ♩ = 184

CLAP

etc.

Fold___ a - noth - er cor - ner, John - ny Brown. Fold___ a - noth - er cor - ner, John - ny Brown.

Fold___ a - noth - er cor - ner, John - ny Brown. Take___ it to your lov - er, John - ny Brown.

Take___ it to your lov - er, John - ny Brown. Show___ her your mo - tion, John - ny Brown.

Show___ her your mo - tion, John - ny Brown. Lope___ like a buz - zard, John - ny Brown.

Lope___ like a buz - zard, John - ny Brown. Give___ it to your lov - er, John - ny Brown.

New words and new music adaptation by Bessie Jones; collected and edited with additional new material by Alan Lomax. TRO—© copyright 1972 Ludlow Music, Inc., New York, N.Y. Used by permission.

East Coast Line

We thought Jacksonville was the magic city of the world, you know, because we heard so much talk of it. And it was on the East Coast Line. . . .

She eats syrup by the gallon, you know; she eats meat by the pound. And by eating all that, she looks <u>good</u>; she's neat in the waist and pretty in the face. . . . She eats bread by the pone—that's cornbread you pat out with your hands. Some peoples make up little bitty pones about as big as your fist, but we used to make up them big old ravish pones; they're really good. . . .

Children are all bottomless pits, and their legs are hollow; but the children of Emancipation sing about how *pretty* you can be if you have good food.

FORM : Ring of children standing and clapping, one player in the center.

LEAD VOICE	GROUP VOICE	ACTION
Way down yonder,		Center player walks (struts)
	Hey,	around inside the ring.
On the East Coast Line,		
	Hey,	
They eat syrup by the gallon,		
	Hey,	
They eat meat by the pound,		
	Hey,	
They eating bread by the pone,		
	Hey,	
And she's <u>neat</u> in the waist,		Center player mimes being
	Hey,	neat in the waist and pretty in
And she's <u>pretty</u> in the face,		the face.
	Hey,	
And if <u>I</u> were you,		Center player "struts" around
	Hey,	inside the ring.
And you were me,		
	Hey,	
I would <u>stop</u> right still,		Center player stops in front
	Hey,	of prospective partner.
And <u>shake</u> it back,		Center player switches hips.

Shake it to the east,
Shake it to the west,
Shake it to the very one
That you love the best.

Center player leaves ring;
partner takes her place.

East Coast Line

Way down yon - der, Hey,* On the East Coast Line,

Hey, They eat syr - up by the gal - lon, Hey, They eat

meat by the pound, Hey, They eat - ing bread by the pone,

Hey, And she's neat in the waist,— Hey, And she's

pret - ty in the face, Hey, And if I were— you,

Hey, And you were me, Hey, I would stop right still,

Hey, And shake it back,— Shake it to the east,

Shake it to the west, Shake it to the ve - ry one that you love the best.

*A minor chord (a, c, e) used throughout on word "Hey."

New words and new music adaptation by Bessie Jones; collected and edited with additional new material by Alan Lomax. TRO—© copyright 1972 Ludlow Music, Inc., New York, N.Y. Used by permission.

Sir Mister Brown

In this play when you dance together you say what kind of lady she is and what kind of person you're dancing with. You claim *she's that way—you know she's not that kind. . . .*

The workshop group persisted in singing *both* the second and fourth lines of this tune with the descending cadence, ending on the tonic note. Mrs. Jones, stating plainly her feelings about the inter-relationship of text and tune, said, "The first time you say it, you're *asking* for her—Sir Mister Brown?" (singing unfinished cadence: B A G B). "The second time, you've done paid for her and you *got* her—Sir Mister *Brown!*" And she ended triumphantly on the tonic note of G.

The Islanders had a lot of fun with this rather satiric lyric, acting out obsequiousness during the first two lines and so on.

F O R M : Ring of children standing, one player in the center.

LEAD VOICE AND GROUP VOICE	ACTION
Mister Brown, Mister Brown,	Center player walks
I come to court your daughter,	around inside ring.
Sir Mister Brown.	
Mister Brown, Mister Brown,	
I'll give you a dollar and a quarter,	
Sir Mister <u>Brown</u>.	Center player stands in front of partner.

Start offbeat clap (lead singer and group)

LEAD VOICE	GROUP VOICE	
Fly round, my lady,		Center player and
	Sir Mister Brown.	partner "jump for joy."
That lady's going to meet you,		
	Sir Mister Brown.	
That big-eyed lady,		
	Sir Mister Brown.	
That cockeyed lady,		
	Sir Mister Brown.	
That one-legged lady,		
	Sir Mister Brown.	
That bowlegged lady,		
	Sir Mister Brown.	

Now Sir Mister <u>Brown</u>

Now Sir Mister
Brown.

Center player joins
ring; partner moves
into center and play
repeats.

Sir Mister Brown

Smooth and stately ♩ = 138

Mis-ter Brown, Mis-ter Brown, I come to court your daught-er, Sir Mis-ter

Brown. Mis-ter Brown, Mis-ter Brown, I'll give you a dol-lar and a quar-ter,

Fast and lively ♩ = 208 *etc.*

CLAP

Sir__ Mis-ter Brown. Fly round, my la-dy, Sir Mis-ter Brown. That

la-dy's going to meet you, Sir, Mis-ter Brown. That big-eyed la-dy, Sir Mis-ter Brown. That

cock-eyed la-dy, Sir Mis-ter Brown. That one-leg-ged la-dy, Sir Mis-ter Brown. That

rit.

bow-leg-ged la-dy, Sir Mis-ter Brown, Now Sir__ Mis-ter Brown.

New words and new music adaptation by Bessie Jones; collected and edited with additional new
material by Alan Lomax. TRO—© copyright 1972 Ludlow Music, Inc., New York, N.Y. Used by
permission.

Way Down Yonder, Sometimes

In this ring play, an account of the doings of magical animals and the courtship feats of human beings is continually punctuated by the chorus's sardonic remark "Sometimes." The tune, when sung and clapped with strong rhythm, will give you an idea of how interesting only four notes can be.

FORM : Ring of players, not holding hands; one center player.

LEAD VOICE	CHORUS VOICE	ACTION
Way down yonder,		Center player walks (struts)
	Sometimes,	around the ring.
Below the log,		
	Sometimes,	
Wild geese are holl'ring,		
	Sometimes,	
Ganders trot,		
	Sometimes,	
Bullfrog marry,		
	Sometimes,	
His mother-in-law,		
	Sometimes,	
Now let's get on board,		Center player stands in front
	Sometimes,	of chosen partner.
I'm going to ball that jack,		Center player balls the jack
	Sometimes,	(see p. 44).
Until my honey comes back,		
	Sometimes,	
I want to rear back, Jack,		Center player (and partner)
	Sometimes,	lean back.
And get a hump in my back,		Center player (and partner)
	Sometimes,	hunch shoulders.
I'm going over here,		Center player takes partner's
	Sometimes,	hand and turns her into
Goin' to get my pal,		center of the circle, taking
	Sometimes.	her place in the ring. Play continues with the new center player.

Way Down Yonder, Sometimes

New words and new music adaptation by Bessie Jones; collected and edited with additional new material by Alan Lomax. TRO—© copyright 1972 Ludlow Music, Inc., New York, N.Y. Used by permission.

Soup, Soup

I like that part about they ain't but the one thing that I dislike. You see in the old times people taught you how to do, and they didn't like you to do things like putting on airs or posing for mens, but they'd yet get down to the raw thing and ball the jack! I thought that was so cute. . . .

The Negro rural community has had its own share of conflict over standards of proper behavior. The whole area of dance has been especially tense because of the direct conflict between ancient African cultural patterns, in which dance is a routine part of almost all human activity, and European Protestantism, in which dance is considered by all except a few dissenting sects to be both worldly and potentially lustful.

On the level of children's activity, both white and black communities have attempted to regard singing games as *playing,* not *dancing,* and therefore allowable, without many restrictions, to the young. The children of both communities have, in turn, fashioned their pastimes in direct celebration of the adult world they saw around them. In this context one can see the irony that Mrs. Jones points out. How pleasant it is to be allowed to demonstrate explicitly and exactly just what it is you disapprove of.

FORM : Ring of players, not holding hands, one player in the center.

LEAD VOICE	GROUP VOICE	ACTION
Way down yonder,		Center player walks around
	Soup, soup.	inside ring.
Below the moon,		
	Soup, soup.	
I got a letter,		
	Soup, soup.	
From Alma Stone,		
	Soup, soup.	
They <u>ain't</u> but the one thing,		Center player picks partner
	Soup, soup.	and stands in front of him.
That I dislike,		
	Soup, soup.	
That's <u>putting</u> on airs,		Center player mimes "put-
	Soup, soup.	ting on airs."
And <u>balling</u> that jack.		Center player balls the jack.

Soup, soup.

That buzzard soup,

Soup, soup.   Center player and partner
That rabbit soup,   ball the jack to each other.

Soup, soup.

That monkey soup,

Soup, soup.

That gopher soup,

Soup, soup.

That elephant soup,

Soup, soup.   Partner moves out to center
                               of ring and center player
                               takes her place; play repeats
                               with new center player.

Soup, Soup

Way down yon-der, Soup, soup.— Be-low the moon, Soup, soup.—

I___ got a let-ter, Soup, soup.— From Al-ma Stone,— Soup, soup.—

They ain't but the one thing, Soup, soup.— That I dis-like, Soup, soup.—

That's put-ting on airs, Soup, soup.— And ball-ing that jack,— Soup, soup.—

That buz-zard soup,— Soup, soup.— That rab-bit soup,— Soup, soup.—
    mon-key   go-pher
    ele-phant

New words and new music adaptation by Bessie Jones; collected and edited with additional new
material by Alan Lomax. TRO—© copyright 1972 Ludlow Music, Inc., New York, N.Y. Used by
permission.

Punchinello

Old Sue, she's going to have to do just about what Sally done. . . .

Apparently this European singing game entered the American game repertoire around the turn of the century in the form of a rather awkward translation that was printed widely in school music texts:

> Ho! look at me,
> Punchinello, funny fellow.
> Ho! look at me,
> Punchinello, funny do.

The form of the dance—a ring with a center player—immediately attracted the children of the Negro community, who then set about remaking "Punchinello" into a completely comfortable play. Mrs. Jones remarked that she had left out "some of the verses about 'who do you choose' and like that because you don't need them."

Instead of the original second and fourth lines, Mrs. Jones sings "Punchinello, follow Sally," and "Punchinello, follow Sue." These phrases may require further changing; as the remark under the title indicates, Mrs. Jones feels a little concern over Sue's presence. (There should be *one* person in the center in a ring play, and on rare occasions, two. Three—Punchinello, Sally, *and* Sue—is certainly too many.) Los Angeles children I have heard playing this popular game don't bother with Sally and Sue at all; they sing "Punchinello, forty-seven" and "Punchinello, forty-two."

Perhaps because of exposure to the textbook version of this play, the students in the workshop were unusually square with this tune, insisting on clapping on the downbeat instead of the offbeat. In an effort to improve the rhythm, Emma Ramsey broke into a fast rumba-like clapping pattern (transcribed in the music over the words "I can do it too"). This, combined with Mrs. Jones's steady offbeat baritone clap, certainly completed the transformation of this somewhat ga-lumphing European dance into one of the most swinging of the Sea Islanders' plays.

FORM: Ring of children standing and clapping; center player in the middle of the circle.

LEAD VOICE	GROUP VOICE	ACTION
Look who is here,		Center player walks
	Punchinello, follow Sally,	around inside ring.
Look who is here,		
	Punchinello, follow <u>Sue</u>.	Center player stops in front of chosen partner.
<u>What</u> can you do?		Center player "makes
	Punchinello, follow Sally,	his motion."
What can you do?		
	Punchinello, follow Sue.	
Well, <u>I</u> can do it too,		Partner imitates center
	Punchinello, follow Sally,	player's "motion."
I can do it too,		
	Punchinello, follow Sue.	Partner takes center ring and game starts over while first center player joins the ring.

Mrs. Jones says that if it's a large ring and you're getting tired, you can sing "We can do it too" and all the ring players can then imitate the dance step of the last center player. This, however, will end the play; the pattern has been destroyed.

Punchinello

New words and new music adaptation by Bessie Jones; collected and edited with additional new material by Alan Lomax. TRO—© copyright 1972 Ludlow Music, Inc., New York, N.Y. Used by permission.

Little Sally Walker

If you got something to move, you can move it. If you ain't got nothing to move, you can't move nothing. . . .

For another example of how a European game can be changed into ring play, here is "Little Sally Walker," long a favorite among British and American children. It is a very old play. In what are perhaps the oldest versions, little Sally's last name is "Water" instead of "Walker" and she is "crying for a young man." Some writers suggest that this play may have grown out of purification ceremonies in ancient British marriage rites.

In sin-conscious early America, however, "Little Sally Walker" became a brief drama about the joys of release from shame; black children undoubtedly learned it from their white neighbors. Mrs. Jones knew three distinct versions. Version One, which she sings in a flowing and unsyncopated style markedly unlike her usual vigorous rhythm and which she says is "the old way to play it," is the one most similar to white versions I have heard. The concluding stanzas of all three versions seem to be Negro additions. "Flying," even to the east and the west, is certainly a less emphatic expression of happiness than "jumping for joy," "shaking it," or "letting your backbone slip." (Mrs. Jones remarked reassuringly one day, "That letting your backbone slip is *good* for you—it'll make you souple all over!")

VERSION ONE

FORM: Ring of children standing; center player sits or kneels in the middle of the ring.

ALL VOICES EXCEPT CENTER PLAYER	ACTION
Little Sally Walker, Sitting in a saucer, Crying and a-weeping Over all she has done.	Center player puts head in hands as though crying.
Rise, Sally, rise. Wipe out your eyes. Fly to the east, Sally,	Center player stands; wipes eyes; arms outstretched and waving, walks to right;
Fly to the west, Sally, Fly to the very one that you love the best.	as above walks to left; as above, goes to face chosen partner.

(Begin strong offbeat clap)
* Now Miss Sally, won't you jump for joy,   Center player and partner
Jump for joy, jump for joy.   jump for joy.
Now Miss Sally, won't you jump for joy,
And now, Miss Sally, won't you <u>bow</u>.

Center player bows; partner
takes place in center while
first Little Sally joins the ring.

VERSION TWO

This version is sung at a faster tempo with strong syncopation
throughout, as well as a decided offbeat clap. The movements are
stylized and should be rigidly held to time with the singing. The
words accompanying the actions are underlined.

FORM : Ring of children standing and clapping. Center player sits in
middle.

ALL VOICES EXCEPT CENTER PLAYER	ACTION
Little Sally Walker,	Center player, face in hands, mimes
Sitting in a saucer,	crying.
Crying and a-weeping over all she have done.	
Oh, <u>rise</u> up on your feet,	Center player stands;
Oh, <u>wipe</u> your cheeks,	wipes cheeks—R L R;
Oh, <u>turn to</u> the <u>east</u>,	turns right step, step, step;
Oh, <u>turn to</u> the <u>west</u>,	turns left—step, step, step;
Oh, <u>turn to</u> the <u>very one</u>	turns to find chosen partner.
that <u>you</u> love the <u>best</u>.	
Oh, <u>shake</u> it <u>to</u> the <u>east</u>,	Hands on hips, switch hips—R L R;
Oh, <u>shake</u> it <u>to</u> the <u>west</u>,	as above—L R L;
Oh, <u>shake</u> it <u>to</u> the very one	as above, alternate hip-switching;
that <u>you</u> love the <u>best</u>.	change place with partner on last word. Partner becomes next Sally Walker.

---

* Mrs. Jones says you can sing "Now let me see how you jump for joy" at the end
of the play so the whole ring can dance at one time.

VERSION THREE

Mrs. Jones's third version, which she learned last and does, indeed, seem more modern, is identical with Version One through the words "Fly to the very one that you love the best," though the tune is sung faster and she claps throughout. The following lines then occur:

Now put your hand on your hip
And let your backbone slip.
Shake it to the east,
Shake it to the west,
Shake it to the very one that you love the best.

Little Sally Walker

(version 1)

Little Sally Walker

(version 2)

Little Sally Walk-er, Sit-ting in a sau-cer,

Cry-ing and a-weep-ing o-ver all she have done. Oh,

rise up-on your feet, Oh,— wipe your— cheeks, Oh,

turn to the east, Oh,— turn to the west, Oh,—

turn to the ver-y one that you love the best. Oh,

shake it to the east, Oh, shake it to the west, Oh,

shake it to the ver-y one that you love the best.

New words and new music adaptation by Bessie Jones; collected and edited with additional new material by Alan Lomax. TRO—© copyright 1972 Ludlow Music, Inc., New York, N.Y. Used by permission.

(version 3)

Now put your hand on your hip and let your back-bone slip.—

Shake it to the east, shake it to the west, shake it to the ver-y one that you love the best.

Uncle Jessie

I tell you what this means, it means a boss man coming across the field. Sometimes he's feeling good, and sometimes he's not. Sometimes he's worried; maybe sometimes he done lost and sometimes he done gained, and I know how he feels. . . . But he still walked like a big-stepping man; he stepped big like he made a thousand dollars. . . . But sometimes he's feeling good and sometimes he's not. . . .

"Uncle Jessie" seems to be one of the oldest of the Islanders' plays; one evidence of its age is the mention of love and power charms in the form of salt, garlic, and onion. The formal dancing by the central partners puts it almost into the category of dance rather than ring play; in action, actually, it feels like a cross between the two.

During the chorus, which may be sung either "Step, Uncle Jessie" or "Walk, Uncle Jessie," the center players dance together as a couple. They hold hands in a skaters' waltz position and either strut or slide in a two-step rhythm:

Step,   Uncle   Jes - sie, step,   step
  R   L slide   R   rest   L   R slide   L   rest

When the partners have two-stepped to the inside limits of the ring, they reverse their direction by turning toward each other and shifting the relation of their arms while continuing to hold hands as before. As Mrs. Jones puts it,

When you go to turn, you don't have to <u>wheel</u>; you just turn like you're <u>sawing</u>. It's beautiful; you step and move together, just right with the song. . . .

F O R M : Ring of players standing and clapping; one player in the center.

LEAD VOICE AND/OR GROUP VOICE	ACTION
Now, here comes Uncle Jessie, Coming through the field With his horse and buggy And I know just how he <u>feels</u>.	Center player walks around in center of ring (in time with the music) acting out Uncle Jessie.
(The next verse may be added now or substituted for the first verse.)	Stops in front of partner (one of the ring players) on the last word of either verse.

Here comes Uncle Jessie,
He's looking very sad.
He's lost his cotton and corn
And everything he <u>had</u>.

Step, Uncle Jessie, step, step,
Step, Uncle Jessie, step, step,
Walk, Uncle Jessie, walk, walk,
Walk, Uncle Jessie, walk.

Center player takes partner's hands in skating position, and the pair two-step together in the center of the circle.

Now, <u>if</u> you want a sweetheart,
I'll tell you what to do,
Just take some salt and pepper
And <u>sprinkle</u> it in your shoe.

Center players drop hands and stand facing each other, shaking right forefingers at each other.
Each center player mimes sprinkling salt in his own right shoe.

Step, Uncle Jessie, step, step,
Step, Uncle Jessie, step, etc.

Center players take hands and two-step together as before.

Now <u>if</u> you want Uncle Jessie
To do what you want him to do
You take some garlic and onion
And <u>put</u> it in his shoe.

Center players repeat finger-shaking as before.

Center players pretend to put something in their right shoes.

Step, Uncle Jessie, step, step,
Step, Uncle Jessie, step, step,
Walk, Uncle Jessie, walk, walk,
Walk, Uncle Jessie, <u>walk</u>.

Center players take hands and two-step as before.

On last word, first center player leaves the center and joins the ring. His partner becomes Uncle Jessie for a repeat of the play.

Uncle Jessie

With snap but not too fast ♩ = 168

Now, here comes Un - cle Jes - sie, Com - ing through the field,

With his horse and bug - gy And I know just how he feels.

CLAP   etc.

Step,— Un - cle Jes - sie, step, step. Step,— Un - cle Jes - sie, step, step.

Walk,— Un - cle Jes - sie, walk, walk. Walk,— Un - cle Jes - sie, walk.

New words and new music adaptation by Bessie Jones; collected and edited with additional new material by Alan Lomax. TRO—© copyright 1972 Ludlow Music, Inc., New York, N.Y. Used by permission.

Way Down Yonder in the Brickyard

And it go on until you get to each one. It's really pretty when you step it together. . . .

In this brief play, dramatic action gives way to a stylized dance step, and the sense of position and pattern begins to dominate over the individual performance of the center player. Because the verse is short, the lead role changes swiftly from person to person. Though clearly a ring play and called so by Mrs. Jones, in action it *feels* like dance. Its simplicity, fast pace, and hot rhythm make it one of the "easiest" plays to learn.

F O R M : Ring of players standing and clapping; one player in the center.

LEAD VOICE	GROUP VOICE	ACTION
Way down yonder in the brickyard,	Remember me.	Center player walks around inside ring.
Way down yonder in the brickyard,	Remember me.	
Oh, step it, step it, step it <u>down</u>,		Center player stops in front of a ring player and both "step it down" (the *dance*
	Remember me.	step) four times.
Oh, <u>swing</u> your love and turn around,	Remember me.	Center player and partner swing halfway around with an elbow swing. This leaves the first player standing as part of the circle; his old partner becomes the new center player for a repeat of the game.

Way Down Yonder in the Brickyard

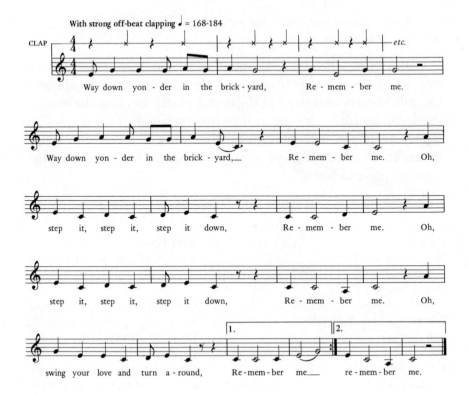

With strong off-beat clapping ♩ = 168-184

Way down yon - der in the brick - yard, Re - mem - ber me.

Way down yon - der in the brick - yard,___ Re - mem - ber me. Oh,

step it, step it, step it down, Re - mem - ber me. Oh,

step it, step it, step it down, Re - mem - ber me. Oh,

swing your love and turn a - round, Re - mem - ber me.___ re - mem - ber me.

Written and adapted by Bessie Jones; collected and edited by Alan Lomax. TRO—© copyright 1972 Ludlow Music, Inc., New York, N.Y. Used by permission.

Way Go, Lily

This is just for exercise, to tell the truth; it's just skipping and getting yourself all limbered up. . . .

Besides getting himself "all limbered up," the child dancing the center role in "Way Go, Lily" is released from the circle to find himself truly the ruler at last. Here again is dance developing out of ring play;* instead of acting out a dramatic scene in front of a chosen successor, the center player makes his ruling position clear by swinging each dancer in turn. At the end, as in ring play, he retires to the circle, leaving to another his dancing glory. The joyous and syncopated tune, punctuated by the ominous word "sometimes," should be paced to fit a skipping tempo.

F O R M : Circle of children standing and clapping; one center player.

LEAD VOICE	GROUP VOICE	ACTION
Way go, Lily,		Center player skips across the
	Sometimes.	ring and swings any player
Way go, Lily,		once around with an elbow
	Sometimes.	swing. Center player con-
I'm going to rule my ruler,		tinues swinging each child,
	Sometimes.	either in turn or at random
I'm going to rule my ruler,		until all have been swung.
	Sometimes.	She leaves the last dancer in
I'm going to rule him with a hick'ry,		the ring to become the next lead player. The song is re-
	Sometimes.	peated ad lib.
I'm going to rule him with a hick'ry,		
	Sometimes.	

Way go, Lily (2)
I'm going to rule my mother, (2)
I'm going to rule her with a hick'ry. (2)

---

* This phrase is meant to be understood in a developmental rather than a historical perspective. Mrs. Jones feels that, *in the social growth of the child,* ring play precedes dance; historically, however, it appears that most of her dances are older than most of her ring plays. Further, the oldest of her ring plays, judging by their texts ("Way Go, Lily" and "Uncle Jessie," for example), are also those most closely akin to dance in their patterning and movements. My own explanation of this is that ring play emerged as an important form among Negro children only *after* the Civil War and that it is an outgrowth of and a response to such post-emancipation institutions as segregation laws and the ghetto.

Way go, Lily (2)
I'm going to rule old Master, (2)
I'm going to rule him with a shotgun. (2)

Way go, Lily (2)
I'm going to rule my sister (father, brother, etc.) (2)
I'm going to rule her (him) with a hick'ry. (2)

The song may be sung in stanza form as above, or the lines beginning
"I'm going to rule my . . ." may be repeated ad lib as many times
as desired.

Way Go, Lily

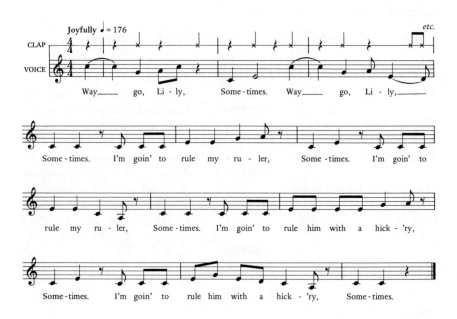

Written and adapted by Bessie Jones; collected and edited by Alan Lomax. TRO—© copyright
1972 Ludlow Music, Inc., New York, N.Y. Used by permission.

Steal Up, Young Lady

Didn't you ever play that play they call "Stealing Partners"? . . .

In a further stylization of play into dance, "Steal Up, Young Lady" is a logical follow-up to "Way Go, Lily." Here, one "steals a partner" by dancing out and swinging one member of a couple; the bereft partner then skips off to steal himself a new mate. It's just skipping and swinging and stealing partners, that's all, as Mrs. Jones says.

The two lines

Steal up, young lady, oh, happy land,
Won't you steal up, young lady, oh, happy land.

may be considered a chorus and may be repeated after each couplet of the song, or they may be inserted ad lib. The dance step is a skip throughout.

FORM: Circle of children standing in pairs and clapping; one extra player is in the center.

LEAD VOICE	GROUP VOICE	ACTION
Steal up-a, young lady,		Center player skips around
	Oh, happy land,	in the ring, chooses one
Won't you steal up-a, young lady,		member of a couple whenever he wishes and skips
	Oh, happy land.	her around with an elbow
If you're going to steal at all,		swing. He has then "stolen" a partner, and the two
	Oh, happy land,	stand in place, forming a
Steal that man, don't steal no boy,		new couple, while the player who has been left
	Oh, happy land.	out skips off to continue
Way down yonder where I come from,		the play by "stealing" himself a new partner. Unlike
	Oh, happy land,	most ring plays, the action
Girls love boys like a hog loves corn,		is not timed to a specific moment in the song,
	Oh, happy land.	though the rhythm should
Way down yonder in the old cornfield,		be kept, of course. The action is continuous until the
	Oh, happy land,	players get too tired to
Black snake popped me on my heel,		go on.
	Oh, happy land.	

I popped my whip, I run
  my best,

                             Oh, happy land,

I run my head in a hornet's
  nest,

                             Oh, happy land.

Steal Up, Young Lady

Steal up - a, young la - dy, Oh, hap - py land,___

Won't you steal up - a, young la - dy, Oh, hap - py land.___

If you're goin' to steal at all,___ Oh, hap - py land,___

Steal___ that man, don't steal no boy,___ Oh, hap - py land.___

New words and new music adaptation by Bessie Jones; collected and edited with additional new material by Alan Lomax. TRO—© copyright 1972 Ludlow Music, Inc., New York, N.Y. Used by permission.

6:
Dances

And the other childrens and I would go in the bottom and have a frolic, instead of going to bed. I was just up for that singing, and I remember they used to say, "Come on, Lizzie!"—they called me Lizzie—"Come on, Lizzie!" and we'd go down a way and we'd have a dance.

Oh, it was pretty. . . . You know, it was just as good as the blues— better, better in a way. When the old folks would go to work or go off or something, we'd put on them long dresses and, boy, we'd have a time. I'd be Annie or Elise or somebody—not mocking, but copying, you know—and have a wonderful time. It was fun for the children to do, because there was much joy to it. . . .

Out of the comforting boundaries of the ring, the grown child dances joyfully into the sometimes rigid, sometimes formless patterns of adult life. He uses the same body articulations, the same "steps," but the dramatic content is more abstract, the patterns more varied, the range of personal choice wider. As an adult, he does not "play" any longer; he dances. He has gone through a long apprenticeship; contrary to what the world around him thinks, he is not a "natural" but a thoroughly trained dancer.

If he lives in a Negro rural community, he lives in a world where everybody can dance a little, and almost everybody does, sometime or another. And it is a world where you don't have to go to a special place or wear special clothes or arrange for special music in order to dance. You can dance in the dust of the backyard, on the porch, on a grass patch; you can sing to yourself for an accompaniment, or clap, or tap your heels on the floor. You can dance with the baby or your grandfather or your sister or just all by yourself. Dancing is all mixed in with life, just as work is, or singing.

We'd sing different songs, and then we'd dance a while to rest ourselves. . . .

This relaxed sense of dancing "a while to rest ourselves" may be one reason for the comparative unimportance of *form* in some of Mrs. Jones's dances. After all, if there is no set place in which to dance and no particular number of people dancing, a formal arrangement such as a square or a longways set or even a couple formation may not be practical.

But as I tried to learn such dances as "Sandy Ree" and "Possum Up a 'Simmon Tree," it seemed to me that Mrs. Jones's point of view was almost *too* casual. The plays and games were quite carefully formalized for the most part, but the shape of the dances seemed to melt and shift just when I thought I had finally understood them. "Well, you *could* do it in a circle, or you wouldn't have to if you didn't want to," Mrs. Jones would remark comfortingly, as I tore up one description after another.

The fact is, we were at cross-purposes. I was thinking about form; she was concerned with content. On a more specific level, the *steps* were what she was interested in—not whether the dancers should stand in parallel lines or in a square. She just didn't care where they stood. This does not seem to be simply a peculiarity of Mrs. Jones's; descriptions I have read of Negro dancing during slavery and on through the minstrel-show era cluster around a detailing of the steps, rather than a picture of the dance as a whole. Since this seems to be a historical fact, perhaps history may give some hint as to the cause of it.

Most writers agree that dance was once one of the most highly developed art forms of West Africa (the area from which most Negroes were brought to this country). Dance accompanied and celebrated all human activity; all significant occasions were marked by dance. Transported as slaves to the United States, the new Afro-

Americans were forced to give up their religion, their languages, their customs, their political institutions—all the formal structures that had held their communities together. Like the drums, the old cultural, social, and political instruments had been destroyed.

The impulse to play upon their instruments—to dance—was not. American Negroes continued to dance, continued through their traditional art form to dramatize and celebrate the importance of life. The old organization, however, was no longer possible—the daylong and nightlong festivals, the masks, the complex choreography of a hunting or a fertility ceremonial in which every member of a tribe danced his own appointed role. It seems very possible to me that in the United States, African dance became fragmented in just the same ways in which the old life patterns became fragmented.

There are some exceptions, of course. One of these is religious dance, for the church has been the only institution of any stability in Southern Negro life for generations. (It is no historical accident that Southern churches were the point of organization for integration activity during the 1960's.) Even during slavery Protestant planters did not forbid—and, in many cases, encouraged—religious activity and association in the slave quarters. Since, in Africa, religious celebrations always involve dance, a new kind of holy dance, the "ring shout," was invented by black worshipers in the Southern states, a celebration both of God and of the constancy of the human spirit.

Since the ring shout is not ordinarily danced by children, a full discussion of it is beyond the scope of this book, though I have included one sample, "Daniel," for illustrative purposes. Still, in contrast with our scattered and inconclusive conversations about other kinds of dancing, it was impressive to watch the Islanders organize an old-fashioned ring shout. The circle must move counterclockwise and in single file. The feet must not leave the floor and the legs must not cross; the heels must be kept down. The gestures must follow the vocal directions of the lead singer. The style, the content, and the form were known to all and understood by all. In the only major social institution where some sort of order and continuity were available to the American Negro—the church—there had also developed an orderly and patterned form of dance.

Another area of dance in which form is relatively fixed has already been discussed: children's play, or what might be called "pre-dance."

This is because from the adult point of view the child's world is an ordered one—or it ought to be; and it is important to remember that the plays in this book were taught *by* adults and were thought of as "good for" children. The child's point of view was expressed by Mrs. Jones in one of her reminiscent moods.

In those days they really danced . . . and people played on their guitars, too. We would do it behind mama and them when we were little—all kinds of rawhides and all kinds of twist-es. And we weren't allowed to do twist-es then, you know, but we would do it after they had gone somewhere; we would do it good. . . .

Even as an adult Mrs. Jones remembered how the children wanted to get out of the circle, wanted to learn the grownup "steps."

The last two dances in the section to follow—"Zudie-O" and "I'm Going Away to See Aunt Dinah"—may be examples of a third kind of attempt at stability. There is some evidence that during slavery Negroes adopted by imitation the formal quadrilles danced by their owners in the "big houses," in an effort to become part of the new society into which they had been transplanted. Mrs. Jones recalls that when she was a girl she would shepherd the smaller children away from the grownups to "have our own frolic, and I'd sing and pat and call the sets."

But these are always described as the "old" dances; they are almost, like the ring shout, fading from memory now. Perhaps their shape was wrong; perhaps they dramatized a kind of social order lacking in meaning to American Negroes. The ring play is still alive even in the harsh and sterile streets of the city ghetto; Afro-American versions of the frontier longways set and the square dance live on mainly in a kind of antiquarian atmosphere.

In any event, outside of religious dance, children's play, and the old longways dances, Mrs. Jones's attention to form was perfunctory; the "steps"—the individual statements of condition and emotion— were what she enjoyed. And so such dances as "Sandy Ree," "Ranky Tank," and "Possum Up that 'Simmon Tree" should be approached casually, as she would approach them: "you could do them in a circle, or you wouldn't have to if you didn't want to." Or you don't even have to dance them; just sit and pat and sing.

Possum-La

In 1937 John A. and Alan Lomax recorded for the Library of
Congress a little Negro girl from Alabama who sang,

Put your hands on your hips and let your mind roll forward,
Back, back, back till you see the stars.
Skip so lightly, shine so brightly,
That is the possum-a-la.

The Lomaxes suggest that perhaps she is actually saying "pas-ma-la,"
a corruption of a French phrase referring to a dance step; this would
certainly fit in well with the rest of her song.

Mrs. Jones's version, however, seems clearly focused on a fat
possum up in a tree, happily gorging himself and littering the ground
below with persimmon seeds. She does know a dance step by the
same name as well, and describes it as being "about like the Kneebone Bend." The "Possum-La" dancer shuffles and "cuts up" casually,
or perhaps skips around in a circle, until the word "possum-*la*," when
he gives a slight jump, or "chug," to one side, landing with his knees
deeply bent. The same action is taken on the word "seed." In the refrain, he makes five such jumps, swinging his body from side to side
and jumping first at one angle and then at another.

F O R M : Indefinite; may be danced alone or in a group. Solo or group
singing with patting, heel-tapping, or clapping. Even the song is
fluid; this is my own reconstruction of Mrs. Jones's highly varied
melody.

Possum up-a that 'simmon tree,
Possum up-a that 'simmon tree,
I don't see nothing but the 'simmon <u>seed</u>.

    Possum-<u>la</u>, possum-<u>la</u>, possum-<u>la</u>, possum-<u>la</u>,
    I don't see nothing but the 'simmon <u>seed</u>.

I want you to catch that possum for me,
I want you to catch that possum for me,
I want you to catch that possum for me,
I don't see nothing but the 'simmon <u>seed</u>.

    Possum-<u>la</u>, possum-<u>la</u>, possum-<u>la</u>, possum-<u>la</u>,
    I don't see nothing but the 'simmon <u>seed</u>.

Possum-la

Highly syncopated; fast, getting faster ♩ = 166-208

Pos - sum up - a that 'sim - mon tree, Pos - sum up - a that 'sim - mon tree, I

don't see noth - ing but the 'sim - mon seed. Pos - sum - la, Pos - sum - la,

Pos - sum - la, Pos - sum - la, I don't see noth - ing but 'sim - mon seed. I

want you to catch that pos - sum for me, I want you to catch that

pos - sum for me, I want you to catch that pos - sum for me, I

don't see noth - ing but the 'sim - mon seed. Pos - sum - la, Pos - sum - la,

Pos - sum - la, Pos - sum - la, I don't see noth - ing but the 'sim - mon seed.

Written and adapted by Bessie Jones; collected and edited by Alan Lomax. TRO—© copyright 1972 Ludlow Music, Inc., New York, N.Y. Used by permission.

Ranky Tank

This one is good for people on their toes. . . .

The morning Mrs. Jones taught the "Ranky Tank," she also gave a subtle demonstration of how culturally varied the goals of teaching can be. One of the white students was having trouble dancing flat-footed; no matter what the step was, inevitably she would rise up on her toes like a ballerina. The rest of us, all experienced teachers and trying tactfully to be of help, worked out little exercises she could do to force her heels down.

Suddenly Mrs. Jones—equally concerned but operating from a completely different cultural basis—remembered this dance. "This one is *good for* people on their toes!" she announced triumphantly. And so it is, for as she demonstrated it for us, it became clear that people who like to dance on their toes can "Ranky Tank" particularly adeptly.

The Islanders had learned the "Ranky Tank" from the people of nearby Sapelo Island; no one was sure just how the dance was organized, but the chant and step were remembered. The step itself would be called a "buzz" step by dance teachers; the weight is kept on one foot while the other toe pushes the dancer along, very much like the motion of a child riding a scooter. The weighted foot "chugs" along on the downbeat, while the pushing toe touches the floor on the offbeat. The dancer can progress either to the right or to the left (depending on which foot is carrying the weight) and in a straight line or around in a circle.

The "Ranky Tank" chant is improvised, with the various lead lines used as the singer thinks of them. It should be chanted strongly with a pronounced anticipation of the downbeat, and a strong offbeat single or double clap. This is a fine practice piece for dancers learning the buzz step; it's fun just to clap to it, too.

F O R M : Indefinite

LEAD VOICE	GROUP VOICE
Oh, ranky tank,	
	Ranky tank.
Oh, ranky tank,	
	Ranky tank.

Papa's goin' to rank,

                         Ranky tank.

Mama's goin' to rank,

                         Ranky tank.

Down in the cornfield,

                         Ranky tank.

I'm goin' to rank,

                         Ranky tank.

Sun is hot,

                         Ranky tank.

See me a-rankin',

                         Ranky tank.

Oh, ranky tank,

                         Ranky tank.

Oh, ranky tank,

                         Ranky tank.

Ranky Tank

New words and new music adaptation by Bessie Jones and The Sea Island Singers. TRO—© copyright
1972 Ludlow Music, Inc., New York, N.Y. Used by permission.

Coonshine

We thought that was good! We'd just get out in the woods and in the bottom and we'd have a time. . . .

I very much regret that I never saw the "Coonshine" dance; all I have to work from is a tape of Mrs. Jones singing the song. I have decided to include it, however, for its fine tune and the further evidence it shows of the antiquity of Mrs. Jones's tradition.

Almost a hundred years ago, George Washington Cable wrote of seeing the Counjaille dance in New Orleans. According to Harold Courlander, it is still remembered in scattered islands through the West Indies and the term "is still used in southern United States waterfront areas to mean moving or loading cotton, an activity that once, in all probability, was accompanied by Counjaille-type songs and rhythms." Mrs. Jones, whose feelings are really quite mixed on the subject of secular dance, might not have wanted to demonstrate the "Coonshine" for me had I asked her to; judging by the lyrics, in her neighborhood, it was considered a somewhat scandalous performance.

Coonshine, baby, coonshine,
Coonshine on the sly,
Mama don't 'low me to coonshine,
Papa don't 'low me to try,
Onliest way I coonshine,
I coonshine on the sly.

    Coonshine, baby, coonshine,
    Coonshine, baby, coonshine,
    Coonshine, baby, coonshine,
    Coonshine on the sly.

Someday I'm goin' coonshine,
Coonshine anyhow,
Mama don't 'low me to coonshine,
Papa don't 'low me to try,
Onliest way I coonshine,
I coonshine on the sly.

    Coonshine, baby, coonshine, etc.

When I get grown, I'm goin' coonshine,
Coonshine anyhow,
Mama don't 'low me to coonshine,
Papa don't 'low me to try,
Onliest way I coonshine,
I coonshine on the sly.

    Coonshine, baby, coonshine,
    Coonshine, baby, coonshine,
    Coonshine, baby, coonshine,
    Coonshine anyhow!

Coonshine

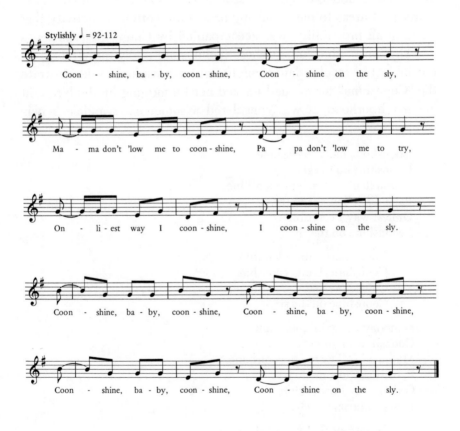

New words and new music adaptation by Bessie Jones; collected and edited with additional new material by Alan Lomax. TRO—© copyright 1972 Ludlow Music, Inc., New York, N.Y. Used by permission.

Sandy Ree

And in that Sandy Ree, you're doing some pretty dancing. You can turn and swing and have a real party out of it. We just shout and dance to one another, or you can have a regular dance . . . but you do it in front of one another.

It's wonderful to see how the children can carry it. I like that because it ain't dead; it'll never die now, because they got it and gone. . . .

"Sandy Ree" was obviously one of the Islanders' favorite dances; they seemed to reserve their fanciest footwork and their hottest clapping for a "Sandy Ree" session. The word itself may originally have been "sangari," an African term, but the Islanders say that the name comes from the way your feet "scrooch up the sand" when the Sandy Ree step is done.

The step itself is an elaboration of the secular shout step described on page 45. Beginners might do well to practice it in the simplest form first: to an even count of four beats, step right, step left, step right, and "chug" backward on the right foot. Repeat to the other side: step left, right, left, and chug backward on the left foot. This may then be fitted to the song as follows:

```
          O-----O  babe,          Sand----y  ree
           R    L    R   chug R L     R   L   chug L
(count)    1    2    3     4    1     2   3     4
```

This step is used throughout the song, but more experienced dancers may want to elaborate it as the Islanders do. To do the "real" Sandy Ree step, the dancer imagines his feet tracing patterns in the sand. On the count of one, instead of just stepping, put the heel down and dig it in by twisting the foot to the side. Steps on the counts of two and three are unornamented; but on the count of four, while chugging on one foot, swing the other around to the front in a half circle, keeping it "low and draggy to scrape up the sand."

The Islanders usually did this dance in couples, facing and working to one another; sometimes each danced alone, sometimes they held right hands across and pulled each other back and forth in what looked very much like the "jive" dancing style of the 1940's. They told me also of a formal way of dancing the "Sandy Ree," in a longways set, apparently, with head and foot couples who "swing and turn partners and go round," but we could never re-create this version satisfactorily. Probably it was much like "I'm Going Away to See Aunt Dinah."

The song has been as hard to pin down as the dance form; the melody varies greatly from stanza to stanza, and the notes as written here should be taken simply as a point of departure. Be sure to accompany it with a strong clap, and don't be afraid of speeding up; this tune gathers momentum as it goes along. Sometimes the Islanders simply used "Sandy Ree" as a background for a clapping practice, or as a song. Either danced or sung, it was certainly not "dead," and I hope, with Mrs. Jones, that "it'll never die now."

> Way down yonder,
>   Sandy ree,
> Where I come from,
>   Sandy ree,
> Girls love boys,
>   Sandy ree,
> Like a hog loves corn,
>   Sandy ree.
>
> (Refrain, to be used ad lib)
> Oh, babe,
>   Sandy ree,
> Oh, babe,
>   Sandy ree,
> Oh, babe,
>   Sandy ree,
> Oh, babe,
>   Sandy ree.
>
> Papa got the shovel,
>   Sandy ree (etc.),
> Mama got the hoe,
> If that ain't farming,
> I don't know.
>
> Dog on the porch,
> Kicking off fleas,
> Chicken in the yard,
> Scratching up peas.
>
> Old brother rabbit,
> Died with a habit,
> In my garden,
> Eating up cabbage.

If I live,
To see next fall,
I ain't gonna plant,
No cotton at all.

Mama in the cotton patch,
Picking up cotton,
Papa in town,
Drunk and sloppin'.

Well, if I live,
And I don't get killed,
I'm going back,
To Jacksonville.

Road is wet,
Woods is muddy,
Daddy's so drunk,
He can't stand studdy.

Down in the bottom,
Cotton goes rotten,
Can't get a bale,
It's no need of trottin'.

Your dog bark,
He don't see nothin',
My dog bark,
He done see somethin'.

One of these days,
And it won't be long,
You'll look for me here,
And I'll be gone.

Sandy Ree

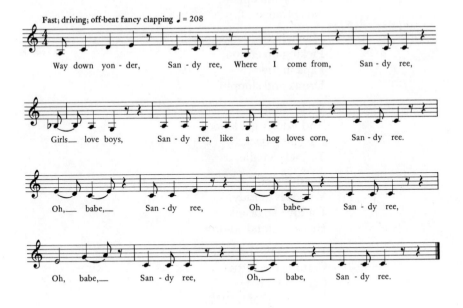

Fast; driving; off-beat fancy clapping ♩ = 208

Way down yon - der, San - dy ree, Where I come from, San - dy ree,

Girls— love boys, San - dy ree, like a hog loves corn, San - dy ree.

Oh,— babe,— San - dy ree, Oh,— babe,— San - dy ree,

Oh, babe,— San - dy ree, Oh,— babe, San - dy ree.

New words and new music adaptation by Bessie Jones and The Sea Island Singers. TRO—© copyright 1972 Ludlow Music, Inc., New York, N.Y. Used by permission.

Zudie-O

You better say "strutting" instead of "trucking." They're about the same, but the old folks just didn't like you to say it so raw. . . .

The term "zudie-o" refers to a movement in the dance in which the active couple, holding hands in a skating position, pull their arms back and forth alternately in a sawing motion to a count of one, two, three, rest.

Pull pull pull   rest pull   pull   pull   rest
Let's go   zudie - o   zudie - o   zudie - o

Pull pull pull   rest pull   pull   pull   rest
Let's go   zudie - o   all   night long

The step used in this dance also takes the same count and is a "strutting" two-step: step forward with the right foot, bring the left foot up to a close, step in place with the right foot, and rest. Repeat with the opposite feet.

R   L   R   rest L   R
We're walking through the al - ley, al - ley, al - ley,

L   rest   R   L   R   rest   L   R   L
We're walking through the al - ley, all night long.

"Zudie-O" is still danced by children in big cities across the country, but Mrs. Jones remembers it as a feature of the country dances of her childhood.

It's fun to play it with a big crowd, hear the children hollering way out yonder in the dark about how they want to go zudie-o too. . . . Let's go zudie-o! . . .

ALL VOICES
Let's go zudie-o, zudie-o, zudie-o,
Let's go zudie-o all night long.

We're walking through the alley, alley, alley,
We're walking through the alley all night long.

ACTION
Head lady and gentleman two-step out to meet each other between the lines, take hands, and "go zudie-o" standing still, while the foot couple does the same.

Head couple two-steps down the inside of the set toward the foot, still holding hands in skating position, while the

Step back, Sally, Sally, Sally,
Step back Sally, all night long.

foot couple two-steps similarly up the set.
Active couples drop hands, face their own partners, and shake right forefingers to the "zudie-o" rhythm.
Verses one through three are repeated until the active couples reach the head and foot respectively, where they step back into line.

And here comes another one, 'nother one,
  'nother one,
Just like the other one all night
  long.
And they're going zudie-o, zudie-o,
  zudie-o,
They're going zudie-o all night long.

The two couples next to the head and foot couples come out and two-step around their partners.
The two new active couples take hands and "go zudie-o," and the dance is repeated.

Mrs. Jones says that the final two couples (the ones at the center of the line) can go to the opposite ends instead of just exchanging places with their opposite couples; this allows them more time to "strut" and also reshuffles the order for the next round of dancing.

Zudie-O

Lyrics under the music:

Let's go zu-die-o, zu-die-o, zu-die-o, Let's go
zu-die-o all night long.— We're walk-ing through the al-ley, al-ley, al-
-ley, We're walk-ing through the al-ley all night long.— Step back,
Sal-ly, Sal-ly, Sal-ly, Step back Sal-ly, all night long.—

2. — And here comes a-noth-er one, 'noth-er one, 'noth-er one, Just like the
oth-er one all night long.— And they're go-ing zu-die-o, zu-die-o,
zu-die-o, They're go-ing zu-die-o all night long.—

New words and original music by Bessie Jones; collected and edited with additional new material by Alan Lomax. TRO—© copyright 1972 Ludlow Music, Inc., New York, N.Y. Used by permission.

I'm Going Away to See Aunt Dinah

They call it the Virginia Reel now. But we played it when we were little—we didn't know what it was. . . .

This Afro-American version of a frontier dance probably dates back to the time of slavery. It might even be called a museum piece, but one afternoon I saw the Islanders lead off on "I'm Going Away to See Aunt Dinah" with close to one hundred dancers in a mammoth longways set. None of the people dancing that afternoon would label this stirring and syncopated tune "old-fashioned" or "quaint."

As Mrs. Jones points out, "Aunt Dinah" is very much like the Virginia Reel. The step throughout is a skip, and it is danced in two parallel lines, one of men and one of women, facing each other. The lines should be spaced far enough apart to allow each facing couple to skip forward for four beats, swing each other for four and skip back to place for a final count of four. Experienced square dancers may find this "move" of twelve counts against a melody of sixteen to be difficult or jarring. In practice it gives an unexpected syncopation to an otherwise routine figure—a three-against-four count (as in "Juba") in still another form.

The dance is performed as follows:

1. Head and foot couples lead off at the same time and skip down between the parallel lines to meet in a group of four at the center.
2. The head man swings the foot lady with an elbow swing, while the foot man swings the head lady.
3. The head couple continues skipping to the foot to take up new places there; the foot couple in the meantime skips up to the head.
4. The new head man and lady skip toward each other (in four skips) and swing once around with an elbow swing, returning to place.
5. Couple number two then swings in the same manner as the head couple, followed by couple number three, and so on down the line. When the new foot couple has finished its swing, the dance repeats. Unlike the Virginia Reel, the head and foot couples stay the same throughout, simply exchanging places, though the Virginia Reel ending could easily be added.

Unlike those in "Zudie-O," the steps are not timed to any particular words in the accompanying song, which is sung ad lib with a strong lead and sharp clapping. On one occasion I asked Mrs. Jones if I had heard the last couplet correctly—was she really "going away in a coconut shell"? She answered enigmatically, "Yes—that's a *hard* nut."

FORM: Longways set; any number of couples dancing in pattern described above.

LEAD VOICE	GROUP VOICE
I'm goin' away,	
	(To) see Aunt Dinah,
I'm goin' away,	
	(To) see my Lord.

(The above lines serve as a chorus and may be repeated ad lib.)

Bake them biscuits, bake 'em brown,	
	See Aunt Dinah,
Turn them flapjacks around and around,	
	See my Lord.
Preacher come to mama's house,	
	See Aunt Dinah,
Set there and eat till his tongue fall out,	
	See my Lord.
Way down yonder in the old cornfield,	
	See Aunt Dinah,
Black snake popped me on my heel,	
	See my Lord.
I popped my whip, I run my best,	
	See Aunt Dinah,
Run my head in a hornet's nest,	
	See my Lord.
One of these days and it won't be long,	
	See Aunt Dinah,
Look for me and I'll be gone,	
	See my Lord.
Yes, I know something that I ain't going to tell,	
	See Aunt Dinah,
I'm going away in a coconut shell,	
	See my Lord.

I'm Going Away to See Aunt Dinah

With drive ♩ = 112-126

CLAP

VOICE

I'm goin' a - way,___ see Aunt Di - nah, I'm goin' a - way,___

see my___ Lord.___ Bake them bis - cuits, bake 'em' brown,___ See Aunt Di - nah,

Turn___ them flap - jacks a - round and a - round, See my___ Lord.___

Daniel

No, the ring plays are not exactly like the ring shouts, because you are playing—you see, the children are playing and they mean *to play. . . . Some ring plays seem just like a shout in some ways but they are plays. . . . [The children] are not shouting and they better not attempt the shouting in those days, you know what I mean, because the old folks would say you were mocking them and then you'd get a whipping. You see, if you're going to play, you* play, *and if you're going to shout, you* shout. *. . .*

As Mrs. Jones makes quite clear, the essential distinction between a ring shout and a ring play is the question of fundamental intent. The ring shout is a religious exercise, a form of worship, born out of African tradition and neatly distinguished from secular activities by its purposeful and delimiting structure. It represents a cultural compromise between two groups: Afro-Americans, who felt that it was right and proper to dance before the Lord, and descendants of Calvinism, who regarded any kind of earthbound joys, especially dance, as sinful. The shout, by its emphasis on observance of form and rule, came *outside the concept of dance* for both groups. For example, if you cross your feet or legs, you are no longer shouting but dancing; and, of course, dancing in church would be regarded as an impious activity by *both* white and black worshipers.

The shout "Daniel" is only one of several practiced by the Islanders. It is mimetic in nature; the participants follow the directions of the lead singer. It begins slowly, as the worshipers move into the counterclockwise motion of the circle with slow steps. The phrase "Shout, believer, shout!"—accompanied by the beginning of the stick beating (a broomstick held vertically and pounded on the floor)—comes at a faster tempo and signals the beginning of the shout step, which is then used throughout the ceremonial. The principal rules are these: the circling motion is continuous; the feet leave the floor as little as possible, especial care being taken that the heels stay down; and the legs do not cross—the trailing foot never passes the leading foot. Following are brief descriptions of the specific motions called for:

SHOUT. A rapid shuffling two-step, the back foot closing up to but
     never passing the leading foot: step (R), close (L); step (R),
     close (L).

EAGLE WING. Arms bent at elbows are flapped slightly by rotating the shoulder joints in parallel motion. This is the same step as the secular "buzzard lope" move.

ROCK. Bending from side to side at the waist; this movement, like all the others, is restrained.

FLY. Arms stretched out at full length and held stiffly are moved in a sailing motion (if the right arm goes up, the left arm goes down in the same axis). The dancer does not flap; he *soars*.

FLY THE OTHER WAY. Circle reverses movement to clockwise direction; flying motion continues as above.

KNEEBONE BEND. A slight sliding jump landing on both feet with the knees bent sharply; the impact should be timed to the word "bend" (the same step as the secular "Possum-La").

FLY BACK HOME. Fly back in follow-the-leader fashion to your seat; this call signals the end of the shout.

F O R M : Circle, clapping if desired; Mrs. Jones occasionally plays tambourine while shouting.* One lead singer, who may dance lead or may beat stick.

LEAD VOICE	GROUP VOICE	ACTION
Walk, believer, walk,†		Circle walks slowly counter-clockwise.
	Daniel,	
Walk, believer, walk,		
	Daniel.	
Walk, I tell you, walk,		
	Daniel,	
Walk, I tell you, walk,		
	Daniel.	
(Tempo almost doubles and stick pounding, if used, begins.)		
Shout, believer, shout,		
	Daniel,	Circle continues in same
Shout, believer, shout,		direction using shout step
	Daniel.	(which continues through-
On the eagle wing,		out).

* As previously mentioned, the term "shout" does not refer to a vocal effect but solely to the dance itself or to the step used in the dance.
† Each phrase sung by the lead singer is repeated four to six times as desired except for the opening phrases, which need only be repeated until the circle is organized.

On the eagle wing,	Daniel, Daniel.	Shout step continues; eagle-wing motion is added.
Fly, I tell you, fly,	Daniel.	Shout step continues with flying motion.
Rock, I tell you, rock,	Daniel.	Shout step with rocking motion.
Fly the other way,	Daniel.	Circle reverses to clockwise direction; shout step and flying motion.
Shout, I tell you, shout,	Daniel.	Return to counterclockwise direction; shout step.
Give me the kneebone bend,	Daniel.	Shout step continues with a kneebone bend as described.
On the eagle wing,	Daniel.	As previously described.
Fly, I tell you, fly,	Daniel.	As previously described.
Fly back home,	Daniel.	Circle breaks and follows the leader out of the center floor, with shout step and flying motion.

Daniel

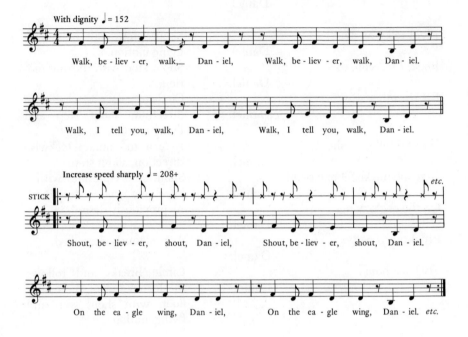

New words and new music adaptation by John Davis and The Sea Island Singers; collected and adapted by Alan Lomax. TRO—© copyright 1972 Ludlow Music, Inc., New York, N.Y. Used by permission.

7:
House Plays and
Home Amusements

They had happy times . . . they <u>made</u> themselves happy. . . .

Country people have always worked hard. But along with their hard work they have also, as Mrs. Jones puts it, looked for ways to *make* themselves happy.

Big jobs, wherever possible, have been combined with social occasions. Barn-raisings, cornhuskings, and quilting bees suggest the remote and vaguely romantic days of frontier America, but they are within the memory of people now living. Mrs. Jones is one.

I've sit underneath the quilts a many a time threading needles, oh Lord. Fun to me, you know, I'd be alone . . . but like if you were going to have a quilting, other peoples would come to you, and no doubt they'd bring their children and we'd all get underneath the quilt and thread needles and it was fun. . . . We'd eat peanuts, you know, sitting under there and thread needles until we'd get sleepy and they'd have to spread a bed out. . . .

Quilting is not patchwork itself but the act of sewing the completed patched top to its filler and backing with thousands of tiny stitches. Short lengths of thread are used so that the thread may not tangle or knot on itself; eight or ten women sitting around a quilt frame could well use the help of sharp-eyed youngsters as the evening wore on and their own eyes tired.

*You be singing hymns and things mostly at quiltings. I never
knowed a stitching song yet—you know, a song about stitching. Not
me. . . .*

Stitching wasn't much to sing about after all; actually songs sung
at work rarely talk about the work at hand. From the perspective of
the present day, a quilting or a cornhusking sounds like an exciting
social affair, but eyes and arms grew tired and backs stiff.

*We'd shell peanuts and shuck corn; we'd shell corn, too. We shelled
it and then you had to drop it with your hand. I dropped many and
many an acre of corn, Lord. And we'd shell the peanuts from house
to house, four or five bushels at your house, and we'd tell the crowd,
just like a quilting. Friends would gather from one house to another
and help shell each farmer's peanuts. And thereby we'd have much
fun—stories, you know, and such different things, and songs. . . .*

And so they "made themselves happy," throwing all the resources
of their imaginations into freeing their spirits from the monotony of
their work—and from the monotony of their surroundings, too. For
it is worth noting that Mrs. Jones speaks of only one place where the
games and dances and parties were held—at home.

During slavery, Negroes were bound to the land they worked; any
Negro found on a public road could be questioned and arrested if he
could show no written pass. On the plantation itself slaves outside
the "quarters" during off hours had to be able to give a good explanation for being found "out of their place." And after emancipation the
resources of the black ghettos in both country and town were too
meager to support public gathering places—the only exception being
the church, tax-free and approved by the white community.

So, except for church meetings and her short schooling, all Mrs.
Jones's recollections of happy times are bound into her concept of
home—her own house and those of her relatives and friends. From
babyhood she had watched the grownups going about their mysterious occupations—working, dancing, talking, singing—all at home,
where a little girl could watch. Her poetic temperament and joyful
appetite for experience developed in the warm and comfortable
places of her childhood—in her own home, around her own house,
in her own mother's kitchen.

We would have candy pullings, and you'd catch it and get it started to pull and I'd hand you one end and you hand me the other one and just pull, boy, pull it until it get real shiny—syrup candy, you know. And then you can wring it and you can twist it and plait it, and I've known four to pull at one time; oh, that's pretty, that's pretty that way! And then when you get through and it looks real light tan and pretty, you put it in a big bowl or plate—they had great big platters in those days, big platters, and they would put the candy on there and then you can cut it and eat it for a long time; that candy's there! . . .

Home was where everything happened.

We would have apple-biting parties, either hang 'em on strings or ducking. And we used to have string chewings—that's a nasty job, ain't it? The apple be hanging in the middle and have two people chewing the ends of the string with their hands behind them. The one that chews the most, open his mouth and gets to the apple, that's his apple. Sometimes they get there at the same time—two big mouths on that one apple!—bite it right in two! . . .

Mrs. Jones's parents were farm people, and their friends and neighbors were farmers, too. As their whole life pattern was centered around food getting and food gathering, food was also the central focus of most of their social activities.

We'd have peanut parchings and egg crackings. . . . Egg-cracking parties are good to have now—I'm supposed to have one as soon as I can when I get home. The adults had egg crackings if they were having something for something, like for the church or the school, for you had to buy the books in those days.

They'd boil a lots of eggs and have a party. And different people come and pay—you buy the eggs—in those days, you know, it would be for a nickel or a dime, that was big money; but nowadays it would be twenty-five on up. But you get one egg, and as many eggs as my egg crack, I win those eggs. You're supposed to hit on the end, not on the side, on that sharp end of the egg—not the round end because we know that is easy to break. But we take the two sharp ends, which is hard to break on the egg, and hit them together; and if mine cracks yours, I win your egg. If yours cracks mine, you win mine, and I go and buy another egg. . . .

> *I'll crack yours and you crack mine,*
> *See whose is thick and whose is fine. . . .*

Papa and them learnt to be schemy; they'd boil a rotten egg. You can't break a rotten egg, period, after it's boiled. That rotten egg would win big batches of eggs! . . . That was a dirty papa; he'd hit it right and do it right, but the egg was crooked! . . . But it wasn't right and they shouldn't have did it, but they did it—it was fun, just win baskets of eggs.

And you have a wonderful time egg cracking. . . . And we would have candy pullings and peanut parchings, and you can ask riddles at home and you can play ring plays, and you can have different parties, all kinds of parties—so many different things to do. . . .

In the next sections of this book, Mrs. Jones describes some of these "many things to do" that are especially *for* children. She divides them into "outdoor games" and "house plays." Both kinds are fun to play and require little, if any, equipment.

Instead of building blocks, the country child of a generation ago piled up towers of living fists. Instead of using doll houses or puppet theaters, he staged dramatic dialogues with his brothers and sisters. The grownups watched and approved, and probably talked about how, in their day, children didn't have to *play* all the time but knew what real work was.

They had happy times. They *made* themselves happy.

William, William, Trembletoe

He's a rogue—a chicken rogue to catch them hens. He sets up till twelve o'clock and goes to old man Chapman's house to catch chickens. . . .

William, William, Trembletoe
He's a good fisherman to catch them hens,
Put 'em in the pens.
Some lays eggs; some don't.
Wire briar limberlock
Set and sing till twelve o'clock.
The clock fell down,
The mouse ran around.
Y-O-U-T spells Out
To old man Chapman's house.
I went down town the other day
I met my brother Jim. (rest)
He had a hammer, he had a nail,
He had a cat with thirty-nine tails.
Some to the east, some to the west,
Some to the evers goo-goo nest.

Another version of the above rhyme served to count out who would be "it" in the "Hide and Seek" games of my own childhood. Mrs. Jones's version, chanted to a strong rhythm, precedes the playing of a game (essentially a series of conversational scenes) that is known throughout the South. This is how Mrs. Jones describes the playing of it.

You spread your fingers out and count on them; if you got a lot of children, you have just one hand of each child. And then you count on their fingers: "William, William, Trembletoe . . ." The last one when the rhyme ends goes out to the evers goo-goo nest; he goes in a corner. And then the rest of us name ourselves, just whisper to one another names, anything we want to name ourselves—elephant or lion or anything we want to—box, shoe, anything—train, cat—just whatever we surmise to name ourselves. We whisper it [the name chosen] to the one who was counting. And then we have an odd [extra] name, too, that nobody is named. Then you ask the one that's standing out in the corner:

When you coming home?

And he say,

Tomorrow afternoon.

And you say,

> What you going to bring?

And he say,

> A dish and a spoon and a fat raccoon.

And then we ask him,

> What you want to ride on?

And we name all those names and in there we call that odd [extra] name. And he have to say [which he wants to ride on]. If he be unlucky and guess the odd name, he have to come on his tiptoes and not let his heels touch, but if he guesses a name that one of the children has, that child have to go after him. If he's too large for the child to carry, he'd just put his hands on his shoulders and come on in home with him. But if he's a small enough child to tote, he totes him, completely totes him, and bring him on to the one counting. And then the counter says,

> What's that you got there?

And the child that's carrying him says,

> A bag of nits!

(That sure sounds rough, but it's a bag of nits.

And the counter says,)

> Shake 'em tell they spit.

And he [the carrier] acts like he's shaking them, and the other one acts like he's spitting. And then the counter asks him [the child being carried],

> What would you rather lay on—a thorn bed or a feather bed?

And if he says a feather bed you just turn him loose, you drop him—don't throw him. But if he say a thorn bed, just ease him down very easy, because a feather bed won't hurt but a thorn bed will hurt—you got to squat down and ease him down very easy. . . . Well, you know most children will pick a feather bed rather than a thorn bed and we had much fun playing that way.

Club Fist

Your fist is a club when you ball it up. . . .

This is a game known around the world. In Yugoslavia the dialogue that makes up most of the game ends:

> Where are the lords?
> They jumped over the fence.
> Where is the fence?
> The ax cut it down.
> Where is the ax?
> Death lies there and shows his white teeth.

The Georgia version of this ancient, widespread, and grimly humorous game involves, as Mrs. Jones puts it, "as many [players] as you want only not too many." The first player puts his right fist on the floor or on a table with the thumb sticking up; a second player catches the thumb in his own fist and leaves his own thumb up. As many players (and hands) as are available catch hold similarly, forming a tower of fists piled one on top of the other. The first player asks:

> What's that you got there?

The owner of the top fist answers,

> Club fist.

The first player asks,

> Want me to take it off, knock it off, or pinch it off?

The top player makes his choice and the first player uses his left hand, which he has kept free, to do as requested. The same conversation is repeated with the owner of each fist; when all have been taken, knocked, or pinched off, a dialogue takes place between the second and first player—the second player asking the questions, the first answering.

> What you got there?
> Cheese and bread.
> Where's my cheese?
> The rat got it.
> Where's the rat?
> The cat caught him.

Where's the cat?
The dog killed him.
Where's the dog?
The stick beat him.
Where's the stick?
The fire burned it.
Where's the fire?
The water squenched it.
Where's the water?
The ox drank it.
Where's the ox?
The butcher killed him.
Where's the butcher?
The rope hung him.
Where's the rope?
The knife cut it.
Where's the knife?
The hammer mashed it.
Where's the hammer?
It's buried round the church door, and the first
        one I see his teeth, I'm going to give him two
        pinches and two hits. . . .

The first player then "cuts the fool" and tries to make the other players laugh—the penalty for "showing his white teeth" being "two
pinches and two hits."

Uncle Tom

It's just a house game, you know—a fun game, to play in the house.

Many "fun" games are concerned with attempts to make another player "show his white teeth." But "Uncle Tom," though it somewhat resembles other, better-known games, has a plot line and a bitter hilarity all its own. It is an uproariously funny game while it is being played, but afterward you realize what you've been laughing at. Southern black children did not have to search far for the models they satirized in this game.

Here is Mrs. Jones's description of how it is played:

There's a crowd of children setting round in a place and you get you some little sticks or things and call them nails. You come around to the children and then you knock to this one's door just like you were at the door, you knock. They say,

Who is that?

You say,

Old Man Tom.

They say,

What you want?

You say,

I want to sell some nails. How many pounds you want?

And they'll tell him [Uncle Tom] one or two pounds or three, and he'll let 'em have one or two or three of those sticks . . . or whatever it is. And then he goes to the next one and say the same way, and they buy the nails and the same thing over. Then he'll go away and stay off a little while—he may change while he's out there, dress all kind of funny ways, you know—put on old crazy ragged clothes or a funny face or old funny hat or anything, you know. Make himself look real ugly and raggedy. Then he'll come back and knock again. They say,

Who is that?

And he say,

   Old Man Tom.

They say,

   What you want?

He say,

   I want you to pay me for my nails, please.

   (*He say it in a funny way, like he was so hongry and tired, you see.*) *And they say,*

   I can't pay.

And he say,

   You can't pay?

They say,

   I can't pay!

He say, like he's crying,

   You ain't going to pay Uncle Tom?

And you're not supposed to laugh or not even smile, just be hard at him, and Uncle Tom have to do all kind of funny things to make you laugh. And if you laugh, then you got to give him the nails back, you see. He got to do all kind of cutting up, dancing and jumping around and making ugly face and all the time asking, "You can't pay? You ain't going to pay Uncle Tom. Poor Uncle Tom, you can't pay?" and all that kind of funny way. And then if he can get you to laugh, he got his nails, and he go to another one and do the same way, with all kind of funny motions.

It's always who can be so hard, you know, and won't laugh, why he'll be Uncle Tom the next time. . . .

Moneyfoot

*Children were honest in those days; they won't do honest now.
. . . They ain't no use your trying it [this game] because they ain't
going to be honest, and they'll peep and they'll look. . . .*

We didn't actually play this game, but it would seem from Mrs.
Jones's description that without either a little dishonest peeping or a
few broad hints it might go on forever. But I am speaking from the
point of view of the middle class, whose houses and lives are choked
with material objects. Mrs. Jones's game reflects those times and
places in our country where a child could lie on his stomach and list
off in a few minutes the things that were in his house. They weren't
so very many; he didn't need to peep. And while he was thinking of
them, he was a "Moneyfoot."

Here is how Mrs. Jones says you play this game:

*The children sit in a circle with their feet stretched out. And the
counter points to each foot and says,*

> One foot, two foot, three foot Sal,
> Bob demidius English mare,
> Mary, tary, moneyfoot!

*And when he says "moneyfoot" and points to that foot, you draw it
up and he don't count it no more. He keeps on counting the others.
Then, quite natural, when you come to both of your feet being
"moneyfoot," then you got no foot to walk on and no foot to count,
then you is a moneyfoot.*

*Then you got to lay down on your stomach, and you close both
your eyes and you're not supposed to peep, and the counter holds
something over you and says,*

> Heavy, heavy, hang over your head.

*And the child lying down is supposed to guess what it is. If he
guesses wrong (like he guesses it's a bottle and it's glasses) the
counter says,*

> I'll lay these glasses here until the bottle comes.

The "counter" then lays the wrongly guessed object down by the child on the floor, sometimes on top of him! He finds a new object to be guessed and holds it up saying, "Heavy, heavy, hangs over your head" again.

Sometimes that child will stay there so long you'll get chairs and blankets and everything in the house by him. If he guesses right, he gets up and you start again.

Jack in the Bush

MABEL HILLARY: *The best way to play this is with peanuts or pop-corn, and that way whoever wins gets to eat all.*

Two players each have an equal number of counters—popcorn, nuts, stones, etc. One picks up a number of his counters, taking care his opponent does not see how many, and holds them out in his closed fist.

> Player 1: Jack in the bush!
> Player 2: I'll ride him!
> Player 1: How many miles?
> Player 2: (Guesses the number of counters.)

If he guesses too many, he must give the first player enough counters to make up the amount guessed. If he guesses too few, the first player must give him the amount lacking. If he guesses right, he wins all the counters in his opponent's fist.

Although Mabel Hillary taught me this game, all the Islanders knew it in varying forms. John Davis had played it:

> Jack in the bush!
> Cut him down!
> How many licks?

In this version, incorrect guesses would be made up with hits. Mrs. Jones had played it as:

> Old gray horse!
> I'll ride him!
> How many miles?

and also

> Eggs in the bush!
> The old hen lay eggs!
> How many eggs?

Mrs. Hillary also remarked that when you played for peanuts, you should say,

> Pinochle mine!

Somewhat surprisingly to me, this was the only gambling game the Islanders taught me. Variations of this game have been reported from many parts of the United States and all over Europe. The idea of guessing what is held in a closed fist is ancient indeed; Xenophon reported a method of cheating in such games!

Bob-a-Needle

It's a game. Of course, it's a play, too, but it's a game, a house game. . . . Or either you can play it outdoors.

"Bob-a-Needle" (bobbin needle?) is, for purposes of this game, a pen, a jackknife, or a small stick of wood that can be passed rapidly from hand to hand. All the players but one stand in a tight circle, shoulder to shoulder, holding their hands behind their backs. The extra player stands in the center of the ring; she closes her eyes and holds the bob-a-needle high over her head in one hand. One of the ring players silently creeps up and takes the bob-a-needle from her hand and puts it behind his own back. The center player then opens her eyes and begins singing the lead line of the song; the players in the circle sing the refrain:

LEAD VOICE (AD LIB)	GROUP VOICE
Bob-a-needle,	
	Bob-a-needle is a-running,
Bob-a-needle,	
	Bob-a-needle is a-running,
Better run, bob-a-needle,	
	Bob-a-needle is a-running,
Better hustle, bob-a-needle,	
	Bob-a-needle is a-running,
I want bob-a-needle,	
	Bob-a-needle is a-running,
Want to find bob-a-needle,	
	Bob-a-needle is a-running,
Going to catch bob-a-needle,	
	Bob-a-needle is a-running,
Turn around, bob-a-needle,	
	Bob-a-needle is a-running,
Oh bob, bob-a-needle,	
	Bob-a-needle is a-running.

The lead singer's lines are extemporaneous and can be sung in any order. Mrs. Jones often sang each one twice.

During the singing, the players in the ring pass the bob-a-needle from hand to hand, trying to move as little as possible in order not to make its location obvious. Bob-a-needle may travel clockwise or counterclockwise, and the players may reverse direction at will. The center player meanwhile reaches around the waist and feels the hands of each ring player in turn; she too may go in either direction, but she may not skip players nor run back and forth across the ring. When the center player reverses the direction of *her* search, she must signal this with the lead line, "Turn around, bob-a-needle!"

This game does not end when someone is caught holding the elusive bob-a-needle. Like most of Mrs. Jones's games that involve "losing," the person caught simply pays a forfeit and/or takes over the center role so that the play can begin again. When the players tire, the accumulated forfeits are redeemed by their owners in a new sequence of play. (See "Pawns," page 166.)

Bob-a-Needle

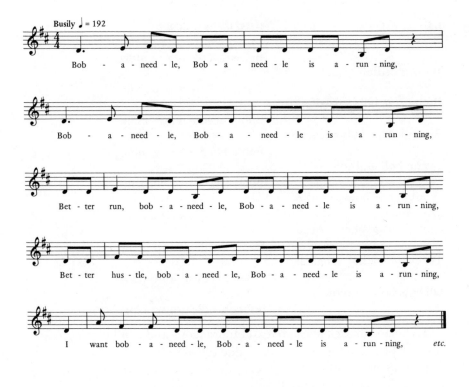

Bob - a - need - le, Bob - a - need - le is a - run - ning,

Bob - a - need - le, Bob - a - need - le is a - run - ning,

Bet - ter run, bob - a - need - le, Bob - a - need - le is a - run - ning,

Bet - ter hus - tle, bob - a - need - le, Bob - a - need - le is a - run - ning,

I want bob - a - need - le, Bob - a - need - le is a - run - ning,   *etc.*

New words and new music adaptation by Bessie Jones; collected and edited with additional new material by Alan Lomax. TRO—© copyright 1972 Ludlow Music, Inc., New York, N.Y. Used by permission.

Whose Bag Is My Gold Ring?

After the summer workshop the Islanders and I met for several afternoons of talk and re-recording before they took the long bus ride back home to Georgia. They remembered some new plays then which we didn't have a chance to try out because there weren't enough of us to make the game go. "Whose Bag Is My Gold Ring?" is one that Mrs. Jones remembered after I had asked her to re-record "Bob-a-Needle" so that I was certain I had the tune right. It is a singing game with a pretty tune.

The players stand in a circle and pass a ring or another object from hand to hand. Unlike "Bob-a-Needle," the player in the middle has his eyes shut or is blindfolded, so the object may be passed in front of the players. As the center player feels in each hand, the other children sing,

> Whose bag is my gold ring?
> My gold ring I lost on the train
> When I went to London to marry.

The child who starts the song each time must have the ring, thus cuing the center player to search in the direction from which the solo voice comes.

When the center player finds the ring, a pawn (forfeit) is given up and play continues as in "Bob-a-Needle."

Whose Bag Is My Gold Ring?

Written and adapted by Bessie Jones; collected and edited by Alan Lomax. TRO–© copyright 1972 Ludlow Music, Inc., New York, N.Y. Used by permission.

Pawns

In such games as "Bob-a-Needle" a player who "loses" does not leave the game, but gives up an article of clothing or some object in his possession to a selected referee, and the play goes on. When the players tire of the first game, the earning back of the "pawns" (the articles given up) forms a kind of coda—a relaxing end play to the game itself. (The Islanders used the term "pawn" for both the forfeited article and the task assigned to redeem it.)

To win back a pawn, a judge and a caller are necessary. The judge sits in a chair; the caller stands behind him and holds a pawned object over his head. The judge should not know what, or whose, the article is.

> CALLER: Heavy, heavy, hangs over your head.
> JUDGE: Is it ladies' wear or gentlemen's wear?
> CALLER: It's [ladies'] wear. What shall be done to the [lady] that owns this wear?

The judge then orders the player in question to perform some action. Some of the "pawns" Mrs. Jones exacted were:

> to bark like a dog
> to crow like a rooster
> to hop like a frog
> to say a speech
> to sing a song
> to wade the green valley (see next play)

Mabel Hillary, of a later generation and "raised up with boys," required more vigorous and difficult pawns:

> to stand on your head
> to walk on your hands from there to me
> to walk like a crab (The player lies down on his back, puts his hands on the floor by his shoulders and pushes up so that his body is held up by his feet and hands. He then "walks," spanking himself on the hips with his hands alternately.)
> to walk like a duck (Player squats down, puts his arms around and then between his legs and holds his ankles while "walking.")
> to roll the pumpkin (Player sits doubled up with arms wrapped around his knees, holding his ankles tightly with his hands, and rolls all the way over.)

Wade in the Green Valley

The one who is wading the green valley don't say a word; he answers by his feet. . . .

This play is actually a "pawn," a task set a player who wants to win back a forfeited article. The judge may tell him to call out a lady of his choice and "wade the green valley with her."

The gentleman then stands on one side of the room with his lady facing him on the other side. He asks her, "Do you like ——?" (some kind of food, or a person, or a color, or anything he thinks of). If she likes it, she takes one step forward; if she does not like it, she takes one step back. If she is indifferent or undecided, she stands still.

Mrs. Jones continues,

Now when you get close, he says, "Would you like a sweet kiss?" and you got to get that, so that's the last of it. Sometimes they take great big steps, if they like what he calls a lot. . . .

This can be played without being a pawn, Mrs. Jones tells me.

Just line your line of children up and let them wade the green valley—just see what would they say with their feet!

In play, this is extraordinarily dramatic; without music or rhythmic accompaniment, the human body makes its statement.

8:
Outdoor Games

That's a good game; it's good for children . . . makes them strong. . . .

Mrs. Jones, vigorous and active in her sixties, firmly believes that running, pulling, jumping, chasing, and wrestling are important for proper physical development and are therefore "good for children." If her group of "outdoor games" is a small one, it is because she includes in this category only those games which *must* be played outside. Ring games, singing games, and many of the plays included in other sections would normally be played outdoors as well, particularly in the community of overcrowded small farmhouses in which Mrs. Jones grew up.

She has put into this section of games, then, only those big-muscle and rowdy activities which could not possibly be played in the house. And it is in this category, too, that the first real signs of organized competition appear. She seems to approve of competition only when it is socially controlled, as it is in play.

So the children, they don't even know how to play those things now, see. But it's just good fun games, keeps you out of devilment, keeps you from fighting. I never had fights with children when I was little—didn't have time to fight, we had to play. When we wasn't playing, we was eating or sleeping or working—and so that was it. But now they got time to talk about the grown things. . . .

Though it seems unlikely that Mrs. Jones *never* had a fight when she was a child, it is surely true that one of the functions of games is to organize and channel the competitive impulse. Today, Mrs. Jones, like most adults, is firmly on the side of peace and quiet.

Actually, the competitive element, even in her "outdoor games," is very slight indeed. Perhaps little girls in Mrs. Jones's "time coming up" weren't encouraged to play competitive games. Perhaps, as an adult, she has forgotten the rougher pastimes of her childhood—or doesn't choose to recommend them to the next generation. In any event, it is fascinating to see how, throughout the sometimes competitive and always strenuous activities she describes in this chapter, there runs the familiar dramatic impulse—the aesthetic goal of the "beautiful play."

Miss Lucy

We used to stand on the step and see who could jump the further in the yard. . . .

Every adult whose childhood was graced by a home with a front or back porch can remember trying to see who could jump the farthest from the top step. Mrs. Jones says,

We used to sing "Miss Lucy" mostly when we played jumping. We'd put a marker out and everybody stand on the top step and jump the same time.

Miss Lucy!
Mama say to send a chew tobacco,
She'll pay you back tomorrow.
Hooray! Let's jump!

Miss Lucy

Words and music by Bessie Jones; collected and edited with new material by Alan Lomax. TRO—
© copyright 1972 Ludlow Music, Inc., New York, N.Y. Used by permission.

Horse and the Buggy

The one who can stand the longest, that's all it takes—that can stand the longest without getting drunk and falling over. . . .

Roger Caillois, in his book *Man, Play, and Games,* categorizes one type of play as "the pursuit of vertigo"; "Horse and the Buggy" certainly fits that description. To play it, two children take hands, their arms either crossed or straight, and wheel around, pulling back from each other so that their momentum increases. On the words "way down low," they stoop down, sometimes getting down on their knees, but the whirling motion never stops nor does the direction of spin change.

At this galloping pace, the call-and-response pattern for the singing is an essential.

> Horse and the buggy,
> > Sail away,
> Sail away, horsey,
> > Sail away.
> Horse and the buggy,
> > Sail away,
> Sail away, lady,
> > Sail away.
> Way down low,
> > Sail away,
> Sail away, lady,
> > Sail away.
> Horse and the buggy,
> > Sail away,
> Sail away, horsey,
> > Sail away.
> Sail away, lady,
> > Sail away. . . .

Mabel Hillary, who demonstrated the game with Emma Ramsey, remarked, "When you play it with the boys and they let go your hands, you *would* go sailing . . . sail right on across the yard!"

Horse and the Buggy

Galloping ♩ = 126

Horse and the bug - gy, Sail a - way, Sail___ a - way, hor - sey, Sail a - way.

Horse and the bug - gy, Sail a - way, Sail___ a - way, la - dy, sail a - way.

Way down low, Sail a - way, Sail___ a - way, la - dy, Sail a - way.

Written and adapted by Bessie Jones; collected and edited by Alan Lomax. TRO—© copyright 1972 Ludlow Music, Inc., New York, N.Y. Used by permission.

Won't You Let the Birdie Out?

Unfortunately I did not see this game being played, as Mrs. Jones only recalled it during a final conversation. From her description, a ring of children stand holding hands tightly while the "birdie" in the center goes around the circle, testing the grip of each pair of hands. Typically, Mrs. Jones acted it out for me in rhythm, pretending to try to break through the hands on the downbeat of each question. She described the lead singer as being the child in the middle, though I imagine he would run out of breath pretty soon, and a member of the ring might well have to take over. The lead should be sung vigorously and ad lib, with any phrases or questions that come to mind, throughout the whole game; the answering chant is crisp. When the birdie finds a weak spot, according to Mrs. Jones, he just *breaks* out.

> Is this door locked?
> > No, child, no.
> Is this door locked?
> > No, child, no.
> Won't you let the birdie out?
> > No, child, no.
> Won't you let your birdie out?
> > No, child, no.
> I'll give you a piece of sweet bread.
> > No, child, no.
> I'll give you a piece of biscuit.
> > No, child, no.
>
> Won't you let your birdie out?
> > No, child, no.   etc.

Won't You Let the Birdie Out?

Briskly ♩ = 176

Is this door locked?— No, child, no. Is this door locked?—

No, child, no. Won't you let the bird - ie out? No, child, no. Won't you

let your bird - ie out?— No, child, no. I'll give you a piece of sweet bread.

No, child, no. I'll give you a piece of bis - cuit. No, child, no.

Written and adapted by Bessie Jones; collected and edited by Alan Lomax. TRO—© copyright 1972 Ludlow Music, Inc., New York, N.Y. Used by permission.

Engine Rubber Number Nine

Most of us will recognize this game as the old familiar "Wood Tag," in which an "it" chases the other players, who may find themselves temporary safety by touching wood. As usual with Mrs. Jones's games, the foreplay is more important than the actual game itself.

The children stand in a line with a "caller" facing them. He points to each in turn as he says,

> Engine rubber number nine,
> Stick your head in turpentine.
> Turpentine will make you shine,
> Engine rubber number nine.

Each time the rhyme ends, the child being pointed to comes to the caller. The last one . . .

is Poison and he has to catch the rest of them and poison them. But as long as they're on wood, they're safe—just put their foot on a little chip or anything. And they'll holler out, "I'm free as a jaybird picking up corn!" because they done got on wood, you see, they're free. . . .

Mrs. Jones says you can say this rhyme for a clapping play if you want to, just like "One Saw, Two Saw" or "One-ry, Two-ry." Similarly, either of those rhymes may be used to start off the game just described.

London Bridge

Scholars seem fairly close to agreement that this traditional European game is a reflection of the ancient custom of offering a living sacrifice to the angry spirit of the river when a bridge is to be built. It is among the most widespread of singing games; the Islanders knew two versions.

Mrs. Jones insisted that she sang the tune "just like the children do now." Later, John and Peter Davis sang the tune most usually associated with the game; both their version and Mrs. Jones's included verses that I found unfamiliar.

FORM : Two children hold hands to make an arch through which the other players pass. All sing,

GROUP VOICE	ACTION
London Bridge is all broke down, All broke down, all broke down, London Bridge is all broke down, Pity poor me.	Children walk through the arch in single file, circling around so the line is continuous.
London Bridge is all built up, All built up, all built up, London Bridge is all built up, Pity poor me.	Circling continues as above.
Catch the one that come by last, Come by last, come by last, Catch the one that come by last, Pity poor me.	Circling continues.

The arched arms come down, catching a player. |
| Give him a kick and send him home, Send him home, send him home, Give him a kick and send him home, Pity poor me. | The players hold the caught child in the circle of their arms and bump him gently with their knees. |

Mrs. Jones continues:

We don't hurt him, just bump him. . . . Then we [the children making the arch] done already whispered to one another which one we are, the United States or London. Then we whisper to the child [and ask] what he'd rather choose, gold or silver. And he got to say;

then he go behind whichever one. . . . The United States is always silver, you know, and London is gold. . . .

The ones that go behind me, they have to protect me. Then afterwards we go to pulling, you know. And the ones who fall is a rotten egg. And all who's behind me is pulling, and all who's behind you is pulling, you know—a string of them—to see who is the best puller.

Peter and John Davis, Emma Ramsey, and Mabel Hillary sang another version; the play was the same, except that they drew a line under the arch, and during the tug of war, anybody who was pulled over the line had to let go and join the other side. Here is how their song went:

> London Bridge is falling down,
> Falling down, falling down,
> London Bridge is falling down,
> Pity poor me.
>
> This is the one that stole my watch,
> Stole my watch, stole my watch,
> This is the one that stole my watch,
> Pity poor me.
>
> Catch that one that come by last,
> Come by last, come by last,
> Catch that one that come by last,
> Pity poor me.
>
> Down to the workhouse he must go,
> He must go, he must go,
> Down to the workhouse he must go,
> Pity poor me.

In the last verse, they may have sung "white house" instead of "workhouse," I am not sure. Since the term "white house" in Negro song generally refers to the plantation mansion, perhaps it doesn't make any difference.

London Bridge

(Mrs. Jones' version)

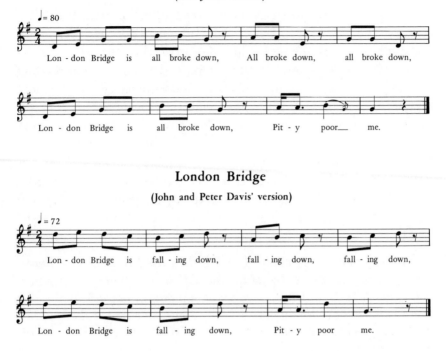

Lon - don Bridge is all broke down, All broke down, all broke down,

Lon - don Bridge is all broke down, Pit - y poor___ me.

London Bridge

(John and Peter Davis' version)

Lon - don Bridge is fall - ing down, fall - ing down, fall - ing down,

Lon - don Bridge is fall - ing down, Pit - y poor me.

New words and new music adaptation by Bessie Jones; collected and edited with additional new material by Alan Lomax. TRO—© copyright 1972 Ludlow Music, Inc., New York, N.Y. Used by permission.

All Hid

This is another game known all over the world. In country after country, the rules for playing "All Hid" or "Hide and Seek" are remarkably similar; the seeker hides his eyes while the other players scatter; at a certain point, usually determined by counting or reciting a rhyme, the seeker goes out to find the hiders; if successful, he races his quarry back "home." If the hider wins the race, he is "free"; otherwise, he becomes the next seeker. The game is mentioned in more than one of Shakespeare's plays; it is played in India and Rumania and during summer evenings in the state of Georgia.

Mrs. Jones rightly assumed that everyone knew the "game" part of "All Hid." She was concerned with the dying element of *play*, and her discussion was so eloquent, I include it almost entire, just as she said it.

Children these days don't play like they used to play—nowhere— mine and no one else's. In "Hide and Go Seek," the children nowa- days play it right quick and angry—I say angry, because if the one that's counting ask them, "Is all hid?" sometimes they'll holler, "Not yet!" and sometimes they'll just throw off and give a kind of a "No!" and all that way. . . .

But in my time coming up, when the person says, "Is all hid?" he said it in a tone *and the children they answered him in a* tone. *And these tones would combine together, which would make a beautiful play.*

And the children don't count now—well, they really does count— nothing but counting. They says, "Onetwothreefourfivesixseveneight- nineten!" But in those days, we had a rhyme that we called counting. Such as, one would go to the base and lean up against a tree and not peeping, because it's not fair, you know, they would hide their eyes and lean against the base and he would say,

> Honey, honey, bee ball,
> I can't see y'all.
> All hid?

And those children would holler back,

> No-o-o!

And the counter would say,

    Is all hid?

And the children would say,

    No-o-o!

And sometimes those children be right close to there—but not too close, you know, not too close for the law of the base, ten feet—but they don't be far and they put their hands up to their mouth or put their heads down and say "No-o-o!" real soft. You see, that make him think they're way off! They sound like a panther! . . .
And then it go on like this (singing):

> I went to the river,
> I couldn't get across,
> I paid five dollars for an old blind horse.
> One leg broke,
> The other leg cracked,
> And great Godamighty, how the horse did rack.
> Is all hid?
>   No-o-o!
> Is all hid?
>   No-o-o!
>
> I went down the road,
> The road was muddy.
> Stubbed my toe
> And made it bloody.
> Is all hid?
>   No-o-o!
> Is all hid?
>   No-o-o!
>
> Me and my wife
> And a bobtail dog,
> We crossed that river on a hickory log.
> She fell in
> And I fell off,
> It left nobody but the bobtail dog.
> Is all hid?
>   No-o-o!
> Is all hid?
>   No-o-o!

One, two,
I don't know what to do.
Three, four,
I don't know where to go.
Five, six,
I'm in a terrible fix.
Seven, eight,
I made a mistake.
Nine, ten,
My eyes open, I'm a-looking!

And they know *he's looking. In other words, he could stop right there at "one, two," and when he stop there, they know they better lay close, because he maybe done left the base then because he say, "One, two, I don't know what to do!" He's looking around then, see, let you know he's about to leave the base. "Three, four, I don't know where to go," because they all are hid, see? "Five, six, I'm in a terrible fix"; see, he's looking someplace. "Seven, eight"—he didn't find nobody there—"I made a mistake!"—see? Then he say, "Nine, ten, my eyes [are] open, I'm a-looking!" and he's going everywhere then, see?*

But the children now don't have that kind of a counting . . . and they won't leave the base! It worries me. I look at them and they won't leave the base, and when the others come, they expect to get their hundred—we called it a "hundred." They call it a base, but in my day, we called it "my hundred." If you make it to the base, if you outrun the counter and get to the base, we called it "my hundred." And you know, when they ask if all is hid, they ask, "All hid?" and they holler back "No!" and all that. . . . You know, it's no play. It's just a snap all the way through. It's no play in it. . . . But we played.

All Hid

Rap Jack

This grim sport was described by Mrs. Jones in one of her reminiscent moods. I have seen references to a similar "game" called "Wrap Jacket"—a form of duel between boys in the midwest—and also to a like activity engaged in by Arawak Indian boys in Guiana. It is such a formless pursuit as to be exceedingly difficult to trace; I include it here as a reminder of the brutality that lies close to the surface of American history.

Mama and them would take those long switches (and in those days we wore those long dresses and we'd hardly ever see our legs and when we did they wasn't rough and tough like these legs we see now—they was tender—the sun didn't shine on them) and they would play Rap Jack, just hit one another with the switches. I've known them to cut through dresses clean, just cut a tear in them. That's the craziest play to play—I nev-er wanted to play that. . . .

Mama used to play it, too—she was seventeen years old—and they'd stand out there, used to rap jack one another—ooh, the womens and the mens, too. The womens would rap jack the men because you see, the men have on pants. You could get to them closer. . . . I've known them to get those switches and let them sit just to play rap jack. And they'd get hard; that's the reason they'd cut through dresses. The women would cut the men's pants, cut 'em, I tell you. They'd have much fun playing rap jack. . . .

9:
Songs and Stories

I like that. I like that because there's so much meaning to it.

This final section, unlike the rest of this book, was not really Mrs. Jones's idea, but mine. Furthermore, when it came to choosing the songs and stories to put in, I found I had to do the job myself. She simply did not behave as though there was a separate category of songs and stories *for* children as opposed to those *for* grownups.

There were a few items, such as "Peep Squirrel" or "I Had an Old Rooster," that she identified as "fun for the children," but most of the time she just told stories and sang songs. Anybody might listen and might like them or not. A story would remind her of a riddle and the riddle of a song and the song of another story, just as a conversation drifts from subject to illustration to a complete change of course. And she told or sang whatever came to mind without seeming to worry too much about whether or not it was "suitable" for a particular age group.

This attitude is remarkably different from her feelings about *activities*. To Mrs. Jones, each play and game has its special role in the progressive development of the child. These she had graded and sorted out—but not the verbal material, not the stories and songs. Actually, the plays and games themselves reflect this feeling. Their actions are ordinarily prescribed and fixed; the accompanying songs are wide-ranging in content and often forthrightly adult.

This distinction, it seems to me, further illuminates Mrs. Jones's basic ideas. Motion (dance-play-game) she seems to see as an acting-out, a practicing of the roles and relationships a child must learn. During play, however, the motion is overlain by song; and the song, then, may be a verbal reflection of the kind of a world the child is going to enter. It is never too early for the child to learn what that world is like, and its complexities are suggested by all the subtle devices of poetry.

Now one can see, I believe, a final extension of the principle of antiphony: the constant and continuous interplay of fantasy and reality. The ring player acts out his dream of romantic availability, while the accompanying singers make remarks about how hard it is to find something to eat. As "Lily" dances out her fantasy of domination ("I'm going to rule my ruler!"), the song's chorus both applauds and cautions her—("Sometimes!"). Sometime, someday, the singers tell her, she will have to go outside the ring.

But Lily needs more than a foretaste of the hardness of life; she needs to dream too. Actually, there would be no *play* without both elements. Both the fantasy and the reality are equal in importance.

Perhaps this is why the Singers could still play children's games with delight, though they were all middle-aged or over, and all people of position and dignity in their own community. The adult could be a child, because the child was already adult. Where does one role end and the other begin? Where does the song give over to the dance, the dance to the game, the ruler to the ruled?

The answer suggested by Mrs. Jones's plays seems to me both terribly simple and terribly complex at the same time. They answer each other—the child and the grownup, the hands and the feet, the group voice and the solo voice, the words and the action, the dream world and the real world, in a continual and mutually supportive conversation.

For a conversation implies both mutual respect and mutual need. The feet and the hands are equally important in the clapping pattern. The solo voice cannot function properly without the supporting chorus, and the other way round as well. For Mrs. Jones, there is no dance without song, and no play without "a story to it." And it is out of this mixture, the interweaving of the solid and day-to-day and the fantastic and poetic that the *meaning,* so important to Mrs. Jones, emerges.

And so it would be a serious mistake, I believe, to think about the games and plays in this book just as motion patterns, to dismiss as irrelevant and nonsensical the tangential and luminous language of the songs which surround them. This is why I have added this final section—a sampling of Mrs. Jones's poetry, song, and story—to provide one further glimpse into the life they all express. To quote Mrs. Jones for one final word:

First you say it (a line from the "Hambone" poem) and then you say it with your hands (clapping). It's all the same thing. . . .

I Had an Old Rooster

Peter [Davis] says he be going out some time he hear one of those birds that holler soon in the morning—maybe it be a jaybird—he say,

> *Laziness'll kill ya!*
> *Laziness'll kill ya!*
> *Wha!*

What the meaning of it is that everything gets up real early in the morning—all but peoples. And those creatures outside would make you know that it's time to get up early in the morning. . . .

All over the world, animals—especially birds—have talked to country people, who have in turn, with their stumbling human tongues, tried to repeat what they have heard. In France, the rooster says "Cocorico!" In England, "Cock-a-doodle-doo!" In Georgia, though, he is more forthright. In a lovely transmutation of sounds, he tells people to get up in the morning and "do early, do early, do."

Mrs. Jones also knows what the jaybirds say, and the owls. Her rooster song goes far back in the Anglo-Irish tradition; her owl story may have been born in the Georgia swamplands. Both themes are centuries old.

> I had an old rooster, my rooster pleased me,
> I fed my rooster on green berry leaves.
> My rooster say cock, cock-a-doodle doodle-doo,
> My rooster say do early, do early, do.
>
> I had an old guinea, my guinea pleased me,
> I fed my guinea on green berry leaves.
> My guinea says pot, pot-a-rack, pot-a-rack,
> My guinea says do early, do early, do.
>
> I had an old turkey and my turkey pleased me,
> I fed my turkey on green berry leaves.
> My turkey says co-look, cook-a-look, cook-a-look,
> My turkey says do early, do early, do.
>
> I had an old hen and my hen she pleased me,
> I fed my hen on green berry leaves.
> My hen say cluck, cluck cluck cluck, cluck cluck,
> My hen say do early, do early, do.
>
> (Spoken:) And going on down in there, he did marry a wife, and

I married a wife and my wife pleased me,
I fed my wife just as I pleased.
My wife she grumbled, she grumbled, she grumbled,
My wife she said do early, do early, do.

I Had an Old Rooster

With a lilt; not fast ♩ = 140

I had an old roost - er, my roost - er pleased me,

I fed my roost - er on green__ ber - ry leaves.__

My roost - er say cock, cock - a - doo - dle doo - dle - doo,

My roost - er say do ear - ly, do ear - ly, do._____

New words and new music adaptation by Bessie Jones; collected and edited with additional new material by Alan Lomax. TRO-© copyright 1972 Ludlow Music, Inc., New York, N.Y. Used by permission.

Owl Talk

I'll tell you a real story, from my grandfather, about what he did that's real. And I feel so good telling this because it's true. He said so.

He was telling us one time . . . You know my grandfather was a great fisherman, and he would go fishing at night sometimes, come home the next morning, on this great creek called Tanyard Creek. And so he said that . . . late in the afternoon about sundown, he said that the hoot owls—we call them whooping owls because they whoops—they would holler and yell at them [the fishermen] that they may stop fishing so that they could catch their own prey. You see, because the owls fish at night too, you know. And grandpa say that it seem to him like the owl would be talking to him. . . .

Late in the afternoon, he say he would hear the old owl way down the creek . . . getting on about night . . . getting hungry . . . and they fishing . . . and he says one owl would holler down the creek and say, [Mrs. Jones sings in a deep whispery voice]

> *Fish done or no done,*
> *When night comes, you go home—mmmmmmmmmmmah!*

He say he hear another old owl, he would holler down the creek and say,

> *If you can't catch a pike fish*
> *You catch a eel and go home—mmmmmmmmmmmmmah!*

So one night he say he notice . . . one would holler and then another. And he say, "I want to know what them things are saying! I believe they is talking!"

So one holler across the woods and he say,

> *Whooo—aaaawww!*

And another say,

> *Ho John!*

And John answer, say,

> *Whooo—aaawww! There's a big dooooo over to my house tonight!*

> *Whooo-aaaall to be there?*

And he say,

> *John the Baptist and his wife and God knows Whooo-aaaall!*

Pretty Pear Tree

Throughout children's folklore runs the stream of man's remote past. The young voices and the archaic words contrast strangely but logically, for in country communities the youngest always learn from the oldest—from the grandfathers and grandmothers who have time to sit in the sun and talk and sing with the children.

The cumulative song, with its slow addition and constant repetition, is one of the oldest ways of teaching and remembering. No one has ever traced all the history of "Pretty Pear Tree" (or "The Green Grass Growing All Round," as it is more frequently titled); perhaps it may reach back to man's ancient concerns with springtime and the growth of plants and the eternal mystery of egg and bird.

Mrs. Jones and the Islanders sing this in full barbershop harmony and in the usual cumulative pattern, adding one new element to each repetition until they end with the "hood on the bird and the bird on the egg, the egg in the nest and the nest on the branch, branch on the limb and the limb on the tree and the tree in the ground and the green grass growing all round." With her practical eye on nature, Mrs. Jones says that the "hood on the bird" must mean that the bird is a woodpecker.

> Pretty pear tree, pretty pear tree,
> Way down yonder.
>> Tree in the ground,
>> The green grass growing all around and around,
>> The green grass growing all around.
>
> And on that tree (and on that tree)
> There was a limb (there was a limb),
> The prettiest little limb (the prettiest little limb)
> I ever did see (I ever did see).
>> Limb on the tree and the tree in the ground
>> And the green grass growing all around and around,
>> The green grass growing all around.
>
> And on that limb (and on that limb)
> There was a branch (there was a branch),
> The prettiest little branch (the prettiest little branch)
> I ever did see (I ever did see).
>> Branch on the limb and the limb on the tree,
>> Tree in the ground
>> And the green grass growing all around and around,
>> The green grass growing all round.

And on that branch
There was a nest, etc.

And in that nest
There was an egg, etc.

And on that egg
There was a bird, etc.

And on that bird
There was a head, etc.

And on that head
There was a hood, etc.

Pretty Pear Tree

With just a little corn ♩ = 76-88

Pret - ty pear tree, pret - ty pear tree, Way down yon - der.____

a tempo

Tree in the ground, The green grass grow - ing all a -

round and a - round, The green grass grow - ing all 'round.

1. And on that tree (and on that tree) there was a limb (there was a
2. And on that limb (and on that limb) there was a branch (there was a

limb), The pret - ti - est lit - tle limb (The pret - ti - est lit - tle limb) I ev - er did
branch) The pret - ti - est lit - tle branch, (The pret - ti - est lit - tle branch) I ev - er did

(All together)

see (I ev - er did see).
see (I ev - er did see).

1. Limb on the tree and the tree in the ground and the
2. Branch on the limb and the
3. Nest on the branch and the
4. Egg in the nest and the
5. Bird on the egg and the
6. Head on the bird and the
7. Hood on the head and the

green grass grow-ing all a - round and a - round, and the green grass grow-ing all 'round.

New words and new music adaptation by Bessie Jones; collected and edited with additional new material by Alan Lomax. TRO-© copyright 1972 Ludlow Music, Inc., New York, N.Y. Used by permission.

Riddles

I would like to ask a riddle of you and you can answer me next year when I come back. . . . I'll ask you one now, and if you can answer it now, I'll appreciate it, but if you can't, well, you rhyme it up by next year. Because the way I tell it, you can just see into it and answer it.

A riddle, for Mrs. Jones, is a puzzle, an intellectual exercise, a problem to be studied and pondered over. The style of riddle play popular today, in which the question is asked and immediately answered by the asker, was disappointing and boring to her. However, not having the year she suggested to wait for the answers, I persuaded her and the other Sea Island Singers into a fast exchange of riddling one afternoon:

BESSIE JONES: What is the difference between an egg and a biddy? Twenty-one days. . . . But that's not a riddle; that's a question. . . .

MABEL HILLARY: Well, what's round as a saucer, deep as a cup, And the Pacific Ocean couldn't fill it up? A sifter. . . .
What goes round the house and can't come in?

BESSIE JONES: It come to the door but it won't come in. (It's the same thing.) It's a path . . . a track. . . . That's a clean house, but I've seen some, the track come right on in!

EMMA RAMSEY: What has eyes and cannot see?

BESSIE JONES: A potato.

JOHN DAVIS: Shoes.

EMMA RAMSEY: Naw, it's a needle!

MABEL HILLARY: Well, what in the world is this that goes all around the town, all down town, all across the country and all across the fields, and then come back home (before they quit making them) and sit in the corner with his tongue hanging out? . . . Shoes. But they don't make too many shoes now with tongues in them.

BESSIE JONES: What is this? You ain't got it and you don't want it but if you had it you wouldn't take a thousand dollars for it. You wouldn't take a *million* dollars for it, as far as that's concerned. . . . A bald head. And what is this?

I went down to the whirly wheely whacker
And I met Bum Backer
And I called Tom Tacker
To run Bum Backer
Out of the whirly wheely whacker.

JOHN DAVIS: That's how come I don't go to England. I don't want to mess with that kind of talk. . . .

BESSIE JONES: Now, Tom Tacker is a dog and Bum Backer is a rabbit. Whirly Wheely Whacker is a garden, because, you see, you're in the garden and you're cutting, you see. You whacks and you whirls—you're turning round—you're wheeling and you're whacking. . . .
And what is this?

I went up my ginga gonga,
I come down my winga wonga,
I looked out of my seenfo,
And I see sainfo eating up sanfo.
I called my two little train-and-trickers,
And put em on sainfo,
And made him not eat up sanfo.

Now sanfo is a potato, because they're forced up from the sand. And sainfo, he eating up sanfo. What eats up potatoes raw? Pigs or hogs, that's correct, and he's eating up sanfo. And so I called my two little dogs and put em on the hog to make him not eat up the potatoes. And so it's I went upstairs and come downstairs and looked through my window—that's a seenfo. You see, when you go upstairs, it's a ginga gonga and when you come down, it's a winga wonga because you come *down* faster. . . .

MABEL HILLARY: What is this?

Whitey went in blacky,
Whitey came out of blacky
And left whitey in blacky?

It was a white hen went in a black stump and she laid a white egg and came out and left the egg in the black stump. . . .
And what is this here?

It can constantly move if it choose to, and it have three legs up and ten legs down . . . and there's a human being involved in it?

Well, there's a man with a washpot turned upside down on top of his head, and that's the three legs up. And the man can walk if he choose to or he can stand still; and therefore he got two legs and he got a horse got four legs and a dog named Bob and Bob have four legs. Therefore, he got ten legs down and three legs up.

JOHN DAVIS: Well, if you had a goose and a fox and a sack of corn and you had to carry them across a river and you couldn't carry but one across at a time. . . . Now if you leave the corn with the geese, the geese going to eat it up. If you leave the fox with the goose, he going to eat *him* up. What would you do?

Carry the geese across and you put the geese over there: then you come back and get the corn. You carry the corn over there, and you carry the geese *back.* *Then* you get the fox and you carry him over, and you come back and get the geese. . . .

MABEL HILLARY: I see a man so ugly he had to slip up on a dipper to get a drink of water and hide behind a washpot for the sun to rise. What's the ugliest you ever see a man?

BESSIE JONES: Those aren't riddles nor either questions. Those are lies.

MABEL HILLARY: Well, the riddles is lies, too.

BESSIE JONES: The riddles is guesswork.

＊ ＊ ＊ ＊ ＊ ＊

I went up the devil's rip rap,
I put up the devil's skip gap.
The devil thought I was so smart
He hitched me to his gocart.
I kicked out from his gocart,
He hitched me to his lead line,
I kicked the devil stone blind.

＊ ＊ ＊ ＊ ＊ ＊

Way Down on the Bingo Farm

The potatoes they grow small because they plant them at the wrong time. You don't plant potatoes in the fall—you dig em. So that's why they eat tops and all, they didn't have anything else to eat. . . .

Mrs. Jones learned this version of a college song from her mother, who had learned it in turn during her school days in rural Georgia. The children marched to it, according to Mrs. Jones's mother. Apparently it must have been the grand march, for

some were turning one way and some the other, and it made a beautiful march. And everyone be on time for the "rig jack jig jack jig" part, and their feet go with the music—"rig jack jig jack jig" [*stop*]. . . .

The phrase "vons of villions" was originally "balm of Gilead," an equally nonsensical expression in this context. Before we had discovered this, Mrs. Jones suggested tentatively that "vons of villions" might be "some kind of a disease that the doctors don't know what else to call it." This would seem to be a most useful term.

> There's a girl named Dinah over there,
> There's a girl named Dinah over there,
> There's a girl named Dinah and her cheeks are made of china.
> You can kiss her if you find her over there.

>> She'll give you vons of villions, vons of villions,
>> Vons of villions, way down on the Bingo Farm.
>> And I won't go there any more,
>> And I won't go there any more,
>> And I won't go there any more, more, more,
>> Way down on the Bingo Farm.
>> And a rig jack jig jack jig,
>> And a rig jack jig jack jig,
>> And a rig jack jig jack jig jack jig,
>> And a rig jack jig jack jig.

> Them potatoes they grow small over there,
> Them potatoes they grow small over there,
> Them potatoes they grow small for they plants them in the fall,
> And they eats them tops and all over there.

> There is maggots in the cheese over there,
> There is maggots in the cheese over there,
> There is maggots in the cheese, you can eat them if you please,
> You'll get maggots in your teeth over there.

Way Down on the Bingo Farm

New words and new music adaptation by Bessie Jones; collected and edited with additional new material by Alan Lomax. TRO—© copyright 1972 Ludlow Music, Inc., New York, N.Y. Used by permission.

Have Courage to Say No

We had schools different to schools now—better than to what I see now. I got a lot of education . . . and the teacher I had, he was a wonderful man, he was really good. They taught you then more Christianity; they taught you good things. And everybody, it looked like, that had understanding, they helped other folks raise their children the right way. Even in school, they help raise children the way they should go. And it wasn't all these juveniles, and all this stuff going on. Although we had mean people ever since the world began, but yet and still the <u>children</u> wasn't that way. The teachers would <u>teach</u> you.

He even taught us about ourselves; he taught the boys and girls how to treat theirselves. He had the big class from the eighth on up to the twelfth, and we'd sit on a different side of the church (we had school in the church) and the little ones on the other side. . . . And he taught the girls how to carry themselves and to keep their bodies clean—the girls especially, because a woman can make a man but very few men can make a woman. A woman when she fall, she's flat as a flounder. You may rise in the sight of God, but people—they'll always have a snare against you. [But] a man can get drunk and [go] naked down the street at night, and tomorrow he's Mister Jack. . . . Well, he taught us these things—how to hold yourself up. . . . And he taught a song to teach boys and girls how to say no. . . .

> Have courage, young girls, to say no,
> Have courage, young girls, to say no,
> Have courage, young girls, have courage, young girls,
> Have courage, young girls, to say no.
>
> Have courage, young boys, to say no, etc.
>
> Have courage, old mens, to say no, etc.

And so on. And he would teach us, and then he would teach us the song.

Have Courage to Say No

Have cour - age, young girls, to say no - o,_____ Have cour - age, young girls, to say no,_____ Have cour - age, young girls, have cour - age, young girls, Have cour - age, young girls, to say__ no._____

New words and new music adaptation by Bessie Jones; collected and edited with additional new material by Alan Lomax. TRO—© copyright 1972 Ludlow Music, Inc., New York, N.Y. Used by permission.

Brother Rabbit and Mister Railroad's Taters

Anyone who loved "Nights with Uncle Remus" as a child or as an adult may find this story vaguely familiar. Actually, it is a retelling of "Brother Fox, Brother Rabbit, and King Deer's Daughter." A point to note is that in both versions the entire plot depends upon the necessity of answering to a call: the principle of antiphony in still another form.

Mrs. Jones told this story with great gusto, pitching her voice up to a thin treble for Brother Rabbit's part of the song, and "bassing" away in a great growl for Brother Wolf.

Brother Rabbit and Brother Wolf were going to see Brother Fox's daughters. Brother Fox had some pretty girls and smart girls . . . oh, and almost everybody called Brother Fox "Mister Railroad," because he was always up and down the railroad tracks stealing chickens.

So, Brother Wolf was very smart and strong and the girls likted him; they would call him to help do different things around the place —that's the story they tell—more than they would Brother Rabbit, because Brother Rabbit's so light and he couldn't do much. Brother Rabbit was light but he liked to do good things and have the girls to call him to help. . . . He got jealous of Brother Wolf.

So, he didn't know any other way to get at Brother Wolf, so he went to Brother Fox's potatoes and he dig up the potatoes in the potato patch—Brother Rabbit did that. He tried to get a trap set for Brother Wolf.

So Brother Fox asked him one day, "Do you know who's going in my potatoes? I want you to watch and help me; somebody's going in my potatoes." (Brother Rabbit says) "I don't know who it is but I sure try to find out."

So, the girls were going to have a big party. Brother Rabbit told Brother Fox, says, "I'll tell you how to do. I found out who's been stealing your taters!" (Taters—they didn't have no potatoes, they had taters in that time.) Brother Fox say, "You did?" Brother Rabbit say, "Yeah, I did!" He say, "I'm going to let him tell you to your face!" Brother Fox say, "Sure enough? You do that for me, I sure be glad; I'll fix him."

All right. Brother Rabbit went on and told Brother Wolf, says, "Brother Wolf, do you know the girls are going to give a party and they want us to play for them? And you've got that big gross voice, you can bass, so I got a little song that we can sing. And when I sing this song, you can bass it, and those girls—oh, those girls be so glad!" Brother Wolf say, "All right!" He's so glad of that, you know, because he want to do everything good for those girls, make 'em happy.

They got right down underneath the hill where nobody couldn't hear them, you know, and Brother Rabbit was teaching him the song. "Now, I'm going to play the guitar and you play the fiddle. When I say,

> *" 'This is the man that stole Mr. Railroad's taters'*

(that was Brother Fox's taters, you know), you must say,

> *'Yes, my Lord, I am!' "*

Brother Wolf say, "All right, how does the song go?" Well, now they begin to stomp:

> *"This is the man that stole Mr. Railroad's taters!"*

(That's Brother Rabbit singing)

> *"Yes, my Lord, I am, am,*

(That's Brother Wolf)

> *"Yes, my Lord I am!"*

Oh, Brother Wolf was just so glad he could bass! Whoo, that was good! And Brother Rabbit just kick up, you know, he was so glad he got him going. They played that for hours under the hill.

They went to the dance that night, setting up there. You know, in that time, in those days, the musicians sets in a corner to themselves, you know. And they sets over there, all tied down, girded down, and they started to play the music. They played other music first, and then they got on to the reel dance for the girls:

> This is the man that stole Mr. Railroad's taters!
> Yes, my Lord, I am, am,
> Yes, my Lord, I am.
> This is the man that stole Mr. Railroad's taters!
> Yes, my Lord, I am, am,
> Yes, my Lord, I am!

And Mr. Railroad stole around there and got Brother Wolf by the collar and jerked him out of there and started beating on him. Brother Wolf asked him, "What's the matter? What I done? What's the matter?" Brother Fox said, "You stole my taters! See, you're the one that's been in my tater patch, eat up my taters." Brother Wolf said, "No, I ain't!" and Brother Fox say, "You just now told me; you <u>told</u> me you're the one that got it. You told me that to my face!" Brother Wolf say, "Brother Rabbit taught me that song! Brother Rabbit taught me to say that!"

And then they got out behind Brother Rabbit. . . . You see, that's the time when Brother Rabbit went and told them, he say, "You can do anything you want to do with me, but just don't throw me in the briar patch!" This story run into that one. . . .

Brother Rabbit and Mister Railroad's Taters

In mock falsetto ♩ = 208

This is the man that stole Mis - ter Rail - road's ta - ters.

In mock bass; growling

Yes, my Lord, I am, am, Yes, my Lord, I am.

Written and adapted by Bessie Jones; collected and edited by Alan Lomax. TRO—© copyright 1972 Ludlow Music, Inc., New York, N.Y. Used by permission.

Old Bill the Rolling Pin

When the mule wouldn't do nothing but the possum-la, that means he'd back around and cut up and like that—like he was dancing. . . .

Mrs. Jones says that Old Bill was a "patteroller" and that people made this song up to make fun of him. During slavery, when Negroes were not allowed to leave their home plantations without a pass, "patterollers" were armed guards, hired to patrol the roads at night, enforcing the pass system. This particular "patteroller" had "big eyes and a double chin," apparently reminding the singers of Mister Frog (the same one who went a-courting and who got "struck by a big black snake"). The mule, who dances instead of working, is not as extraneous as he may seem either.

> Now, Old Bill the Rolling Pin this morning,
> Now, Old Bill the Rolling Pin this morning,
> Now, Old Bill the Rolling Pin,
> He's up the road and back again,
> Big eyes and double chin this morning.

I geed to the mule but the mule wouldn't gee this morning,
I geed to the mule but the mule wouldn't gee this morning,
I geed to the mule but mule wouldn't gee,
I knocked him side the head with the singletree this morning.

> Now Old Bill, etc.

I hawed to the mule but the mule wouldn't haw this morning,
I hawed to the mule but the mule wouldn't haw this morning,
I hawed to the mule but the mule wouldn't haw,
He wouldn't do nothing but the possum-la this morning.

> Now Old Bill, etc.

Mister Frog went swimming down the lake this morning,
Mister Frog went swimming down the lake this morning,
Mister Frog went swimming down the lake,
But he got swallowed by a big black snake this morning.

> Now Old Bill, etc.

(Sung to chorus melody)
Mrs. Duck went swimming down the lake this morning,
Mrs. Duck went swimming down the lake this morning,
Mrs. Duck went swimming down the lake,
But she got struck by a big black snake,
Poor thing, her neck got breaked this morning.

Old Bill the Rolling Pin

Rabbit and the Possum

MRS. JONES: My father used to sing this when I was little childrens. . . . I still sings it to little children—you know, where the
rabbit and the possum are going up the hill.

You know, the rabbit's always cunning and sharp and dirty,
they say, but he was scared of that possum because he's a big
thing and ugly, too. And so they was walking up a hill, as they
always walked together in the forest, and so the possum—you
know, the possum's got a pocket underneath his stomach—and
in that pocket the possum had a forty-dollar bill. (You know
there isn't any such thing as a forty-dollar bill.)

So the rabbit, he noticed it, and the rabbit, he didn't know
how to get that money. He knew he couldn't take it; he couldn't
robber. So they went on up there and the rabbit looked at the
possum, say, "Possum, let's play seven-up." The possum say, "All
right." They started playing seven-up. They played and played
and the rabbit knew he could beat him because he's cunning. He
won all Brother Possum's money.

Brother Possum looked at him mean and bad, you know, and
kind of grinned, and the rabbit knew good and well he better not
bother that money because the possum's going to knock him
down. And so that rabbit just got him a *quick* lick, and he knock
Brother Possum and Brother Possum fell. (You know the possum
will fall stiff every time you hit him.) And the rabbit grabbed
that money and over the hill with it and he said, *"Fare* you well!"
So that's a song we sing.

> Rabbit and the possum going up the hill,
> Rabbit knowed the possum had a forty-dollar bill.
> Rabbit say, "Possum, let's play seven-up!"
> Rabbit win the money but he's scared to pick it up.
> Rabbit hit the possum, the possum fell,
> Rabbit grab the money, say, "Fare you well!"

A lot of the white childrens like to play that down where I was
nursing. I'll play that little song and then I'll make like I'm
hitting on 'em, hitting the possum. Then they'll fall just like
they're the possum. . . .

MABEL HILLARY: The way I heard it was that the rabbit told the possum that the possum was brown and he was white and they was going to play seven-up, but they weren't going to be like the Negro and the white man. You see, it was the Negro and the white man was playing seven-up, and the Negro won the money and was scared to pick it up.

BESSIE JONES: That little song I know about ain't it hard to be a farmer—that goes in there, too. The colored man win the money but he's scared to pick it up. But we don't say that; we say it's a farmer—it's all the same. . . . It's about it's hard to be a farmer. . . .

(singing)

> Ain't it hard, hard, hard,
> To be a farmer, a farmer, farmer, farmer,
> Ain't it hard, hard, hard,
> You can't get your money when it's due.

> A farmer and a white man was working on a freight,
> Was going out soon but it gets that late.
> White man takes up the farmer's time.
> It always leave poor farmer behind.

> A farmer and a white man was playing seven-up,
> The farmer win the money but he's scared to pick it up.
> The farmer hit the white man, the white man fell,
> The farmer grabbed the money and run like hell.

> The farmer and a white man was walking cross the field,
> Farmer stumbled up on the white man's heel.
> White man cussed and the farmer grinned—
> He knocked that farmer up under his chin.

JOHN DAVIS: Sometimes the white man can't get his money when it's due any more than the farmer. . . .

PETER DAVIS: Mr. Ed Young told me that he ain't never going to eat no more possum because they laugh too much and they ain't nothing funny. . . .

Rabbit and the Possum

Gaily ♩ = 144

Rab-bit and the pos-sum go-ing up the hill. Rab-bit knowed the pos-sum had a

for-ty-dol-lar bill. Rab-bit say, "Pos-sum, let's play__ sev-en-up!" The

Rab-bit win the mon-ey but he's scared to pick it up. Rab-bit hit the pos-sum, the

pos-sum fell,__ Rab-bit grab the mon-ey, say, "Fare you__ well!"

Written and adapted by Bessie Jones; collected and edited by Alan Lomax. TRO—© copyright 1972 Ludlow Music, Inc., New York, N.Y. Used by permission.

Ain't It Hard to Be a Farmer

With a little blues ♩ = 112

CHORUS

Now ain't it hard, hard, hard To be a farm - er, a farm - er, farm - er, farm - er, Ain't it hard, hard, hard, You can't get your mon - ey when it's due.

VERSE

Farm - er and a white man was work - ing on a freight. Was go - ing out soon but it gets that___ late. White -man takes up the farm - er's time. It al - ways leave poor farm - er be - hind.

Words and music by Bessie Jones; collected and edited with new material by Alan Lomax. TRO—
© copyright 1972 Ludlow Music, Inc., New York, N.Y. Used by permission.

Peep, Squirrel

It seems right somehow to bring our book back full circle and
end, as we began, with one of Mrs. Jones's songs that she says is
especially *for* children. You can sing "Peep, Squirrel" while the children dance, or while you're bouncing a child on your knee; or, at a
slower pace, it makes a fine song for a tired baby and a warm lap and
a rocking chair. Mrs. Jones says that the "ya di da di deedy um" is the
sound of the squirrel's feet scuffling in the leaves, and she sings this
song in a somewhat dry and whispery voice and paces it slowly to fit
a squeaky chair.

And while she rocks and sings, her fine imaginative mind,
nourished by the deep springs of her tradition, sharpened by her sixty
years' experience and understanding, ranges slowly over the many
surfaces of her little nonsense song.

Peep, squirrel,
    Ya di da di deedy um,
Peep, squirrel,
    Ya di da di deedy um.

Hop, squirrel,
    Ya di da di deedy um,
Hop, squirrel,
    Ya di da di deedy um.

(Each line is repeated as above.)

Run, squirrel,
    Ya di da di deedy um.

Come here, mule,
    Ya di da di deedy um.

Whoa, mule,
    I can't get the saddle on.

Hold that mule,
    I can't get the saddle on.

Go that mule,
    I can't get the saddle on.

Go that squirrel,
    I can't get the saddle on.

Ya di da di deedy um, a
Ya di da di deedy um, dum!

She is searching for *meaning*—for some statement, however fragmentary or slight, about the human condition. "It have to be *about* something." And so, one day, she told me that there was a "story to that song," and, as she told it, the song came alive.

About a little boy in the woods, a little small boy about six years old or better. He seed this squirrel and he couldn't catch the squirrel and he wanted to catch the squirrel. But the squirrel was too fast for him, playing with him, playing around in the leaves. The squirrel would peep at him and go on up in the tree, you know, and every time the squirrel would go in the leaves, the boy said the leaves would say "ya da deedy um!" (You know—the little feet running in the leaves, "ya da deedy um!" so that's where the "ya di da di deedy um!" come in.)

He couldn't catch the squirrel and he told him hop, and he'd see the squirrel hop, and he'd run and everything, and he couldn't get that squirrel. And then he see an old mule out there in the pasture not far from there—an old mule walking around, done quit working an' everything, old pet mule. He figured that big old mule could help him get that squirrel, so he call him for help, he call the mule to come here, mule. (The mule didn't know nothing about hunting no squirrel.)

So an old piece of saddle was out there. He picked up the saddle and he gonna do like he seen other people do—throw the saddle on the mule so the mule could help him catch the squirrel. And he couldn't get the saddle up. Every time he tried to throw the saddle, it would hit around the mule's leg; and the mule wouldn't kick him, he'd just kind of walk off from him. The mule didn't want to bother with him; he didn't want to hurt him.

And the squirrel was still running up and down around in the leaves and the tree. So finally, the mule got tired, because he couldn't get the saddle on, and he went to running off, and that scared the squirrel worse, and the squirrel went to running off. So it's "Yonder go that mule!" and "Yonder go that squirrel!" And the boy is standing looking—the mule going one way and the squirrel going the other way—"ya di da di deedy um, ya di da di deedy um dum!" That's why we wind it up with "dum!" because he couldn't hear it no more. . . .

So they made a song of it. The song comes after the story, quite natural, you know, almost always. It have to be about something for it to come. . . .

Peep Squirrel

Steadily and evenly ♩ = 152

Peep, squir-rel, Ya di da di dee-dy um, Peep, squir-rel, Ya di da di dee-dy um.
Hop, Hop,
Run, Run,

Come here, mule,_ Ya di da di dee-dy um. Come here, mule,_ Ya di da di dee-dy um.

Whoa,_ mule,_ I can't get the sad-dle on. Whoa,_ mule,_ I can't get the sad-dle on.

Hold that mule,_ I can't get the sad-dle on. Hold that mule, I can't get the sad-dle on.
Go that mule,_ Go that mule,
Go that squirrel, Go that squir-rel,

Ya di da di dee-dy um, a ya di da di dee-dy um, dum!

New words and new music adaptation by Bessie Jones; collected and edited by Alan Lomax. TRO—©
copyright 1972 Ludlow Music, Inc., New York, N.Y. Used by permission.

Note to Scholars

1. The work done on this collection was the result of about one month's direct observation of Mrs. Bessie Jones and the Sea Island Singers, as described in the Introduction; during this time, I recorded about forty hours of tapes, including interviews, demonstrations, and teaching sessions. I have further used tapes of interviews loaned to me by Alan Lomax and Ed Cray, as indicated in the acknowledgments.

2. Almost every game has thus been recorded at least twice. I have used and compared all versions; some of the printed texts are portmanteau versions combining several of Mrs. Jones's performances of the same game. Tempo has been recorded, wherever possible, from a tape of the game while it was being performed. Where I have not, for one reason or another, actually seen the game being played, I have mentioned this fact in the head notes.

3. All italicized head notes are direct quotes from taped interviews with Mrs. Jones except where noted. In the case of all but the most generalized observations, these have been remarks made directly about the game being described. I have edited them, in some cases, for comprehensibility; they are essentially verbatim.

4. The musical transcription has been somewhat simplified, due to the impracticality of indicating all of Mrs. Jones's melodic variations. Slides and scoops have been largely eliminated or, where especially important, indicated by grace notes. The original key (usually quite low, because Mrs. Jones's voice is an extraordinarily deep alto) has been raised to a more singable and readable level. Syncopation has been simplified though not eliminated.

5. Unless specified, the entire repertoire may be taken as having come from Mrs. Jones, who seems to have taught the rest of the group. This does not preclude, of course, the possibility that they already knew her version or others. It

has proven impossible, unfortunately, to establish the exact provenience of each item—that is, which come from the mainland and which from St. Simons Island. Mrs. Jones's own memories on exactly where she first heard which song or play were often at sharp variance with those of the other Islanders.

6. Sources consulted for historical data, as well as notations of other published versions (for comparison) have been listed for each song in the section titled "Annotations."

B.L.H.

Annotations

These references in one sense take the place of footnotes; in another, they are designed to aid those who may be interested in investigating individual songs or games more intensively. In the list that follows, where no relevant information or parallel versions have been discovered, the title of the item has simply been omitted.

"Go to Sleepy, Little Baby"
    Cf. Brown, vol. 3, pp. 150–53; Lomax (4) pp. 14–15; Scarborough, pp. 145–49; Seeger (1), p. 65; Trent-Johns, pp. 20–21; Work, p. 250.
"This Little Piggy"
    Cf. Baring-Gould, pp. 233 and 235; Brown, vol. 1, pp. 185–87; Opie, pp. 348–50; Northall, pp. 416–20.
"Finger Names"
    Cf. Baring-Gould, p. 234; Brown, vol. 1, p. 188; Northall, pp. 415–16.
"Patty Cake"
    Cf. Abrahams (1), p. 158; Baring-Gould, pp. 239–40; Brown, vol. 1, p. 198; Opie, pp. 341–42; Northall, p. 418.
"Tom, Tom, Greedy-Gut"
    Cf. Brown, vol. 1, p. 177; Opie, p. 390; Northall, p. 188.
"Green Sally Up"
    Cf. Abrahams (1), p. 72; Brown, vol. 1, p. 172; Talley, p. 116.
"One-ry, Two-ry" and "One Saw, Two Saw"
    Cf. Abrahams (1), pp. 146–47; Baring-Gould, pp. 249–50; Bolton, pp. 96–101; Brown, vol. 1, pp. 163–64; Coffin, p. 191; Emrich, p. 100; Jones (for clapping), vol. 1, p. 31; Newell, pp. 197–200; Northall, pps. 344, 348–49; Opie, pp. 335–37.

"Head and Shoulder, Baby"
    Cf. Abrahams (2), p. 132.
"Hambone"
    Cf. Parrish, pp. 114–16; Scarborough, pp. 46–50; White, p. 218; Talley, pp. 190–95 (rhyme).
"Juba"
    Cf. Courlander (1), p. 192; Nathan, pp. 443–46; Parrish, p. 116; Parsons, pp. 199–200; Scarborough, pp. 98–99; White, pp. 161, 163; Talley, pp. 9, 179, 296–97; Turner, p. 101.
"Skip to the Barbershop"
    Cf. Durlacher, p. 11; Abrahams (1), p. 65; Emrich, p. 232.
"Just from the Kitchen"
    Cf. Courlander (2), p. 67; Parsons, p. 201; Johnson, p. 170.
"Shoo, Turkey"
    Cf. Carawan, pp. 132–33; Gomme, pp. 85, 94; Parsons, pp. 200–201; Saxon, p. 446; Talley, pp. 78–79; Johnson, pp. 166–67; Brewer, pp. 371–72; Coffin, pp. 181–82.
"Knock Jim Crow"
    Cf. Nathan, pp. 50–52; Opie, pp. 244–45; Scarborough, p. 127; Talley, p. 13; White, pp. 162–63; Lomax (4), p. 78 (for background).
"Josephine"
    Cf. Parrish, pp. 106–7; McIntosh, p. 24.
"Elephant Fair"
    Cf. Brown, vol. 3, p. 219; Randolph, vol. 3, p. 207; Talley, pp. 159–60.
"Green, Green, the Crab Apple Tree"
    Cf. Beckwith, pp. 62–63; Brown, vol. 1, pp. 56–57; Gomme, vol. 1, pp. 170–83; Carawan, p. 129; Newell, p. 71; Northall, p. 362.
"Johnny Cuckoo"
    Cf. Botkin, pp. 328–30; Brown, vol. 1, pp. 89–93; Chase, pp. 16–19; Gomme, vol. 2, pp. 233–55; McIntosh, pp. 96–97; Newell, pp. 47–50; Talley, p. 85.
"Oh Green Fields, Roxie"
    Cf. Talley, p. 81; Courlander (1), p. 280; (2), p. 69; Newell, p. 56.
"Go In and Out the Window"
    Cf. Beckwith, pp. 67–68; Brown, vol. 1, pp. 119–22 and vol. 3, pp. 108–9; Chase, pp. 14–15; Gomme, vol. 2, pp. 122–43; Newell, pp. 128–29; Randolph, pp. 336–38.
"Draw Me a Bucket of Water"
    Cf. Baring-Gould, p. 259; Brown, vol. 1, pp. 142–46; Chase, pp. 24–25; Gomme, vol. 1, pp. 100–108; McIntosh, p. 100; Saxon, p. 447; Brewer, pp. 371–72; Northall, pp. 395–96.
"Nana, Thread Needle"
    Cf. Beckwith, p. 38; Chase, pp. 30–31; Brewster, pp. 174–75; Gomme, vol. 1, pp. 119, 145–46; vol. 2, pp. 384–87; Parsons, pp. 180, 202; Northall, p. 397.
"Sir Mister Brown"
    Cf. Abrahams (1), p. 204; Parsons, p. 178.
"Soup, Soup"
    Cf. Saxon, p. 446; Brewer, p. 371; Coffin, p. 183.

"Punchinello"
 Cf. Ruth M. Coniston, *Chantons un Peu.* New York, 1929.
"Little Sally Walker"
 Cf. Beckwith, pp. 78–79; Brown, vol. 1, pp. 130–31; Courlander (1),
 pp. 153–54, 275, 278; Courlander (2), p. 75; Gomme, vol. 2, pp. 149–
 79; Jeckyll, pp. 190–91; Newell, p. 70; Scarborough, p. 142; Trent-Johns,
 pp. 24–25; Northall, pp. 375–78; Abrahams (1), p. 114; Bolton, p. 120.
"Uncle Jessie"
 Cf. Abrahams (2), pp. 129–30; Abrahams (1), p. 62.
"Way Down Yonder in the Brickyard"
 Cf. McIntosh, pp. 2–3.
"Way Go, Lily"
 Cf. Brewer, p. 370.
"Steal Up, Young Lady"
 Cf. Botkin, p. 318; Brown, vol. 1, pp. 101–3, 159; Lomax (2), p. 501;
 Scarborough, p. 116.
"Possum-La"
 Cf. Botkin, pp. 295–96; Brown, vol. 3, pp. 206–7; Jeckyll, p. 214; White,
 p. 237; Talley, pp. 34–35.
"Ranky Tank"
 Cf. Beckwith, p. 61; Carawan, p. 131.
"Coonshine"
 Cf. Courlander (1), p. 161; Talley, p. 1; White, pp. 162–63.
"Sandy Ree"
 Cf. Courlander (2), pp. 70–71; Parrish, pp. 99–101.
"Zudie-O"
 Abrahams (2), pp. 14–17; Trent-Johns, pp. 14–17.
"I'm Going Away to See Aunt Dinah"
 Cf. (for verses about blacksnake) White, pp. 245–46.
"Daniel"
 Cf. (for background) Courlander (1), pp. 194–200; Lomax (4), p. 335;
 Turner, p. 202.
"William, William, Trembletoe"
 Cf. Beckwith, pp. 12–13; Brewster, pp. 177–78; Brown, vol. 1, pp. 134–
 37, 160–61; Opie, p. 224; Parsons, p. 203; Johnson, p. 65.
"Club Fist"
 Cf. Beckwith, pp. 19–20; Brewster, pp. 30–31; Brown, vol. 1, pp. 66–68;
 Gomme, pp. 117–19; Newell, pp. 234–35; Johnson, p. 167; Coffin, p. 180.
"Uncle Tom"
 Cf. Brewster, p. 23; Northall, pp. 407–8.
"Moneyfoot"
 Cf. Beckwith, p. 26; Gomme, vol. 2, pp. 449–50.
"Jack in the Bush"
 Cf. Brewster, pp. 8–9; Brown, vol. 1, pp. 60–61; Gomme, vol. 1, pp. 187,
 218; Newell, pp. 147–48; Coffin, p. 180.
"Bob-a-Needle"
 Cf. Courlander (1), p. 159; Jeckyll, pp. 196–97. Compare "Thimble
 Game," McIntosh, p. 110.

"Whose Bag Is My Gold Ring"
    Cf. Brewster, p. 19; Newell, p. 51.
"Pawns"
    Cf. Gomme, vol. 1, p. 143; Newell, p. 143.
"Wade in the Green Valley"
    Cf. Brewster, pp. 153–54.
"Horse and the Buggy"
    Cf. Brewster, p. 165; Brown, vol. 1, p. 153; McIntosh, p. 24; Newell, p. 170; Talley, p. 20.
"Won't You Let the Birdie Out?"
    Cf. Gomme, vol. 1, pp. 50–51, 142–43, 146–47.
"Engine Rubber Number Nine"
    Cf. Brewster, pp. 65–66; Brown, vol. 1, pp. 71–74, 168; Gomme, vol. 2, pp. 292–94; Newell, pp. 158–59; Abrahams (1), pp. 48, 184; Emrich, p. 99.
"London Bridge"
    Cf. Baring-Gould, pp. 254–57; Brown, vol. 1, pp. 137–40; Gomme, pp. 192–99; Newell, pp. 204–11; Opie, pp. 270–76; Parsons, p. 182; Coffin, p. 176.
"All Hid"
    Cf. Brewster, pp. 42–45; Brown, vol. 1, pp. 37–38; Gomme, vol. 1, pp. 211–14; Newell, p. 160; Johnson, p. 166.
"Rap Jack"
    Cf. Brown, vol. 1, pp. 157–58; compare "Whipping Toms," Gomme, vol. 1, pp. 217–18.
"I Had an Old Rooster"
    Cf. Brown, vol. 3, pp. 172–74; Newell, p. 115; Parsons, p. 184; Talley, p. 145.
"Pretty Pear Tree"
    Cf. Brown, vol. 3, pp. 184–85; Newell, pp. 111–13; Randolph, vol. 3, p. 213; Scarborough, p. 359.
"Riddles"
    Cf. Scarborough, p. 20; Taylor, p. 35, p. 72 (nos. 199, 200), pp. 152–53 (no. 454), p. 325 (no. 867), p. 649 (no. 1593); Johnson, pp. 156–60; Brewer, pp. 347–52; Coffin, pp. 161, 167, 168; Parsons, pp. 151–175; Emrich, pp. 17, 29, 69.
"Way Down on the Bingo Farm"
    Cf. Randolph, vol. 3, p. 384.
"Brother Rabbit and Mister Railroad's Taters"
    Cf. Harris, pp. 68–94; Talley, pp. 265–67; Johnson, p. 142.
"Old Bill the Rolling Pin"
    Cf. Brown, vol. 3, pp. 154–65; White, pp. 229, 245–46.
"Rabbit and the Possum"
    Cf. White, pp. 385–86; Brown, vol. 3, p. 548; Talley, pp. 31–32.
"Peep, Squirrel"
    Cf. Botkin, pp. 159–60; Courlander (1), p. 160, and (2), p. 71; Seeger (1), pp. 18–19, 64; Scarborough, pp. 134–36; Talley, p. 78.

Selected Bibliography

An old joke points out that if you steal from one person, it's plagiarism, but if you steal from a hundred, it's original research. I assume the latter activity is what I have been up to, for I find that listing all the books and journals consulted in preparing this manuscript is really impractical. This bibliography, then, contains only those works which I have referred to most frequently and which I would especially like to recommend to the attention of others.

Abrahams, Roger D. *Jump Rope Rhymes: A Dictionary.* American Folklore Society Bibliographical and Special Series, Vol. 20. Austin: University of Texas Press, 1969. (1)

Abrahams, Roger D. "There's a Black Girl in the Ring" from *Two Penny Ballads and Four Dollar Whiskey: A Pennsylvania Folklore Miscellany,* Kenneth Goldstein and Robert Byington, eds. Hatboro, Pa.: Folklore Associates, 1966. (2)

Baring-Gould, William S. and Ceil. *The Annotated Mother Goose.* New York: Clarkson Potter, 1962.

Beckwith, Martha Warren. *Jamaica Folk-Lore.* American Folk Lore Society Memoirs, Vol. XXI. New York: G. E. Steckert, 1928.

Bolton, Henry Carrington. *The Counting-Out Rhymes of Children.* New York: D. Appleton Co., 1888.

Botkin, Benjamin A. *The American Play Party Song.* New York: Frederick Ungar Publishing Co., 1963.

Brewer, J. Mason. *American Negro Folklore.* Chicago: Quadrangle Books, 1968.

Brewster, Paul G. *American Nonsinging Games.* Norman: University of Oklahoma Press, 1953.

Brown, Frank C. Collection of *North Carolina Folk Lore.* Volumes I, III. Newman I. White, ed. Durham, N.C.: Duke University Press, 1952.

Caillois, Roger. *Man, Play and Games.* (Paris: 1958). Trans. by Meyer Barash. New York: Glencoe Press, 1961.

Carawan, Guy and Candie. *Ain't You Got a Right to the Tree of Life,* New York: Simon and Schuster, 1966.

Chase, Richard. *Hullabaloo & Other Singing Games.* Boston: Houghton Mifflin, 1949.

Coffin, Tristram P. and Hennig Cohen. *Folklore in America.* New York: Doubleday & Co., 1966.

Courlander, Harold. *Negro Folk Music U.S.A.* New York: Columbia University Press, 1963. (1)

————. *Negro Songs from Alabama.* New York: Wenner-Gren Foundation, 1960. (2)

Dundes, Alan. "*On Game Morphology: A Study of the Structure of Non-verbal Folklore.*" *New York Folklore Quarterly,* Dec. 1964.

Durlacher, Ed. *Singing Games for Children.* New York: Devin-Adair, 1945.

Elder, J. D. *Song-Games of Trinidad and Tobago.* Hatboro, Pa.: Folklore Associates, 1965.

Emrich, Duncan. *The Nonsense Book of Riddles, Rhymes, Tongue Twisters, Puzzles and Jokes from American Folklore.* New York: Four Winds Press, 1970.

Emrich, Marion Vallat and George Korson. *The Child's Book of Folklore.* New York: Dial Press, 1947.

Erikson, Erik F. *Childhood and Society.* New York: W. W. Norton (revised 2nd edition), 1963.

Gomme, Alice Mertha. *The Traditional Games of England, Scotland and Ireland.* Volumes I and II. (London: 1894 and 1898). New York: Dover reprint, 1964.

Gorer, Geoffrey. *Africa Dances.* (London: 1935). New York: W. W. Norton, 1962.

Harris, Joel Chandler. *Nights With Uncle Remus.* Boston and New York: D. Appleton Co., 1911.

Herskovitz, Melville. *The Myth of the Negro Past.* (New York: 1941). Boston: Beacon Hill Press reprint, 1958.

Hughes, Langston, and Arna Bontemps. *The Book of Negro Folklore.* New York: Dodd, Mead & Company, 1958.

Huizinga, Johan. *Homo Ludens: A Study of the Play Element in Culture.* (Paris: 1951). Boston: Beacon Hill Press reprint, 1955.

Jeckyll, Walter. *Jamaican Song and Story.* (New York: 1907). New York: Dover reprint, 1966.

Johnson, Guy B. *Folk Culture on St. Helena Island.* (U. of North Carolina Press: 1930). Hatboro, Pa.: Folklore Associates reprint, 1969.

Jones, A. M. *Studies in African Music,* volumes I and II. London: Oxford University Press, 1959.

Lomax, Alan. *Folksongs of North America.* New York: Doubleday Doran, 1960. (2)

————. *Folk Song Style and Culture.* Washington, D.C.: American Association for the Advancement of Science, 1968. (1)

————. *The Rainbow Sign.* New York: Duell Sloan and Pierce, 1959. (3)

Lomax, John A. and Alan. *Folk Song U.S.A.* New York: Duell, Sloan and Pearce, 1947. (4)

McIntosh, David S. *Singing Games and Dances.* New York: National YMCA Press, 1957.

Muir, Willa. *Living with Ballads.* New York: Oxford University Press, 1965.

Nathan, Hans. *Dan Emmett and the Rise of Early Negro Minstrelsy.* Norman: University of Oklahoma Press, 1962.

Newell, William Wells. *Games and Songs of American Children.* (New York: 1903). New York: Dover reprint, 1963.

Nketia, Kwabena. *African Music in Ghana.* Evanston: Northwestern University Press, 1963.

Northall, G. F. *English Folk Rhymes.* (London: 1892). Detroit: Singing Tree Press reprint: 1968.

Opie, Iona, and Peter Opie. *The Oxford Dictionary of Nursery Rhymes.* London: Oxford University Press, 1961.

Parrish, Lydia E. *Slave Songs of the Georgia Sea Islands.* (New York: 1942). Hatboro, Pa.: Folklore Associates reprint, 1965.

Parsons, Elsie Clews. *Folk-Lore of the Sea Islands, South Carolina.* Cambridge: American Folk Lore Society Memoirs Vol. XVI, 1923.

Paskman, Dailey, and Sigmund Spaeth. *Gentlemen, Be Seated.* New York: Doubleday Doran, 1928.

Randolph, Vance. *Ozark Folksongs,* Vol. I, II, III. Columbia, Mo.: State Historical Society of Missouri, 1948.

Saxon, Lyle, Edward Dreyer, and Robert Tallant, eds. *Gumbo Ya-Ya.* Boston: Houghton Mifflin, 1945.

Scarborough, Dorothy. *On the Trail of Negro Folk-Songs.* (Cambridge: 1925). Hatboro, Pa.: Folklore Associates reprint, 1963.

Seeger, Ruth. *American Folk Songs for Children.* New York: Doubleday Doran, 1948. (1)

Seeger, Ruth. *Animal Folk Songs for Children.* New York: Doubleday Doran, 1948. (2)

Staff of Music Department, Minneapolis Public Library. *Index to Folk Dances and Singing Games.* Chicago: American Library Association, 1936; suppl. 1949.

Sutton-Smith, Brian. *"Sixty Years of Historical Change in the Game Preferences of American Children." Journal of American Folklore,* 1961.

Talley, Thomas W. *Negro Folk Rhymes.* New York: Macmillan, 1922.

Taylor, Archer. *English Riddles from Oral Tradition.* Berkeley: University of California Press, 1951.

Trent-Johns, Altona. *Play Songs of the Deep South.* Washington, D.C.: Associated Publishers, 1944.

Turner, Lorenzo Dow. *Africanisms in the Gullah Dialect.* Chicago: University of Chicago Press, 1949.

Waterman, Richard A. *"African Influences on the Music of the Americas." Acculturation in the Americas,* Sol Tax, ed. Chicago: University of Chicago Press, 1952.

White, Newman Ivey. *American Negro Folk Song.* (Cambridge: 1928). Hatboro, Pa.: Folklore Associates, reprint, 1965.

Work, John W. *American Negro Songs and Spirituals.* New York: Bonanza Books, 1940.

Discography

The real musical experience can never be written down. The most detailed notations, the most precise and thorough descriptions, have no "sound." To try to help the reader compensate, I am appending two lists of records. The first contains a listing of commercially available recordings which contain performances, by Mrs. Jones, of some of the material included in this book. The second list includes some recordings containing performances by children of their own traditional games and plays; some are similar to Mrs. Jones's repertoire and some are not. All are worth attention.

Performances by Bessie Jones:

American Folk Songs for Children. Southern Folk Heritage Series. Atlantic 1350.
   "Go to Sleep, Little Baby"
   "Hambone"
   "Johnny Cuckoo"
   "Sometimes (Way Down Yonder)"
Deep South—Sacred and Sinful. Southern Journey Series. Prestige/International 25005.
   "East Coast Line"
Georgia Sea Islands, Volume II. Southern Journey Series. Prestige/International 25002.
   "See Aunt Dinah"

Game performances by children:

Afro-American Blues and Game Songs. Ed. by Alan Lomax. Library of Congress recording AAFS 14.

Been in the Storm So Long. Spirituals, Shouts and Children's Game Songs from Johns Island, South Carolina. Folkways FS 3842.

One Two Three and a Zing Zing Zing. Street games and songs of the children of New York City. Ed. by Tony Schwartz. Folkways FC 7003.

Play and Dance Songs and Tunes. Ed. by B. A. Botkin. Library of Congress recording AAFS L9.

Skip Rope. Thirty-three skip rope games recorded in Evanston, Illinois. Folkways FC 7029.

Index

75 76 77 10 9 8 7 6 5 4 3

Tides of Light

Bantam Spectra Books by Gregory Benford

ACROSS THE SEA OF SUNS
GREAT SKY RIVER
HEART OF THE COMET (with David Brin)
IN THE OCEAN OF NIGHT
IF THE STARS ARE GODS

TIDES
OF LIGHT

Gregory Benford

BANTAM BOOKS
TORONTO • NEW YORK • LONDON • SYDNEY • AUCKLAND

TIDES OF LIGHT
A Bantam Spectra Book / February 1989

Library of Congress Cataloging-in-Publication Data

Benford, Gregory, 1941–
  Tides of light.

  I. Title.
PS3552.E542T53 1989   813'.54   88-7545
ISBN 0-553-05322-1

Published simultaneously in the United States and Canada

Bantam Books are published by Bantam Books, a division of Bantam
Doubleday Dell Publishing Group, Inc. Its trademark, consisting of the
words "Bantam Books" and the portrayal of a rooster, is Registered
in U.S. Patent and Trademark Office and in other countries. Marca
Registrada. Bantam Books, 666 Fifth Avenue, New York, New York 10103.

PRINTED IN THE UNITED STATES OF AMERICA

WAK   0 9 8 7 6 5 4 3 2 1

*This novel is for two dreamers
who nonetheless get their numbers right:*

Charles N. Brown

and

Marvin Minsky

PART ONE

ABRAHAM'S STAR

ONE

The Cap'n liked to walk the hull.

It was the only place where he could feel truly alone. Inside *Argo* there was always the rustle of movement, the rub of humanity kept two years in the narrow though admittedly pleasant confines of a starship.

And worse, when he was inside, someone could always interrupt him. The Family was getting better at leaving him alone in the early morning, he had to give them that. He had carefully built up a small legend about his foul temper just after he awoke, and it was beginning to pay off. Though children might still rush up to him and blurt out a question, lately there had always been an adult nearby to tug the offending youth away.

Killeen disliked using implied falsehoods—he was no more irritable in the morning than at any other time—but it was the only way he could think to get some privacy. So no one hailed him over ship's comm when he was out here. And of course, no ship's officer would dare pass through the lock and seek to join him.

And now there was a much better reason not to come out here. Hull-walking just made you a better target beneath the ever-watching eyes above.

Out here. Killeen had been thinking so firmly about his problems that he had, as was often the case, completely forgotten to admire the view. Or to locate their enemy escort.

His first impression, as he raised his head to let in all the sweep of light around him, was of a seething, cloud-shrouded sky. He knew this was an illusion, that this was no planetary sky at all, and that the burnished hull of the *Argo* was no horizon.

But the human mind persisted in the patterns learned as a

1

child. The glowing washes of blue and pink, ivory and burnt orange, were not clouds in any normal sense. Their phosphorescence came from entire suns they had engulfed. They were not water vapor, but motley swarms of jostling atoms. They spilled forth light because they were being intolerably stimulated by the stars they blanketed.

And no sky back on Snowglade had ever crackled with the trapped energy that flashed fitfully between these clouds. Killeen watched a sprinkle of bluehot light near a large, orange blob. Its wobbly curves fattened like ribbed, bruised sausages. It coiled, clotted scintillant ridges working with snakelike torpor, and then burst into luridly tortured fragments.

Could this be the weather of the stars? Snowglade had suffered from a climate that could turn suddenly vicious, and Killeen supposed the same could be true on the unimaginably larger scale between suns. Since he didn't understand the way planets made weather, or the complex fabric of tides and currents, air and water, it was no great leap for him to suppose some similar shadowed mystery might apply to the raging lives of stars.

Anger forked through this sky. Behind them spun the crimson disk of the Eater, a great gnawing mouth. It ate suns whole and belched hot gas. In *Argo's* flight from Snowglade, which swam near the Eater, they had beaten out against streaming, infalling dust that fed the monster. Its great disk was like burnt sugar at the rim, reddening steadily toward the center. Closer in swirled crisp yellow, and nearer still a bluewhite ferocity lived, an enduring fireball.

Looking outward, Killeen could see on the grandest scale the structure his Aspects told him should be there. The entire galaxy lurked like a silvery ghost beyond the swarthy dustlanes. It, like the Eater, was a disk—but incomparably greater. Killeen had seen ancient pictures of the regions beyond the Center, a lake of stars. But that lake did not ripple and churn. Here tides of light swept the sky, as though some god had chosen Center as her final incandescent artwork. Their target star spun ahead, a mote among wrack and storm, and all their hopes now bore upon it.

And floating in this seethe, their enemy.

He squinted, failed to find it. *Argo* was nearing the verge of a jetblack cloud. The distant mech vehicle probably lay somewhere within the obliterating darkness there. Abraham's Star was struggling free of the massive shroud. Soon *Argo* could peer through the shredding fringes of the cloud to find her planets.

A notion tugged at Killeen but he shrugged it aside, caught up in the spectacle all around him. The heavens worked with ribbed and scaly light, like luminescent beasts drowning in inky seas.

What were the chances, he wondered, that merely showing himself out here would tempt the mech vehicle to skewer him with a bolt? No one knew—which, in the paradoxical logic of leadership, was why he had to do it.

Killeen had started this hull-walking ritual a year before, at the urging of one of his principal Aspects, a truly ancient encased personality named Ling. Revered and respected, the Aspect had been given to Killeen by the Family with high attendant ceremony in *Argo*'s central hall. Ling was the last remaining true starship Cap'n in the Family chip inventory. The micromind had commanded a forerunner of *Argo* and had exciting though often unintelligible yarns to tell.

Yes, and following my advice is bringing a reward.

Thinking about Ling had brought the Aspect's firm, Cap'nly voice sounding in Killeen's mind. He let a skeptical frown cross his face and Ling picked it up.

You make this hull-walk serve the added purpose of displaying your personal calm and unconcern in the face of the enemy.

Killeen said nothing; his sour doubt would faintly trickle down to Ling, like runoff from a rainstorm. He kept up his pace, making sure his boots got a firm magnetic clamp on the hull before he freed the following leg. Even if he kicked himself free of the hull, there was a good chance that his low trajectory would carry him into a strut or an antenna downhull from him. That would save the embarrassment which he had often suffered when he had started this ritual. Five times he had been forced to haul himself back to the ship using a thrown, magnet-tipped line. He was sure crew had seen it, too, and had gotten a good laugh.

Now he made it a point not to have his line even within easy reach on his belt. He kept it in a leg pocket. Anyone watching him from the big agro pods downhull would see their Cap'n loping confidently over the broad curves of the *Argo*, with no visible safety line. A reputation for dashing confidence in his own abilities might come in handy in the difficult times to come.

Killeen turned so that he was facing the pale yellow disk of

Abraham's Star. They had known for months that this was the destination of their years-long voyage—a star similar to Snowglade's. Shibo had told him that planets orbited here as well.

Killeen had no idea as yet what kind of planets these might be, or whether they held any shelter for his Family. But *Argo's* automatic program had brought them here, following knowledge far older than their forefathers. Perhaps the ship knew well.

In any case, the Family's long rest was nearing an end. A time of trials was coming. And Killeen had to be sure his people were ready.

He found himself loping harder, barely skimming the hull. His thoughts impelled him forward, oblivious to his loud panting inside the cramped helmet. The rank musk of his own sweat curled up into his nostrils, but he kept going. The exercise was good, yes, but it also kept his mind away from the invisible threat above. More important, the hard pace cleared his mind for thinking before he began his official day.

Discipline was his principal concern. With Ling's help he had drilled and taught, trying to fathom the ancient puzzles of the *Argo* and help his officers become skilled spacers.

This was his ambiguous role: Cap'n of a crew that was also Family, a circumstance which had not arisen in the memory of anyone living. He had only the dry advice of his Aspects, or the lesser Faces, to guide him—ancient voices from eras marked by far greater discipline and power. Now humanity was a ragged remnant, scurrying for its life among the corners of a vast machine civilization that spanned the entire Galactic Center. They were rats in the walls.

Running a starship was a vastly different task from maneuvering across the bare, blasted plains of distant Snowglade. The patterns the Families had set down for centuries were nominally based on crewing a ship, but these years under way had shown how large the gap was. In a tight engagement, when the crew had to react with instant fortitude and precision, Killeen had no idea how they would perform.

Nor did he know what they would have to do. The dim worlds that circled Abraham's Star might promise infinite danger or easy paradise. They had been set on this course by a machine intelligence of unknown motives, the Mantis. Perhaps the dispersed, anthology intelligence of the Mantis had sent them to one of the few humanly habitable planets in the Galactic Center. Or perhaps they were bound for a site which fitted the higher purposes of the mech civilization itself.

Killeen bit his lip in fretted concentration as he loped around the *Argo*'s stern and rounded back toward midships. His breath came sharply and, as always, he longed to be able to wipe his brow.

He had gambled the Family's destiny on the hope that ahead lay a world better than weary, vanquished Snowglade. Soon now the dice would fall and he would know.

He puffed heavily as he angled around the bulbous lifezones— huge bubbles extruded from the sleek lines of the *Argo*, like the immense, bruised bodies of parasites. Inside, their opalescent walls ran with dewdrops, shimmering moist jewels hanging a bare finger's width away from hard vacuum. Green fronds pressed here and there against the stretched walls—a sight which at first had terrified Killeen, until he understood that somehow the rubbery yet glassy stuff could take the pokes and presses of living matter without splitting. Despite the riot of plant growth inside, there was no threat of a puncture. *Argo* had attained a balance between life's incessant demands and the equally powerful commandments of machines—a truce humanity had never managed on Snowglade.

As he slogged around the long, curved walls of the lifezones, here and there a filmy face peered out at him. A crewwoman paused in her harvesting of fruit and waved. Killeen gave her a clipped, reserved salute. She hung upside down, since the life bubbles did not share *Argo*'s spin.

To her his reflecting suit would look like a mirror-man taking impossibly long, slowmotion strides, wearing leggings of hullmetal, with a shirt that was a mad swirl of wrinkled clouds and stars. His suit came from *Argo*'s ancient stores and had astonishing ability to resist both the heat and cold of space. He had seen a midshipman carelessly back into a gas torch in one, and feel not a flicker of the blazing heat through its silvery skin.

His Ling Aspect commented:

A reflecting suit is also good camouflage against our mech companion.

This sort of remark meant that the Aspect was feeling its cabin fever again. Killeen decided to go along with its attempt to strike up a conversation; that might help him tickle forth the slippery idea that kept floating nearly into consciousness. "The other day you said it wasn't interested in me anyway."

I still believe so. It came upon us as though it would attack, yet over a week has passed as it patiently holds its distance in a parallel path.

"Looks like it's armed."

True, but it holds its fire. That is why I advised you to hull-walk as usual. The crew would have noticed any reluctance.

Killeen grumbled, "Extra risk is dumb."

Not in this case. I know the moods of crew, particularly in danger. Heed me! A commander must imbue his crew with hope in the mortal circumstances of war. So the eternal questions voice themselves again: "Where is our leader? Is he to be seen? What does he say to us? Does he share our dangers?" When you brave the hull your crew watches with respect.

Killeen grimaced at Ling's stentorian tones. He reminded himself that Ling had led far larger ships than *Argo*. And crew *were* peering out the frosted walls of the lifezones to watch their Cap'n.

Still, the magisterial manner of Ling rankled. He had lost several minor Faces when Ling's chip was added, because there wasn't enough room in the slots aligned along his upper spine. Ling was embedded in an old, outsized pentagonal chip, and had proved to be both a literal and figurative pain in the neck.

He gazed once more at the streaming radiance that forked fitfully in the roiling sky. There—he saw it. The distant speck held still against a far-passing luminescence. He watched the mote for a long moment and then shook his fist at it in frustration.

Good. Crew like a Captain who expresses what they all feel.

"It's what *I* feel, dammit!"

Of course. That is why such gestures work so well.

"You calc'late *everything*?"

No—but you wished to learn Captaincy. This is the way to do so.

Irritated, Killeen pushed Ling back into his mind's recesses. Other Aspects and Faces clamored for release, for a freshening moment in his mind's frontal lobes. Though they caught a thin sliver of what Killeen sensed, the starved interior presences hungered for more. He had no time for that now. The slippery idea still eluded him and, he realized, had provoked some of the irritation he had taken out on Ling.

If crew were already harvesting, then Killeen knew he had been running a bit too long. He deliberately did not use the time display in his suit, since the thing was ageold and its symbols were a confusing scramble of too much data, unreadable to his untutored mind. Instead he checked his inboard system. The timer stuttered out a useless flood of information and then told him he had been running nearly an hour. He did not know very precisely how long an hour was, but as a rule of thumb it was enough.

He wrenched the airlock stays free, prepared to enter, looked up for one last glimpse of the vista—and the idea popped forth, unbidden.

In a heartbeat he turned the notion over and over, inspecting every nuance of it, and knew it was right.

He studied the sky, saw the course *Argo* would follow in the gradually lifting gloom of the cloud-shadow. If they had to, there was enough in the sky to navigate by eye.

He cycled through the axial lock, passed quickly through the tight zero-g vapor shower, and was back inside the spun-up corridors within a few minutes.

Lieutenant Cermo was waiting for him at the midships gridpoint. He saluted and said nothing about Killeen's lateness, though his irrepressible grin told Killeen that the point had not slipped by. Killeen did not return the smile and said quietly, "Sound quarters." The way Cermo's mouth turned down in utter dismayed surprise brought forth a thin smile from Killeen. But by that time Cermo had hurriedly turned away and tapped a quick signal into his wrist command, and so missed his Cap'n's amusement entirely.

TWO

He directed the assault from the hull itself—not so much because of Ling's windbag advice, Killeen told himself, but because he truly did get a better feel of things out there.

So he stood, anchored by magnetic boots, as sunrise came.

Not the coming of sunlight from a rotating horizon, a spreading glory at morning. Instead, this false dawn came as a gradual waxing radiance, seen through billowing, thinning grit.

Killeen had noticed that soon *Argo* would pass across the last bank of clotted dust that hid Abraham's Star from them. The swelling sunburst would come as the ship very nearly eclipsed the mech vehicle that was escorting them inward toward the star.

—Still don't see why the mech won't adjust for that,— Cermo sent from the control vault.

"It will. Question is, how fast?"

Killeen felt relaxed, almost buoyant. He had committed them, after a week of vexed, fretting worry. If they entered the inner system around Abraham's Star with an armed mech vessel alongside, a mere quick command from elsewhere could obliterate *Argo*. Best take it out now. If that proved impossible, this was the time to know it.

He searched the quilted sky for a single figure.

—Approaching on assigned path,— Gianini sent.

This young woman had been chosen by Jocelyn to close with the mech. Killeen recalled that she came from Family Rook and knew her to be an able crewwoman. He followed standard practice in letting his lieutenants choose specific crew for jobs; they knew the intricacies of talent and disposition far better than he. Gianini had fought mechs back on Snowglade, was seasoned and twice wounded.

And Killeen found her—a distant dot that sparkled amber and yellow as Abraham's Star began to cut through the shrouding clouds that hung over his shoulder, filling a quarter of the sky.

The brooding mass had lightened from ebony to muted gray as it thinned. Shredded fingers of starshine cut the spaces around *Argo*. And Gianini sped toward the mech, using the sudden rise of brilliance at her back to mask her approach.

A tactic. A stratagem. A life.

A necessary risk, because the mech was too far away to hit with their weapons, which were designed for battles fought on land. *Argo* herself carried no weaponry, no defenses.

—I'll hit it with microwave and IR, then the higher stuff.— Gianini's voice was steady, almost unconcerned.

Killeen did not dare reply, and had ordered Cermo not to allow any transmissions from *Argo*, lest they attract the mech's attention in the ship's direction. Gianini's directed transmissions back could not alert the mech vehicle, though.

As they had calculated, Abraham's Star began to brim with waxy radiance. Rays refracted through Killeen's helmet, sprinkling yellow across his lined face. He found he was clenching and unclenching his hands futilely.

Do it now, he thought. *Now!*

—Firing.—

He strained, but could see no change in either the dot that was Gianini or the dark point where the mech moved against the blue background glow of a molecular cloud.

—I can't see any effect.—

Killeen grimaced. He wanted to give an order, if only to release his own tension. But what would he say? To be careful? A stupid, empty nattering. And even sending it might endanger her.

—Closing pretty fast.—

Gianini was a softening yellow dot approaching a vague darkness. Action in space had an eerie, dead-silent quality that unnerved Killeen. Death came sliding ballistically into the fragile shells that encased moist life.

Starshine from behind him swelled and blared and struck hard shadows across *Argo*'s hull. He felt how empty and barren space was, how it sucked human action into its infinite perspectives. Gianini was a single point among a countless plethora of similar meaningless points.

He shook off the thought, aching to *do* something, to be running and yelling and firing in the midst of a suddenly joined battle that he could *feel*.

But above him the dots coalesced in utter silence. That was all. No fervor, nothing solid, no sure reality.

Burnished sunlight raked the hull around him. Time ticked on. He squinted at the sky and tried to read meaning into mere twitches of random radiance.

—Well, if that don't damn all.—

What? he thought. His heart leaped to hear Gianini's voice, but her slow, almost lazy words could mean anything.

—This thing's had its balls cut off. Ruined. All those antennas and launchers we saw in closeup, 'member? Their power source is all blowed away. Nothin' here that works 'cept for some drive chambers and a mainmind. Guess that's what led it our way.—

Killeen felt a breath he had been holding forever rush out of his chest. He chanced a transmission. "You're sure it can't shoot?"

—Naysay. Somethin' pranged it good. A real mess it is here.—

"Back off, then."

—You want I should skrag the mainmind?—

"Yeasay. Leave a charge on it."

—Doin' that now.—

"Get clean clear before you blow it."

—I'll put it close, be sure.—

"No contact, just leave it—"

In Killeen's ears screamed the horrible sound of circuit ringing—a long high oscillating twang as a load of electrical energy bled off into space, acting as an involuntary antenna as raw power surged through it.

"Gianini! Gianini! Answer!"

Nothing. The ringing wail steepled down into low frequencies, an ebbing, mournful song—and was gone.

"Cermo! Suit trace!"

—Getting nothing.— Cermo's voice was firm and even and had the feel of being held that way no matter what.

"Damn—the mainmind."

—Figure it was on a trigger mine?—

"Must've."

—Still nothing.—

"Damn!"

—Maybe the burst just knocked out her comm.—

"Let's hope. Send the backup."

Cermo ordered a crewman out to recon the mech vehicle. But the man found Gianini floating away from the wrecked craft, her systems blown, her body already cold and stiff in the unforgiving vacuum.

THREE

Killeen walked stiffly down the ceramo-corridors of the *Argo*, his face as unyielding as the walls. The operation against the mech was a success, in the sense that a plausible threat to the ship was removed. They had detonated the charge Gianini had left behind on the mech, and it had blown the vehicle into a dozen pieces.

But in fact it had been no true danger, and Killeen had lost a crewwoman discovering that fact.

As he replayed their conversation in his mind he was sure he could have said or done nothing more, but the result was the same—a second's carelessness, some pointless close approach to the mainmind of the vehicle, had fried Gianini. And had lessened Family Bishop that much more, by one irreplaceable individual.

Numbering fewer than two hundred, they were perilously close to the minimum range of genotypes which a colony needed. Any fewer, and future generations would spiral downward, weighed by genetic deficiencies.

This much Killeen knew, without understanding even a smattering of the underlying science. *Argo's* computers held what they called "DNA database operations." There was a lab for biowork. But Family Bishop had no Aspects who knew how to prune genes. Basic bioengineering was of marginal use. He had no time and even less inclination to make more of such issues.

But Gianini, lost Gianini—he could not so brusquely dismiss her memory by seeing her as simply a valuable carrier of genetic information. She had been vibrant, hardworking, able—and now she was nothing. She had been chipstored a year ago, so her abilities survived as a spectral legacy. But her ghostly Aspect might not be revived for centuries.

Killeen would not forget her. He could not.

As he marched stiffly to his daily rounds—delayed by the assault—he forced the somber thoughts away from him. There was time for that later.

11

You are acting wisely. A commander can feel remorse and can question his own orders—but he should never be seen to be doing that by his crew.

Killeen gritted his teeth. A sour bile settled in his mouth and would not go away.

His Ling Aspect was a good guide in all this, but he still disliked the calm, sure way the ancient Cap'n laid out the precepts of leadership. The world was more complex, more darkly crosscurrented, than Ling ever allowed.

You assume too much. I knew all the tides that sweep you, when I was clothed in flesh. But they are often hindrances, not helps.

"I'll keep my 'hindrances,' little Aspect!"

Killeen pushed Ling away. He had a role to fulfill now and the small chorus of microminds that he felt calling to him could be of no help. He had followed Ling's advice and decided to continue with the regular ship's day, despite the drama of the assault. Returning to ordinary routine, as though such events were within the normal course of a ship's life, would help settle the crew.

So he had told Cermo to carry on as planned. Only now did he realize what that implied.

Killeen rounded a corner and walked toward the open bay where the crew of the morning's watch waited. Halfway there Cermo greeted him with, "Punishment hour, sir?"

Killeen stopped himself from clenching his jaws and nodded, recalling the offense from yesterday.

Cermo had caught a crewwoman in the engine module. Without conferring with his Cap'n, Cermo had hauled her—a stringy, black-haired woman named Radanan—unceremoniously out into the lifezone, barking out his relish at the catch. The deed was publicly exposed before Killeen had a chance to find other means to deal with it. He had been forced to support his officer in the name of discipline; his Ling Aspect had drilled that principle into him.

"Yeasay. Proceed."

"Could give her more, y'know."

"I said proceed."

He had firmly resolved to speak as little as possible to his officers during ordinary ship operations. He was like a drinker who could not trust himself to stick to moderate amounts. In Family meetings he gave himself a little leeway, though. There, eloquence and even outright oration served his ends. He knew he was not very good at talk, and the briefer he was the more effect it had. As *Argo* had approached this star system he had gotten more and more terse. There were days when most of the crew heard him say only a short "ah-mmm" as he pointedly cleared his throat at some demonstrated inadequacy.

As they made their way to the central axis Killeen set his face like stone. He was ashamed of his aversion to watching punishment. He knew that to punish a crewmember was a sign of his own failure. He should have caught the slide in behavior before it got this far. But once the event had occurred there was no turning back.

In this case, Radanan had been trying to sneak into the thrumming dangers of the engine zone as they decelerated. This alone would have been a mild though flagrantly stupid transgression. But when Cermo caught her she had bristled, bitterly angry, and had called on some friends nearby, trying to provoke a minor mutiny.

A wise Captain hands out rougher justice than this.

His Ling Aspect offered this without being summoned. "She just screamed and swore some, is all," Killeen subvocalized. "And was stupid enough to take a poke at Cermo."

Mutiny is a capital offense.

"Not on the *Argo*."

She'll incite others, harbor resentment—

"She was looking for food, just a minor—"

You'll lose control if—

Killeen damped the Aspect's self-righteous bark into silence.

Evidently Radanan had been looking for a way to scavenge something extra, though Killeen could not imagine what she thought she might find. Usually, crew were caught pilfering food, an outcome of the strict rationing Killeen had imposed for a year now.

The watch crew stood a little straighter as Killeen came into the area. Radanan was at the center of a large circle, since this was both a shipboard matter and a Family reproach. She looked down dejectedly. Her eyes seemed to have accepted already the implications of the cuffs around her wrists that held her firmly to a mooring line.

Cermo barked out the judgment. Two crewmen stood ready to hold Radanan at the elbows in case she should jerk away from the punishment. She bleakly watched as Cermo brought out the short, gleaming rod.

Killeen made himself not grit his teeth. He had to enforce his own rules or else nothing he said would be believed. And he did blame himself. The woman was not overly bright. She had originally been a member of Family Rook.

By tribal consent, all those who had chosen to set off in the *Argo* had realigned, so that they constituted a new Family composed of the Bishops, Rooks, and Kings. They had elected to term it Family Bishop still, and Killeen had never been sure whether this was a tribute to him, a Bishop, or a simple convenience.

At any rate, as he watched the hard rod come down upon Radanan's buttocks, he thought it seemed unlikely that a woman small-minded enough to venture into dangerous territory in search of an oddment would benefit from so crude a tactic as flogging. But tradition was tradition. They had precious little else to guide them in this vast darkness.

A dozen cuts of the rod as Family punishment, each one counted out by a midshipman. And as ship's punishment, twelve more. Radanan held herself rigid for the first six and then began to jerk, gasps bursting out from behind clenched teeth. Killeen thought he would have to turn away but he made himself think of something, anything, while Cermo ran the count to twenty.

Then she collapsed to the deck.

"Belay that!" Killeen said sharply, and the awful business was over. She had stumbled so that she hung by her wrists. That took matters beyond anything he would tolerate and gave him grounds to call it off four strokes short.

He struggled for something to say. "Ah-mmm. Very well, Lieutenant Cermo. On to the day's orders, then."

Killeen turned and left quickly, hoping that no one noticed that he was sweating.

FOUR

He made his way in a sour temper through the slick corridors connecting the life vault with the central axis spiral. His anger with himself could find no clear expression. He knew he should have become hardened to the necessity of imposing punishment. Barring that, he should have been clever enough to find a way around the situation that Cermo's quick action had forced on him.

A whiff of sewage wrinkled his nose. He hastened past. All of third deck was sealed off. Even so, some sludge had leaked into ventilation shafts here, and crew somehow never got it all cleaned out. The problem had started a year ago with clogged toilets. Attempts at repair damaged the valves and servos. The waste had spread through the third deck until work details gagged, fainted, and refused to go in. Killeen had been forced to seal the deck, losing bunking quarters and shops.

He irritably demanded of his Ling Aspect, "You're *sure* you can't remember any more about pipes and such?"

Ling's reply was stony:

No. I have informed you often enough that I was brought up through the combat ranks, not the engineers. If you had not let ignorant crew tinker with the problem—

"I got no engineers know 'bout that, in chip or living. You savvy so much, why can't—"

If you'll read the ship's flow diagram—

"Can't! They're too 'plexified. It's like tellin' what a woman thinks by studyin' every hair on her head."

Even a ship like this, though far advanced beyond some I commanded, requires intelligence to run. If you'll institute the study sessions I recommended long ago—

15

"Make Family sit and decipher for weeks?" Killeen laughed dryly. "You saw how far I got with that."

Your people are unlike anyone I ever commanded, I'll grant that. You are from a society that scavenged and stole for a living—

"Won battles 'gainst the mechs, you mean. The food and 'quipment we got was war booty."

Call it what you will. Such training is a far cry from the discipline and skill needed to fix even a broken sewer connection. Still, with time and proper training—

Killeen piped the Ling Aspect back down again; he had heard all this before. Ling knew of the Chandelier Age, when humans had great cities in space. Cap'ns had made year-long voyages between Chandeliers, braving the increasing mech raids. Ling himself had functioned then as a full interactive Personality. The Family could no longer maintain Personalities, so Ling was available only as the lesser, truncated projection—an Aspect.

Ling invariably recommended the strict discipline necessary in the Chandelier Age. Superimposed on that, though, was an older theme. The original, living Ling had come from the fabled Great Times, or possibly even beyond. The Aspect's memory flattened time distinctions, so it was hard to tell which facet of Ling was speaking. The sensation of having at the back of his head a voice from an unimaginably grand past, when humans had lived free of mech dominance, made Killeen uneasy. He felt absurd, maintaining the persona of a confident Cap'n when he sensed the supremely greater power of lost ages.

As he climbed up the axis, saluting crew as he passed, he was uncomfortably aware of the scuffs and dings the walls had suffered. Here a yellow stain covered a hatchway. There someone had tried to cut away a chunk of hardboard and had given up halfway through, leaving a ragged sawtooth slash. Random chunks of old servos and electronics packages had been chucked aside and left, once they proved useless for whatever impulse had made crew yank them out of some locker.

Argo's systems could handle nearly any threat, but not the insidious barrage of ignorance that Family Bishop served up. Their lifelong habits told them to strip away and carve up, haul off and make do, confident that mech civilization would unthinkingly replenish everything. Scarcely the talents appropriate to a starship crew. It had taken Killeen quite a while, and some severe public whippings, to get them to stop trying to harvest random gaudy bits from the ship's operating parts.

He would have to order a general cleanup again. Once clutter accumulated, crew slid back into their old habits. The last week, distracted by the mech escort, he had let matters slide by.

Breakfast was waiting in his cramped quarters. He slurped up a hot broth of savory vegetables and gnawed at a tough grain cube. The day's schedule shimmered on the tabletop, a 3D graphic display of tasks to be done about the ship.

He did not know how this was done, nor did he care to learn. These last years had so saturated him with the Byzantine lore of the *Argo* that he was content to master what he had to, and leave much else to the crew. Shibo had ferreted out this particular nicety; she had an unerring instinct for the ship's control systems. He wished she were here to share breakfast, but she was on watch already at the helm.

A knock at the door proved to be Cermo. Killeen had to smile at the man's promptness; on Snowglade he had been called Cermo-the-Slow. Something in *Argo*'s constrictions had brought out a precision in the man that contrasted wildly with his muscular bulk. Cermo now wore an alert expression on a face which Killeen had for so long seen as smooth and merry. Short rations had thrust the planes of his cheeks up through round hills of muscle.

"Permission to review the day, Cap'n?" Cermo asked snappily.

"Certainly." Killeen gestured to a seat across the table.

Killeen wondered idly if one of Cermo's Aspects had been a starship crewman. That might explain how naturally the man adjusted to ship life. Cermo's round, smooth face split with a fleeting grin of anticipation whenever Killeen gave an order, as though it summoned up pleasant memories. Killeen envied that. He had never gotten along well with his Aspects.

Cermo launched into summary of the minor troubles that each day brought. They were all hard-pressed, running a huge star-sailing machine bequeathed to them by their ancient forefathers and foremothers. Though each crewman carried Aspects of former Family members—which could help with some of the arcane ship's lore—vexing problems cropped up daily.

As Killeen talked with Cermo his left hand automatically tapped his cube of baked grain on the shiny ceramic table. Two years before, a crop-tending crewmember had been browsing among

the agricultural storehouse. She had mistakenly read a label wrong
and not bothered to consult with one of her Aspects to get it right.
Blithely she had accidentally released a self-warming vial of frozen
soil-tenders. They were ugly, slimy things, and the woman had
been so badly startled that she dropped the vial. Some had inched
their way to freedom before the crewwoman raised the alarm. In
the rich loam of the gardens, carrying with them not only their
own genes but also an anthology of lesser mites, the worms
wreaked havoc.

Killeen's rapping brought two small, squirming weevils wrig-
gling from the tan grain cube. He swept away the tiny things and
bit into the hard, tasty knot. It was hopeless to try to wipe them
out now that they had spread. As well, he still objected to harm-
ing living things. Machines were their true enemy. If lesser life
got out of its rightful place, thanks to human fumbling, that was no
excuse to strike against the fabric of living beings. To Killeen this
was not a moral principle but an obvious fact of his universe, of
unspoken Family lore.

Cermo sat uncomfortably in a small chair, cheerfully jawing on
about the woman's punishment and all the supposed benefits of
discipline that would unfold from it.

He should be the one carrying Ling, not me, Killeen thought.
Or maybe it was easier to take a hard line when final responsibility
wasn't yours.

He had seen that years before, when Fanny was Cap'n. Her
lieutenants had often favored tough measures, but Fanny usually
took a more moderate, cautious course. She had kept in mind the
consequences of decisions, when an error could doom them all.

It occurred to Killeen that his own hesitant way in those days
might have been what made Fanny advance him up the Family's
little pyramid of power. Maybe she had mistaken that for a wary
sense of proportion. The idea amused him, but he dismissed it;
Fanny's judgment had been far better than his, better than that of
anyone he had ever known except for his father, Abraham. Killeen
had enjoyed some success, due mostly to outright luck, but he
knew he could never equal her abilities.

"The Rooks 'n Kings always grumble 'bout a whipping if it's
one *their* folk," Cermo said. "But they get the point."

"Still bitching over how I chose my lieutenants?"

He had made Cermo and Jocelyn, both Bishops, his immediate underofficers. Lieutenant Shibo was both Chief Executive
Officer and Pilot. She was the last survivor of Family Knight.

Though she had lived with the Rooks, everyone considered her a Bishop because she was Killeen's lover.

Of such Byzantine issues was policy made. In the difficult days following liftoff from Snowglade, Killeen had tried using Rooks and Knights as Lieutenants. They simply didn't measure up. He had wondered if their time living in a settled village had softened them. Still, he saw that his decisions had not been politically wise. Abraham would have finessed the matter in some inconspicuous way.

"Yeasay," Cermo said, "but no worse than usual."

"Keep your ear on the deck. Let me know the scuttlebutt."

"Sure. There's some who talk more'n they work."

"That's private Family business."

"Could use a touch of the crop, I'd say."

Experience told him that it was best to let Cermo go on for a while, exhaust the subject of crew discipline. Still, he wished he were breakfasting with Shibo, whose warm, sure silences he found such a comfort. They understood each other without the endless rattle of talk.

"—train 'em, get 'em savvy out the techtalk in ship's computers."

"You think the younger ones'll do better at it?" Killeen asked.

"Yeasay. Shibo, she says—"

Cermo was always coming up with another scheme to get more of the Family trained. The simple fact was that they were hardened people and didn't learn technical matters easily. Families traded knowhow, but their ageold tradition was as craftsmen and craftswomen, not as scientists.

He nodded at Cermo's enthusiasm, half-listening, his attention focused all the while on the incessant ship noises. The muffled thud of heels, a gurgle of fluids in pipes, a subtle creaking of decks and joints. But now there was a lower note, coming from the rub of interstellar dust against the giant balloonlike lifezones.

The strumming sound had gathered over the last weeks, a deep voice that spoke in subliminal bass notes of the coming of the beckoning yellow star. Decelerating, *Argo* swooped among thickening dustclouds that shrouded this side of the coming sun. Mottled dustlanes, cinder-dark, cloaked their view of the inner planets.

The low, resonant bass note kept its unnerving, constant pitch. Sometimes in his sleep he imagined that a slow, solemn voice was speaking to him, the words drawn into a dull moan that forewarned doom. Other nights it was a giant's drunken boom hurling slurred words at him, the tones shaking his body.

He had immediately shrugged off these rough visions; a Cap'n could not afford to harbor such gloomy and irrational thoughts. Still, the hum now came creeping into his hands as they rested on the table. As a boy he had not known the stars were other suns. The spilling fluid flow of gas and smoldering dust about Galactic Center had seemed inconsequential, forever silent and distant.

Now the thick churn sang against *Argo*, a quickening wind driven by the galactic wheel. The *Argo* had somehow tapped this gale, he knew, harnessed its unseen dynamics. The massive, dusty currents smothered suns and silted planets with grime, so his Arthur Aspect said. The moaning that ranged and stuttered through *Argo* seemed to wail of dead worlds, of silted time, and of the choked-off visions of lost races he would never know.

The tabletop between them flickered abruptly. Shibo's chiseled features appeared, flattened and distorted by the angle. "Pardon," she said when she saw Lieutenant Cermo. "We have clear view now, Cap'n."

"You see more inner worlds?"

"Aye, a new one. Dust hid it before."

"Good detail?"

"Aye, sir," Shibo said, her glinting eyes betraying a quick, darting enthusiasm. If it had been just the two of them, she probably would have thrown in a dry joke.

Killeen made himself take his time finishing the bowl of green goulash and then savored the last dregs of his tea. He spoke slowly, almost casually. "Take a sure sighting, using all the detectors?"

"Course," Shibo said, a small upturning of the corners of her lips showing that she understood that this show was for Cermo's benefit.

"Then I'll be along in a bit," Killeen said with unexcited deliberation. He had seen his father use this ruse long ago in the Citadel.

Cermo shifted impatiently in his chair. They all wanted to know to what world two years of voyaging had brought them. Many still felt that the Mantis had sent them toward a lush, green world. Killeen was by no means convinced. He trusted no mech. He still remembered with relish their obliteration of the Mantis in *Argo*'s exhaust wash at liftoff.

He took his time with the tea, using it to consider the possible reactions of the Family if their expectations were not met. The prospect was sobering.

He debated having another cup of tea. No, that would be too much torture for Cermo—though the man had certainly seemed to like handing it out to the Radanan woman earlier.

Forgoing the tea, he nonetheless put on his full tunic and walked rather more slowly than usual around the ship's axis and up one level.

His officers had already assembled in the control vault when Killeen arrived. They were staring at the big display screen, pointing and whispering. Killeen realized that a proper Cap'n would not allow such milling in the confines of the control vault, despite the fact that this was a completely natural reaction to years of long voyaging.

He said sharply, "What? Nobody's got jobs? Lieutenant Jocelyn, how's the patching going in the dry zone? Faldez, those pipes still clogged in the agro funnel?"

His stern voice dispersed them. They left, casting quick glances back at the display screen. He wanted them to see that he had not deigned even to look at the image there, but had tended to ship's business first.

They could not know that he kept his neck deliberately turned so that temptation would not slide his eyes sideways to catch a glimpse. He exchanged a few words with several departing officers to be sure his point was made. Then he turned, pursing his lips to guard against any expression of surprise that might cross his face, and stared directly into their destiny.

FIVE

Two years before, Cap'n Killeen had flinched when he saw the ruined brown face of his home planet, Snowglade, as *Argo* lifted away.

Now, with heady relief, he saw that the shimmering image before him did not resemble that worn husk. Near its poles small dabs of bluewhite nestled amid gray icecaps that spread crinkled fingers toward the waist of the world. But these features came to him only after a striking fact:

"Wrong colors," he said, startled.

Shibo shook her head. "Not all. Ice is dark, yeasay. But middle is green, wooded—see the big lakes?"

"Pale areas in between look dead."

"Not much vegetation," Shibo conceded.

"What could cause . . . ?" Killeen frowned, realizing that he would need to know some planetary evolution, in addition to everything else.

Shibo said, "Could be these clouds did that? Dust killed plants, dirtied up the ice, turned it gray."

Killeen sensed that it would not be wise to admit complete ignorance in front of Cermo, who had remained.

"Might be. Plenty dust still around. That's why we're coming in at a steep angle." Killeen studied the planet's crescent for signs of human life. The nightside was utterly dark, though even if he had seen lights they might easily have been cities built by mechs.

Cermo said hesitantly, "Sir, I don't understand. . . ."

Normally it was a bad idea to explain the basis of your decisions to underofficers, his Ling Aspect had said. But it was also a good idea to train them; the days ahead would be dangerous, and if Killeen fell, his replacement would need to know many things.

"These little black blotches—see them?" Killeen pointed as the scale of the viewing screen enlarged, bringing in the hot disk of the parent star. Beyond it, the broad, banded grins of two silvery gas giant planets hung against a speckled tapestry of molecular clouds. Tiny smudges freckled the image, motes that ebbed and flared from day to day.

"This star, it's ripped apart a passing cloud. There's lots of these blobs in the plane of the planets."

Killeen paused. The three-dimensional geometry had been easy for him to see in Aspect-provided simulations, but now it was hard to make out in a flat grid projection like this.

"So I directed us in at a steep angle," he said, "cutting down into that plane. That'll avoid running into small clouds that we might not detect. *Argo* won't hold up if we get blindsided by one of those."

He watched fondly as Shibo's exoskeleton whirred as her hands passed over the control boards. Its polycarbon lattice made swift, sure movements. For Killeen one of the many delights of *Argo's* slow spin was that she seldom needed her mechanical aid except for quick precision. In Snowglade's heavy gravity she had used it continually just to keep up. A genetic defect had given her only normal human strength, which was much less than the Families' level.

Still, the simple sight of her made him smile. Momentarily the day's weight lifted.

She brought up wildly different views of the planetary system, images colored in splashes of violent reds, tawny golds, cool blues. Killeen knew these arose from different spectra, but could not say how. They showed grainy specks orbiting between the planets— small knotty condensations that hailed incessantly in toward all the stars at Galactic Center. These had been caught by Abraham's Star and now pelted its planets unmercifully.

"Bet it makes for a dusty sky down there," Shibo said reflectively. She thumbed up a speckled orange display which highlighted five cometary tails. They lay above and below the plane of the planetary orbits, gaudy streamers that pointed inward like accusing fingers.

Killeen caught her meaning. "I don't believe, though," he made himself go on with casual assurance, "that the dust could snuff out life. This planet's suffered infalling grime before. You can see the forests have survived. It can still shelter us."

Shibo gave him a wry sidelong glance. She sometimes fed him hints like this, enabling him to seem to have thought problems through before they came up. It was a great help in slowly building a crew, Killeen thought, if the Cap'n happened to love the Chief Executive Officer. He resisted the temptation to smile, sure that Cermo would guess his thoughts.

"Any moons?" he asked stonily.

"None I can see so far," Shibo said. "There's something else, though. . . ."

Her slender arms stretched over the controls, calling forth functions Killeen could scarcely follow. Far out he saw a nugget of bronzed hardness.

"A station." She answered his unspoken question.

Cermo gasped. "A . . . a Chandelier?"

"I can't make it out well enough. Could be."

Killeen asked, "Can't we see better? If we wait till we're closer, could be dangerous."

She thought, punched in an inquiry. "No, not this way. There's another lensing system, though. Needs be hand-deployed on the aft hull."

"Do it," Killeen ordered. Of Cermo he asked, "Who's got suit duty?"

"Besen," Cermo said. "But she's young. I'd—"

"Use the assigned crew. Besen's quick and smart."

"Well, still, Cap'n—"

"They'll never learn if they don't face problems." Killeen could remember his father saying exactly the same, refusing to shield Killeen from tough jobs when he was a boy.

He studied the small bronze speck for a long moment, then asked Shibo to give the natural light view. In true human spectrum the thing glittered with jewellike warmth, but under maximum magnification he could make out no structure.

Quite possibly this was a human outpost. Perhaps—Killeen felt a racing excitement—it was indeed an ancient Chandelier, those legendary edifices of crystalline perfection.

He had once seen one through a 'scope on Snowglade, so far away that he could make out no detail. He had caught only the strange glimmering presence of it, the suspicion of beauty lying just beyond perception. The possibility of finding something man-made, hanging in this roiling vault of troubled sky, was enough to summon up his profound respect and awe for the ancient masters who had made *Argo* and the even older Chandeliers. That he might see one closely—the thought made him lean toward the screen, as if to force answers from it.

Besen arrived, a young woman of hard eyes and soft, sensuous mouth. She had a strict crewlike bearing and came to attention immediately after entering the control vault. "Sir, I—"

Killeen's son, Toby, dashed in through the hatchway before she could finish. He was gangly, a full head taller than Besen, and panted heavily. "I—I heard there's some hullwork needs done."

Killeen blinked. His son was flushed with excitement, eyes dancing. But no Cap'n could allow such intrusions.

"Midshipman! You were not ordered here. I—"

"I heard Besen's call. Just lemme—"

"You will stand at *attention* and shut *up!*"

"Dad, I just want—"

"Stand fast and belay your tongue-wagging. You are *crew* here, not my son—got that?"

"Uh . . . yeah . . . I . . ."

"Stand on your toes," Killeen said firmly. He clasped his hands behind him and jutted his chin out at the undisciplined young man his own boy had become.

"Wh-what?"

"Deaf, are you? You will stand on your toes until I am finished giving orders for Midshipwoman Besen. Then we will discuss the proper punishment for you."

Toby blinked, opened his mouth to speak, then thought better of it. He swallowed and rose on his toes, hands at his side.

"Now," Killeen said slowly to Besen, who had all this time remained standing at attention, eyes ahead—though at the word *tongue-wagging* a quick grin had flashed across her face. "I believe Officer Shibo has instructions for your task. Perform it with all good speed."

SIX

Besen proved equal to the demands of finding and extruding from the ancient ship's hull the needed opticals. They followed her progress on the main monitor. Killeen gave Toby a dressing-down in front of Cermo and Shibo, knowing that through Cermo the story would get through the ship faster than if he had played it over full comm. All the while Toby had to remain on his toes, even after the ache began to twist his face with grimaces and sweat beaded on his brow. In this contest between father and son there could be only one winner—Family legacy and the demands of the ship itself required that—but Toby held out as long as he could. Finally, in the middle of a deliberately protracted lecture by Killeen on the necessity of following orders exactly, Toby toppled over, crashing to the deck.

"Very good. Lesson finished," Killeen said, and turned back to the main display screen.

Besen had adroitly arranged the fibery, translucent opticals, which were too delicate to be permanently exposed. She tilted their platform so they could find the tiny glimmering planet that lay swaddled in the dusty arms of the star's ecliptic plane.

Shibo brought up an image from it quickly. Killeen watched the watery light resolve, while Toby got up and Lieutenant Cermo ordered him back to station. It had been a hard thing to do but Killeen was sure he was right, and his Ling Aspect agreed. The inherent contradictions involved in running a crew that was also a Family demanded that difficult moments not be avoided.

"What . . . what's that?" Cermo asked, forgetting that it was a good rule never to question a Cap'n. Killeen let it pass, because he could well have asked the same question.

Against a mottled background hung a curious pearly thing, a disk penetrated at its center by a thick rod. Strange extrusions pointed from the rod at odd angles. Instinctively Killeen knew it was no Chandelier. It had none of the legendary majesty and lustrous webbed beauty.

"Mechwork, could be," he said.

Shibo nodded. "It circles above the same spot on the planet."

"Is there some way we can approach the planet, keeping this thing always on the other side?" Killeen asked.

He still had only a dim comprehension of orbital mechanics. His Arthur Aspect had shown him many moving displays of ships and stars, but little of it had stuck. Such matters were far divorced from the experience of a man who had lived by running and maneuvering on scarred plains.

Once, when Killeen had asked if a ship could orbit permanently over a planet's pole, Ling had laughed at him—an odd sensation, for the tinny voice seemed to bring forth echoes of other Aspects Killeen had not summoned up. It had taken him a while to see that such an orbit was impossible. Gravity would tug down the unmoving ship.

"I can try for that in the close approach. But even now this thing could have seen us."

"We will avoid it then, Officer Shibo. Give me a canted orbit, so this satellite can't see us well."

Shibo nodded, but by her quick, glinting eyes he knew she understood his true thoughts. Soon he had to decide whether they would pause in this system at all. The Mantis, that frosty machine intelligence of Snowglade, had set them on this course. But if the planet ahead proved to be mech-run, Killeen would take them out of the system as swiftly as he could. But where was the crucial choice to be made? No experience or Family lore told him how to decide, or even when.

He left the control vault and walked through the *Argo's* tight-wound spiral corridors. Inspections awaited, and he took his time with them. He kept his pace measured, not letting his interior fever of speculation and doubt reveal itself, so that passing crew would see their Cap'n moving with an unconcerned air.

There was a gathering, humming expectancy in the air as they plunged toward their target star. Soon they would learn whether they came to a paradise or to another mech-run world. The planet's strange, discolored face had given him no answers, and he would have to deflect questions from Family members who so desperately wanted assurances.

Walking through a side corridor, he heard a faint scrabbling noise from an air duct. Instantly he sprang up, unslipped the grille, and peered inside. Nothing.

The sound, like small feet scrambling away, faded. A micro-mech, certainly.

Try as they might, the crew had never destroyed all the small mechs left in the *Argo* by the Mantis. The remaining machines were almost certainly unimportant, delegated to do small repairs and cleaning. Still, their presence bothered Killeen. He knew how much intelligence could be carried in a fingernail's width; after all, the chips lodged along his spine held whole personalities. What were even such small mechs capable of doing?

He had no way of knowing. There had been disturbing incidents during the voyage, when problems mysteriously cleared up. Killeen had never known whether the ship had repaired itself with deep, hidden subsystems, or whether the micromechs were at work, following their own purposes.

No Cap'n liked to have his ship at the control of anyone but himself, and Killeen could never rest comfortably until all the micromechs were gone. But short of some drastic remedy, he saw no way to rid himself of these nuisances.

Vexed, he took a moment for himself and stopped at a small side pocket just off the spiral corridor. Here was the only room in *Argo* devoted solely to honoring their link to antiquity. It was large enough for ceremonies such as marriages or deaths, which Killeen had duly performed in the last two years, and dominated by two iron-dark slabs on two walls.

These were the Legacies, *Argo*'s computer memories said. They were inscribed with spidery impressions that glinted in all colors if a light shone upon them. A digital language, clearly, though couched in terms even the *Argo* programs could not unravel. The ship had severe instructions to preserve these tablets, embedded in the ceramo-walls, against all depredations. Clearly here was some incomprehensible clue to the origin of humans at the Center, and perhaps much else—but Killeen had no idea how to pursue this avenue.

He came here, instead, to sit on a simple bench and think. The looming, somber presence of the twin-slab Legacies gave him a curiously calming sensation of a firm link to a human past unknown and yet magnificent. In ancient days humans had built ships like this, plied the thin currents between suns, and lived well, free of the grinding presence of vastly superior beings.

Killeen envied the people of that time. He paused now to run his palms over the smooth surface of the Legacies, as if some fragment of ageold vision and wisdom could seep into him.

Now that the problems of Cap'ncy beset him, he thought often of Abraham and all those from times before. They had led the grudging retreat before the mechs. They had given everything.

To Killeen and the Bishops fate had granted a shred of hope. A fresh world, new visions. He could liberate his people or he could lose their last gamble.

And this opportunity had come just one bare generation late. Abraham would have known what to do now. Abraham had been a natural leader. His sunbrowned, easy air had commanded without visible effort. Killeen missed his father far more than he had in the days after Abraham's disappearance at the Calamity when Citadel Bishop fell. Time and again he had wondered what his father would have done. . . .

He sighed and got to his feet. His hand brushed the Legacies once more. Then he turned and left, the mottled brown face of the nearby planet framed in his right eye, so that he could study new pictures as they arrived.

He was mulling over this vision so deeply that he didn't hear the running feet in the spiral corridor. A body slammed into his shoulder and spun him around.

He fetched up against the wall, the wind knocked out of him. His son peered into his face. "You all right, Dad?"

"I . . . didn't hear . . . you coming."

Besen and three others came running up, their hot pursuit of Toby brought to a halt as they saw the Cap'n.

"We were just, y'know, playin' a li'l kickball," Toby said sheepishly, holding up a small red sphere.

"It's lots fun, on the axis," another boy said.

"Yeasay, funner with low grav," Besen put in. Her eyes were zesty and bright.

Killeen nodded. "Glad you're keeping your legs in shape," he said. A meaningful glance at the others prompted them to leave him alone with Toby.

"You steamed 'bout what happened in the control vault?"

Toby chewed at his lip, conflict warring in his face. "Don't see why you had to roust me."

"I won't give you the discipline lecture, but—"

"Glad 'bout *that*. Been hearin' nothin' *but* that from you."

"You haven't given me much choice."

"And you aren't givin' *me* much chance."

"How you figure?"

Toby shrugged irritably. "Ridin' me alla time."

"Only when you force me."

"Look, I'm just tryin', that's all."

"Trying too hard, maybe."

"I'm tired out from just sittin'. Wanna *do* somethin'."

"Only when you're ordered."

"That's it? No—"

"And you'll belay your gab when I give you an order, too."

Toby's lip curled. "That your old Ling Aspect talkin', right? What's 'belay' mean?"

"Means *stop*. And my Aspects are—"

"Ever since you got it, seems like *it's* givin' the orders."

"I take advice, certainly—"

"Seems like some old fart's runnin' *Argo*, not my dad."

"I keep my Aspects under control." Killeen heard his voice, stiff and formal, and made himself say more warmly, "You know what it's like sometimes, though. You've had two Faces now for—what?—a year?"

Toby nodded. "I got 'em runnin' okay."

"I'm sure you do. They ride easy?"

"Pretty near. They give me tech stuff, mostly."

"But you can see, then, how you look at some things differently."

"Get tired, just sittin' 'round tryin' to fix stuff."

"When the right time comes—"

Toby's mouth warped with exasperation. "Me an' the guys, Besen, all of us—we wanna be in on what happens."

"You will be. Just hold back some, yeasay?"

Toby sighed and the tightness drained slowly from his face. "Dad, it's like there's . . . there's no time anymore when we're just . . ."

"Just us?"

Toby nodded, swallowing hard.

"You better 'member, I'm Cap'n now a lot more often than I'm your father."

Toby's jaw stiffened. "Seems you come down special hard on me lately."

Killeen paused, tried to see if this was so. "Might be."

"I'm just tryin', is all."

"So'm I," Killeen said quietly.

"I don't want to miss out on anythin' when we hit ground."

"You won't. We'll need everybody."

"So don't leave me out, just 'cause I'm . . . you know."

"My son? Well, you won't stop being that, but sometimes maybe you'll wish you weren't."

"Never."

"Don't think you'll get special jobs, now."

"I won't."

"Son? None this changes what we are, y'know."

"I guess." Toby's face seemed strained and flattened in the enameled light. "Only . . . it's not like the old times."

"When we were runnin' for our lives? I'd say this is sure as hell better."

"Yeah, but . . . well . . ."

"Hard times only look all right when you're lookin' back from good times."

Toby's face relaxed a fraction. "I guess."

"Between us, time makes no difference."

"I guess."

SEVEN

Toby went back to his kickball in the spiral axis. Killeen warned them to be careful and not get in the way of crewwork, but never considered ordering them to stop. As near as he could tell, humanity had come into being on the move, designed to chase small game that bounded around very much like a ball, and he wasn't about to get in the way of so basic an impulse. It kept the crew in condition and smoothed out antagonisms, too.

But not all. As he passed a maintenance pocket he came upon a dozen Family huddled around a small fire of cornhusks and dried cobs. Killeen disliked the sooty stains this practice left on the ship's walls, but he understood the reassurance of a communal fire. In dimmed light the crackling yellow tongues forked up like wild spirits, casting fluttering shadows among faces intent with their discussion.

He expected a lot of earnest talk now; the ship echoed with chatter and hoteyed gossip. To his surprise, this knot of idlers included First Mate Jocelyn.

"Cap'n!" she hailed. She was a stringy, middle-aged woman with quick, canny eyes. She wore the coverall appropriate for shipwork, free of snags and covered with zippered pockets. The sewing and metal-shaping skills of the Family had come to the fore during the two years of voyaging from Snowglade, giving every Family member a sturdy wardrobe fashioned from organiweave and from the fiber of plants from the lifezone bubbles.

Killeen made a clipped half-salute, a gesture he had perfected. It carried greeting and acknowledgment, but also reminded that he was in his official Cap'n capacity, not functioning as simply another member of the Family. He was about to move on when Jocelyn said loudly, "We're figurin' on takin' that station, yeasay?"

Killeen was stunned. "How—" he began, then stopped himself. He must not betray surprise that word of the station had

32

gotten around so fast. Shiptalk was legendary. "—you mean?" he finished.

He knew that the old formalisms of Family speech dictated that he should say "*do* you mean"—long hours spent with his Aspects had made the ancient, smoother speech patterns almost second nature to him, and he customarily used them to distance himself. But casual crewtalk might be the right approach now.

"Heard there's a big mech place up ahead," one of the men said slowly.

"Word gets 'round," Killeen admitted, settling onto his haunches. This was the ageold posture the Family had adopted while on the move, always ready to jump and move in case of surprise. Here it was meaningless, of course, but it underlined their common past and equality. Everyone in the circle was also squatting, some clutching small bottles of flavored water. A midshipman offered Killeen one and he took a swig: rich aromatic apricot, the fruit now flowering in the lifezones.

"Yeasay," Jocelyn said. "We'll be having a gathering?"

"Don't see why," Killeen answered carefully.

"Battle plans!" a burly crewman exclaimed loudly.

"And what battle's that?" Killeen countered quietly.

"Why, 'gainst that mechplex," the man said. Several grunts of agreement came from the knot.

"You sure it's a mechplex?" Killeen asked mildly.

"What else's it?" a deckwoman demanded.

Killeen shrugged, eyeing them closely. They seemed worked up by the prospect of an attack, faces pinched and drawn. "We'll see."

"Can't be anythin' but human or mech," Jocelyn said, "and it's sure as hell not human."

"We'll attack no mechplex without getting its measure first," Killeen said.

"Surprise it!" the burly man said hoarsely. Killeen suspected the man had been drinking something beyond flavored water. Indeed, in several faces here there was a glow, a certain careless droop of lip and eye, that told him much. A clear violation of regs. But he reckoned that this was not the best moment to challenge them. Something more was going on and he needed to find out what.

"Coming at it from an empty sky—that's a surprise?" He chuckled.

"We killed the mechs aboard here!" the man countered.

"We had *real* surprise then. They weren't ready for an assault at liftoff. We had that one chance, sweep the ship clean, and we took it." Killeen shook his head. "Won't get that chance again."

This seemed to silence most of them; there had been restless mutterings around the circle for the last few moments. Killeen still could not see where these ideas had come from. For some time now he had watched the Family acquire the usual bad habits of an outdoor folk forced to live too long in cramped quarters: drinking, stimwires, gambling, random pointless quarrels.

Beyond those infractions, which he could deal with in the usual ways, there had gradually risen a harder problem. They regaled one another with gaudy tales of past battles, grand adventures bloated beyond recognition. Killeen himself could recall all too clearly those years spent on the run across Snowglade—his frequent chilling fear, the sickening indecision, the many scrambling retreats from humbling defeats. Now, as the tales had it, everyone (but usually most notably the narrator) had been valiant, savvy, quick, and steadfast, a dreaded scourge of mechs.

But there was something more than empty bravado here. He watched the snapping flames, smoke licking at his eyes with a sting he almost welcomed. The sooty tang brought forth innumerable memories of hard nights spent peering dejectedly into guttering campfires, fearing every odd sound that came ringing out of the darkness. The corncobs gave off a sweeter taste than the bite of woodsmoke, but the gathering pall did encase this nook in a comforting blue fog, a momentary signature of their mutual dependence.

He felt a restive mood building and kept his silence, letting it grow. Finally Jocelyn edgily broke the silence with, "Near as I 'member, Fanny said that we should never leave a mechplex at our back when we're advancin'."

Heads nodded all around the circle. Killeen sipped thick apricot nectar to cover his surprise. So it was Jocelyn talking up these ideas, harking back to the old Cap'n, Fanny. Though Fanny had been dead years now, cut down back on Snowglade by the Mantis, she still exerted a profound influence in the Family. Killeen himself had respected and loved her beyond saying. Innumerable times, during their long voyage, he had asked himself, *What would Fanny do now?* and the answer had guided him.

But this was different. Jocelyn was using Fanny's legend to sow trouble among the crew.

"She also said, don't take on enemies you don't need." Killeen looked deliberately around, locking eyes with each of the crew in turn. "And 'specially when they're bigger'n you."

Some murmuring agreement welcomed this. Jocelyn didn't look directly at Killeen, but said, "If we can't take a station, how'll we do with that whole damn planet?"

Killeen knew he had to be careful here. There was a tense expectation in the air, as if Jocelyn had summed up what they all felt. This was a Family talk, and she had kept it just beyond the strictures of ship discipline. He could cut off Jocelyn right now, show his anger, but that would leave unanswered questions, and irritations among the crew. He decided to not invoke his rank. Instead, he laughed.

Jocelyn had not expected that. His dry chuckle startled her.

Then he said with a halfsmile, "That's your killer-Aspect talkin' again, right?" He turned to the rest. "Jocelyn now, she's loaded in five new Aspect chips in just the last year. One's a Cap'n who specialized in leadin' charges 'gainst the mechs—just 'bout the only maneuver he knew, I'd guess, 'cause he sure didn't live long. That Aspect gives great advice, he does—only it's always the same."

Several around the circle smiled. Granted, the Family would never have survived this voyage without the Aspects' vast hoard of advice on the ancient human tech which had built the *Argo*. But their hovering presences perpetually yearned to be tapped more fully into their host's sensory net, to gobble hungrily of the very air and zest that life brought. Aspects could never be truly content. They came from many eras and their advice often conflicted. Occasionally one dominated its host's thinking. Letting an Aspect get out of control was humiliating.

Muscles bunched in Jocelyn's long jaw. "I speak for my*self*, not for some dusty Aspect," she spat out.

"Then you should avoid fights when you can." Killeen kept his voice wry and friendly.

She said sharply, "Like this one?"

So she had gotten the hint and still chose to make this public. Very well. "Now that you mention it . . ."

"Some of us think Family honor demands—"

"Honor's the first thing that falls on a battlefield," Killeen said dryly.

He immediately regretted having interrupted her, because Jocelyn's eyes narrowed angrily. "We should take that mechplex 'fore it attacks us."

"Our target's a world, not a tin box in space," Killeen said easily. He knew he would come out ahead if he let her lose her temper.

"With that in our hands, we can control what reaches the surface!" she said excitedly.

"And alert whatever's on the surface before we can land the *Argo*," he said.

"Well, Fanny would never—"

"Lieutenant Jocelyn, belay that Fanny stuff. *I'm* Cap'n now."

She looked startled. He had always thought that she was best at following a planned tactic. She fumbled when time came for fast footwork and a shift of attack. "Uh, aye-aye, but—"

"And I say we're going straight in. Got that? We'll skip the station."

"Damnall, that station'll give us—"

—Cap'n!—

The call came not from the circle but from Killeen's own belt. He was startled at the tinny voice that spoke from his waist: Shibo.

"Yeasay," he answered. Abruptly he lost interest in Jocelyn. Shibo seldom called on ship comm. For her to do so meant something important.

—The board— Shibo began, but Killeen cut the switch. He never allowed crew to overhear officers' messages unless he wanted to leak something deliberately.

He got up, nodded briskly at Jocelyn, and set off up the spiral to the control vault. He disliked leaving his dispute with Jocelyn hanging. He had blunted her momentum, but left a core of resistance in her still. And ambition, as well.

When he came through the hatch, Shibo was standing with uncharacteristic immobility, meditative: her arms wrapped around herself, thumbs hooked into her shiny black exskell ribs. Normally her hands would be moving restlessly over the boards, summoning forth the *Argo*'s energies and microminds.

"Cap'n, I have a problem. New kind, too." Her luminous eyes and chagrined mouth could not conceal her alarm.

"Is it the station?"

"In a way." Her exskell shifted like a cage of black bones, framing her gesture: something halfway between a shrug and a vexed wave of dismissal. "The board is frozen. I can't dictate trajectory anymore."

"Why not?"

"Some override command."

"From where?"

"Maybe 'From when?' is the right question."

"The Mantis?"

"Could be. It's taking us on a slightly different tack from planetary rendezvous."

"You can't countermand it?"

"No."

When Shibo admitted defeat he was sure she had struggled with the problem to her limits. He frowned. "Where are we going?"

"Toward that station. Against our will."

EIGHT

Deep bass moans ran the length of *Argo*, like the songs of great swollen beasts.

The dust outside hummed and rubbed against the lifezone bubbles as the ship decelerated. It was as though the thin flotsam of the Galactic Center, spiraling in toward the shrouded star ahead, played the *Argo* like a great taut instrument. Melodies of red lightning danced about the burnished bow.

Killeen watched the approach of the station. He stood with his back to the assembling crew and peered through the forward port. Their trajectory ahead was clear. *Argo* was coming down to fly parallel to the station's great circular plain, skimmed along it by unseen forces. Shibo could do nothing with *Argo*'s helm.

He allowed himself a smile of self-derision. His proud show of decisiveness had come to nothing. Jocelyn's cagey—and insubordinate—egging on of the crew, and her public disagreement, had angered him. She had taken advantage of the Family context to attack his piloting decisions. Now, ironically, her whetting of appetites for action served his purposes.

He had to rouse the crew for an assault that promised little success. They were going in against unknown opponents, across a mechtech terrain they had never seen the likes of before. Hard-learned Family tactics would mean nothing here—perhaps worse than nothing, for they might well be exactly the wrong thing to do.

The swelling disk below revealed its silvery intricacies as he watched. At their present speed, blunted somehow by the station as they approached, it would take over an hour to reach the central tower. If that was their destination, he had time to carry out the ruse he had planned. If not, there was a surprise squad set at a spot mechs would probably not anticipate.

Killeen wore his full ceremonial tunic of blue and gold over his gray coverall, and a full belt of tools and weapons beneath that.

He would waste no time changing if events interrupted the ceremony. Battle squads were poised at every small lock of the ship, ready to pour forth on signal. The remaining crew, gathered here, were for effect. Killeen had no way of knowing if whatever ran the station had already planted bugs on the hull, listeners powerful enough to pick up conversation. But he had to allow that this might be true, and use it against the enemy if he could.

Ahead, the scintillant, perfectly circular disk filled half the sky. Phosphorescent waves spiraled inward on the disk, their troughs brimming silver, their peaks moving rims of gold. The luminescence hovered like a fog over the actual metalwork of the disk. Arcs formed at the disk's rim, where they washed and fretted in random rivulets.

Somehow this chaos resolved itself into distinct waves which grew and glowed with each undulation, oozing inward to join a whirlpool that twisted with majestic deliberation toward the towering spike at the disk center. That bristly central axis harvested the inward-racing waves in a spray of rainbow glory as they hammered against its ribbed base.

Jutting above and below the disk, the light-encrusted central tower tapered away, many kilometers long. Web antennae bristled along it. One end of the tower poked into a vapor of forking flux that burned steadily, silent and ivory against the backdrop of a passing dustcloud. The other ended in a burnished stub.

The waves seemed to be drawing *Argo* down in a long, scalloping glide across the circular plain. Bulkheads crackled and the deck rippled in sluggish, muscular grace, like something roused from sleep. Killeen fretted about how much of such flexing the ship could take.

Shibo said to him quietly, so the gathering Family behind them could not hear, "Lie doggo?"

"A little longer. Looks like whatever's bringing us in is taking no other precautions."

"Maybe it thinks we're a mech ship?"

"Hope so." Killeen watched luminous discharges warp and merge in the plain beyond. He had the sensation of skating over a huge sea, and remembered the time he had spent in a place like this—the interior digital world of the Mantis, a great gray ocean of the mind.

"What now?" she prompted.

"We zag against their zig."

He turned when he sensed the room become still. Lieutenants

Cermo and Jocelyn had ranked and ordered the Family into lines precise and attentive.

This was the atmosphere he wanted, had carefully programmed. Here, he reflected, was all of humanity he would probably ever know again. The nearest brothers were back at Snowglade, an unfathomable distance behind. For all he knew, this small band might well be the only shred of their race that yet lived.

"Dad? Uh, Cap'n?"

He turned, startled, to find Toby at his elbow. "You're out of ranks, midshipman," he said severely.

"Yeah, but I gotta carry this damn thing, and it's 'cause a *you*." Toby twisted his neck uncomfortably at the cowling that wrapped around his shoulders, snug against his helmet ring.

"You'll carry your designated 'quipment into battle," Killeen said stiffly.

"This'll just slow me down!"

"It will give us a good view of all the action around and in front of you. Someone has to carry the area-survey eye." Killeen used the connective words *of* and *to*, which were absent in ordinary Family speech, to lend distance and Cap'nly reserve.

It failed to work with Toby. "*You* got me saddled with this, right?"

"Lieutenant Cermo chooses gear."

Toby sneered. "He knew just what you wanted."

"Cermo assigns jobs, picks the most able," Killeen said tightly. "I'm proud that he deemed my son capable of such an important job."

"Dad, I'll be a slow target with this rig on, crawlin' 'round down there. I'll get pushed back to the second skirmish line."

"Damn right. I'll want views from the second line, not the first."

"That's not fair! I want—"

"You'll get back in rank or else you won't set boot outside," Killeen said sharply.

Toby opened his mouth to protest and the Cap'n spat back, "*Now!*"

Toby shrugged elaborately and marched stiffly back to his position in the third left-flank squad. He stood beside Besen, the dark-eyed young woman; Killeen often saw them together these days. True, they served in the same squad, but that probably concealed more than it explained.

Killeen hoped the Family had not overheard them and thought

they were just bantering casually. Somehow, given his inability to conceal his emotions where his son was concerned, he doubted that. As if to confirm this, Besen cocked an eyebrow at Toby. Killeen realized that he and Toby must have been quite obvious to everyone in the large room.

He suppressed an irritated grimace and nodded curtly to Cermo. The inspection began. Killeen walked down the ranks, Lieutenants Cermo, Jocelyn, and Shibo at one pace behind. He scanned each crewmember closely. Faces well remembered, faces which had grown healthier with rest and better food. But also faces that had time to see that the old ways of Family fidelity and organization did not suit well the running of a true starship. Faces that doubtless hatched half-thought-through plans to better themselves by bending Family and crew discipline.

With the press of deadly necessity gone, the sprouts of individual ambition grew in fertile soil. Would they fare well in battle after such indolence? A host of tiny impressions collected in Killeen's mind. He would digest them later, during his solitary walks on the hull, to form the raw and instinctive material for furthering the efficiency of the ship—if they ever again flew the *Argo*. Yet the ritual was worthy in and of itself.

The Family had added thirty-two newborn on the voyage. Mothers tended the young at the rear of the domed assembly room. Killeen wondered if those children would ever stride the soil of the world far below, proud and free. Or, indeed, of any world at all.

It was time. Before the action to come, it would be best to remind them of who they were. He began to read the ancient Family Rites.

His Ling Aspect had provided the text from ancient times. The planet-bound Citadels of Snowglade had neglected the spacefaring rites. But here they fitted perfectly.

It was a code black and stern, full of duty and tradition and larded throughout with dire warnings of the punishment which would befall any Family member who transgressed it.

Many of the arcane passages made no sense to Killeen at all. He read one such without letting the slightest suggestion of a frown of incomprehension cross his brow. "No Family shall countertack or polyintegrate more than two separable genetic indices in any one birthing, using artificial means. Penalty for this is expulsion of both parents and child for the lifetime of the engendered child."

Now what did *polyintegrate* mean? And how could anyone tinker with the traits of his or her children-to-be? True, Killeen had heard whispered tales of ancient crafts like that. They were buried in the mists of mankind's origins in the Great Times. This passage indirectly vouched for the ancient origin of the Families, which was, he supposed, reassuring. The human vector had been set long ago, and its opposition to the mechs was a truth which emerged from time immemorial.

Something about the droning passages, saddled with legalisms and prickly with techterms, caught and held their attention. The Family stood stiffly with solemn, set faces. As Killeen launched into the long, rolling sentences detailing the depredations of the mechs, and the valiant efforts every Family member was expected to take to oppose them, they stirred. A boy in the front row, Loren, had eyes that seemed to fill his face. Tears welled in those eyes and trickled down, unnoticed by the boy. He had a faraway look, perhaps dreaming of classic battles and brave victories that were to be his.

In a sudden bitter gust Killeen wondered if these old, lofty sentiments would armor Loren against mech shots. He had seen more than one boy blown to red jelly—or worse, his mind sucked of self, the once-vivid eyes blank and empty.

This sudden lurch of emotion did not make him miss a syllable of the reciting. He went on to the finish, projecting the stern moral tones that were right and effective, even though within him doubts fought and sputtered.

Now for the added touch:

"In furtherance of these high aims I have a new name to bestow. Tradition grants Cap'ns the right to name a fresh-found star system. I have already seized this right. The blazing opportunity before us is Abraham's Star."

They cheered. Abraham's legend endured still.

"To the crew of a ship falls the time-honored right to name a discovered world. Your council has picked one hallowed and vibrant—New Bishop."

He finished and, following tradition, the Family shouted "Yeasay! Yeasay! Yeasay!" and broke into a raucous symphony of howls and calls. A few, thinking of the battle ahead, indulged in rude obscenities. Some were ingeniously impossible, describing acts of unlikely sexual passion between mechs of astounding geometries.

Killeen stepped back, his mind coolly distant from the effect he had sought. Humans could not press the attack without heightened adrenaline and hormone-driven zest. Mechs could simply switch on, but humans who would risk their lives needed a powerful cocktail lacing their veins.

Killeen realized now that in these last years he had come to think of the Cap'ncy as a welter of endless detail. To be a good shipman meant mastering the countless minute but important elements of lifezone regulation, of pressures and flows, of servos and engines. Only the memories of the Aspects had gotten him and his crew through the blizzard of petty mysteries that allowed life to survive this harshest of all realms.

But now he felt returning his older, original sense of what a Cap'n needed. Bold initiative, laced with sober calculation. Ingenuity and quickness. Moral and physical courage, both. Tactful handling of Family who were in ship's terms underlings, but in the full compass of life were the dearest people he would ever know.

Those were the crucial qualities. He only hoped he had some of them. So much depended on him, and he had only his memories of Fanny and of Abraham—whose wind-worn face swam before him now, split by a fatherly grin—to guide him.

His personal sensory net resounded with pinpricks. Timing was essential now, and he wanted the mech acoustic bugs—if any—to register human zest and celebration, and so be unprepared for what came next.

"Cap'n!" Cermo called.

As the Family dissolved into chattering knots, Killeen turned to Cermo and from the corner of his eye caught a hint of movement upon the immense perspectives outside.

They were moving swift and sure toward the central axis. Fresh energies surged on the intricate disk floor below them. It was as though the activity he glimpsed took place beneath a tossing ocean, and he could catch only a flickering of a vastly larger plan beneath the waves. Oblong forms shot swiftly among bulky pods. Machines whirled on rails, angularities moved like schools of darting fish—yet it all had the appearance of orderly labor, carried out beneath the surging bands of luminescence.

Bass notes rolled through the deck. Metal rang.

Something felt for purchase on the *Argo*'s outer skin.

Killeen switched to his shielded comm frequency and whispered the code: "Hoyea! Hoyea!"

He patched a line in from Shibo's control survey. It bloomed in his left eye, a view uphull from the lifezone bubbles. Against the *Argo*'s burned and nicked hull, those moist, filmy swellings seemed like abnormal growths run wild. From small slits in the opalescent bubbles came quick, darting figures. They shot downward, through the roiling waves of electroluminescence, and into the protecting grooves of the disk.

Killeen blinked twice and got a view looking forward. Long, tubular mechs had appeared from somewhere and were moving rapidly toward the airlocks of the *Argo*. He nodded to himself, seeing only the flexing forms that flew to meet them.

Good timing. They would be at the locks in a few moments, undoubtedly sent by the mechmind to take advantage of the momentary human rituals.

So the mechs in this station knew something of humans— enough, at least, to recognize them as enemies. That could be useful. Killeen had learned certain patterns of thought from the Mantis, oblique ways of viewing humanity. Mech ways were now more intelligible, though no less hateful.

These station mechs were probably following the orders of the Mantis, sent before the *Argo* lifted from Snowglade. Whatever the intention of the Mantis in sending *Argo* here, the Family was united on one point—they would destroy whatever agency tried to control them. They had smashed the small mechs aboard *Argo* immediately after liftoff. At the slightest sign of interference they would attack the station. Some thought the Mantis's plans may have been benign, but they were a minority.

Killeen stood amid the fading revelry of the Family, seeing and hearing nothing except the silent drama beyond the hull.

"Arm!" he whispered over comm. Ringing clicks answered him.

Slender, coiling forms now neared the main and side locks of the *Argo*. Killeen waited until the first made contact. It wriggled, forming a hoop around the lock door. Killeen saw small borers fork out, bite into *Argo*'s hull. The others had reached their locks, were settled—

"Fire!" Beside each lock the planted mines exploded. Each made a billowing blue-shot cloud that ripped through the mech bodies, shredding them.

Killeen allowed himself a smile. This first blow had gone well, but now there would be lives at risk with every turn of events. He became aware that the assembly room had grown silent, pensive, watching him. He blinked, dispelling the outside visions. Cermo stood at his elbow. He breathed in luxuriantly, pierced by the strange pulsing pleasure of being again, after so long, in the thick of action.

"Posts!" he shouted. "Form the star!"

NINE

Airless, silent, the metallic landscape rose against the distant mottled black like a gleaming promise of perfect order. Watching the view, Killeen thought it amusing that his job was to smash such smug geometric certainty, to bring living chaos.

He stood in the control vault, Shibo at his side. This was the first time he had commanded an intricate movement of the Family without actually being there, participating. Family Bishop had a long tradition of Cap'ns who fought and risked and died with their fellow Family. Now, operating from a true ship for the first time in long ages, that was impossible. Only from here could he monitor all the small teams who swarmed over the tower, seeking the mainmind.

The shifting scene on the main screen was a direct feed from the all-scanner on Toby's back. Killeen's eyes narrowed at each flicker of fresh movement on the disk plain, letting his own reflexes respond to the images. His hands tightened, unclasped, tightened again.

Shibo looked at Killeen shrewdly. "You told Cermo, pick Toby?"

"Naysay."

"Truly?" She seemed surprised.

"I 'spect Cermo chose Toby 'cause he's quick. Sure, some crew'll see this as pure favor. But if I overruled him, showed any interference for Toby . . ."

"I see."

"It's a tradeoff. This scanner slows you down, makes you easier to hit. But—"

"It gives you a chance to warn him if he's missing something."

His mouth twisted with irritation. "Naysay! I was going to say, it puts him in the second skirmish line."

"Which is safer."

"Course."

46

He turned to see Shibo's silent wry smile. He was about to bark a challenge at her when he paused, made himself step out of his Cap'n persona, and found himself making his "um-hmm" of grudging amusement. She understood him perfectly, and when they were alone was unwilling to let him get away with the Cap'n role completely. He was about to kiss her—which was easier for him than speaking—when the screen above shifted.

Toby was striding quickly across the disk plain, having trouble finding boot-grip. He was down in one of the myriad open-topped "streets" that crisscrossed the disk, for unfathomable purposes. The tower loomed directly overhead, larger than the eye could take in.

What had caught Killeen's attention was Toby's long leap out of the "street," which had protected him so far. He rose to the tower side, applied his magnetic coupler, and was drawn with a harsh clank to the studded tower wall.

Two other suited figures joined him. They raced along the wall, letting their boots seize and thrust. A thick-lipped opening appeared over the horizon of the tower's curve. The three dropped down it. Killeen saw that one was Besen, her white teeth the only feature visible inside her helmet amid the yellow sunlit glare.

A sizzling report echoed. Something spat microwave bursts at them from a side passage. Low-level mechs always imagined they could kill with mech weapons, never realizing that organic forms could shut out the electromagnetic spectrum and still function quite independently.

Killeen was glad he had sent them in with their inboard receivers completely dead, except for the link through Toby's all-scanner. Toby and Besen surged after the bulky mechs and blew neat holes in each.

The squad twisted deeply into the tower. They worked without crosstalk, giving the mechs no electromag-tag. A hard yellow glow beckoned down a narrow tunnel and Toby did not hesitate to plunge after it.

Killeen drew back, the lines of his face deepening, but he said nothing. Momentarily he turned to tracking the other squads, giving maneuvering orders.

The attack was going exceedingly well. The squads flanked and parried and thrust with agile verve. The mechs were inept and uncoordinated, once their initial plan failed. They probably planned to humble *Argo* with a show of force. These were guard forces, not fighters.

Well ordered, however. I suggest you be careful as the line progresses into the interior. A slow defense can nevertheless draw the swift, unthinking attacker into a trap.

This interjection from his Ling Aspect reminded Killeen to order the side squads to attack the comm lines they met. They responded quickly and severed several obvious lines. Killeen worried about the nonobvious ones. His Ling Aspect seized this opportunity to hold forth.

You display a tendency toward far too clipped and brief orders, I have noticed. The great ancient generals kept their heads, remember, and did not allow the disorder of battle to affect clarity. For example, a land general of far-ancient days, named Iron Wellington, was directing a grand battle called Waterloo when he saw a fire threaten to break his troops' line. He sent a note which read, "I see that fire has communicated from the haystack to the roof of the chateau. After they will have fallen in, occupy the ruined walls inside of the garden, particularly if it should be possible for the enemy to pass through the embers to the inside of the house." Graceful, accurate—and all written while on horseback under enemy fire, in the midst of a raging military crisis. That should be your aim.

Killeen grimaced, and his Arthur Aspect piped in:

I cannot but note that the message contains both a future subjunctive and a future perfect construction—remarkably difficult forms even in relaxed circumstances.

Arthur was a scientist and lightning calculator from the Late Arcology Era. He was precise, prissy, and invaluable. Killeen pushed away both Aspects. He watched as Toby's squad came coasting into a vast bowl lined with scintillant panels. Killeen recognized this from Aspect-pictures he had seen years before. An old-style trap using crossfiring lasers.

"Get out!" he sent on a tightbeam channel.

Toby heard him, veered left. Acceleration slammed perspectives into a squashed blur.

The screen gave quick glimpses of convoluted conduits, incised slabs of pale orange, tangles of wiring. Bolts snarled around them, ricocheting off curved metallic surfaces. Burnt-gold electrical overloads arced ahead of them along the side shafts.

"Mines," Killeen sent. "Seal up."

Though the fast-moving picture kept plunging down a wide tunnel, Killeen could hear the faint *snick* of Toby's suit closing all possible current-carrying leaks. Voltages lurked all around them, lying in wait for humans who could scarcely take a simultaneous unshielded Volt and Amp, so delicate were their interiors.

Killeen checked with several squads who had entered the tower. They were meeting the same clumsy defenses. The twisting warrens of dense circuitry made it hard to figure the location of the mainmind. No Family had ever entered such a place. Experience could not guide them.

Stranger still, there was obvious damage to some passages. A fight had raged here before. The cuts looked fresh, too. His Ling Aspect said:

Perhaps this explains the rudimentary resistance we are meeting.

"How?"

If someone else has taken this station, they might have left it with token forces.

"Some rival mechs?" Killeen knew mech cities sometimes fought one another, competition run amok. Maybe the Mantis's reception committee had been knocked off?

Perhaps. We may discover more at the mainmind.

Killeen watched the teams move on a 3D projection of the tower. Shibo entered fresh information as the teams reported in. Quickly, blocks of detail filled in the large blank spaces in the tower projection.

Killeen thought he saw a pattern in the snaking tunnels. The station's many corridors and shafts did not center on the disk plain. Instead, they necked toward a point high above that, in the northern end of the tower.

He sent orders to the teams to vector that way. Then he turned his attention back to Toby's scanner feed. It provided the most complete views, which the *Argo's* systems immediately integrated into the station 3D map.

Toby was plunging down a hexagonal shaft. Besen flew ahead of him. They both moved adroitly in the zero gravity, maneuvering with experience born of daily drill on the *Argo*.

Ahead was another squad, which had reached the nexus first. They were attaching inputs to a huge blank cube.

—Mainmind,— came a comm signal.

"Looks like."

—Wiring so can blow it, Cap'n.—

"Yeasay."

Toby landed on the bulwark cube, boots thumping. Killeen watched leads attached, holes bored with quick darting laser punches.

Mechs appeared nearby, obvious and awkward. They died in bursts of ruby phosphorescence. Killeen frowned. The mechs seemed unusually slow and stupid. Had they simply gotten un-used to human combatants?

A motion caught his eye. Indices showed a higher radiation count. . . . *even a slow defense can draw a swift, unthinking attacker into a trap* . . .

"Exit now!" he sent to Toby. Relayed, the order provoked a hurried finish to the mining.

"Leave the extra charges!" Killeen shouted.

—But they're primed,— Toby sent. —I gotta—

"Even better. Go!"

Something appeared at the far end of the shaft. It was big and moved quickly but Killeen's warning had gotten the squads clear. The approaching shape did not have a good angle to shoot.

The two squads raced away into an exit tunnel.

"Blow those extra charges," Killeen ordered.

—But they're just floating,— Toby answered. —Won't hurt the mainmind.—

"Do it!"

The answering percussive punch came rattling through the electromagnetic spectrum. A strange, descending wail cut across the noise. Killeen frowned. The dwindling shriek was like the cry of a dying animal. Mechs never gave such a sound.

The big thing must have been caught as it passed the mainmind. Killeen guessed that it was the controlling influence here. Only luck had let the squads escape. But there were still plenty of dangers.

Toby's relayed images showed them racing into a tunnel that led straight away from the mainmind.

"No," Killeen sent. "Take one that has turns. They'll have ambushes on the fast routes. And the turns will block the blast."

In eerie stretched silence he watched the seconds tick on. The screen darted and swerved and lurched as Toby made maximum speed in the zero gravity. The boy could windmill his arms and get his feet into position for a land-and-repel with perfect timing. The screen whirled as Toby tumbled in the closed, narrow spaces. This swept twirling spotlights over the mad rush of mechtech that came streaming up from darkness and vanished just as quickly.

At last they came to a long tunnel that showed starlight in a distant circle. Toby ram-accelerated toward it. The screen suddenly jerked.

"The mainmind's dead," Killeen said. "That was an electromagtag burst from it as it blew."

—Great!— Besen burst in.

Killeen tensed. Toby tumbled soundlessly in the yawning blackness. Ghostly arms reached out nearby, blue and flickering, searching for something to scorch. Further, Killeen knew, there were other presences called Inductances and Resistors and Capacities which played mysterious but perhaps fatal roles in these electrodynamic corridors. He had learned to use them, but their deep essences eluded the practical programs he had studied.

Toby veered. Three squads followed him in a quick dash for the opening.

Then the screen showed only swirling stars and the harsh yellow-white of the disk plain.

Toby spun and looked behind. From the tower opening came a crumpled form in a shiny suit, drifting with the still-dancing radiance that had almost reached the main party.

Killeen watched as the view approached the coasting body. He recognized the backpatch of Waugh, a woman originally of the Family Knight, now a Bishop. The form did not move.

It spun in stately revolution, as solemn and uncaring as a planet in its gyre. Toby approached carefully. Within the helmet was shadow.

Then Killeen noticed a small dark patch on Waugh's boot, a flaw perhaps struck by a near miss during the attack. It was a small hole, hardly deep enough to break the suit's vacuum seal. But it had allowed a voltage in and was rimmed by a burnished halo. Killeen saw that Waugh's helmet was slightly swollen and distended. He understood then why they could not see into it. Carbon black masked the faceplate. He was grateful for this small fact, because then he could not see inside, where Waugh's head had exploded.

TEN

The memory came back to him as he ate the celebratory dinner. Waugh, a good crewwoman he had not known well. She had paid the price for his decisions, and he would never know if somehow the cost could have been less.

Fortunately, her genetic material and eggs were preserved by *Argo*'s surgery. We must take measures to ensure that all Family can contribute to future generations' genetic diversity. I advise—

"Shut up!" Killeen muttered. His Arthur Aspect had no sense of time and place and decency and Killeen was not in a mood for his coolly analytical views. He glanced up from his serving of baked savory eggplant and saw that no one had noticed his exclamation, or else were too polite to show it. Ignoring outer manifestations of Aspect conversations was now considered good manners. *Argo*'s soft life was at least making the Family more refined.

He could not help reliving the battle, a habit he had picked up through the years on the run on Snowglade. The Family always held a Witnessing if a member was wounded or killed in an attack, and this time there had been Waugh and Leveerbrok, both brought down by electric weapons. So the Witnessing summoned up the mourning, and then the Family broke into smaller families and guests for a meal which put the dead behind them and made muted merriment over the victory. Killeen had seen many such, most celebrating nothing more than escaping another mech ambush or pursuit. It was pleasant to greet this meal as a Cap'n fresh from his first engagement, an intense action swiftly won.

"I sure hope next time you saddle somebody else with the scanner," Toby said, passing an aromatic zucchini casserole.

Killeen allowed himself a slight smile. "Cermo makes minor staffing decisions," he said curtly.

"Oh, come *on*, Dad," Toby said. "You're frappin' over."

"I'm what?"

"Frapping over," Besen explained, pronouncing the words carefully. "It means dodging."

"New lingo for young Turks?" Shibo asked.

Toby and Besen looked blank, but the second young guest, Midshipman Loren, said brightly, "Well, guess we sorta have our own way, y'know, talkin' things out."

"Turks?" Toby persisted.

"Old expression," Shibo said. "The Turks were an old Family who lived vibrantly."

This was news to Killeen, who had never heard the term either, but he did not show this. He was fairly sure that if the Turks had been a Family, it must have been long before human-kind came to Snowglade. Perhaps they had inhabited the Chandeliers, or even had come from ancient Earth. Shibo had made good use of the years of voyaging, communing often with her Aspects, learning much. Along with tech help, Aspects and even the lesser Faces prattled about their own lost times and traditions.

"Yeasay," Killeen said, "the Turks fought hard, ran swift." He saw Shibo give him a skeptical glance but kept on. "They never had a better day than the one you brought off, though."

"Yeasay, we blasted 'em," Loren said, eyes bright.

"Took those mechs clean," Toby agreed.

Besen nodded. "New kind mechs, too."

"You noticed," Shibo said approvingly, passing a platter of mustard-laced ship's biscuits.

Toby looked insulted. "Why, course we did. Think we can't remember, can't tell a navvy from a Snout?"

Besen said mildly, "Those were Snowglade mechs. Why should here have same mechs?"

Toby answered, "Mechs're ever'where, that's why."

Loren was taller than Toby but thinner, and this gave the steep planes of his face a look of studious care. "Who says?"

Toby snorted. "Family lore. Mechs're all over Galactic Center."

"Maybe they're adapted for each star," Loren said reasonably.

Toby had no answer to this, but Besen pursed her lips and observed, "Mechs could adapt faster on a planet, sure. It's life that has a hard time."

"Life?" Toby asked indignantly. "We can zig and zag faster'n *any* mech ever did."

"No," Besen said patiently, "I mean *real* adapting. Changing the body, stuff like that."

Killeen gave Shibo a veiled look of approval. For midshipmen they knew a lot more than he had at that age. "How were these mechs here?"

Toby snorted. "Slow as sundown."

Loren said more judiciously, "They seemed disorganized. Couldn't form up right."

"Dont think they were fighters," Besen said.

"They sure fought enough," Toby said. "I 'member *you* dodgin' plenty bolts."

Killeen leaned forward quizzically. "Besen, why you think they weren't fighters?"

She paused, aware that the Cap'n had been letting them pour forth their own ideas, and now suddenly feeling self-conscious. "Well . . . they had grapplers, screwjacks, poly-arms. Work 'quipment."

"They tried fryin' us," Toby pointed out.

Besen held her ground. "Those microwave disks were prob'ly comm gear, not weapons."

"How 'bout that thing almost caught us at the mainmind?" Toby pursued.

Besen paused reflectively. "I'm not sure."

Killeen watched her carefully. Whatever had been lurking near the mainmind had disintegrated when the cluster charges went off. The Family had found only meaningless fragments. There had been chunks of fleshy stuff, but mechs on Snowglade had often used compounds which mimicked the self-repairing chemistry of life.

Besen went on, "Don't think we'll savvy out the answer till we meet the mechs who made the station."

"C'mon, you're just inventin' boogeymen." Toby chuckled.

"I know navvy-class mechs when I see 'em," Besen said. "That's all we saw in the station. The higher-class mech was at the mainmind."

"You dunno that," Toby said. "We never got a good look."

"Stands to reason." Besen gave Toby an affectionate, bemused look. "Station was already damaged. Prob'ly some mech faction took it from another. We caught 'em before they could build up defenses again, I figure."

Killeen watched Toby wrestle with the idea. The boy was bright but he let his enthusiasm cloud his thinking—or replace it.

Toby began, "Even if it was a manager mech or somethin', we were faster."

"We got lucky, is all," Besen said.

"*Luck?*" Toby looked insulted. "We were quick!"

"If Cap'n hadn't made us drop everything and run, we'd be mechmeat."

Killeen was glad to see Besen not meekly following whatever Toby said. There was in the Family a regrettable tendency of adolescent females to accept their boyfriends' views of the world. The generations of sedentary life in the Citadels had somehow instilled that. The Long Retreat after the Citadel Bishop fell had seemed to erase this, but a scant few years aboard *Argo* now threatened to bring such customs back. He wanted his midship-women to give no ground to the usual swaggering male self-assurance, to develop their burgeoning ability to lead. In a battlefield crisis, such timidity could prove fatal.

Killeen shared the Family's traditional view that females usu-ally made the best Cap'ns. Conventional wisdom held that once women were through their adolescent-romantic phase, and had reared children, their abilities could again come to the fore, especially diplomacy and compromise. They could ripen as mates and execu-tive officers into Cap'ns. But the Family had no time now for such extended, subtle, and probably wasteful methods. He had to encourage independent thinking in everyone, and to hell with the ageold mating dance.

"I think the same," Killeen said.

Besen brightened. Toby looked surprised, though he quickly covered it by slurping at his cold potato soup. "But Waugh and Leveerbrok might disagree."

Besen's face darkened. Killeen instantly regretted being so blunt. He couldn't get the hang of handling young crew. "But you're right. I think they made mistakes."

Loren nodded soberly. "Didn't stop, didn't fix up their suits when they took hits."

"True," Shibo said emphatically. Killeen caught her veiled glance, which told him that she was coming to his rescue even though she saw what a clumsy lunk he was. "Got laser punctures into circuitry. Didn't slap-patch. Voltage found 'em."

Killeen was still unclear about the difference between Volts, the powerful spirits that inhabited mechs, and Amps, the mysteri-ous sense of quick flow that somehow aided the Volts to seek and move within the world of the machines. Volts embodied intent, and Amps were the runners who carried out those intentions, against the Ohms. He expected he never would fathom such lore.

He had heard the scientific explanation but couldn't keep it straight.

Instead, like all the Family, he treated the scientific underpinning of his world as a set of colorful spirits and personalities, elementary animations and wills which orchestrated events he could not see. Learning to use them meant boring study of the proper rituals—connecting leads, punching in numbers and commands, arranging wires and knobs and minute chips—which induced proper behavior in the entities who inhabited the interior of the *Argo*'s myriad complexity.

He sensed living motivations inside dead matter, but imagined that this came from humanity, animating the ancient human tech with fresh force. Mechtech, though, was inherently dead and beyond human understanding. It came from more recent and higher evolution of the galaxy, he knew, but he despised it for what it did to humanity—and for its indifference to the pain and anguish and inexpressible poignancy of what every human felt instinctively and mechs in their remorseless certainties so clearly could not.

"Yeasay," Killeen added. "The Volts hid in the shafts. Like mines; the mechs didn't have projectors themselves. Carelessness killed Waugh and Leveerbrok."

This pronouncement brought silence and stony, downcast glances to the table. Killeen bit his lip, wishing he could have made the point more smoothly. Better to get it over soon, though, before the experience faded. "So it went," he said cheerfully. "But you three—you were fast and sure and damnfine."

He raised a glass of alky-laced cider and they all followed suit. There was a traditional toast at every post-Witnessing dinner, and this seemed a good way to break the mood. They murmured assent and Killeen said, "Clean the table, too." They all cast puzzled glances at him.

"Didn't Family Knight have such a custom?" he asked Shibo.

"Eating all food?"

"After a Witnessing, yeasay. It shows confidence in the future, gathering energy for coming battles and victories."

Shibo shook her head. "Family Bishop big eaters anyway."

"Porkers," Toby put in timidly, "compared with Knights."

"Guess it got started in the bad years at Citadel Bishop," Killeen said. "I was small, barely 'member 'em. Ending the meal was the best—crunchy, salty."

Shibo arched an eyebrow at him. "What was?"

"The food? Crawlers. Insects."

They all looked shocked. Shibo said disbelievingly, "You ate?"

"Oh, yeasay. Times were when that was all we had."

"Ate *crawlers?*" Toby asked open-mouthed.

"Was fair—ate only ones that crawled onto our crops, tryin' eat our own food. Turnabout's fair, yeasay?"

To their continuing shocked looks he added, "Had 'em salted, crisped up over the Family fire. In big baskets, mixed in with whatever crop they were tryin' eat themselves."

Loren swallowed with difficulty and the others looked down at their plates. "Eat up, now," Killeen said, and could barely suppress his impulse to laugh.

Shibo's lips played with a smile and then took a solemn, thin line as she caught on. This bit of foolishness had gotten their minds off Waugh and Leveerbrok. Further, Killeen judged, the midshipcrew would all soon hear of how the Cap'n had eaten crawlers and been glad of it. It did no harm to have stories of the hard oldtimes circulating, and it helped build the tenuous communality that they would surely need.

Killeen finished the scraps of fleshy black eggplant and stringy beans on his plate. He said nothing as the others started up smalltalk again, for without his anticipating it, a dark mood had stolen over him.

He had enjoyed this meal in the company of his son and friends, but throughout it he had been unable to remain simply the father. He could not shuck off the role of Cap'n merely by shedding his tunic and emblem. Loren and Besen were Toby's friends but they were midshipcrew, too, and a good Cap'n had to seize every chance of training them. Comfortable though they had all gotten during the long voyage, there was no room for easeful life now.

The experience of watching his son dodge and dart through murky alien passages had filled Killeen with horror. He had suppressed it then, but now it all came out in a black and foul mood that fed on him even as the others resumed their bantering. They were speculating on what lengths Families might've gone to for gruesome victuals in the past—or themselves, in the future—and he knew they were trying to draw him out. But he could not get the images of the assault from his inner eye.

To these three midshipcrew, happily joshing one another, the action had been an exciting triumph. To Killeen it had conjured up memories of dozens of battles and all the anguish they brought.

The young had not yet learned that death was not a dramatic outcome of a heroic charge. Instead, it came with a sudden sound and a Family member nearby falling, already crisped or fried or spat by a projectile weapon. They were gone before they knew they'd been hit. And who got hit depended on a thousand factors you could never judge in advance: positions, terrain, speed, color of body armor, vagaries of mech movements and aim, endless details that shifted every moment. So death was random and meaningless—that was what you learned on the field. And all the Witnessing and ceremonial dinners could not erase that penetrating fact.

How had his father handled this knowledge? Abraham had never seemed bothered by the losses suffered on the raids he led out of the Citadel. Even the worst moments had not seemed to damp that wry spirit. Yet they must have. That was the difference between him and Abraham, Killeen thought. He had to struggle to keep up the facade of Cap'n. To Abraham there had not been any falsity. Abraham had been the real thing.

He saw he had been silent too long, and opened his mouth to rejoin the conversation. Before he could speak, Cermo's signifier beeped from his finger-coder. All at the table heard it and fell silent, knowing that Cermo, who was on watch, would not call unless it was important.

Killeen tapped his wrist. "Report?"

—Cap'n, there's something happenin' on the planet.— They all could hear the tension in Cermo's voice.

"Another shuttle coming up?" Already a shuttlecraft from the surface of the planet had arrived. The Family had easily overpowered the two mech pilots. The ship had been filled with machined parts.

—Nossir, it's—it's—you come see.—

"I'm on my way," Killeen said, getting up. Having to end a meal this way irritated him and he added, "You should sharpen your descriptive powers." The phrase had the right edge of old-style Cap'nly speech, and he felt a certain pleasure in that.

—Sorry, Cap'n.— Cermo's small voice was chagrined. —What it is . . . well, there's some *ring* around the planet. And it's gettin' brighter.—

Killeen felt a cold apprehension. "It's in orbit?"

—Nossir. Looks like it's . . . it's cuttin' through.—

"Through what?"

—Through the whole damn planet, sir.—

ELEVEN

At first Killeen did not believe that the image on the large screen could be real.

"You check for malfs?" he asked Cermo.

"Aye-aye, sir. I tried. . . ." The big man's forehead wrinkled. Cermo labored hard, but to him the complexity of the command boards was a treacherous maze. Shibo gently took over from him, her hands moving with rippling speed over the touch-actuated command pads.

After a long moment she said, "Everything checks. That thing's real."

Killeen did not want to believe in the glowing circle that passed in a great arc through free space and then buried a third of its circumference in the planet. Without understanding it he knew immediately that this was techwork on a scale he could never have imagined. If mechs did this here, they had blundered into a place of danger beyond his darkest fears.

"Magnify," he ordered curtly. He knew he had to treat this without showing alarm.

The hoop was three times larger than New Bishop. Its brilliant golden glow dimmed even the crisp glare of Abraham's Star. As the image swelled, Killeen expected to see detail emerge. But as the rim of New Bishop grew and flattened on the screen, the golden ring was no thicker than before, a hard scintillant line scratched across space.

Except where it struck the planet's surface. There a swirl of fitful radiance simmered. Killeen saw immediately that the sharp edges of the ring were cutting into the planet. New Bishop's thin blanket of air roiled and rushed about the ring's sharp edge.

"Max mag," he said tensely. "Hold on the foot, where it's touching."

No, not touching, he saw. Cutting.

The bluehot flashes that erupted at the footpoint spoke of vast catastrophe. Clouds of pitted brown boiled up. Tornadoes churned near each foot—thick rotating disks, rimmed by bruised clouds. At the vortex, violence sputtered in angry red jets.

Yet even at this magnification the golden hoop was still a precise, scintillating line. On this scale it seemed absolutely straight, the only rigid geometry in a maelstrom of dark storms and rushing energies.

Toby and Besen and Loren had followed them to the command vault and now stood against the wall. He felt their presence at his back.

"It's moving," Besen whispered, awed.

Killeen could barely make out the festering footpoint as it carved its way through a towering mountain range. Its knife-edge brilliance met a cliff of stone and seemed to simply slip through it. Puffs of gray smoke broke all along the cut. Winds sheared the smoke into strands. Then the hoop was slicing through the peak of a high snow-topped mountain, not slowing at all.

He peered carefully through the storm. Actual devastation was slight; the constant cloudy agitation and winds gave the impression of fevered movement, but the cause of it all proceeded forward with serene indifference to obstacles.

"Back off," he said.

Shibo made the screen pull away from the impossibly sharp line. The hoop pressed steadily in toward the center of New Bishop. No longer a perfect circle, it steadily flattened on the side that pushed inward.

"Lined up with pole," Shibo said. "Watch—I'll project it."

A graphic display appeared alongside the real image.

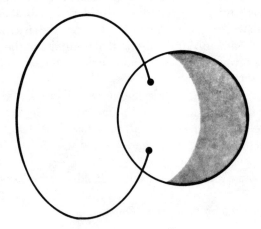

Cleaned of clouds, the planet's image shone brightly. The hoop's flat side was parallel to the axis of New Bishop's rotation.

"Not natural," Cermo said.

Killeen smothered the impulse to cackle with manic laughter. *Not natural! Why, whatever makes you say that, Lieutenant Cermo?*

Yet in a way his instincts warred with his intelligence. The hoop shared a planet's smooth curves, its size, its immense uncaring grace. Killeen struggled to conceive of it as something made by design. This was tech beyond imagining. Mechs, he knew, could carve and shape whole mountain ranges into their strange, crackling cities—but this . . .

"It's moving toward the poles," Shibo said, her voice a smooth lake that showed no ripples.

The hoop glowed brighter and flattened more and more as its inner edge approached the center of New Bishop. Killeen felt suspended, all his hopes and designs dashed to oblivion by this immense simple thing that sailed so blithely through a planet.

"Where . . . where'd it come from?"

Cermo bit his lip in frustration. "From *nowhere*, Cap'n, I swear. When I saw it first it was dim, just barely there."

"*Where?*"

"It was startin' in on cuttin' the air. Musta come from further out and just ran smack into New Bishop."

Killeen did not believe this for a moment. He scowled.

Shibo said, "It lit up on impact?"

Cermo nodded. "I'd seen it before if it was bright."

"So it's drawing its light from what it's doing to the planet," she deduced, her eyes distant. "That's why we didn't see it before."

Killeen wondered momentarily how she could remain so abstract while confronting events so huge. His own imagination was numbed. He struggled to retain some grip on events by digressing into detail. "How . . . how thick is it?"

Shibo's glance told him that she had noticed the same strange sharpness. "Smaller than the *Argo*, I'd judge," she said, her eyes narrowing.

"That small," Cermo said distantly, "but it's cutting through all that."

Shibo said, "Planet does not split."

Cermo nodded. "It's holdin' together. Some places you can see where the thing's cut through rock and left a scar. But the rock closes up behind it."

"Pressure seals scar again," Shibo agreed.

"It's no kind knife I ever saw," Killeen said, and instantly regretted making such an empty statement. In the face of a thing like this, the crew had to believe their Cap'n wasn't as dazed as they were. Doubtless, many had already seen the golden hoop from other parts of the ship. It might throw them into blind panic. Killeen's own impulse had been to get away from the thing as fast as possible. That might, indeed, be the smart thing to do. But they had come so far. . . .

Toby asked, "D'you think . . . maybe it's not like a knife at all. Could be some thing lives off planets? Eats 'em?"

The idea was both absurd and also not dismissable, Killeen thought. Reasonableness was no guide here.

"If it eats all that rock, howcome it's so thin?" he said with elaborate casualness. Besen laughed merrily and somehow the meaningless joke relaxed the small party.

"Why would mechs make it, then?" Toby persisted.

Killeen noted ruefully that no one considered for a moment the possibility that humans might have 'factured such a thing. The glittering, jewellike Chandeliers had been the peak of human endeavor, ages ago. The numbing simplicity of this glowing ring immediately spoke of an alien mind at work here, acting through majestic perspectives.

The mute indifference of this glowing thing was the final judgment against them all, Killeen thought. Their endless ruminations and longings had invested their destination with such weight, and now this silent slicing of their freshly named world ended all speculation. Fragile humanity could not live on such a vast canvas, the plaything of forces beyond fathoming. Their quest had ended in disaster even before they could set foot on the soil of their new paradise.

"Hey, maybe *Argo* can do somethin' 'bout that thing," Toby said eagerly.

Loren joined in. "Yeasay, ask the systems if they can cook up somethin' for that."

Killeen had to smile, though he did not take his eyes from the screen. A sixteen-year-old boy knew no constraints, could imagine no problem that he could not meet with the right measure of savvy and sheer boundless bursting energy. And who was he to say no?

"Try," he said to Shibo, gesturing with one hand.

She worked over the control pads for long moments, lines creasing her face in concentration. Finally she slapped the console and shook her head. "No memory. *Argo* doesn't recognize this thing."

Killeen summoned up all his Aspects. They were happy for even momentary attention but only one had any useful idea. This was Grey, a woman from the High Arcology Era. She was a somewhat truncated personality, suffering from sentence-constructing disability because of a transcription error a century before. She knew scientific and historical lore of her own and earlier times. Her voice was halting and cluttered with purring static, heavily accented with the dust of time.

> *I believe it . . . is what was called by theoreticians . . . a "cosmic string." They were known . . . in Chandelier Age . . . but only theory . . . hypothetical objects . . . I studied . . . these matters in . . . youth . . .*

"Looks real to me," Killeen muttered to himself.

> *We believed . . . they were . . . made at the very earliest moments . . . of . . . universe. You can envision . . . at that time . . . a cooling, expanding mass. It failed . . . to be perfectly symmetrical and uniform. Small fluctuations produced . . . defects in the vacuum state . . . states of certain elementary particles—*

What the hell's that mean? Killeen thought irritably. He was watching the hoop slowly cut through a slate-gray plain. Around him the control vault had fallen into numbed silence. His Arthur Aspect broke in:

> I believe matters could proceed better if I translated from Grey for you. She is having difficulty.

Killeen caught the waspish, haughty air the Aspect sometimes took on when it had been consulted too infrequently for its own tastes. He remembered his father saying to him once, *"Aspects smell better if you give 'em some air,"* and resolved to let them tap into his own visual and other sensory web more often, to stave off cabin fever. He murmured a subvocal phrase to entice the Aspect to go on.

> Think of ice freezing on the surface of a pond. As it forms there is not quite enough area, perhaps, and so small crinkles and overlaps appear. These ridges of denser ice mark

the boundary between regions which did manage to freeze out smoothly. All the errors, so to speak, are squeezed into a small perimeter. So it was with the early universe. These exotic relics are compacted folds in space, tangles of topology. They have mass, but they are held together primarily by tension. They are like cables woven of warped space-time itself.

"So what?"

Well, they are extraordinary objects, worthy of awe in their own right. Along their lengths, Grey tells me, there is no impediment to motion. This makes them superconductors! —so they respond strongly to magnetic fields. As well, if they are curved—like this one—they exert tidal forces on matter around them. Only over a short range, however—a few meters. I should imagine that this tidal stretching allows it to exert pressures against solid material and cut through it.

"Like a knife?"

Indeed—the best knife is the sharpest, and cosmic strings are thinner than a single atom. They can slide between molecular bonds.

"So it just slides right through everything," Killeen mused to himself.

Yes, but, well—think of what we witness here! A flaw in the continuity of the very laws that govern matter. Nature allows such transgressions small room, and the discontinuity derives a tension from its own wedged-in nature—a stress that communicates along its stretched axis. And so we can see this incomparably slim marvel, because it is bigger than a planet along its length.

"So why's this one cutting through New Bishop? It just fall in by accident?"

I sincerely doubt that such a valuable object would be simply wandering around. Certainly not at Galactic Center, where entities are sophisticated enough to understand their uses.

"Somebody's usin' it? For what?"

That I do not know.

Grey's wispy tones sifted over Arthur's:

I heard of astronomers . . . observed distant strings . . . but no record . . . of use. Were born . . . as relativistic objects . . . but slowed down . . . through collisions with . . . galaxies . . . finally came to rest . . . here . . . at Center . . .

When her voice faded Arthur said:

I would imagine handling such a mass is a severe technical difficulty. Since it is a perfect superconductor, holding it in a magnetic grip suggests itself. The sure proof of my view, then, would be fluctuating magnetic fields in the region near the outer part of the hoop.

Killeen recognized Arthur's usual pattern—explain, predict, then pretend haughty withdrawal until Killeen or somebody else could check the Aspect's prediction. He shrugged. The idea sounded crazy, but it was worth following up.

To Shibo he said, "Can *Argo* analyze the magnetic fields near that thing?"

Without answering, Shibo set up the problem. When she thought intensely, Shibo seldom spoke.

Toby stepped forward eagerly. "Magnetic fields! Sure, I shoulda thought. That magnetic creature, right? 'Member, back on Snowglade? It told us then—look for the *Argo*, it said. You think it's maybe followed us here, Dad?"

His Ling Aspect spat immediately:

This is a grave crisis you face. Do not let crew get out of hand or you will have even greater difficulty.

Killeen understood Toby's exuberance, but Ling was right: Discipline was discipline. "Midshipman, you'll kindly remain silent."

"Well, yessir, but—"

"What was that?"

"Uh . . . aye-aye, sir. But if it *is* the EM—"

"You'll stand at attention, mister, against the wall." Killeen saw that Besen and Loren were grinning at their mate's dressing-down, so he added, "All three of you—attention! Until I say otherwise."

He turned his back on them and Shibo was at his elbow. "*Argo*'s detectors report strong fields there. Changing fast, too."

"Um-hmm," Killeen murmured noncommittally. He outlined to Cermo and Shibo, and the eavesdropping midshipmen, what Arthur had conjectured. He resorted to simple pictures, describing magnetic fields as stretched bands that seized and pressed. Nothing more was needed; explanations of science were little better than incantations. None of them had a clear notion of how magnetic fields exerted forces on matter, the geometry of currents and potentials such a phenomenon required, or the arcane argot of cross vector products. Magnetic fields were unseen actors in a world unfathomable to humans, much as invisible winds had driven Snowglade's weather and ruffled their hair.

Cermo said slowly, "But . . . but what's it *for?*"

Killeen said tersely, "Keep a sharp eye." Cap'ns did not speculate.

"Maybe caused those gray, dead zones on the planet." Shibo pointed to the devastated polar regions, which the hoop was now approaching.

"Um-hmm," Killeen murmured noncommittally.

He felt instinctively that they should not fasten on one idea, but leave themselves open. If New Bishop was not a proper refuge for them, he wanted to be damn sure of that fact before launching them on another voyage to some random target in the sky. Now that he had a moment to recover, even this gargantuan glowing hoop had not completely crushed his hopes that they might scratch out an existence here.

"Why's it happening now?" Shibo mused.

"Just as we arrive?" Killeen read her thoughts. "Could be this is what the Mantis wanted us for."

"Hope not," Shibo said with a sardonic twist of her lips.

"We had plenty bad luck already," Cermo said.

Shibo studied the board. "I'm getting something else, too."

"Where?"

"Coming up from near the south pole. Fast signals."

"What kind?"

"Like a ship."

Killeen peered at the screen. The glorious squashed circle had cut slightly farther into the planet. It was still aligned with its flattened face parallel to the rotation. He estimated the inner edge would not reach the planet's axis for several more hours at least.

As it intruded farther, the hoop had to cut through more and more rock, which probably slowed its progress.

Shibo shifted the view, searching the southern polar region. A white dab of light was growing swiftly, coming toward them. It was a dim fleck compared with the brilliant cosmic string.

"Coming toward us," she said.

"Maybe cargo headed for the station, if they're still carrying out business as usual." He cut himself short; it did no good to speculate out loud. A crew liked a stony certainty in a Cap'n; he remembered how Cap'n Fanny had let the young lieutenants babble on with their ideas, never voicing her own and never committing herself to any of their speculations.

He turned to Cermo. "Sound general quarters. Take up positions to seize this craft wherever it comes in."

Cermo saluted smartly and was gone. He could just as easily have hailed the squads of the Family from the control vault, but preferred to go on foot. Killeen smiled at the man's relishing this chance to take action; he shared it. Pirating a mech transport was pure blithe amusement compared with impotently watching the hoop cut into the heart of their world.

The three midshipcrew left hurriedly, each taking a last glance at the screen where two mysteries of vastly different order hung, luminous and threatening.

TWELVE

Killeen glided silently around the sleek craft, admiring its elegant curves and economy of purpose. Its hull was a crisp ceramo-steel that blended seamlessly into bulging flank engines. The capture had been simple, flawless.

The squad that had seized it hovered near both large airlocks in the ship's side. They had waited here in the station's bay, and done nothing more than prevent six small robo mechs from hooking up power leads and command cables to the ship's external sockets. Without these, the craft floated inertly in the loading bay.

It was clearly a cargo drone. Killeen was relieved and a little disappointed. They faced no threat from this ship, but they would learn little from it, as well.

> It is of ancient design. I recall the mechs' using such craft when they transported materials to Snowglade. I believe I could summon up memories of how to operate them, including the difficulties of atmospheric reentry. They were admirably simple. People of times before mine often hijacked them for humanity's purposes.

Arthur's pedantic, precise voice continued as Killeen inspected the loading bay. Arthur pointed out standard mechtech. The Aspect was of more use here, where older, high-vacuum tech seemed to have changed little in the uncounted centuries since humanity had been driven from space altogether. On Snowglade the mechs had adapted faster than humans could follow, making the old Aspects nearly useless. Arthur's growing certainty about their surroundings in this station began to stir optimism in Killeen.

> Flitters! See there?

A squad member, exploring nearby in the station, had fumbled her way through a lock. A large panel drew aside, revealing a storehouse of sleek ships similar to the cargo drone they had just seized.

> These are quick little craft that can reach the surface with ease. I remember them well. We termed them Flitters because they move with darting ease in both atmosphere and deep space. Admirable for avoiding interception. That was before the Arcologies lost control of their orbital factories. Before the mech grip on Snowglade grew so tight.

Killeen ordered some fresh squads to inspect the storage bay and estimate the carrying capacity of the Flitters. The Family had explored only a fraction of the station, so it was no surprise that this storage-and-receiving bay had eluded them. Killeen had hoped such a place might turn up; the incoming vessel had simply pointed the way.

A signal came on comm from Shibo. —Something's happening with the hoop.—

Killeen quickly made his way through shafts and tunnels to the station's disk surface. He had to juggle his elation at finding shuttle ships which could take parties to the planet surface, against the unyielding fact that something vast was at work on New Bishop.

The vision that confronted him was mystifying. The hoop had nearly reached the polar axis, he saw. But it was not moving inward now. Instead, it seemed to turn as he watched. Its inward edge, razor-sharp and now ruler-straight, was cutting around the planet's axis of rotation. In a simulation provided by Shibo he saw the hoop spinning about its flattened edge.

STATION
•

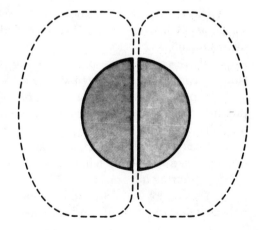

—It slowed its approach to the axis,— Shibo sent. —Then started revolving.—

"Looks like getting faster," Killeen said.

A pause. —Yeasay . . . the magnetic fields are stronger now, too.—

"Look, it's slicing around the axis."

—Like cutting the core from an apple.—

"Revolving . . ."

—Yeasay. Picking up speed.—

As he watched, the hoop revolved completely around the axis of New Bishop. The golden glow brightened further as if the thing was gaining energy.

"Pretty damn fast," Killeen said uselessly, wrestling to see what purpose such gigantic movements could have.

The simulation grew more detailed as Shibo's uncanny sympathy with *Argo*'s computers brought up more information.

He said quizzically, "That dashed line further out—"

—That's this station. We're clear of the string,— Shibo sent.

"More like a cosmic ring," he mused. *Wedding band,* he thought. *Getting married to a planet . . .* "It hitting anything?"

—Naysay. Nothing's orbiting near it.—

"Looks like somethin' in high polar orbits." He had picked up some of the jargon from his Aspects but still had trouble with two-dimensional pictures like this simulation.

—That's small stuff. Too far away to tell.—

"Much around the middle?"

—The equator? More small things. And a funny signal. Looks very large one moment, then a little later it reads as small.—

"Where?"

—Close in. Just skims above the atmosphere, looks like.—

"Sounds like mechtech. We've poked our hands into a beehive. Damn!"

—There's more. I've been scanning New Bishop. Picking up faint signals that seem human-signified.—

"People?" Killeen felt a spurt of elemental joy. A human presence in this strange enormity . . . "Great! Maybe we can still live here."

—I can't tell what the signals say. Might be suit comm amped way up. Like somebody talkin' to a crowd.—

"Try getting a fix on it."

—Yeasay, lover.— She added a playful laugh and he realized he was being too brusque and Cap'nly.

"You can get even in bed tonight."

—That an order?—

"You can give the orders."

—Even better.—

He laughed and turned back to the spectacle.

His mind skipped with agitated awe. It had been sheer bravado, he thought, to name this sun Abraham's Star. A tribute to his father, yes, and with a sudden wrenching sadness he wished desperately that he could again talk to Abraham. It seemed he had never had enough time to learn from his father, never enough to tap that unpretentious certainty that Abraham had worn like a second skin.

He recalled that weathered yet mirthful face, its casual broad smile and warm eyes. Abraham had known the value of simple times, of quiet days spent doing rough work with his hands, or just strolling through the ample green fields that ringed the Citadel.

But Abraham had not been born into a simple time, and so he had come to be a master of the canny arts humans needed. Killeen had absorbed from him the savvy to survive when they raided mech larders, but that was not what he remembered best. The wry, weary face, with its perpetual promise of love and help, the look that fathers gave their sons when they glimpsed a fraction of themselves in their heirs—that had stayed with Killeen through years of blood and fear that had washed away most of the Citadel's soft images. He could not recall his mother nearly as well, perhaps because she had died when he was quite young.

And what would Abraham say, now that his son had named a star for him that was a caldron of vast forces, beside which humanity was a mere fleck, a nuisance? Some promised land! Killeen grimaced.

The hoop had finished its first revolution and begun the second, hastening. Its inner edge did not lie exactly along New Bishop's axis but stood a tiny fraction out from it.

As Killeen watched, the cosmic ring finished its second passage, revolving with ever-gathering speed. The hoop seemed like a part in some colossal engine, spinning to unknown purpose. It glowed with a high, prickly sheen as fresh impulses shot through it—amber, frosted blue, burnt orange—all smearing and thinning into the rich, brimming honey gold.

—I'm picking up a whirring in the magnetic fields,— Shibo sent.

His Arthur Aspect immediately observed:

That is the inductive signal from the cosmic string's revolution. It is acting like a coil of wire in a giant motor.

"What *for?*" Killeen demanded, his throat tight. Without ever having set foot on it, he felt that New Bishop was *his*, the Family's, and not some plaything in a grotesquely gargantuan contraption. He called up his Grey Aspect.

> *I cannot . . . understand. Clearly it moves . . . to the beck . . . of some unseen hand . . . I have never heard . . . of mechs working on such a scale . . . nor of them using a cosmic string . . . To be sure . . . strings were supposed . . . in human theory . . . to be quite rare. They should move . . . at very near the speed of light. This one must have . . . collided with the many stars . . . and clouds . . . slowing it. Someone captured it . . . trapped with magnetic fields.*

Arthur broke in:

> A truly difficult task, of course, beyond the scope of things human—but not, in principle, impossible. It merely demands the manipulation of magnetic field gradients on a scale unknown—

"What's your point?" Killeen demanded. Though the Aspect talk streamed through his mind blindingly fast, he had no patience for the smug, arched-eyebrow tone of Arthur's little lectures. Equations fluttered in his left eye. They were leakage from Arthur; or maybe the Aspect thought much mumbo jumbo would impress him. Killeen grimaced. The Aspect had now assimilated Grey's memories and was working with them. Grey's dusty presence faded as Arthur continued crisply:

> Simply that the cosmic string is clearly employed here in some sort of civil-engineering sense. Shibo detects the strong inductive electromagnetic fields generated by its revolving, but surely this cannot be the purpose. No, it is a side effect.

"Why slice in when the cut seals up right away?"

> Indeed. A puzzle, surely. Still, I can admire this object for its beauty alone. Grey tells me that they ascribed the very formation of the galaxies, and even whole clusters of galaxies, to immense cosmic strings, at the very dawn of our

universe. Rings were once truly, cosmologically huge. Galaxies formed from the turbulence of their passing, like whorls behind a watercraft. As time waxed on, cosmic strings twisted on themselves, breaking where they intersected. Coiled strings did this repeatedly, proliferating into many lopped-off loops—such as this magnificent fossil, apparently.

"Look, what's that thing *doing?*"
Somewhat miffed, Arthur said coolly:

We will have to deduce its function from its form, obviously. Note that the absolutely straight inner edge of the hoop stops short of exactly lying along the planet's axis. This cannot be a mistake, not with engineers of this ability. Clearly this offset is intended.

The hoop revolved faster and faster. Through Shibo's comm line he could hear the distant *whump-whump-whump* of magnetic detectors in the control vault.
"Why line up along the poles?" Killeen persisted.

I would venture to suppose that this quick revolution evokes a pressure all around the polar axis. The faster the string revolves, the more smoothly distributed is this pressure. It slices free the rock close to the axis. This liberates the inner core cylinder it has carved away, frees it from the planetary mass farther out. The results of this I cannot see, however.

"Humph!" Killeen snorted in exasperation. "Let me know when you have an idea."

THIRTEEN

He returned to the labyrinth of corridors within the station's disk. Over comm he summoned two more squads to explore the Flitters. They met him at the bay and he gave instructions for trying to revive the craft. The Family might need to flee soon. How they could get past the revolving hoop to reach New Bishop, though, he had no idea. Maybe the cosmic string would go away. Maybe it would stop. All he could do was be sure the Family had the capability to move swiftly and then pray that some opportunity came from that.

Around him midshipmen and other crew hurried, searching for the right cables, calling raucously on the comm lines for input from the *Argo*'s ancient computer memory. Commandeering mechtech was always chancy, dangerous business.

Killeen saw that the first squad had breached the incoming Flitter's hold. They were prying forth crates. No time to see what these held; he ordered the space cleared in case they should need it. He was uncomfortably aware that they had taken the station at a particularly lucky moment. Some vast experiment was going on around New Bishop, and they had sneaked in while attention was focused on that. Whatever called the tune in this star system was distracted. But for how long?

Killeen fell to helping one work gang unload cargo. He enjoyed the heft of real labor, using his hands, and it cleared his mind for some unsettling questions.

Had the course settings of *Argo* somehow taken this cosmic string into account? He remembered that the Mantis, years ago, had conferred with the recently revived intelligences buried in *Argo*—human-programmed machine minds of undoubted loyalty to humankind. Had the Mantis set this course for *Argo*, knowing that they would arrive when the golden hoop was at work?

It seemed fantastic, so specific a prediction at such a range, like describing the clouds over a particular mountaintop five years hence—but not, he supposed, truly impossible. Such ability, if real, simply underlined again the unreachable heights of machine intelligence. Killeen accepted this without a second thought; he had never known a time when the predominance of mechminds was not obvious.

Killeen thrust speculations aside. Events rewarded the prepared, and he intended to act.

"Come on," he called to one of the newly arrived squads. "These ships—try figurin' them out." He led them toward the Flitter which had just arrived. The squad unloading it had been forced to rejack the ship into the power cables from the station in order to get the cargo-hold doors to open.

"Cap'n, put me in charge," Jocelyn said at his elbow. "I'll get this one up'n runnin'."

About her eyes there was a concentrated look of unbending discipline. She was one officer he could rely on to do a job on time and without error. Lean and fit, the *Argo* years had not softened her. She was trouble only when she got to talking with the others.

"Good," he said. "I want as many Flitters running as we can manage."

"Enough so can carry all the Family?" she asked.

"Yeasay." She had already guessed his intention. They were too exposed here. The station was some sort of shipping nexus in an economic scheme he could not imagine, but he knew that whatever truly ran the station would not long tolerate them. Their victory over the mech attendants had been exhilarating but too easy. The true governing intelligence was elsewhere.

As if to confirm this, Shibo broke in on comm. —I'm picking up another ship coming at us. Moving fast. It's a lot bigger, too.—

"Time to pay the piper," Killeen said, repeating a mysterious phrase his long-dead mother had used. The last musician had vanished from the Family a century ago.

Jocelyn had heard the comm on overlap circuit. "Think it's a boarding party, Cap'n?" she asked sharply.

"Um-hmm," Killeen said. He did not like being prompted by crew, especially when they were right.

"We can take them right here, when they come into the bay," she said.

He shook his head. "They won't be that dumb, whoever they are. Even ordinary defensive mechs, barely better than navvys, would see that."

"We can catch 'em as they come in over the disk," she persisted.

"*If* they come that way. Suppose they dock up at the end towers?"

"There?" She frowned. "We haven't got out there yet. Hadn't thought . . . But what'd be the point, puttin' a dock that far away?"

"Boardin' when there's trouble down here, that's why," Killeen said irritably. He disliked discussing tactics with crew, even officers, because they kept him from clearing his mind of all extraneous ideas. He needed to concentrate, decide on the best odds in the battle he knew was coming. There could be no other meaning to another, larger ship coming along the same trajectory that the Flitter had followed.

"Got that first craft up and running?" he asked.

"Uh—" Jocelyn touched her left temple and conferred with her squads over comm. "Yeasay, Cap'n. The other Flitters will take a while. Y'know—rev up, check out, things like that."

"But the first one?"

"It's ready."

"Good. Let's move it out from the station."

Jocelyn blinked, surprised. "Uh, why?"

Killeen gave her a mirthless smile. "Just do it."

"I don't—"

"*Do* it, Lieutenant."

"Yessir!"

Killeen made his way up through the open cargo hold of the Flitter just as the doors began to close behind him. He wanted to get a full view of the station, and this was a quick way. It would be a while—he checked with Shibo and got an exact figure, 1.68 hours—before the large craft could arrive.

He wanted to see what he could use for maneuver, what the station could do as a defensive fortification. The immense crackling energies that worked over the disk surface would presumably not hinder the humans as they moved and fired at the incoming antagonist, since they had not reacted to the *Argo* as it approached. But he could be sure of nothing.

IIe wormed his way through narrow dark passages and soon he was in the cramped control room, a geometrically precise cylinder densely rimmed with electronic gear.

Jocelyn was floating beside some complex mechtech. "I've just 'bout got it revved up, Cap'n," she began. Then something abruptly shifted. Killeen could feel ratcheting signals course through his own sensory net.

The Flitter moved under him.

"What—?"

Jocelyn's eyes widened. "I—I dunno. This ship's movin'—but I didn't start it."

Killeen sprang to the end of the long cylinder. It was transparent and showed the wide loading bay beyond . . . which was drifting silently away.

"We're pulling out."

Jocelyn cried, "But I didn't—"

"I know. Something else is."

The loading bay coasted away and he saw that they were backing out the entrance tube. The Flitter buzzed and clicked under them, finding its head.

Killeen switched to general comm. "Unjack all Flitters!"

Faint confirming replies came back.

"What's doing this?" Jocelyn asked, punching in commands on her wrist module. They had no effect.

"That big ship coming toward us. It's overriden our work."

"Maybe we can get out." Jocelyn tried to open the cargo-bay doors. No response.

"We're trapped," Killeen said. His mind raced through possibilities. Did the approaching ship know humans were inside here?

There must be an emergency exit from this craft, something manually activated. The design of the Flitter was strange, seeming to follow no pattern of bilateral symmetry even though the exterior features and hull did. He would have to explore it carefully and see what resources they could marshal.

Whatever was coming would probably unlock the Flitter to see what sort of vermin it had caught inside. He had a quick image of himself and Jocelyn being plucked forth and held up to the light by something immense and terrible.

Jocelyn gazed with a pale, stricken expression out the viewport. They were out of the bay now and the Flitter had made a powered turn. Now it accelerated steadily away from the station, which turned in luminous silvery glory below them.

Jocelyn gritted her teeth but did not give way to excitement. She was a good officer. Killeen knew she thought she should rightfully be Cap'n. Women had usually led the Family, and Jocelyn had been Cap'n Fanny's best lieutenant.

But her normally brisk voice shook slightly as she turned to him. "Why's . . . why's it want this Flitter?"

"We'll find out," Killeen said.

PART TWO

STARSWARMER

ONE

Clinking
clacking
jittering,
Quath strode the slashed land.

A final hill loomed between her and the Syphon. Quath articulated widely, legs grating, yawning—and surged over the apex.

A stone outcrop shattered against her underbelly and ground away with a brittle shriek. Quath tuned out the wail of tearing metal, even as she felt the alloy rip. A storage vat popped, the sulfuric mix gurgling out.

She peered ahead. There, blooming skyward in golden plumes, would grow the Syphon.

<Where are you, slit-eye?> came a burst in Nimfur'thon's sweet-sour tongue.

<Coming askew you, monopod,> Quath spat in reply, though hissing with warm friendship to take the sting from her jibe. To call anyone one-legged was a deep insult within the elaborate status-conventions. But the image of anything hopping about on one pod was also funny enough to be a joke among friends.

<You will stumble, prang yourself, and be late.>

<You told me you would be far from the Syphon. Yet I read you to be ahead of me.>

<Catch me!> Nimfur'thon sent.

<You are too close!>

<For you, maybe. Not for me.>

Quath rumbled on, edging closer to the place where the Syphon would come. Already clouds writhed red and tortured overhead. The golden carving line had already passed once within

79

view. Soon it would reappear, casting stark shadows. It could sear if Quath and Nimfur'thon got too close.

<The Tukar'ramin specifically *warned* us! Modes of the jet can snarl outward.>

When she and Nimfur'thon had boasted and challenged each other to come out here they had both been brave beyond question. Now Quath felt timid strains lacing her speech, fed from her subminds. Those were always cautious. They demanded incessant consultation. They made basso doubt and hesitation ride out beneath her carrier wave. She hated how these unwanted clues to her inner nature slipped through her filters, making her easy to read.

Nimfur'thon said confidently, <They are mere statistical fluctuations, low-limper friend. Feedback stabilization will catch the bulge and tuck it back into its mother sac.>

Quath stopped to measure her position, using fixes on two nearby peaks. No moons circled this world; for easy navigation, she sighted on the high station captured from the mechs by her brood. This glimmering spoil of warfare pleased Quath's subminds, a sign of their thundering success on this world. They had deftly gutted the mech-station superintendents, the Horde of Podia descending with complete surprise and zestful courage. Quath was proud to be part of such a daring thrust into an inner mech province.

Quath surged downhill—clanking, jingling, ringing—as her pods found footing on skittering stones. She arrowed on Nimfur'thon's peeping redness. Calmly, letting no color into her warble, she said, <Still, we *are* very close. . . .>

<Monopody, you are. Stop worrying!>

Quath's mind clogged for an instant as she sensed a servo whine hotly—*eeeeeeii*—in a forepod. She thought of the Tukar'ramin safely working in the Hive, beyond the brimming ridgeline. She and Nimfur'thon should be there, celebrating with the rest of the Hive's brood.

Quath had tramped these hills many days with Nimfur'thon as they labored together. They had struggled with the fluxtube cannisters. Nimfur'thon had splintered a pod bone when a bulkhead tipped over. She had been unable to walk without agony until Quath fetched an artificial replacement.

Nimfur'thon's new pod shaft worked better than her natural organic one, as usual. Quath envied Nimfur'thon the fresh pod, making her faster; she had no natural pods left at all. Nimfur'thon's long, prickly body gleamed with purpose, nearly all of it covered in metallic cowlings.

The Hive had seen cause to outfit both Quath and Nimfur'thon with the latest in advanced cybertech, whole subsystems of handsomely self-powered organs and limbs and antennae. They were honored to be so chosen, but that did not leach from them the free high spirits of the young.

<Has memory fled you, Quath? We swore to slip away and meet, to brave fierce energies and watch the plasma dance on the hills!>

<I—we have—>

<Your ossicles overload at this small flight?> Nimfur'thon sent in sharp chatter. In parallel she lifted a singsong, *I, we have! . . . I, we have!* on a sour sideband of her carrier, taunting.

<No, I—I—>

<A groveling ground-burrower you become, *Cicada*-Quath. Your thorax trumpets, but at the cusp moment—>

<Enough, cyst-sucker! I shall soon be upon you!>

Quath's bravado rang false. Like all her ground-burrowing race, she was terrified of heights. And even more of flying. Her subminds pealed their alarm. She mustered all her courage.

With a lurch Quath birthed a rosy egg of flame beneath her. She jetted up a granite-flecked cliff face. All through Nimfur'thon's chiding Quath had been planning, vectoring. Now, expending all her reserve in one spurt, Quath arced up the stony wall and—fuel guttering out in black fog, rockets choking down—she scrabbled at the boulders of the peak.

Clutched.

Teetered on the brink.

Fanned the blue air—

—and caught.

—*Jitjitjit-eeeee*—screamed a linkage, but Quath scrambled to safety, feeling the safety-warmth as her center of gravity slid into snug position above solid ground. Her hot fear changed to pride.

<Pay homage here!> Quath barked.

<How did you—? Ah, squeezed out your last dollop of fuel. Not wise.> Nimfur'thon was a squat disk on the plain below.

<*You* bray of wisdom? *You*, who jibed me into ambling here?>

Quath felt suddenly exposed on this high point. She spied sheets of phosphorescence hanging in the air—near, chillingly near.

Nimfur'thon's rippling signal now betrayed a thin thread of doubt.

<The Syphon forms,> Quath cried.

Yellow steam gouted from far hills. Mudworked buildings crescented that ridgeline, temporary housings for the fluxtube formers.

<Go down the reverse side, Quath. Away from the Syphon.>

Quath scrambled downslope, sending boulders clattering with her bumpers. <And you? We must hurry.>

<I will cross this plain. We will meet in that low rut, there>— Nimfur'thon squirted a vectored grid image—<and watch the Syphon.>

Quath gave a heaving grunt as she geared up in haste.

Nimfur'thon called boisterously, <We *deserve* a good gaze at it. This is our first, not like a vinegar-souled multipodder who is bored with it all. We have labored hard for these moments.>

Quath ignored these repeated justifications and focused on the skittering gang of rocks that herded before her, racing and leaping downhill. No moment to be buried in the embrace of pebbles, no. She skirted a ledge, made a grinding controlled slide—

<Quath—there are animals here!>

<Impossible. This area was burnt fine.>

<No, I have stirred them out with my pounding. They swarm from their pits.>

Quath turned and crosshaired Nimfur'thon on the plain. Dots jiggled about her graywhite disk. <Flyers. Birds.>

<No, Noughts. They are the worst. Pests, into everything.> Nimfur'thon fired flame into the dots. They blackened and tumbled.

<Are you sure they are not mechs?> Quath felt real fear. They had vanquished the main forces, but vagrant mechs still roamed the hills.

<No, nothing so dangerous. Still—so many!>

<Move on! We have mere moments!>

<No. I sense there are more pests here. What if they have gotten into the fluxtube formers? They could spoil the Syphon.>

<Forget them. Run!> Quath lurched at full gear down a narrow ravine.

<I can pick up their thrummings now,> Nimfur'thon cried. <There are many here. They stretch in long lines.>

<Seeking food. Grazers. But you must leave that exposed plain. *Now.*> Chuffing, clenching, she jounced down the steep cleft.

<We must call upon the Tukar'ramin. These pests could even be *inside* the fluxworks—>

<Then they shall soon be scoured *out*. Witless one!—We cannot call the Tukar'ramin. Forgotten, have you, that we are here without mandate?>

<Ah, *there*—I have flamed the last. If there be more—>

<Forget them!>

<You are right. I come.>

The sky crinkled. Golden wealth spun toward them.

<*Fly!* Time does not allow—>

<I am. I fire—>

The sky shattered.

Quath skidded to a stop, tucked in pods, and—*snick!*—clapped fast her ports and shields. Rushing air sang an ionized blue.

From beyond the low hills a golden wall advanced. The glowing line had passed to the north as its revolutions increased. The grand Cosmic Circle revolved faster, its beats making a blur. The spinup had formed a steady cutting pressure. Now the wall of gold moved outward from the pole, a nearly perfect cylinder that stood and pointed through the sky.

A nearby flux station sent forth its strumming magnetic whorls, which seized the passing distant string and flung it on its way. Thousands of similar stations all tugged and pushed the spindly, rushing line on its path around the planet's pole.

This tube of dancing light, the Syphon, bled color into the bruised sky, fed ripening pink to red to orange. Wind howled and clutched at Quath's rim, thin fingers to tip her over. Quath tuned frantically to the brood's channel, to call out. Instead she was flooded by the brood's view from the far ridgeline.

The fluxtube grew straight and true from the skirt of hills. It bit the ceiling of clouds, boiling them away in a purple flash. Dark mottlings shot up, up—in an instant heat had cleared the ivory clouds.

Now the black of vacuum appeared, a spot forming high above, a target coming into being as the arrow shot through it. Stars winked new.

The upper link was forged as the tube opened on the clean vacuum of space. Quath watched writhing amber and gray motes climb, her eyes smarting, awed. The brood sent forth a chorus of applause, popping and frizzing song.

Complete! came the Tukar'ramin's warm signal.

Now the Syphon hummed with new life deep in the rock. The tube walls kept back the pressing solid rock on all sides—except at the core. There immense pressures forced more metal into the tube with each revolution. Vast stresses fought along the tube walls. The strumming tube gnawed, burning a cylinder of stone free of its mother world. The top faced vacuum, while below liberated pressures pushed the freed rock upward.

Flowing is, the mellow, unhurried voice of the Tukar'ramin came—and the fluxtube suddenly filled.

Pearly, transparent walls of force dulled to gray. A plug of rock was streaming out.

Quath called, <Nimfur'thon!> in the roaring, pelting gale. The wind's pebbled teeth clattered on her skin. <Nimfur'thon!>

<Here. I landed, but am exposed.>

<Hold there!>

<Blinded, we are, my monopoddy. This grimy breeze—>

A rolling blast burst over the hills. The fluxtube brightened. The cylinder filled, gold to red to white.

<The core!>

—And out it spurted.

Their lance had now struck to the treasure of this world. The tube throat was artfully shaped, fattening slightly as the whitehot metal funneled up. The gusher of molten metal rushed from the vast core pressures into the void of space. Riches squirted up and out, fleeing the groaning weight.

Quath squinted. The fluxtube walls' glow hurt her many eyes. She submerged in the flood of the Tukar'ramin's view.

Delicate streamers of green and amber danced—precious metals, the only hoard this wretched world boasted. The Tukar'ramin's view tilted, following a black fleck of impurity up the glowing pipeline, starward, into sucking void, high beyond air's clutching.

There, flexing magnetic fields peeled away streamers, finding orbits for the molten pap. The yellowing, shuddering fluid, free of gravity's strangle, shot out into the chill. Returned to the spaces it once knew, the metal coldformed, mottled, its skin crusted brown with impurities. The birthing thread creaked and groaned in places as it unspooled. It fractured in spots, yet kept smoothly gliding along its gentle orbit.

Cooling, it grayed.

Graying, the threads wove.

<Quath! Something—>

Dazed, she fixed on Nimfur'thon. But the signal cut off.

She sent a burst to the Hive through a haze of noise. An answering tone came, and the brood view at once tilted back down the glowing strand of metal, veering into the slumped hills.

A hurricane wind had flushed clear the air. The eerie light of the core metal dappled the plain with shadows. But something wavered—

The tube. It twisted, hummed, curled into a helix, straightened again. Light surged the walls.

A bulge formed. Grew.

Quath watched the image, awash in it. The fattening fluxtube rippled. Flexed. And looped suddenly, faster than the eye could follow. Out, across the plain. Its metal soup escaped. A blinding white ball spilled over, splintering rocks, spreading.

The gray pancake of Nimfur'thon crouched in a shallow draw. Rock above her singed where the bubbling liquid touched. The tide hesitated and then lapped over, blackening, blackening, blackening everything.

<Nimfur'thon!>

Now the images came too fast to comprehend.

The legs jerking. A ripping scream. Footpads melting where they touched bubbling white. Nimfur'thon turning, her pods splintering. Skin popping open. Guts pouring out—to flame into brown smoke.

Nimfur'thon's walking pods melted slowly into the ooze. Her manipulating pods clutched frantically at the sky, as if to pull herself up.

Orange plumes cracked the upper bulkhead. Armpods beat at the flames in spasms. Yellow tongues ate. A bulkhead blew open. Gobbets spattered.

This was the way Quath would remember Nimfur'thon. The vision seared away all other memories. For what seemed a long time Quath could see nothing but this licking moment of death. Her opticals registered other inputs, but her mind rejected them. She stood frozen. Silent. She began to tremble.

TWO

The Syphon guttered out. Colossal magnetic knots crimped the flow. The glowing wall of pressure became again the lone cosmic string, its golden razor beauty hanging at the poles of the planet. A calm returned. Above, a dark tangle of coldhardened core metal orbited. Forms moved among this newly grown maze, polishing, cutting, making vast works.

The helical instability was diagnosed. There was indeed sign of Nought interference.

Labor parties crossed the plain toward the fluxworks. They carried Nimfur'thon's remains, sectioned, back to the Hive. Few spoke to Quath, not because they considered her shamed—inspection of Nimfur'thon's tracer log showed the risk was her own—but rather because they were busy restoring the fluxtube projectors, which had fused to slag.

As the teams labored, Quath sloughed back to the Hive. Her joints and seams ached from pinprick damage. Danni'vver, assistant in training to the Tukar'ramin, sent beeping questions during Quath's march, asking details of how the two had maneuvered so close, and—from supple dartings of phrases—sensed the cloud that now descended over Quath.

There followed a rest period which Quath tried to embrace. She failed. She felt in the warren walls the strumming of motion from other multipodia, who did not rest. She listened to the urgent, fever-shot data that would not let her sleep.

The looping instability was a setback, throwing off their schedule. Legions of their fellow strandsharers orbited far in space beyond the Cosmic Circle. They awaited the gouts of metal to begin their weave. The pace in the Hive must quicken, then. Finally she silenced her subminds' irksome voices. She fell into a slumber gratefully, legs folded close and tight in the slick webbing; for something dark pursed her.

Quath woke panting, pods tangled, the speckling of her tra-

cheae bulging red, yellow, red again in hasty rhythm. A buzzing
call for her echoed through the groined alcove. Quath answered
and found a summons from Danni'vver.

She dismounted anxiously. Her mind was a snarled maze. Her
hydraulics knotted and filled with a pressing ache.

Hastily she smeared a vomit drop on an acid spore. This eaten,
Quath hobbled forth, favoring one leg which had splintered a
knee. She limped through vaults astir with work. A pentapod
hailed, but otherwise she was ignored. This was nothing new, and
in fact was what Quath desired this day. The weight that had
descended upon her did not welcome company.

<You realize that you are blameful?> droned Danni'vver at
the entrance to the central chasm.

<Of necessity.>

<Your Ascension will be slowed.>

<Yes.>

<Addition of a manipulating arm, to render you>—Danni'vver
consulted her slate, rather than look directly at Quath—<pentapod,
will be delayed.>

<Yes.>

<It is good that you reconcile so easily. Some do not have that
ability, though they be myriapodia.>

<Yes.>

Danni'vver flicked open a port in her barnacled hide. Moistly
she studied Quath for a long moment and said, <Despite your
error, the Tukar'ramin will enter you.>

Quath felt the spaces within her suddenly burst. Fear flooded
out. Awe squeezed her spiracles shut until the air wheezed through
tight slits. Embarrassed, she was sure Danni'vver would notice.
The wall parted with a soft rumble that covered Quath's rasping
breath. Quath teetered forward on stiffening limbs. She knew she
would be seen for what she was.

Terror pins you.

The shimmering thought came as she gazed up, tilting to
register the height. A vast bulk moved in the webs. Moist beads
drifted in a tingling cloud. Massive arched stoneworks gave the
hushed air a pressing weight.

Quath began, <Abbess, I have abysmal sorrow—>

Do not attempt to state your inner self. I see.

Vibrant light played in the Tukar'ramin's body, which spanned
the upper chasm. Quath had never been alone with such an

august being. She struggled to take it all in. The bulbous presence bristled with uncountable legs.

She felt a probing. Fine wires laced through the muddy inside of her. She dully sensed a phantasm dancing, spinning—and then gone, evaporated.

It is not Nimfur'thon's death that infests you.

The words rang cold though they floated awash and welcoming in Tukar'ramin's warm sea.

<No. I fear some, some—>

Cease. The weight you carry must be lifted by degrees. Immersion in our Path will help.

<I *know* the Path.>

No myriapod can trace more than a branch or two of the Path, Quath'jutt'kkal'thon. Do not add arrogance to your burden.

<I—> The pressing fear welled up again and Quath sucked in breath to cry out.

I see it. Know it. But you must journey through that mossing.

<But I—>

The Factotum will show you the Chronicle to a depth you have not seen. Explore it. See the sweep of us. This will restore you.

Quath left, stumbling on numbed pods, spiracles sucking and bristling in agitation.

THREE

Within the Chronicle, time engulfed Quath.

The Factotum—a dry, fussy sort—had left her moored in a cloying mesh that reeked of use by many bipodia. This place was usually used for the elementary education of the very young, the slow-witted.

Quath could barely remember that phase. She had been totally natural, then, with no machine-augmented capacity. Weak, soft, dumb. She had memorized the Verities of the Chronicle, of course. Now it all felt useless to her. She had lost her faith.

So now she was back here. Among the smells of youth. Helmeted, pinpricked in all her senses.

And before her gaze the vast story opened.

She knew the outlines, had learned this lore without ever truly thinking about it. Images of antiquity flitted by. For the ancient multipodia life was uncaring, a sweet gambol. Even myriapodia lounged amid luxuriant sticky strands. They basked, pap-gorged.

Yet in time the race spread over the homeworld. The sciences and philosophies of those distant times were numbed by the pervading slackness.

The podia had not always been this way. In early drawings fierce, long-extinct animals took the pincer in their throats, struggled mightily, went still. Lazy though they had been, the ancients had cleared their world of such vermin.

Unchallenged, the race lounged. But their parent star had arced into the inner precincts of the Galactic Center. Mechs began to foray into the realm of the podia. The enormity of mech purpose became clear. Only by reproducing at a fevered pace could the podia match the mechs' expansive verve.

Their slit-eyed spirit revived. After that came scientific discoveries that made sense of all things.

What is your concern? The Factotum was ever alert, feeding Quath a torrent of data, all encoded in hormonal tangs and filigrees.

<I . . . I am here because the Tukar'ramin . . .>
You would like some educational facet of the Chronicle?
<Very well.>

Quath was in a vagrant mood. Her mind skittered on the surface of a teardrop that shimmered like a planet, surface tension tugging her to skate on its icy sheen. She braced herself as finely orchestrated scents began singing "Harnessing the Collapsed Stars."

The introduction quickly shuffled through conventional lore. Suns' deep fires inevitably ebbed. The nearly burntout stars imploded, their pyre a flash seen across the galaxy. The smaller ones left cores of pure neutrons. Spinning, their polar caps spitting out particles, they beamed frantic searchlights, pulsing steadily: galactic lighthouses. A useful source of energy.

Once the spinning slowed, podia could approach. Teams of strandsharers blocked the circling streams of particles, dammed the energy, silencing the pulsar, converting it to useful purposes.

They had found that mechs were drawn to pulsars, not only for their wealth of energy but for gargantuan scientific experiments. The purpose of these elaborate works, carried out above the poles of pulsars as they gushed electron-positron plasmas, remained unknown.

Mechs had stimulated suns to supernova throughout the zone surrounding Galactic Center—apparently, to generate pulsars. By laying traps for mech squadrons in near pulsars, the podia had enjoyed their first military successes.

Without warning, terrible fear welled up. Quath met it for the first time in the images swimming before her.

A nebula shimmered with the delicate pink of birthing stars. Nearer, a pulsar flickered, gravestone for a vanquished sun.

Across the thin sheet of light oozed a dustcloud, blotting the nebular face—a precise image of the death that awaited all the podia, all beings, everything.

Nimfur'thon—first singed brown and then blackening, her flesh crisp and brittle, cracking away.

Nimfur'thon was nothing now, gone. Quath felt sadness for her strandsharer, for the spirit that had quadded simply with her in the Hive warrens. But that sadness was the mere skin of the beast that slouched below, the thing that Quath could not voice to herself until this moment, as the dustlanes blotted the nebula's fair glimmering.

Dust. Darkness. All-swallowing death.

Quath felt a chill of dread, not for Nimfur'thon but for herself.

Quath pressed for the Factotum.

Yes? Your instruction is not complete—

<Forget that. I want the Chronicle again. Tell me about the Interlopers.>

The usual history was there, in abundance. How the ages-long war with the mechs began. How the race had seen the challenge. How the highest of all the podia, the Illuminates, understood what the landscape of science had implied: the holy cosmic view.

But not all agreed. Dissenters called the Interlopers opposed the Synthesis. Debate raged. Finally, all disagreement was banished, liberating the energies of the race. Then, knowing the truth, the race went on to—

Quath clicked off this standard stuff.

Yes?

<The Interlopers—their teachings? Those are not mentioned.>

That is not customarily requested.

<I do now request it.>

Was there a hesitation? *Well. I suppose . . .*

A gloss of more history. Dates, places, facts—planets and aeons, now all faded. Then, plunging on, Quath was suddenly in the midst of the Interloper vision, as quoted in their texts.

The death of the individual was a fact, they said, brute and unavoidable. There was no rebirth for each of the podia. There was *no* hidden message in science.

A resonant, silky voice sang from some ancient bower:

IT IS OUR STATION TO LIVE WITHIN LAWS THAT GIVE US BEING, BUT OFFER OF THEMSELVES NO PURPOSE OR PROMISE, NO TRIUMPH AS A SPECIES. THE UNIVERSE ALLOWS US A PLACE IN ITS SYSTEMATIC WORKINGS BUT ONLY CARES FOR THE SYSTEM ITSELF, NOT US.

Quath gasped, to see such things so baldly stated.

Yet she felt an answering dread inside herself, a swelling feeling of greeting. These ideas she too held. The crisping moment of Nim'furthon's death had brought these thoughts forth. They would not submerge again, ever. She listened further to the soft, confident voice that chanted its final truth:

EVEN THIS MANNER OF STATING THE TRUTH MISLEADS. THE WORLD OUTSIDE OURSELVES IS IN FACT INCAPABLE OF CARING. WE EXIST

AS RANDOM HAPPENINGS IN A WORLD WHICH IS ORDERLY
IN ITS LAWS, BUT WITHOUT ANY PLAN BEYOND
THE GRAVID WORKINGS OF DYNAMICS.

Quath recoiled, as though an eating strand had suddenly writhed and turned into a serpent.

Here it was, what she had feared. Now it was substantial and unmoving, a solid chunk of history. Other podia had seen the same vast chewing abyss. The world was a rotten, hollow thing. One touch and it split.

Quath's hearts pumped erratically; she could sense each thumping liquid surge through a different tube. Hormones showered her, rendering with tangs and savory threads the dry drumroll of history.

The heretics easily refuted the Synthesis by which Quath had lived. History, carved by a different knife, became unrecognizable. There was talk of religious mania induced by the merciless, unending mech war.

But the Synthesis was *not* religion, Quath argued to herself, it was a philosophical *discovery*. Religions had come and gone before. None had caused the podia to rise as one.

Unrelenting, the hormone-savored logic rolled on, over Quath's objections. The Illuminates had come into full being in that vastly ancient time. Their iron rule prevailed.

Images flared, one by one: spindly podia smashing nests, cutting strands. Disbelievers gutted, wailing, and left hanging to shrivel under strange suns.

The Synthesis spoke of rational podia seeking the light, Quath heard. But she could not quell her own thoughts. Did *this* look like the labors of logic? How could the Synthesis be so sure of its assumptions?

She abruptly yanked away. The Factotum must have been watching closely. *You leave?*

Angrily, Quath spat, <Yes, yes. So?>

It is not done. No benefit accrues from— and the Factotum launched into a hoary, cobwebbed oration.

<Surely, Factotum, surely,> she interrupted. <I am disturbed by the heretical lies, that is all. Forget what I said.>

Quath realized that the Factotum would take the words literally and erase the conversation. Perhaps that was just as well. The poor creature could not deal with these questions.

Perhaps, Quath told herself grimly, no podia could.

Then why was she so burdened?

FOUR

Bəq'qdahl clacked by, moving rapidly and well.

<Confluence will begin soon,> she called.

<What?> Quath, distracted by a robot resetting the sleeve of her injured leg, glanced up.

<The confluence for Nimfur'thon, slit-eye.>

Beq'qdahl canted her forelegs back with easy grace, her thorax colors and fuzzed eyes rippling with wry humor. Eyelet hairs dilated outward in waves to signify strandsharer fellowship. She added, <You have not forgotten already, I hope?>

Quath burned with embarrassment. Whenever she thought of Nimfur'thon the persistent nightmare flooded all other memories. <Of course not. Some mourn in private.>

<A point. I will see you then.>

Quath decided to cover her confusion with a sly dig: <I have not noticed much public mourning, however.>

Beq'qdahl caught the hint in the words. <Meaning we all should do what you do not?> She pursed her anal cavity to show her remark carried sting.

<At least I haven't been striving to transfer into orbital weaving.>

<So you haven't. A good idea not to. You are inexperienced.>

<Your eyes grow drool-dimmed,> Quath said sharply. <You mistake this crippled leg shell. I carry four pods, as you.>

<And have done so longer, I'm sure you will soon add.>

<The thought does leap to the lobes.>

<Very well.> Beq'qdahl settled into knee-cock, *raak, raak*. <You think I overclimb?>

<You came here a quad. I spanned less area than you, it is true, but I did have four legs. I still do. We all aspire to do orbital weaving, of course, but your arrogant attitude—>

<You are a grub indeed. My ambition is to replace the Tukar'ramin herself.>

Quath smoothed her eyelet hairs and oozed red pap through them to show lacings of anger barely held in check. <Incredible!>

<Not so. I am not a ground-hugger like you.>

Quath flared. Her fear of heights and of flying was a barb in her flesh. <You fever-dream. Next you will say you intend to become an Illuminate.>

Beq'qdahl was surprised. <Dung-speaker! Be careful. The Illuminates transcend us utterly. Someone may overhear.>

<They came from such as us,> Quath said.

<But are far augmented beyond our realm.>

<No one is beyond question.>

<True, but it is smart to pretend otherwise.>

Quath spat back, <I want the truth, whatever it is. I will pretend nothing.>

A pause. <Does something vex you? You speak brave words but your cilia, your thorax spectrum—they say otherwise.>

Disquiet darted through Quath. Could Beq'qdahl read what she truly felt? Did Beq'qdahl know her doubts? Exposure could ruin Quath's future.

Quath started to compose a crushing remark and then thought better of it. <My thoughts are my own.>

<Very well. I hope your precious selfhood remains composed, even after I am promoted above you.> Beq'qdahl clattered her ossicles in jeering symphony, excreting bile juice from their seams, flooding the tunnel with an acrid smoke.

<If we be rivals, let there be no pretending otherwise!> She exited, clanking a rear waste port.

Quath brushed away a ratlike service robot which was polishing its handiwork, Quath's new pod. Beq'qdahl was a competitor, of that one could be sure. For a passing moment Quath had wanted to unburden herself to Beq'qdahl. That would have been an error. No one could help. But still . . . if she could find even a gesture, a word . . .

Stamping heavily out of the tunnel to try the fixed pod, ringing and clacking, she noticed a reference output in the ceramic wall. Something nagged at her, something from the simmering anxiety within. She punched for General Information, gave indices, and scanned the flowing text:

THE SYNTHESIS: (1) REALIZATION THAT A CONTINUITY EXISTS BETWEEN INERT MATTER, THROUGH THE GRAND DESIGN OF THE EARLY UNIVERSE, AND INTELLIGENT LIFE TODAY.

NOW ACCEPTED BY ALL, THIS COSMIC PERSPECTIVE MAY
BE SEEN AS A CULMINATION OF ALL THE ANCIENT RELI-
GIONS, THOUGH OF COURSE IT IS ERECTED ON A FIRM
FOUNDATION OF SCIENTIFIC . . .

Continuity. That meant things went on. Stated so baldly, in
austere and objective lines, the phrases had a certain power.

A tiny crevice, but Quath took shelter there.

FIVE

The podia assembled for the confluence in a cavern deep in the Hive burrows. They had carved it when first arriving here, even while they ripped and scoured whole mech legions. This cavern recalled their ancient origins. Watery images of the mingling, chattering podia reflected from the steepled, glossy walls. Scrabbling pupa had polished the rude stone while they mewled and played.

Danni'vver appeared at the entrance of the confluence portal. She issued the ritual call, syllables booming down from the arched ceiling.

For this occasion none wore the gray, rough work sheaths of laborers. Instead, there were ample ballooned legments. Some sported rosy crescents of flapping headdress. Fuzzed cilia rippled. Rainbow washes of sweet-scented pus set off artfully inflamed eyelets. Teased tracheae plumes and carapaces of steel-blue sheen exalted their wearers. Some played with pearly castanets of animal bone jangling from each legjoint. Old myriapodia showed fresh encrustations of mica or baked pumice.

Those recently promoted found opportunities to display the gleaming leg they had earned, polished and bright amid the tangle of their tarnished pods. Others flaunted ringing, coppery antennae. Or huge ebony tusks. New quartz lenseyes oozed spectra like jewels in oil. Those recently augmented with artificial digestive tracts sported swollen bladders which throbbed with recently pulped food.

The tardy podia swarmed up the laddered strands and into the confluence hole. As they creaked into knee-cock, Nimfur'thon's image formed above them. The traditional invocation began. A resounding voice thanked the laborers for quitting their tasks, to come and honor a fallen strandsharer. Quath paid close attention though some nearby buzzed with gossip. Then—incredibly!—the Tukar'ramin appeared on high far above Nimfur'thon.

Everyone gaped. Never had the Tukar'ramin deigned to come before them all. <What! Why?> someone blurted.

Seeming not to notice the shock she had caused, the Tukar'ramin filled the huge chamber with her resonant voice. She intoned the Verities. Quath listened intently as the ancient story unfolded, trying to pry fresh meaning from it.

The litany was, of course, quite true and grand. It told how perturbations clumped balls of spinning gas, which in time flattened into galaxies. The collapsing cores of young galaxies then flared hot: quasars. Those death throes were burning beacons across an abyss so vast that distance dimmed them to pinpricks of radiance. Yet the podia had deduced that at their center lurked immense black holes of a billion stellar masses or more, holding in a vast grip the surrounding roiling dust.

So it was in all galaxies, down to our very own. *The black holes spin and suck, spin and suck,* the Tukar'ramin said.

So the grip of matter's evolution went on. Accretion disks swirled about the black holes. Tidal forces ground stars to dust. Inductive electrodynamic fields drove great swarms of particles out from these disks, like geysers. Only in the benign outer districts of a galaxy are there mild conditions for the origin of organic life.

Thus do we glimpse across the refracting curvature of the universe itself only the pyres of huge ancient catastrophes. The burning of matter itself. The graves of suns. The Tukar'ramin made the spectacle unfold before them. Galaxies churned and flared and died across the walls of the chasm.

Yet this was only the opening act in a grand drama. In the quiet, unseen, wheeling disks of ordinary galaxies, the Verity went onward. Stars baked heavy elements. Carbon wedded to oxygen, phosphorus, nitrogen, hydrogen. They thrived. Planets spun. Life struggled up.

Opposing this flowering of natural workings were the mechs. They pitted themselves in vicious, eternal war with sovereign life.

Quath became drowsy. Many legs rustled impatiently. Multipodia nearby sent covert chatter on their private bandwidths. The Tukar'ramin surely overheard them, but still droned on. The familiar litany:

Noughts. Life that was Nought mastered the energy resources of a world. These were simple, unsophisticated races. The first stage. Divine evolution decreed that Noughts must leave the stage. Their lands became grist for the next stage.

Primes. Life coming to Prime converted whole stars to useful purpose: the second level. Their works could be seen across the galactic arms, those chasms of dark and confusion. Such races wrote their names large on the open slate of dumb, blank matter.

The podia were surely Primes now—this much they had risen. They knew their purpose.

Starswarmers. This was the podia's goal. Starswarmers mastered the colossal energy sources of the galaxy itself.

Such a torrent, used to signal across the gulf between galaxies, could send word of the podia to the entire universe. This was their destiny: Starswarmers.

If the podia could master the energy of the center of their own comparatively mild and inconsequential galaxy, they could yet play a role on the largest of all stages, the singing communications between the great lakes of stars. Thus could they harvest the lore of ancient times and share the gathering destiny of other Starswarmers.

The Summation, the merging of all that was best in the universe, would follow.

The Tukar'ramin followed the ageold text, as handed down by the Illuminates:

*—all strandsharers, near and far, flat and thin, sorbed and laced. *All* shall lick of it in company. That supreme moment shall surely come, when mind dominates matter at last and turns it to the purposes of the Swarmers. The race to entropy death shall be halted. Mind will rule. As the atoms of our bones and metals were cooked in the first stars, so shall we return to oneness with the universe and . . .*

Something coiled inside Quath. In the spiral arms flaring with crisp orange supernovas she saw not stars coming out of nothing, but instead black dust eating all, a relentless tide of filth that swamped the ember ruby suns—

<But what of *us*?>

Her voice shattered the Verities. The confluence ceremony fell into shocked silence. Quath discovered she had risen from kneecock to full stature.

You have a question? That is proper, my strandsharer.

But no one ever asked questions in confluence, ever, and everyone knew it.

<Why do you say we will be rejoined in the Summation?>

All life will find rebirth.

<Where will we be hiding in the meantime?>

In waiting.

<Will we know it?>

In a sense.

<Even though we're dead? Like Nimfur'thon?>

It will be like sleeping time.

Above, the Tukar'ramin loomed vast and glistening, anchored to gossamer strands. Quath heard a muttering of discontent around her. But she pressed on:

<All of us there, together?>

Information does not ever truly vanish in the universe, if we can elude entropy's gnawing jaws. That is our aim.

<But we haven't! We are only *beginning* to be Starswarmers.>

Quath'jutt'kkal'thon . . . Using Quath's full name, the Tukar'ramin lowered a probiscus encrusted with fertile sensors, peering. Her cilia rippled with concern. *It is better to think of the Summation as something far larger than yourself. For such it is.*

<Of course, I know, but—>

*We live on in the sense that our works live. What we *are* lives. Our vector sum abides in the universe forever.*

<But are we *conscious* of it?>

That, I think, is unknown.

<But it's the whole point!>

I do not believe so.

This reduction of the center of the matter to, to an *opinion,* stunned Quath. Without this peg the edifice collapsed.

<Will the Illuminates survive forever?>

That is not given to us to know.

Several of the elderly myriapodia sent discreet low-frequency signals to Quath, urging an end. Other podia murmured and rustled.

Remember, it is the essence of us which propagates.

More homilies. Quath felt a sudden rush of embarrassment at being so exposed. They all mutely accepted, all of them. They kept silent. Which meant that none truly believed. Only stupid, blind Quath still questioned.

This has proved to be a blossoming exchange. Are your quandaries resolved?

<I . . . yes.>

I suspect you are more disturbed by Nimfur'thon's passing than the rest of us. Know that we understand.

<I . . . I know.> To cover her fear and confusion she retreated

into the ritual of <I give thanks.> Quath returned to knee-cock, *raak, raak.*

Podia nearby pinched their cilia in disapproval. Beq'qdahl openly jibed.

The *unfalum,* their shared holy food, passed from pincer to pincer. Quath took a strand numbly, engorged it, and began to pull the sticky wad into strings. The manipulae inside her mouth tugged the sweet filaments and spread them into sheets, expanding the surface area. Fine-boned manipulae pressed these against tasting buds, to heighten the sense. Quath sat and worked her mouth, as did the others.

Why was she alone burdened with these doubts? Quath wondered. Yet she could not give them up.

The confluence ended with singing and smacking noises as they devoured the last of the *unfalum.* Quath made a show of clenching her thorax, but no matter how thinly she pressed the *unfalum,* somehow Quath could not swallow, could not truly eat of the essence of their shared vision.

SIX

That evening she podded away from the Hive, which floated shadowlike above a wrecked dry plain. She wandered among the hills north of the Syphon. Tomorrow she would return to the ferment of work, but now something drew her out of the secure warrens.

The land trembled as though this planet were breathing. If so, Quath thought in her distraction, the world would begin to gasp its last quite soon enough. Inexplicably, the image disturbed her.

A roof of clouds drifted overhead, bellies bulging blue with rain. A wan glow from the setting sun drenched the landscape in lazy oranges and reds. Quath shifted to transopticals and saw the Cosmic Circle in orbit, inert and dull without the prodding of the podia's magnetic fields.

She longed to labor up there, to help fling the incredible sharpness of the Circle into the breast of this dying mudball. *That* was glory, honor, destiny.

The Circle was the most precious of her race's natural resources. The names of the podia who had found and captured the Circle would ring down through history forever. Possession of the Circle gave the podia the key to slitting the throats of whole worlds. They had used it against the mechs who opposed their move into Galactic Center.

It could be hurled against mech craft at immense speed. After it had chopped ships, there was a way to make it suddenly radiate enormous bursts of electromagnetic radiation, frying all unprotected mechs within an entire solar system. The Circle Masters were benefactors and warriors beyond all comparison in the history of the podia. Quath was proud to tread the ruptured ground beneath their handiwork.

On this rumpled plain mech ruins clogged the ravines. Smashed mech factories gaped like rotted teeth. Mech carcasses still smoked from past battles. Podia had stripped others of useful parts so that

101

only the shell remained. Quath swelled with pride at the devastation her kind had wrought.

Even this lightly defended world had demanded the best of the podia. They had fallen upon it while the local mechs were beset by internal struggles. The Illuminates had detected signs of exceptionally vicious mech intercity competition. Those wise beings had then ordered the Hives to descend. Once enough of the surface was secured for construction of the magnetic clamping stations, the Cosmic Circle had been brought into play. Their victory here opened the possibility of penetrating into the mech fortress stars even closer to the tantalizing core of the whirlpool galaxy.

A herd of grazing animals caught sight of Quath and scattered, pell-mell. Even for animals, they seemed stupid and graceless. To think Nimfur'thon had hesitated a precious time too long, out of concern over such base creatures! This was a crude planet, incapable of hatching more than Noughts in its scum of sea and sky.

Some scattered Noughts—mere planet-bound creatures, with crude devices—remained here. Only after the mech defeat had the podia even noticed them. Disemboweling their world would finish such trivial beings.

Yet some podia still fell to their assaults. Even such minor creatures could hurl podia into the blackness that Quath now knew to be everywhere, behind each apparently solid object.

As it had swallowed Nimfur'thon, so it would, inevitably, suck down Quath, the Tukar'ramin, everyone, everyone and everything, making a vile joke of continuity.

Quath plucked up a boulder in irritation and flung it skyward, arcing toward a distant herd of dull-witted grazers. The stone smashed great holes as it bounded through them, felling a few. Smaller animals hopped in panic from their holes. They melted into the shadowed dusk and Quath turned, weary, back to the floating alabaster mountain that was the Hive.

The Syphon lanced skyward again. This time the Cosmic Circle held steady in its course and the Syphon did not snake sideways. No burning lash fell, letting streaming yellow gush forth.

The podia took special care with this first successful firing. The Circle spun perfectly, caressed by sinewy fields. They would have to repeat the exercise many times before abandoning this scrap of a world, each time made a bit more difficult because of the shifting pressures below as the planetary mantle collapsed.

Quath took refuge in the bustle of work. She volunteered for excess time at the feedback-stabilization monitor. Canted forward to sense the rippling green display, integrating differential inputs, she felt the pressing hollowness of life lift away. If there was no redeeming facet in things, at least there was this: A blur of activity hid the fact that activity meant, finally, nothing.

As the Syphon steadied its rush of core metals, the Hive lifted farther. Quath watched from a viewing blister. The ground below heaved and broke, spurting fountains of dust. The land groaned. Pebbles rattled on the blister's underbelly. Animals stumbled in panic as hills slumped. Pits opened beneath their feet.

Quath felt her resting strands quiver and she turned, away from the chaos outside. Beq'qdahl nimbly enveloped herself in a webbing, saying, <A good show.>

<Yes.>

<I think we'll start mining tomorrow.>

Quath allowed herself a glance at Beq'qdahl's large, hairy mass. <You're looking forward to it?>

<Isn't everybody? It's a chance to show what you can do on your own.>

Quath had not thought of mining that way, but Beq'qdahl's self-assurance made the point obvious. With each sucking of the Syphon the crust churned, exposing fresh seams of rare minerals. Many ores were needed in the thermweb weaving now going on in orbit. To thread the great bands of coldformed nickel-iron required bonding pastes and weldings, so freighters lofted a steady stream of mixed materials from the surface.

Captured mech ships and a large orbital station aided this. Quath and Beq'qdahl had both been privileged to pilot flights to the captured mech station, the nearest they had gotten to where the orbital weavers conjured their deft magic.

No hope of such lofty labor now. All surface-working podia had to find rich upturned seams. All who could be spared became prospectors.

<It is boring work,> Quath said.

<So say they who do not do it well.>

<I would prefer focusing the Syphon.>

<That's just puzzle-work. No real zest in it.>

<It is *intellectually* more difficult to—>

<Oh, never would I question your intellectual *credentials*.>

Beq'qdahl dipped her proboscis sarcastically, impaling on it a burr of spitfood. <Particularly after your brilliant cross-examination of the Tukar'ramin.>

Quath bristled cilia. <I was seeking answers.>

<To grub-stupid questions. What does all that *matter*?> Beq'qdahl plucked a mite from a moist slickstrand.

<It is everything.>

<Talk, mere talk. We are here to *act*.>

<But what is the purpose, when—>

Beq'qdahl leaned closer gracefully, her hydraulics wheezing. <The purpose, slit-eye, is to get into orbit. To *weave*, not hug the ground like a grub.>

Quath framed a reply and suddenly saw that Beq'qdahl would be a success. Beq'qdahl's smooth, successful, uncaring manner came naturally because she was in touch with deeper wellsprings, she sensed the way things truly were. And in that clear world, the Synthesis was talk and the Summation a promised sugar dollop meant to quiet children, not a thing podia took seriously for long. That world was real. Relentlessly real.

SEVEN

Gathering call, came the beep, slicing through Quath's concentration. She crunched over crumbling slag and looked for silvery green streaks.

Gathering call.

She slipped a needle into the flaking silver-green, measured and clattered her ossicles in frustration. The stuff wasn't *palazinia.* Finding a lode of *palazinia,* the rarest of the bonding pastes, would have been a coup. This scrap, glinting falsely—Quath kicked at it—was worthless.

Gathering call.

She answered, dreading.

Rendezvous! Noble Beq'qdahl has found a deep seam of—

Savagely she clicked the message off. Another feat for Beq'qdahl.

This was the fifth important find since the prospecting and mining had begun, *all* Beq'qdahl's. Most of the other podia were kept busy mining Beq'qdahl's discoveries, leaving the field clear for Beq'qdahl to find more, to stand out even better. Quath had pondered giving up prospecting—she wasn't good at searching; she moped and rambled when she should scuttle, ferretlike, poking into every cranny—and becoming a miner. But something inside made Quath keep on, trying to best Beq'qdahl. She would *not* yield the ground so easily. If only—

Quath'jutt'kkal'thon. Summons!

<I was delayed. Am proceeding to—>

No. Do not rendezvous. Return to the Hive. To the Tukar'ramin.

Down slippery strands slid the Tukar'ramin, a great glistening mass of polished steel and grainy carapace. Gusts of warm well-being spread through Quath as feelers stole into her mind, sensing all. Nervous, jittery tensions smoothed away.

Rejoice, small one.

<All celebrate, in your presence.>

105

No formalisms please; they tax the mind by seeming to mean something. Rejoice, because you need no longer slough the crumbled land. I know you dislike that.

<I have been so . . . obvious?>

The Tukar'ramin drew Quath nearer, washing her with comfort and forgiveness.

Your doubts drag at every step you make.

<I have kept to the task.> The words came out more stiffly than she intended, but Quath clutched at the phrase out of a sense of dignity.

Must you always go sober-suited?

<I . . .> She hesitated. How to tell this most enfolding of all creatures that the snug universe was a vortex, sucking them all down to nothing? <I am a mere quadpodder and more solitary.>

But Beq'qdahl is solitary, too. Alone, seeking rare soils. Her pods do not shamble as yours do.

Beq'qdahl again! Quath said primly, <We each have our ways.>

But you are none of you alone! Faint, chiding exasperation. *We are bound on the great, final task. The thermweaves we spin around this star will clasp firm its burning energy. Our fellow podia will soon harness the crackling electrodynamics of the Galactic Center which rage nearby. Soon we shall combine all such energies. Thus gathered, and the mechs banished—and who can doubt that we shall do so, given our great victory here?—we can use the tamed power to communicate with other Starswarmers in far galaxies.*

<I fully perceive this. Yet—>

*I lick you do not. We span the galaxy to bring *meaning* to matter. Not simply within our own minds—the castles of besieged reason—but in the stars themselves.* She made the eight-legged sign.

Quath shuffled, not knowing what to reply.

I sense your unease remains.

Quath sent a sharp command to her podding subtask brain, willing its nervous dance to cease. <I, I have no vector.>

When the Tukar'ramin spoke again, gaudy hormonal spurts brought a new gravity to the resonant words. *You are a manifestation of a rare trait in our kind, Quath'jutt'kkal'thon.*

Afraid of exposure, she answered, <My doubts are only temporary, I assure you—>

No. The deep secret behind our expansion from our home system I shall now reveal to you. Long ago, we encountered a race of small beings who explained the nature of the coming mech onslaught. Our savants of that time saw that our own lazy nature meant that we would fall before the mechs. So we blended genetic material with the small ones, to amplify our aggressive side.

<They must have been fierce.>

They were. I do not know what physical form they took, but they were both canny and persistent. In selecting these subtle mental traits from their DNA—for we shared that fundamental helical carrier—we necessarily incorporated other facets of them. One such is a capacity to doubt, to question.

<I got their fierceness, too,> Quath said with false bravado.

Perhaps. But you are surely the rare form we call a Philosoph. The conventional wisdom of the Synthesis, as handed down by the Illuminates, is enough for most. Even those who do not believe—such as Beq'qdahl—function well within that context. But leadership of our race depends on the Philosophs.

<Leadership?>

Eventually, yes—if you display the questing mind we need.

<I . . . I . . .>

This deep trait is what has plunged you into bleak despair after Nimfur'thon's burning. It brings pain, but can also bring wisdom.

<A cursed inheritance,> Quath said bitterly.

On the Tukar'ramin's great wrinkled hide flashed a hormonal code. *We will encrust you. A small addition for your new task.*

<The prospecting—>

Is not spiritually fitting for you. We are lacking labor in the Hive itself, due to the mining. Here I will sense you better, as you work. There—you have the code? Apply to the Factotum and be encrusted with your new tool.

A gesture told Quath her audience was done. She skittered away. Liberation from prospecting! And an encrustation—!

Next to promotion, which would mean an added pod, encrustation was the highest tribute to a podder. Quath could preen in the warrens, displaying her addition without baldly announcing it. A plus, definitely. Yes. Her spirits rose.

Quath clattered past Danni'vver, hurrying to the nearest terminal. She beeped the code number and awaited the news, her servos humming. She could ponder the odd news of her nature

later, when there was time. After all, she was a Philosoph—
whatever that strange name implied.

The screen flickered fretted ivory. An image of the new tool
formed.

Gorge rose in Quath, an acrid blue that rasped her thorax.
Swimming before her was a stapling gun. A simple, brainless tool.
A simpleton encrustation so low as to be an insult.

EIGHT

The days passed with an ache in each hour.

Quath had some use of the stapling gun, occasionally tacking machines and crates to the Hive walls in the company of a rabble of robots she directed. The small Hive creatures squeaked and jibbered in their stuttering minilanguage. Quath felt a stab of embarrassment whenever an acquaintance happened by.

But in time this faded. After all, she was laboring, like all the podia, and gradually she came to feel that this was her rightful station. Facts had their own hardness, but one could sleep upon them.

Quath did not mind the studied way some myriapodia now ignored her conversation. There was always someone to talk to, anyway. The myriapodia were distant and boring, in truth; they cared only for their many mechanical jewelments, and how to acquire yet one more.

Aeons ago the idea must have seemed a good one, Quath thought: augment the podia as they aged, to use their experience and shore up the stiffening organs. But now these encrusted mammoths preened more than they worked. And the Quath they snubbed, the quadpodder they passed without seeing as she labored among brainless robots—-that Quath knew that these bright myriapodia would inevitably vanish forever, no matter how many stringy muscles and clogged veins they replaced.

One night Quath passed a gang of miners and prospectors as she returned alone to the communal webbing, down the inert gray arterial corridors. One called out, <Come, pay respect!>

<To whom?> Quath asked, tired.

<Beq'qdahl! The Tukar'ramin has newly six-podded our friend!>

<For what?> Quath had heard no news.

<You jibe, wall-tacker.>

<No. For what?>

<She found a rich new seam of *palazinia* today.>

<I see. A lucky find.>

<More than luck! Craft! Spiracles that sniff out rarity. That we go to celebrate!>

Beq'qdahl came into view. Three podia escorted her. The fresh leg gleamed silver and Beq'qdahl bowed toward them, articulating well, with color splashes at her throat that were almost convincingly humble. But her eyes drifted randomly, fogged, unattended by a saturated brain. <Come with us, Quath'jutt'-kkal'thon.> Her voice was thick from excess of celebration.

<I am rather tired. . . .>

<Don't you *want* to celebrate?> a quadder shouted. <Beq'qdahl has been double-promoted, *cicada*. A rare honor!>

<I realize.>

<You're buzzed that Beq'qdahl is now a hexpodder, while *you* remain with four. That's *it*, isn't it?>

<I am really not in the mood—>

<Grub! Rotten *cicada*!> The wobbling quadder lurched toward Quath, threatening.

Quath skittered aside. Another farted sourly in contempt, spewing an acrid yellow cloud. Beq'qdahl pretended indifference, studying the grainy walls.

Quath ducked down a side passage and away, to the moist gossamer communal bedding, to sleep.

Sleep.

Yet sleep came fitfully, laced by hot lightning behind the eyes.

Quath tossed and clutched at her smooth bed weavings. At times she awoke and then it was the long Dreamtime when they journeyed from her homeworld at far below light-speed. They had hung in swaying pearly sacs and voyaged through the notsleep, bodies slowed, minds floating among fog-racked visions best forgotten later. . . .

Just before dawn the distant sounds of Beq'qdahl's celebration finally died away. Quath expected deep sleep at last. Instead she awakened soon with tingling palps, flushed with a vision.

The Tukar'ramin, shrunken and old, lecturing. Not the enduring, enfolding Tukar'ramin she knew, but a doddering old podia who repeated the rote wisdom of the dead past. Despite the technical magic that let the Tukar'ramin span the gulf between minds, and heal, she was still an ancient podder, no more.

In the dream Tukar'ramin had described how the mechs would fall before the podia and the cutting Cosmic Circle, vanquished by life triumphant.

In the dream Quath had cried, *You know our mission is empty!* and the Tukar'ramin, shocked, fell crashing into brass and ceramic and gristle and withered bony parts. Thorax and antennae clattered on the warren floor. She fell and fell and fell—endlessly, authority squeezed to nothing beneath the crushing weight of remorseless time.

Awakening, Quath saw for a glimmering moment that her preoccupation with death held a clue. Somehow, this bore upon all events here at Galactic Center. But how? The small traces of Philosoph that laced thinly through her gave no clue.

NINE

Once more the Syphon sucked hard. Again the planet's husk cracked and spat vast plumes of brown dust.

It was fortunate that this world had no major oceans, or a different fraction of the crumpled crust would have been submerged with each Syphon firing, impeding the mines. That fact had helped select this world for the thermweaving. It overrode the absence of moons, whose ripping apart would have provided convenient building materials. What's more, there was a curious, ancient orbital device at the equator, which the podia might find useful later.

But now, word came of disturbances aloft. The podia used the captured mech orbital station as a shipping depot. But something had now intruded into the depot, delaying transports. This news was buried in the rush of Hive labor. Quath did not bother herself with such large problems, though she still ached to work in orbit, above the seethe of dust and gravity. She did her tasks and sought solace in marveling at progress beyond her Hive.

Already the podia had captured a small fraction of this yellow star's light. Their weaving proceeded apace in orbit, deploying broad planes ribbed with photosensitive silicon. When finished, the weave would be only a framework, of course, for later expeditions. They would render the planets into light-sopping materials—a tedious task—in preparation for harnessing the star's total flux.

By the time that happened, Quath expected she would be long dead, and the dream of Starswarmers touching between galaxies in the Summation would be, for Quath, dust. The others did not see this, or care. It was one thing to know in an abstract way that one day you would die, and another to wake in the night and feel your hearts thumping. To delve into your subtask brains and feel the prickly oxygen entering bloodstreams, the slow sluggish purr of tissues rebuilding, a hydraulic tug where titanium met carti-

112

lage, the dull orange burning of stored calories . . . and know they
will cease, you will plunge into blackness.

With repetition these somber moments lost some of their bite.
Quath began to see herself as a simple being, humble before the
brute facts of living. She labored with the ratlike robots, using her
massive stapler when great strength was needed, followed orders,
and kept to herself. From murmurs of transmissions in the Hive
corridors she overheard more talk of Beq'qdahl's successes.
Beq'qdahl is rising, the myriapodia observed. As though Beq'qdahl
were a confection baking, puffing itself up, and they were indirectly
the cooks. To Quath these matters no longer stung.

Thus she was not disturbed, when work teams reorganized,
that Tukar'ramin ordered her to accompany Beq'qdahl as an equipment carrier. Being a young Philosoph did not free one from the
rub of the world.

Ahead rumbled the bulky Beq'qdahl, legs scrabbling on rocks.

Her crescents of phosphorus made a small splotch of day amid
the night. Quath lurched behind, jumping at each tremor of the
rock for fear that another shifting of the crust had begun. Overhead hung the Cosmic Circle, its aura dull when not in use. The
sharp stars were eyes staring out of a swallowing abyss.

<Hurry. I want to probe this outcropping.> Beq'qdahl trans-
mitted only clipped, efficient messages.

Quath labored forward under her load of acoustic sensors. The
Tukar'ramin had given Beq'qdahl a complete analytical station, so
that tests could be made in the field. The components were bulky.
Quath also carried Beq'qdahl's extra boosting rockets, for escape
should magma spurt over the crumpled hills.

<Quick—a differential spectrometer.>

Quath supplied it. Dawn broke as the sun ripened behind
thinning clouds. Quath thought of Nimfur'thon and their gambols
on these lands, then sprinkled with green. A very long time ago.

From behind a tilted shelf of rock ambled a flock of animals. It
was surprising, Quath reflected, that they had survived the land's
heavings. The next round of Syphon firings would surely end life
on this world.

Something whined off Beq'qdahl's high turret.

<Do not jostle me.>

<I did not.>

<I said . . .>

The animals quickly spread among the shattered boulders. Something thudded into Beq'qdahl's flank. A pod jerked in spasm.

<They are throwing pebbles?> Beq'qdahl asked.

<No. Those are weapons.> Quath felt a flare of hot pain. Another shot sang off Beq'qdahl's bronzed turret.

<These are more than animals.>

<A reasonable hypothesis,> Quath answered mildly.

<But the Tukar'ramin said there were no significant Noughts! No civilization. No artificed works. Only the mechs.>

<So she did.>

Two quick bursts caught Quath in the side. She drew up a battered palp. A salty pus oozed forth.

<Evidently the inspection was cursory,> Quath said evenly.

<You miserable arachnida! These have *weapons*!>

<Yes, with considerable momentum density, as well. Simple, but—>

Beq'qdahl's shrill cry pierced the air. Her fifth pod split ripely and belched a foul smoke.

<I am injured! Injured! Help me boost.>

<A minor breaching.>

<Minor? I feel *pain*.>

<Your waste system has ruptured.>

<Give me the extra boosters!>

Quath abruptly pitched forward. Her rear bulkhead puckered around two steaming holes.

<Off your knees! The boosters!>

<H-here.>

Beq'qdahl strapped on the blue cylinders. Sharp shots rang on her carapace.

<When you are above these Noughts . . .> Quath spoke slowly, <sweep the backwash over the ground. The flames will—>

<Maneuver where they can shoot into my underbelly?> A harsh laugh. <You *are* a grub.>

<Stay, then. We can perhaps ride over them and, and crush—>

<Flee, fool! This is not our task. Clearing of Noughts requires real weapons.> Beq'qdahl's infrared antennae wobbled and sheared away with a grating noise. <Agh!—what pain! I'm leaving!>

<I . . . I'm trapped here.>

<I will go ahead, summon aid. You . . . you boost as far as you can and, and wait.> She finished hurriedly and made ready. Near misses hummed in the air.

Quath felt a stabbing gouge in her third pod. The gray

animals—no, Noughts, she corrected herself—were nearer. They were fanning out. Metal glinted in their small feelers.

When Quath glanced skyward again, Beq'qdahl was a yellow dot arcing toward the distant Hive. Quath knew that even if she had boosters, she would lose valuable moments overcoming her own subminds. Their fear of flying was almost unmanageable.

Resigned, she turned to study the Noughts with no weapons to repel them. Small pellets ate—*snick! ping!*—at her skin. She hoisted her own boosters and locked them into sleeves, shrugging off the small bites as the Noughts' shots nipped at her. Small, but so many.

As she articulated a telescoping arm, something caught her attention. Her stapler gleamed in the dawnlight.

The humble stapler which drove forked brackets into the Hive rock. No weapon at all . . .

Quath started to run. And then stopped. The Noughts could follow, after all. If she stood she would retain at least her dignity, if not her life.

Quath turned and faced the enveloping tide of piping Noughts. Something in her wanted this.

She raised the stapler and sighted along it with three eyes. A Nought charged into her center of focus and she fired. The staple split a rock, missing the Nought. She corrected. Fired. Another miss.

Quath felt a strange soothing calm. Shots struck her palps, fracturing one away. Steadily she calibrated and aimed. The stapler jerked. A Nought crumpled and fell into a gully.

The next gray target bobbed and weaved. Quath compensated and caught it on the third shot, splitting the thing in two. Beneath the gray shell it oozed sap.

High, frantic calls piped from the Noughts. Many ducked behind outcroppings. Quath quickly shot three.

Their weapons peppered her, stings nicking at her concentration. She killed five more.

They crowded in now, skipping like mites from one shadowed refuge to the next. Staples plowed through the soft, unarmored Noughts.

Her side dimpled and a hard wave of pain lanced through her. She lurched, gasping. Oil bubbled from two pods. Her remotely actuated hydraulic cylinders did not respond. She was trapped here.

She dashed sideways to elude a wedge of them and a massed

volley slammed her into a rock face. Her lenses fogged. Oxygen processors rasped. Fiery fingers pulled at her guts.

Here it is, Quath thought. *I have met it.* Blackness closed in.

Drifting . . .

Swimming . . .

Darkness came . . . slow . . . slow.

Yet time ticked on.

In her blurred sensate swamp Quath felt a brush of cool air, like the plasma wind which stirs the banks of dust between suns. Watery images floated in her eyes. She oxidized sugars with nitric acid, splitting open her internal mucus pouches to hasten the mix. She strained—

With a gathering rush her boosters fired, yellow columns singing. A cold fierce joy burst in her.

She landed unsteadily. Noughts swarmed after her. She set herself with a cool certainty and aimed. Fired.

Forked staples cut into the Noughts. Clanking, rumbling, surging, she moved—and boosted again, firing as she flew.

The Noughts in their gray suits exploded when the staples caught them. Guts spilled on crushed rock.

A pleasant fever swept over Quath as they fell under her hail of staples, puny voices screaming, rasping for a last suck of air.

Quath pushed them back across the field. Their firing slowed, ceased. They fled. She swiveled and searched out the few gray dabs remaining. They cowered in their hiding holes, bleating in fear, little better than animals.

Each became a small detail that Quath settled with the quick sharp stutter of the stapling gun. Each ended with a little cry, as if what awaited were a surprise.

When she sliced the last one through, Quath stood alone, gasping, her mind fuzzed. She attached a hook and line to a Nought body which was still in one piece and hauled it up for a better view. In the absolute silence of the battlefield her driving servo scratched, demanding oil. Her joints trembled with strain. The Nought body turned on the hook. Quath plucked at the gray skin. Filmy, it tore away.

The gray suit shucked off, much the way this world would soon become a husk. The Nought slipped free.

At first Quath saw only the gangling appendages with their awkward, splayed ends. Two for walking, two for manipulations. The joints were slight pivots, surely not capable of withstanding much stress.

Yet as Quath studied the creatures she saw how the wrinklings and knottings of its skin told how the thing lived. Patches of curdlings at the midjoints of the shorter pods, evidence of wear. A funguslike growth above and below the eyes, to cup warmth about the small brain. Another dark patch, lower, to shelter a tangle of equipment.

Quath traced the fine pattern of fleece that wove about the body, following what she could see were flow lines water would make as the thing swam. A beautiful design. So this Nought was a swimmer, yet it could walk, after a fashion.

She clamped the skull and turned the spinal juncture until a click came. She sent a subsonic hum along the body. With care she lifted the skull. The skeleton came free, sliding up out of the meat.

To Quath this gesture brought into the air a fresh and wonderful vision. The chalky bones were not crude and heavy. They seemed delicately turned, fitting snugly together—thin where waste would slow the beast, strong where torques and forces found their axis.

The center held a finespun cage of calcium rods. Ribs. They blossomed into a brittle and precisely adjusted weave, a song of intricate design and wonderful order that Quath could sense trilling through the webbed intersections.

Yet this Nought-thing was a pest. It crawled on the ground and probably never noticed the stars. It had mastered at best the trifling resources of its pitiful little world. Its crude weapons were barely better than the teeth and hooves of dumb animals.

Quath spun the skeleton, marveling at it. Inside her a chorus swelled over her weak, doubting voices. She swept aside the bleak landscape of small-minded logic, the fears which had ruled her.

Here at last was the truth made manifest. Her faith returned.

Reason resonated here. A universe which spent such care on loathsome, useless Noughts surely could not make the whole drama pointless by discarding it all, by letting blackness swallow everything, by letting Quath'jutt'kkal'thon ever finally fail, fail and die.

PART THREE

A MATTER OF MOMENTUM

ONE

Killeen smacked his gloved palm against the alien bulkhead. "Damn!"

Then he heard Jocelyn coming back and made himself take long, calming breaths. It was never a good idea to let an officer, even one as disciplined as Jocelyn, see the Cap'n in a pure, frustrated fit of anger.

"Nothing," she reported. "Couldn't see a damn thing happening anywhere in the ship."

Killeen nodded. He had been certain the craft was completely dead to their commands, but they had to check every possibility. There was precious little else they could do.

He remembered that during the assault on the station he had regretted that, as Cap'n, he was no longer in the thick of things. Well, now his wish had been granted. . . .

Their Flitter had been under way for over an hour. A steady throb of motors gave a slight acceleration toward the aft deck. In these skewed hexagonal compartments this was a particularly awkward orientation, intended for some odd mech purpose.

Jocelyn pulled herself deftly over a tangle of U-cross-section pipes that emerged from the floor and arced into the outer hull. Killeen peered into the mass of wires and mysterious electronic wedges that he had uncovered beneath a floor hatch. He called up his Aspects—Arthur for the electronics craftsmanship of the Arcology era, former Captain Ling for the starship lore of millennia earlier, and even Grey, aloof, sophisticated, so remote as to be nearly inaccessible. No matter who he summoned, none of the ancient personalities offered anything useful. Ling came the closest.

119

The external entity's means of controlling this craft may be insidious ... note how none of your precautions prevented Mantis from re-asserting itself, upon our arrival. Your mastery over Argo was illusory.

"You mean we never stood a chance," Killeen said bitterly. "Never did, never will."

Long ago, before my time, before Grey's, before even the epoch of the great Chandeliers, it is said that our ancestors once challenged the mechs. Higher entities were forced to acknowledge our existence, rather than delegating our elimination to minuscule mechanisms such as you knew on Snowglade.

It was difficult for Killeen to picture a being like *Mantis* as "minuscule," though Mantis itself had said that this was so. Killeen's mind could not encompass the heights Ling was implying— heights once assaulted by humanity before the long, grinding fall.

As for your present problem, there is a simple solution. A way to prevent the outside entity from controlling this craft.

"How's that?"

By destroying its means of receiving instructions. Go outside and wreck the antennae.

Killeen laughed so coarsely that Jocelyn looked up from her useless labor under the floorboards. "Already thought 'bout that. We can't *get* outside!"

Before Ling could respond he swept the irritating Aspect to the back of his mind. He tried again to call Shibo on comm.

Reception had improved since the last try, though it still faded in and out, washing her voice in soft static. To him it sounded beautiful.

—How are you doing?— she asked, tense with concern.

"Survivin'. I miss you an' Toby. How is he?"

—Toby's fine. He's up here on the Bridge with me and Cermo. We're trackin' you.— There was a pause.— You're still headed for rendezvous with the approaching ship. It's hell just sitting here. Can't budge *Argo*, come after you.—

"Did you try painting the hull with insulator? It might keep out whatever's jammin' the controls."

—Yeasay. No good. It's Mantis programs that've got us stuck here, embedded too deep.— Her level voice could not hide from him her tight apprehension. —Looks like that method worked on the other Flitters, though. They're under our control now. We'll have 'em charged up soon.—

Implied, but unspoken, was the fact that none would be ready in time to rescue Killeen and Jocelyn. Jocelyn reacted to this by spitting on the cabin wall.

"All right," Killeen said. "Shibo, I want you to form up the family. Issue provisions. Full field gear."

—For what?—

"For abandoning the station. Take the Family away."

—But *Argo*!—

"We'll have to abandon *Argo* too. Detach the farm domes. We discussed that. They're self-sustaining. Drag 'em along. But get out within twenty hours."

—But we can defend the station!— It was Toby's voice, rent with frustration, breaking in.

"Son," Killeen said. "Get off the command comm."

—I say we can *take* these damn mechs!—

Before Killeen could cut his son off, Shibo interjected agreement.

—Yeasay. We'll stay with *Argo*, fight off anything that comes.— Shibo's voice was filled with fierce commitment. Her motivation warmed him, but it frustrated Killeen that he could not make her see.

Lieutenant Cermo's forceful voice joined in.

—Fight higher-level mechs? From a *fixed* position? Crazy! Naysay!—

Shibo's reply sounded uncertain. —We'll sucker 'em in, jump 'em.—

—They'll expect that!— Cermo spoke louder than necessary.

—These mechs're puny!— Toby interrupted again. —We took 'em easy.—

Cermo's reply was bitter. —Those were just night watchmen. Just wait'll the Marauder class mechs show up. I tell you we can't fight things at that level. Not from fixed positions. At least not without help from something like the Mantis.—

—You Mantis-followers!— Toby grated. —Mantis's mechs were gonna meet us here, you thought. Where were they? They got beat by something else before we ever arrived.—

—Exactly my point! Whatever beat Mantis's allies is gonna come back here soon. It's already got th' Cap'n.—

"Cermo's right," Killeen told them, glad that his second lieutenant was showing some sense. He was about to add more praise when Cermo took a completely unexpected tangent.

—Thanks, Cap'n. That's why I say we head right *now* for broken ground. Head for territory where we know how to fight, like in the old days, and where *we* can find allies.—

"You can't mean . . ."

—Yeasay! Head for the surface.—

"No! Take the Flitters outward! You can reach the fourth planet. It's got ice, carbon. We got some Aspects who 'member that kind of life. You can set up domes."

But Cermo cut in again.

—*Argo* brought us here for a *reason*, Cap'n. Some of us say let's go down and find out what that reason is.—

"But those reasons may be obsolete! They *probably* are, if Mantis's allies have lost. Anyway, what about the others in the Family? Those who *don't* trust Mantis?"

That had always included the majority of *Argo*'s crew. Killeen had long counted on their support to overcome the mysticism, or gullibility, of the faction willing to put its faith in the promises of a mech, even a "different" mech as unusual as Mantis. Killeen was confident peer pressure would bring Cermo around.

But Shibo's next words cut the deck from under him.

—The majority say we should stand an' fight for the station,— she said in a low, bitter voice he could barely make out. —But the Cap'n has convinced me we can't. Given that, Cermo's right.—

"No! Take the *Argo*. Run!"

—If we take the Flitters maybe I can find you later.—

"Not much chance I'll be alive long. Somebody wants a look at Jocelyn 'n me. Don't 'spect it's just friendly interest."

Cermo said, —Cap'n, we vote for goin' down.—

"And I say you *don't*."

With less heat now Cermo sent, —The Mantis . . .—

"We're masters of our own lives, dammit!" Killeen shouted.

—The Mantis had somethin' in mind,— Cermo said stolidly.

"So what? Think it planned that cosmic string? Shibo! What's it doing?"

In reply she sent a simulation picture that fluttered in his left eye.

The revolving hoop shaded the entire planet. From the small opening along the axis dark pencil-thin strands shot upward. Both poles vented streams of matter. Yellow metal-lava struck vacuum and exploded into banks of fog. From the vapor came long, thin threads.

"Looks like buildin' somethin'," Killeen said.

—Gutting the planet while they do it,— Shibo agreed.

Killeen said sharply, "You'll do as I order. Shibo, you sounded the gathering call yet?"

Shibo replied reluctantly, —Yeasay.—

"Good. Now—"

—I got Flitters ready, too. They're set up for easy destination programming. Files on the *Argo* showed me how. I've got them set for planet approach.—

Killeen saw bitterly that she had thought this through thoroughly. She could probably bring it off, too. Shibo was a wonder at ferreting out mechmind ways. "Naysay! Something awful's going on here. Get away!"

—Sorry, lover. You're outvoted.— Shibo gave the words a lilt but he could feel her tension.

"As Cap'n I—"

—If you want legalisms, try this, — Shibo cut in sternly. —You've been shanghaied off. As acting officers we're expressing the Family's decision.—

"Naysay! You can't—"

—Listen!— Her voice suddenly flared with genuine anger. He could imagine her suddenly widened eyes, her clenched teeth. Emotions seldom broke her calm surface, but the effect was spectacular, like an unleashed force of nature. —We'll try saving you. But we're holding with our dream.—

"Shibo, I want—"

—Lover, you *know* I can't just sit here and do nothing.—

Killeen made himself pause. His frustration should be directed against whatever had seized this ship, not against this most precious of all women. "All . . . all right. No way I can stop you, is there?"

Cermo answered with surprising warmth, —Naysay. None.—

"Where'll you go?"

A pause. He imagined that she was holding herself in check too. The thin strand connecting them seemed to sing with unspoken thoughts. —You . . . 'member that signal from New Bishop?—

"Yeasay. Had human indices, you said."

—I got a better fix on it. Voices. Near the equator. We'll try for that.—

"Well . . ."

—There're *people* down there. That convinced a lot of us. If we can't defend *Argo*, we'll go down and join our kin.—

It made sense. Killeen reluctantly admitted that Shibo and Cermo had logic and human fellowship on their side.

"The string, though!" he shouted, pounding the console. "How can you get past it?"

—It whirls round for a day or so, then stops,— Shibo said. —We'll spread out from the station. When the string stops, we'll hit the atmosphere.—

"Too risky."

—Lover . . .—

For a long moment they said nothing. The purr of static seemed almost like a background chorus to poignant, unspeakable thoughts.

"When . . . when'll you leave?"

—Soon. We're nearly ready. I . . we'll . . . try . . . pick you up . . . you . . . hide from whatever's in that ship . . . if we can . . . get in close . . . otherwise . . .—

Her voice faded in and out. Killeen listened intently for some last contact with her. Finally he switched off the static and realized he had been holding his breath.

Jocelyn looked at him expectantly. Killeen had no ideas and did not want to show it. He clamped down his jaw muscles, knowing this gave him a stern look, but this time he valued it more because it compressed his helpless frustration.

"They want to keep us in here till . . ." Jocelyn plainly could not think of a way to finish.

"Yeasay. Till they can flush us out, step on us."

"Haulin' us out this far, maybe they just want get some idea 'bout what we are, 'fore they go into the station."

"Seems reasonable. Mechs're careful."

"Even dead, we'll give 'em info," Jocelyn said flatly.

He saw her meaning. "Yeasay."

"We better get out 'fore we arrive."

Anger brimmed fresh in him. He needed to think but the blind rage seethed nearly beyond control. His hands ached to smash and tear.

At that moment he saw the glimmer of an idea. Evolution's mute legacy of hormones had made him get angry, and maybe that was the right thing after all. Use his rage, yes.

"Let's have some fun," he said with a thin smile.

"Huh?"

"This ship's got some onboard mind, even if we can't reach it. Let's give it a problem. A *big* problem."

Killeen picked up a metal rod he had wrenched free from a mech loading mechanism. With a spurt of joy he brought it down on the U-shaped pipes. One, two, three blows—and a pipe dented. Fractured. Split to let hiss forth a green gas.

"Seal up!" Jocelyn cried with alarm. They both twist-locked their helmets as the gas filled the ship with a billowing emerald fog.

Distant warnings wailed, keening in his sensorium. Killeen waved Jocelyn to follow and moved as quickly as he could through the snaking tunnels of the Flitter. There had been a small side lock that they could not open, but now, if they confused the ship's internal systems enough . . .

The lock was a simple exit chute with a large dimpled cap. They had spent a lot of time trying to lever it open, and now Killeen simply slammed his metal rod into the thing. He chipped its finish and broke off the side flanges. Jocelyn had caught his meaning, too, and had found a shaft of heavy composite brass. She flailed at the lock with relish, grinning.

After the first rush of rage Killeen reflected that this at least cleared their heads. It burned up oxygen, but he didn't have much hope of using his full reserve anyway. He knew he had blundered badly and was going to pay for it.

More alarms hooted through his sensorium, electromagnetic spikes of mech dismay. Killeen chopped down on power cables. Sparks jumped. He was wearing his rubber gloves to avoid the usual shocktraps but the surge still blinded him—breaking down the air, forking orange fingers into the deck. The green gas was thickening. Killeen smashed a panel of controls, denting the side and ripping wires.

And the lock popped open. Killeen stared at it. Brilliant stars beckoned. He had only an instant before the *whoosh* of escaping air drew him headfirst toward the open lock.

He windmilled his arms in the storm. This made him strike the yawning mouth sidewise, so it could not swallow him. Jocelyn slammed into his legs. He wrenched sidewise. That gave her a shove toward the floor, where she could grab at the base.

But securing her cost him his precarious hold on the lip of the lock. The rising gale's shriek clutched at him. He tried to sit up. A giant hand pushed him heavily back. Small mouths sucked at his arms, legs, head—

Something struck him solidly in the neck and abruptly he was in the lock, battering against the side in a green-tinged darkness—

—and was out, free, whirling away from the shining skin of the Flitter.

Tumbling. Spinning.

He vectored hard to correct his plunge. A jumble of impressions began to make sense.

He hung on the dayside of New Bishop, far from the station. He was near a pole. Far below the ruddy twilight stretched shadows of mountains across beaten gray plains. Toward the equator green life still clung in valleys and plains, where forests thickened.

All this lay behind the incandescent golden blur of the cosmic string. It spun with endless energy. One edge of it arrowed straight down toward the pole. The other side bulged out far beyond the planet's equator.

The hoop spun faster than the eye could follow. A hovering tapestry spread over the entire world. The polar axis was clear now. Killeen could see no dark jet of metal spewing up. But glinting craft lingered still.

Now he was going to get a close look. He was nearly over the pole. Far away, nearly over the soft curve of the world, arced vast gray warrens. The fabricated fruit of the recently ejected core metal, he guessed.

This he took in with the barest glance, unable to react— because something came looming into his view, swelling with the speed of its approach.

The ship was far larger than the mech Flitter, which now floated like a helpless insect beside a predatory bird as the craft slowed and stopped. The comparison came to Killeen because of a certain tantalizing, evocative sweep of the larger ship's lines. It had flared wings made of intricate intersecting pentagons, as though spun out from a single thread. Its forward hull bulged like a gouty throat. Blackened thrusters at its rear puckered wide. His Arthur Aspect remarked serenely:

While the Flitter expresses mech rigidities, this huge craft seems sculpted to express underlying body symmetries. Aspect Grey tells me this is a characteristic of organic intelligence, not mech. Still, I fear these are not the familiar bilateral forms made by humans.

"Jocelyn! There's something out here. Hide!"

Faintly she sent in answer, —Yeasay. Flitter's nearly stopped anyway.—

The ships now hung together. Killeen wondered if this had been their intended destination. If so, perhaps all their mad raging had only succeeded in getting him free a few moments early, as the Flitter was allowed to void its irritant.

He jetted around the Flitter, calculating that the larger ship might miss him in the clutter of debris that had spewed from the lock. If he could somehow stay free, he might find out what manner of being flew the strangely shaped ship.

Speculation ceased. A form rushed forth from a darkened oval hole in the craft's side, moving far swifter than a human could. It headed for him.

Killeen sped away. There was nowhere to go but he was damned if he would wait to be caught. His turn brought into view the pole again, and the golden glow of the spinning hoop below. The shimmering covered all of New Bishop except for the small open cylinder at the pole.

Killeen tried to angle away from the onrushing form and gain the small shelter of the Flitter. A glance behind him showed that the thing was closing fast. He veered.

At each darting turn it came closer, following him with almost contemptuous ease. It loomed so near now that Killeen could see bossed metal studded with protuberances. Between riveted coppery sections was a rough, crusted stuff that seemed to flex and work with effort.

He realized abruptly that the thing was *alive*. Muscles rippled through it. Six sheathed legs curled beneath, ending in huge claws.

And the head—Killeen saw eyes, more than he could count, moving independently on stalks. Beside them microwave dishes rotated. It had telescoping arms socketed in shiny steel. They ended in grappling arrays of opposing pads.

The thing was at least twenty times the size of a human. A bulging throat throbbed beneath stiff-crusted graygreen skin. Its rear quarters were swollen as though thruster tubes lodged there. Yet they were also banded with alternating yellow and brown rings, like the markings of a living creature.

Killeen guessed that this was what had been near the mainmind of the station. But that one had been much smaller. This was another order of being. It united the forms of both mech and life.

This was all he could think before gaping pads clasped him in a rough but sure embrace.

The thing brought him up toward its moving eye array. It

studied him for a long moment. Killeen was so rapt upon the orange ovals that only after a moment did he notice the steady tug of acceleration.

The thing was hurtling him forward. Not back to its ship, but toward the pole. It tossed him from one array of pads to another, letting him tumble for seconds in space before snagging him again.

Like a cat playing with a mouse,

his Arthur Aspect said mournfully.

"What's . . . a cat?"

An ancient animal, revered for its wisdom. Grey told me of it.

Killeen's mind whirled, empty of terror or rage.

He felt only a distant, painful remorse at all he was about to leave behind—Toby's laughter, Shibo's silky love, Cermo's broad unthinking grin, the whole warm clasp of the Family he had failed, and would now die for in a meaningless sacrifice to something beyond human experience.

He tried to wrench away from the coarse black pads. They seemed to be everywhere. A brutal weight mashed him down. A long, agonizing time passed as he struggled to breathe.

He wondered abstractly how the thing would kill him. A crushing grasp, or legs pulled off, or electrocution . . .

In sudden rage he tried to kick against the pads. He got a knee up into them and pushed, struck sidewise with his arms—

—and was free. Impossibly, he glided away at high speed from the long, pocked form of worked steel and wrinkled brown flesh. It did not follow.

He spun to get his bearings and saw nothing but a hard glow. He was close to the hoop. No, not merely close—it surrounded him.

Killeen looked behind him. Above the fast-shrinking alien hung at the end of a glowing tube that stretched, stretched and narrowed around him as Killeen watched.

He was speeding down the throat of the pipe made by the whirring hoop. Shimmering radiance closed in.

He righted himself and fired his jets. The alien had given him a high velocity straight down into the hoop-tube. If he could correct for it in time—

But the brilliant walls drew nearer.

He applied maximum thrust to stop himself, even though that meant his fuel would burn less efficiently. His in-suit thrusters were small, weak, intended only for maneuvers in free-fall.

He plunged straight down. The alien had so carefully applied accelerations that Killeen did not veer sidewise against the hoop walls. He was falling precisely toward the pole of New Bishop. Through the shimmering translucent walls he could see a dim outline of the planet, as ghostly as a lost dream.

His thrusters chugged, ran smoothly for a moment, then coughed and died. He fell in sudden eerie silence.

He had been simpleminded, thinking that the alien anthology of flesh and steel would kill him in some obvious way. Instead, from some great and twisted motive, it had given him this strange trajectory into the mouth of a huge engine of destruction.

At any moment, he supposed, the tube would vent more liquid metal outward. In an instant he would vanish into smoke.

Vainly he tried his sensorium. No human tracers beckoned. He grimaced, his breath coming rapidly in the sweat-fogged helmet.

The shimmering walls drew closer. He almost felt that he could touch them, but kept his arms at his sides. He fell feet first, watching a small yellow dot between his boots slowly grow. His Grey Aspect said distantly:

This is . . . wondrous work . . . such as I . . . never studied . . . comparable to the constructions . . . in ancient times . . . of mechs themselves . . .

His Arthur Aspect remarked:

We are inside the bore of the tube that stretches out along the polar axis. Let us hope the entire tube has been emptied by the alien mining operations. It appears we do have a quite exact trajectory. The alien sent us falling straight along New Bishop's spin axis. We may well fall all the way through the planet.

Killeen tried to think. "How long will that take?"

Let me calculate for a moment. Yes, I retained the data on New Bishop which Shibo announced . . . which yields . . . I am performing the dynamical integral analytically . . .

Across Killeen's field of view appeared:

$$\text{time} = \left[\frac{\pi}{2} - \tan^{-1} \frac{V}{R\sqrt{\frac{4\pi}{3}G\rho}} \right] \left[\frac{3}{4\pi\,G\rho} \right]$$

Time to pass through to the other side of the planet is 36.42 minutes. I would advise you to start a running clock.

Killeen called up a time-beeper in his right eye, set it to zero, and watched the spool of yellow digits run. He could make no sense of them, and in his life had never needed more than a rough estimate of minutes elapsed—and then only when timing the beginning of an assault. Let the Arthur Aspect read it. Time was of no importance when the outcome was so barrenly clear.

TWO

Quath'jutt'kkal'thon surged with pride.

Powerful acceleration pressed her into the rough webbing. She sang to herself of the adventure to come, the first fruit of her new status in the Hive.

Beq'qdahl called, <See the thermweb!>

Quath could have tapped into the general ship's electro-aura, but she chose to lean forward and watch through the optical port. They were well above the smooth blue curve of this world. The Cosmic Circle hung still in the distance, gray and serene. Soon it would begin winding up again. More core metal would be needed for . . . She searched the starry dark. *There!*

The thermweb was a slate-dark lattice, hard to see. Some strands of it were nearly complete, knotted at the intersections by pearly bonding dollops larger than mountains. The total span showed a distinct arc and its far edge lay beyond the horizon.

Quath narrowed her vision. She could see podia working on the immense girders and vaults—forming, shaping, cutting, polishing. Soon the thermweave would be ready to harness the outpouring solar energy of the nearby star, and the mission of Quath's race could carry on with its inexorable momentum.

But first there were minor details to clear up. Quath and Beq'qdahl had been sent up in this shuttlecraft to take care of a nuisance which had infested the former mech orbital station.

For Quath this was a great honor. She had distinguished herself in the battle with the Noughts. The Hive's supreme arbiter, the Tukar'ramin, had witnessed Beq'qdahl's cowardly flight. So Quath had been decorated with gaudy new additions to her body parts, including two fresh legs. In the corridors she was spoken of as Quath-the-Terror and She-Who-Fights.

And now this: a mission to squash an infestation in orbit. Honor! Opportunity!

A vicious pest had occupied the station, killing a minor functionary. The orbital laborers were too busy to tend to the task, and so had delegated it to the lower-rank ground podia. Still, this was surely more than Quath had dreamed she could achieve, a strand far higher in the social web.

<I have extracted the mech shuttle ship and am speeding it to rendezvous with us,> Beq'qdahl said.

Quath gibed at her, <I favor striking directly at the station.>

<No doubt you would. Barge in without thinking, without knowing what you face.>

<Courage shall carry us through!>

<I prefer assessing risk.> Beq'qdahl was still sensitive about the embarrassing encounter with the Noughts.

Quath said slyly, <Reports from our mech slaves imply these are mere Noughts infesting the station. Surely caution is unnecessary when stamping out mere—>

<I shall decide what is necessary here.>

Quath saw Beq'qdahl's design. She wished to recoup her repute. A quick engagement could indeed restore her good name. Perhaps the Tukar'ramin had allowed the two of them alone to come on this mission for just that reason.

Quath fretted. She had assumed that *she* was being honored here. Now she saw that perhaps the Tukar'ramin was simply guarding Beq'qdahl's stature, with Quath along as a safeguard. In case Beq'qdahl bungled matters, Quath-the-Nought-Slayer could save the day.

<Suffice to say that I wish to take a sure and steady course,> Beq'qdahl said.

Quath hesitated. After all, action in orbit was a great privilege. She scintillated her pore hairs to show agreement. <What can I do?>

<We shall soon meet the mech ship. I commanded it to withdraw from the station and meet us here, for inspection. Internal signals show it contains some Noughts. We shall take their measure.>

<Ah!> The Tukar'ramin placed a high value on stamping out the Noughts, ever since they had damaged the magnetic flux stations. The very death of Nimfur'thon might have arisen from Nought vandalism, causing the Syphon to snarl. Quath relished the opportunity to squash more of these dwarf enemies.

They swooped around the bowl of the planet. Below them the Cosmic Circle tilted on the far horizon and began with gravid grace to spin again. Its length shimmered brilliantly as it converted a small fraction of the mass at the core into self-energy.

Quath watched this with humble awe. She saw they would intersect the shuttle ship near the pole, where they could well witness the working of the Cosmic Circle.

She hoped to approach it, sense its cyclic power. There was a legend among the podia that the Circle, their most potent tool and weapon, radiated an enhancing aura. Podia who ventured near were ensured of longer life.

Quath thought this was probably worthless legend, but she was not absolutely sure. Why not test it? After all, she was a Philosoph.

Her conversion to an inner certainty of her own immortality, which had come as a blinding insight on the battlefield, had now echoed down through her life. She no longer questioned the ultimate rightness and central position of the podia, and of her place in the scheme of the galaxy. The calming reassurance of her conversion was an ever-present joy.

Yet, oddly, when she had related this to the Tukar'ramin, that great entity had seemed unmoved.

Quath watched as they approached the shuttle ship. She tensed with excitement as Beq'qdahl commanded, <You may inspect the Noughts. I am releasing them now. Meanwhile, I shall ready our assault guns.>

Quath clanked and rasped as she made her way through the lock. She was fully charged in all reservoirs and capacitances. Her body prickled with the desire to vanquish.

She launched herself through the lock into the cool embrace of high vacuum. Pleasurable waves swept across her tough self-skin, the original organic hide she had been born with. She had thought of covering it with body armor or some useful appliance, but the charm of true flesh outweighed utility. She was nostalgic for her earlier, purely organic self. To erase all dependence on flesh would be too great a breaching with her past, too soon. Time enough for that later, when she had climbed on up to greater strands in life. Only the Illuminates, it was said, were totally augmented. Those vast, wise beings had attained the ultimate synthesis of flesh and mechanism.

The shuttle ship hung nearby. Quath saw immediately that a cloud of junk spun lazily away from the small aft lock. Amid the twirling stuff was a silvery Nought.

She shot toward it. Yes, it was the same boring bipedal sort that she had slaughtered in plenty on the battlefield. The mirror finish to its skin spoke of a high-quality technology, an insulating texture. Perhaps the Nought had stolen this material from the podia's stores in the orbiting station. This suspicion flared hotly in Quath. She sped to intersect the pitifully slow passage of the Nought.

She caught it easily. Its struggles were comically weak.

<What form is it?> Beq'qdahl asked.

<One you ran from, remember?>

<Do not aggravate me, I warn you. Report!>

<Negligible tech evident, though its suit is of high level. It is moving its limbs as though it walks on two, works with the others. No augmentation that I can see. Probably a raw animal form, really.>

<They should be simple to eradicate.>

<Yes. Shall I peel back the suit, to check it in detail?>

<I do not like to witness the disgusting raw form of animals, Quath.> Beq'qdahl sniffed. <That is beneath my dignity.>

<Oh, most sorry.> Quath suppressed her jangling mirth.

<Finish up, then. Enough inspection.>

<Could we not watch the Syphon, Beq'qdahl? See, it brims nearby.>

<I perceive no purpose—>

Quath felt an idea percolate up from one of her subminds. <Wait! This Nought has caused us trouble, yes?>

Beq'qdahl's voice betrayed interest. <What of it?>

<Noble Beq'qdahl, I have in mind an amusing game. . . .>

THREE

Killeen fell.

It had taken him years to truly get used to the sensation of free-fall, and that had been outside *Argo,* in the silent enormity of open space. It had been possible then to convince his reflexes that he was in some sense flying, airy and buoyant, oblivious to gravity's cruel laws.

But here . . . Here he plunged downward between mottled glowing walls that rushed past with dizzying speed. He *felt* the silvery rim of New Bishop thrusting up to meet him as the planet flattened into a plain. Crinkled mountains grew, detail getting finer with every moment. Through the gauzy sheen of the whirling cosmic string he watched the planet grow.

The polar region still held a few rivulets of white, snow from what must have once been an icecap. The land had a naked look, pale and barren, as though recently exposed. It stretched away, filling half his sky beyond the glowing translucent walls of the hoop-tube. The ravaged land was rutted by fresh rivers that poured over jagged scarps. He could see rough roads cut by treads, broad tracks of churned mud.

The ground hurtled up, a vast hand swatting at him, and he flinched automatically. He plunged toward a broad hillside—

—braced himself for the impact—

—and felt nothing.

Instantly he shot through into a dim golden world, alone.

Glowing walls gave some light but he could see nothing beyond them. Far below, between his boots, was a glaring yellow point. Arthur's voice came to him:

I have conferred with Grey. She unfortunately knows nothing more of this than I. We are left with only educated guesses. This tube is indeed empty, free even of air. We are inside the planet now. I estimate our speed at 934 meters per second.

135

Dark mottled shapes soared up toward him and flashed soundlessly past in the walls. "Headed for what?"

> If the alien cyborgs have constructed this miraculous planet-
> coring device with the precision I would expect of them, I
> predict we shall plunge entirely through the center and out
> to the other side.

"What's a cyborg?" Killeen asked, to focus his mind. His Grey
Aspect answered faintly:

> *Half-organic being . . . half-machine . . . I could not ascer-*
> *tain . . . exact proportions . . . from such hasty observation*
> *. . . historical records . . . spoke of such a race . . . in very*
> *early days . . . the Great Times . . .*

"Skip that! How can I get *out?*"
Arthur replied crisply:

> We cannot. By thrusting the cosmic string to very near the
> planetary axis, the cyborgs ensured that there is no spin
> along this tube. Matter coming up from the core—or down
> from outside, as we are—will suffer no slow drift, and so
> should not strike the walls. In addition, uniquely to this
> choice they have adroitly made, there is no Coriolis force
> which would deflect us.

Killeen could not follow the jargon but he understood it was all
bad news.

Despite the glowing walls the light around him was dimming.

He fought down rising panic. Part of his fear came from the
simple fact that he was falling at greater and greater speeds, and
sheer animal terror threatened to engulf him. Against this consuming fear he fought like a man hammering at a dark wave which
loomed ever higher. His breath caught. He forced his throat to
open, his lungs to stop their spasmodic heaving.

Grainy, blurred shapes flashed past. These were features in
the rock, illuminated by the thin barrier of the rotating hoop.

The yellow glare below had swollen to a brilliant disk. He
could feel now through his sensorium a bone-deep bass *whuum-*
whuum-whuum-whuum of the spinning magnetic fields.

"Maybe . . . maybe I can reach the walls. Is there any way I
can slow down?"

Killeen felt Arthur's sharp, peeling laugh. A circle appeared in his left eye. It billowed into a sphere—the planet—with a red line thrust along the axis of revolution. A small blue dot moved inward near the top of the axis, just below the surface.

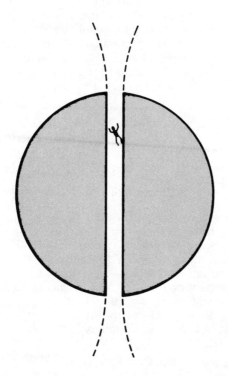

We have now acquired a speed of 1,468 meters per second. The hoop material, remember, is extremely dense—many millions of tons per kilometer. All packed into a thread which hardly spans an atom's width, whirling at immense speed. If you were to strike that matter at our present speed, your hand would vaporize.

Killeen's breath came in fast, jerky pants. "Suppose they get some core metal in here, comin' out, and we meet it."

I don't suppose I have to analyze that possibility for you.

"No, guess not."

Killeen cast about for some idea, some fleeting hope. The walls were nearly dark now, the radiance of the hoop somehow absorbed by the rock beyond. Smoldering orange-brown wedges shot past—lava trapped in underground vaults, great oceans of livid, scorching rock.

I would suppose that the hoop-tube is left to stand empty at times. Perhaps the cyborgs are now working on some minor repairs. Or perhaps they simply pause to let the orbited teams which are fashioning the first batch of core metal do their work. In any case, assuming the cyborg above did not simply throw us in to see us boiled away by a gusher of iron, there is another fate.

Killeen tried to calm himself and focus on Arthur's words. The walls seemed closer as he fell, the tube narrowing before him. He pulled himself rigid and straight, arms at his sides, feet down toward the yellow disk below that grew steadily. He blinked back sweat and tried to see better.

I believe we have passed through the crust and are now accelerating through the mantle. Note that the occasional lava lakes are getting larger and more numerous. Temperature increases here by about 10 degrees centigrade every kilometer we fall. This will continue until the temperature exceeds the melting point of simple silicate rocks. Then— drawing on studies of similar planets—we will enter an increasingly dense and hot core. At this point the rocks will be fluid and at about 2,800 degrees centigrade.

"Howcome rock doesn't fill up this tube?"

The hoop pressure, which is truly immense. Grey calculates—

"And the heat? The hoop stops that?" Killeen asked, seeking reassurance, though he already suspected the answer.

Heat is infrared electromagnetic radiation. The hoop is transparent to it. All light passes through it—which is why we see now the dark rock beyond. Soon, though, the silicates will begin to glow with their heat of compression.

"What'll we do?"

The heat radiation exerts a pressure. But this is symmetric, of course, acting equally in all directions. So it cannot push us toward one wall in preference to another. But it will cook us quite thoroughly.

"How . . . how long?"

Passage through the core . . . about 9.87 minutes.

"My suit—it'll silver up for me."

True, it already has. And I calculate we might survive one
entire passage if we seal up completely, close your helmet
visor, damp all inputs. Perhaps the cyborg understood that;
it may know a good deal about our technology. Yes, yes . . .
I am beginning to see its devilish logic.

Killeen shut down his suit inputs. He left only a slight lightpipe
for optical images. His suit skin reflected the blur of thickening
light around him with a mirror finish. The walls rushing past
were turning ruddy, sullen. "Where are we?"

We must be approaching the boundary at which iron melts.
This reddening probably signals the transition from the mantle to the outer core. We can expect some varying magnetic
fields now, since this is the region—so theory says—where
the planet's field is born. Large currents of molten metal
eddy about, carrying electrical currents, like great wires in a
generator station. New Bishop's spin serves to wrap these
around, creating current vortexes, which in turn stir up
magnetic whorls.

"Damn, it's getting hot already."

External temperature is 2,785 degrees centigrade.

Killeen clicked down his visor. He fell in complete blackness.
He wondered if he could stand the heat in utter isolation, plunging faster, faster, ever faster. . . .
Again he struggled to slow his breathing. If he was to live
through even the next few minutes he would have to think clearly.
The dark might help that as long as he could keep his natural
reactions from running away.

Luckily, the added speed imparted by the cyborg will take
us through that much faster. I register external temperature
now at well over 3,000 centigrade. Here—one of the suit's
lightpipes will give us a faint image, which is all we need in
such a place.

"Damnall, *think!*"

I am. I simply do not see any way out of our dilemma.

"There's gotta be *some* way—"

The existence of a well-defined problem does not imply the existence of a solution.

"Damn you!"
Years before, Killeen had suppressed his Aspects when they threatened to overwhelm him. Now he felt the risk in that. Arthur was a disconnected intelligence, serving as a mere consultant mind. Without nature's primitive surges of alarm, like adrenaline, Arthur remained aloof. Still, his coolness kept the less-used Aspects and Faces from intruding on Killeen with their panics.
"Look, we get through this, we'll be back outside, yeasay?"

Yes. But that is the devilish nature of this cyborg's trick. We are participating in an ancient schoolboy's homework problem—a shaft through the planet, with us as the harmonically oscillating test mass.

"What . . ."
Killeen suddenly saw what Arthur meant. He watched as in his eye the blue dot shot through the core and on, out through the other side of the red tube. It rose toward the surface, its velocity dwindling in gravity's grip, then broke free above the surface, still slowing. After hesitating at the peak it began falling again, to execute another long plunge through the heart of the spitted planet.

We can perhaps survive this one passage. But another, and another?—so on, ad infinitum?

"There must be a way out."
Killeen said this with absolute conviction, even though he had no knowledge of the physics underlying Arthur's colorful display. Even if a gargantuan alien had made this incinerating rattrap, it could have made a mistake, left some small unnoticed exit.
He had to believe that or the panic which squeezed his throat would overwhelm him. He would die like a pitiful animal, caught on the alien's spit and roasted to a charred hulk. He would end as a cinder, bobbing endlessly through the central furnace.

We might possibly try something at the very high point, when the hoop begins to curve over far above the pole. We should come to rest there for a brief instant.

"Good. Good. I can maybe pump some this cooling stuff—"

Refrigerant fluids, yes, I see. Use them in our thruster. But that would not be enough to attain an orbit.

"How about the hoop? Maybe I could bounce off it up there, where it's spinning. I could pick up some vector, get free."

Killeen felt Arthur's strangely abstract presence moving, pondering, consulting Ling and Grey and some Faces, as though this were merely some fresh problem of passing interest. Falling in absolute blackness, he felt his stomach convulse. He clamped his throat shut and gulped back down a mouthful of acid bile.

Now a strange sound came to him. Beneath the ratcheting *whuum-whuum-whuum* of the revolving hoop he heard bass gurglings and ringing pops.

We are picking up the whorls of the planetary magnetic fields in the core. They sound remarkably like organ notes.

The long, strumming, hollow sounds broke Killeen's attention. He imagined they were majestic voices calling out to him, beckoning him into the utter depths of this world. . . .

No. He shook himself, gasped, and switched the lightpipe image into his left eye.

The walls outside bristled with incandescent heat, cherry red. Globs of scorched red churned in the walls.

"Stop your calculatin'! Give me an answer."

Very well. The idea might be marginally possible. I cannot estimate with certainty. However, it would require that we be close enough to the hoop-formed wall. The cyborg has placed us exactly in the center of this tube, as I measure. We need to move perhaps a hundred meters before we will be within the pressure shock wave of the hoop as it turns.

"How far's that?"

About as far as you, ah, *we* can throw a stone.

"That's not so hard. I can use that cooler stuff—"

Extract it now and we will die in seconds.

"Damnall. I'll do it when we're clear, then."

That is tempting, but I fear it would not be effective. The tube opens as it rises toward the surface. Here the tube wall is only a stone's throw away. By the time we are clear of the core, the walls will be too far to reach in time—unless we begin to move now.

"Yeasay, yeasay—*how*?"

Even a small pressure applied now would give us enough push to reach the wall during the rise out.

"Pressure . . ."

Killeen frowned. The claustrophobic suit filled with the sound of his own panting, his sour sweat, the naked smell of his fear. He felt nothing but the clawing emptiness of perpetual falling, of weightless anxiety. He squinted at the tiny image that came through the lightpipe.

The walls outside were flooded with fire. The nickel-iron core only a short distance beyond raged and tossed with prickly white compressional waves. He flew close to livid pink whorls that stretched for tens of kilometers, yet passed in a few seconds of harsh glare. The hoop's constant *whuum-whuum-whuum* stormed in his teeth and jaws with grinding persistence.

For a crawling moment he remembered a similar time long ago on Snowglade. He had gone flying with his new wife, Veronica, and Abraham. Near the Citadel there had been an ancient tunnel through a mountain, dug during the High Arcology times. The prickly desert wind swept through it and funnels artfully increased the gale speed. Where the tunnel turned abruptly vertical the wind could support a man with wings. He had cast off into the roaring stream and circled around the tunnel's wide oval bore. Veronica followed, grinning and wide-eyed. By canting their wings they could soar and plunge and bank about each other. Abraham then came swooping down, his yells swept away in the howl. They had labored against the battering wind and then harvested its incessant pressures, merrily spiraling around one another, aloft on the moment . . .

All gone, a time lost forever . . .

Now . . .

His tongue seemed to fill his throat. Searing air bit in his nostrils. His suit was close to overheating. He realized he was nearing the point where his grip on himself would slip. He would do something rash to escape the heat and he would die.

But something Arthur had said plucked at his memory. Even a small pressure . . .

"The light. You said something about it pushing us."

Yes, of course, but that acts equally in all directions.

"Not if we turn some of the silver off."

What? That would— Oh, I see. If we slightly lessen the silvering on the front of us, say, by robbing the autocircuits there of power . . . yes, then the light will reflect less well. We will be pushed in that direction by the light striking us from behind.

"Let's do it. Not much time."

But the heat! Lessening the reflection heightens the absorption.

Killeen had already guessed that. "Show me how to taper down the silver on my chest."

No, I don't— The temperature outside, it's 3,459 centigrade! I don't—I can't take—

"Give the info. *Now.*" Killeen kept his mind under tight control. This was the only way, he felt sure of it, and seconds counted.

Not now, no! I'll—I'll think of something—something that will work—yes, work when we get through the core. I'll review my back memories, I'll—

"No. *Now.*"

He felt the Aspect's fear, surging now nearly as strongly as his own. So the chip-mind had finally broken, revealed the fragments of its residual humanity.

Deliberately he reached within himself and smothered Arthur's objections. It called plaintively to him in a small, desperate whine. Killeen clamped down, forced Arthur back into a cranny.

"*Now.*"

FOUR

Beq'qdahl's ribbed pores flared a deep, angry yellow.

<The Noughts flee already!>

Quath quickly peered ahead, using the sharp infrared. Motes were spreading away from the outline of the approaching station. <They are quick of wit.>

<No, it is *we* who are as thick as grubs!>

<They seem to have mastered the mechanisms of those shuttlecraft soon enough.>

<They had time, monopody! *You* were playing your addled prank.>

Quath bristled. <We both took part in the little amusement.>

<*I* wished to get on with our assault.>

Quath said as mildly as she could, <Then you should not have helped calculate the precise velocity and angle for my flinging of the little Nought.>

<I—I was sucked in. I had no idea we would suffer such delay, and miss these vermin. We were to take samples, remember?>

Quath watched the shuttles speed away, spreading like fragments of an explosion. A nice escape. Already some swept in close to the glow of the cosmic string, which was rotating on a test run, to try new magnetic flux generators at both poles. The test would last only a bit longer, and would not suck more metal from the core unless there was a pressure failure. The string would keep the Noughts from reaching the upper atmosphere, but as she watched the shuttles they mingled with the great slabs of freeze-formed nickel-iron that laced the high orbits.

Clever pests! She hungered to crush them.

Amid that complex stockpile they could hide quite well, and no doubt planned to do so. These were no mere ground-grubbed Noughts, no. As soon as the cosmic string slowed, they would slip into the planet's atmosphere and air brake. With each working of the Syphon quakes rocked the planet, but that would scarcely prevent their landing. Once down, they could find easy refuge in the jumbled countryside.

<I shall make clear the cause of this foolish mistake,> Beq'qdahl said ponderously.

Quath spat back, <And I shall rely on the inboard timeline recordings, which will show what a trifling time we spent on our game.>

<You would—?>

<Of course.> Such a measure might not carry significant weight with the elders of the Hive, but Quath was determined to try.

Beq'qdahl paused, obviously reconsidering. Their ship cruised along its approach orbit. The station ahead seemed inactive now. Its bays yawned empty, shuttle ships gone.

A mech-slave signal peeped forth on the main board before Quath. A large craft hung near the station, probably the Noughts'.

<We can search that cobbled-together ship,> Beq'qdahl said.

<I doubt any Noughts remain there,> Quath said.

<Still . . .>

<And it looks to be a cramped, skinny ship. We will have to wedge ourselves into its bowels and search thoroughly.>

<Well, perhaps I can take another position in this entire matter,> Beq'qdahl said judiciously.

<I should hope so.>

<After all, we have rid the station of pests, have we not?>

<True—and without firing a shot.>

<We can report to the Hive that the mere sight of us approaching, and our ferocious battlecries, frightened them off.>

<I do not recall that I issued any cries.>

<I did. And so I shall report.>

Quath decided not to challenge this small lie. <Do you think we will be believed?>

<Surely so!>

Quath relaxed somewhat. She watched one of the fleeing shuttlecraft on the horizon, where it took up orbit above the aura of the Cosmic Circle. Alarm shot through her. <That is the shuttle we intercepted!>

Beq'qdahl ratcheted her pods in disbelief. <No! You were to commandeer it!>

<I did,> Quath cried in frustration.

<Then there must have been another Nought inside. It has seized the vessel.> Beq'qdahl's electro-aura seethed with malice.

Acrid hormones flooded the cabin as both of them suffered involuntary embarrassment. Their bodies acted to rid their lymph chambers of the corrosive chemicals generated by their sudden, spiky emotions.

Quath said darkly, <This is a deep humiliation.>

<Yes, and *your* fault.>

<That will not exempt *you*, noble pus-sucker.>

Beq'qdahl saw Quath's threat. Her head swiveled and turned indigo in confusion. <We will both be held accountable?>

<Of course.>

Bitter cadences of violent color washed over Beq'qdahl. <There must be *some* way to recover.>

<We could simply not speak of the mission,> Quath said. <As long as we satisfy the minimum requirements, perhaps no attention will be paid. After all, this is a minor task.>

<We must bring back some of the vermin for analysis, remember,> Beq'qdahl said sourly.

<Ah . . .> Quath recalled. It had seemed a small matter at the time they received their orders. <To see if they are the same Noughts which have pestered us.>

<And very nearly killed me,> Beq'qdahl added sharply. She still seemed to take that past battle as a personal affront.

<The Tukar'ramin prefers certainty in these matters,> Quath answered diplomatically. <And such caution is well repaid, in this case. These Noughts are canny, if they are the same as the pack I slaughtered.>

Beq'qdahl fretted. <I would like to cover every possible source of complaint.>

Quath did not relish the prospect of having to run down one of the quick, darting shuttles, then pry it open and rummage inside for a sample Nought. They might easily squash them all and then have to go after yet another shuttle. All that, in full view of the thermweave crews who worked in preparing the great metal-mountains. Was there some other way . . . ? She poked at her subminds, rummaging for any notion that might help. They chorused their partial visions.

Beq'qdahl said, <I am quite certain, however, that this taking of a sample is a minor matter. Surely the Hive will not fault us for such a negligible—>

<Wait,> Quath said brightly. <Wait, I have an idea.>

FIVE

The yellow-white hell soared away above Killeen's head. The walls nearly seeped a sullen red, but even this was a relief after the incandescent fury that dwindled now, a fiery disk fading above him like a dimming, perpetually angry sun.

Killeen panted deeply, though it seemed to do no good. Prickly waves washed over him, bringing him unbearable itches that moved in restless storms across his skin. His lungs jerked irregularly. His arms trembled. Muscles and nerves fought their private rebellions and wars.

But he had managed to keep his arms and legs straight. The light pressure would not have forced him in only one direction if he had spun or tumbled.

Had it been enough? The long minutes at the core had crawled by, bringing agonizing lungfuls of scorched air.

Now the searing ebbed slightly.

We are, after all, just another radiating body. We can only lose heat by emitting it as infrared waves. So we must wait for cooler surroundings before this intolerable warmth can disperse.

His Arthur Aspect seemed remarkably collected, given the hysteria which had beset it only minutes before. "How . . . how 'bout that cooling thing?"

You mean our refrigerator? It can only function by ejecting waste heat at a cooler sink. As yet there *are* no colder surroundings, as you can see.

"So we wait till we get out?" It seemed an impossibly long time. Between his boots he could see the blackness of the planet's mantle, thousands of kilometers of dead rock they must shoot through before regaining the dark of space itself. And there he would somehow have to make good this attempt, or else he would slow and pause and then plunge again. He wished again that he had saved his thruster fuel. It would give him some freedom, some hope of being something other than the helpless, dumb test particle in a grotesque experiment.

We do have some fluids we could eject, but . . .

"But what? Look, we try everything. Got no hope otherwise."

The refrigerant fluids. We could bring them to a high temperature and vent them.

"Think it'll help much?"
To lose the coolant meant he would have no chance whatever if he failed up ahead and fell back into the tube. He would fry for sure.

I cannot tell how much momentum we picked up from that maneuver. Pushing a large mass such as ourselves with mere light pressure . . .

Killeen gave a jittery laugh. "I'm the mass here—you weigh nothin' at all. And don't you worry 'bout calculatin' what'll happen. Time comes, up at the top of this hole, I'll have to grab whatever's in sight. Fly by the seat of my pants, not some eee-quation."

Then I should vent the refrigerant fluids?

"Sure. Bet it all!" Killeen felt small icy rivulets coursing along his neck as he let the Aspect take fractional control of his inboard systems.

I am warming the poly-xenon now.

"And when you spray it, just use the spinal vents. That'll give us another push in the right direction. Could make the difference."

Oh, I see. I did not think of this possibility.

"Trouble with you Aspects is you can't imagine anythin' you haven't seen 'fore."

Let us not debate my properties at quite this time. We are rising toward the surface and you must be ready. I believe the wall you face is nearer now. Notice the sparkling?

"Yeasay. What's it mean?"

That is where the mantle rock is forced by sidewise pressure against the passing cosmic string. It is disintegrated on impact. I cannot see whether it is somehow incorporated into the string, or whether it is simply forced back. For whatever reason, the rock is held back. Clearly, the cyborgs must relax this hoop pressure somehow, down in the core, in order to fill this tube with the liquid iron we saw before.

"Maybe they just slow it down some? Let the iron squish in a li'l 'fore the next time the string comes whizzin' by?"

In the midst of techtalk he lapsed back into the short, clipped speech of his boyhood in the Citadel. The carefully assumed veneer of Cap'n rubbed away under the press of action. Killeen fumbled with the suit refrigerator controls. He knew he had to understand more about the hoop.

Possibly. Clearly the rotating string exerts great pressure against these rocks.

Killeen watched the quick flashing in the walls. For him to see these sparks at all, they must be enormous, since his speed took him by kilometers of the ruby-red rock in an instant. He had no bodily sensation of speed, but knew from the 3D simulation Arthur ran in his left eye that he was rising toward the surface, slowing as gravity asserted itself.

He had to find a way to escape the tube, but no idea came to him. He had nothing he could throw to gain momentum. The coolant jet throbbed behind him, but relative to the blur of motion in the walls he could not tell whether it did any good. It occurred to him that if he was too successful he would crash into the speeding wall and be torn to pieces in an instant. Somehow the abstract nature of these things, the dry, distant feel of science, frightened him all the more.

The tube is flaring out. We are approaching one side of it, but I cannot judge our velocity well. As we rise, the hoop curves away to make its great arc outward. The majesty of it is impressive, I must say. No mechtech I have ever heard of matches this. Grey says the historical records suggest even greater works near the Eater.

"Forget that. What can I *do*?"

I am trying to see how we can use our situation, but I must say that a solution continues to elude me. The dynamics—

"We're gettin' close. Come on!"

The rock around him had already ceased glowing. Beyond the walls lay complete darkness. He could not understand how he could be moving up from the center of New Bishop and yet still feel that he was falling. No matter; science was a set of rules to him, and this was simply a rule he did not comprehend.

The tunnel was broadening. A shimmering golden passage flared gradually as he gazed between his boots at shards of light that rushed toward him. More vast lava lakes, brimming with angry reds. The injury to the whole axial length had brutally shoved great masses together, making the walls around him froth with the planet's jagged orange wrath.

Again he thought of what would happen if he could do nothing up ahead. The cool logic of dynamics would, Arthur said, fling him back into the core. The heat would kill him on the next pass. Or if it managed only to send him into delirium, there would be another cycle, and another, and another. . . . He would bob endlessly, a crisp cinder obeying simple but inexorable laws.

Instantly he was swimming in light.

Stars bloomed beneath his feet. A bowl of brilliant gas and suns opened as he shot free of the planet's grasp, above the twilight line. After the sultry darkness this sky was a welcoming bath of colors and contrasts.

Out, free!

He could feel his suit cool as it lost heat to the cold sky. It went *ping, pop* as joints contracted. Wrinkled hills rose above his head, the whole landscape stretching as it drew away. Here, too, was the stripped look, as though the polar ice had only recently been vanquished.

The golden walls fell away from him on one side, but in front of him the radiance did not fade or recede. It was much closer. He *had* gained some significant speed, then.

But now he was losing his speed along the tube. He watched

the planet above his helmet turn into a gigantic silvery bowl. The dawnline cut this bowl in half. A ruby skyglow of dustclouds and stars dominated the wan day.

As he rose the world's curve brought into view a far-off scruff of woodland and stark, jutting mountains. Fluffy white clouds clung to shallow valleys.

His rate of rise dwindled. The far side of the hoop-tube was bending away. In front of him the glow was brighter. He took a few moments to be sure he was in fact curving over along with the hoop walls. Could he see the flicker of motion from the rapidly rotating string? He had begun to think of the walls as solid, and now he became aware of their gauzy nature.

> The cosmic string can exert pressure only when it is very near you, of course. You will not in fact strike the cosmic string itself, I judge.

"Thought you said it'd take off my hand."

> I have conferred further with Grey. She believes that normally a string would function like a scythe. However, this highly magnetized string is different. Until now you were moving with respect to the string at high speeds. Now you will have a low relative velocity, but only for a brief moment. At such speeds the string's magnetic fields will repulse your metallic boots and suit.

"Huh." Killeen supposed this was good news, but the Aspect spoke as though this was just another dispassionate physics problem. "Look, you save any that cooler stuff?"

> Yes, I had anticipated that we might need another push. But there is very little. I needed it all to keep us from losing consciousness back there, and so—

"Get ready."

Already he could detect no further shrinking in the wrecked face of New Bishop below. He must be near the top of his swing.

"Fire it!"

He felt the jetting pressure at his back. The glowing hoop-tube curled away like an opening funnel. Beyond he could see the gossamer surface generated by the globe-spanning cosmic string. It appeared now to wrap the world in a ribbony stranglehold.

The venting at his spine gurgled to a stop.

Whuum-whuum-whuum, the magnetic rotor sang.

Vibrant, intense glow spread all around him. He windmilled his arms and brought his boots down toward the golden surface. It pulsed with freshening energy.

He felt as though he were a fragile bird, vainly flailing its wings above a sheet of translucent, wispy gold. Falling toward it. Performing his own sort of experiment . . .

The impact slammed him hard. It jarred up through his boots like a rough, wrenching punch. He had crouched, letting his legs absorb the momentum. Suddenly he was shooting along the surface of the sheet.

It has conveyed impulse to you, an infinitesimal fraction of its spinning energy.

Killeen felt himself loft slightly higher. Then he came down toward the sheet again. He had shot sidewise, away from the polar axis, going out on a tangent like a coin flung off a merry-go-round.

He hit again. This time the jolt twisted his ankle. It felt like a hand grabbing at him, then losing its grip. But it gave him another push—outward.

I estimate you are gaining significant velocity from these encounters. It is difficult to calculate, but—

Killeen ignored the tiny piping Aspect. His ankle ached. Was it broken?

He had no time to bend over and feel it. The shimmering plain came rising toward him again, hard and flat.

He grunted with pain. The shock caught his feet and flung him off at a steep angle, twisting him with a sharp, wrenching stab.

You will have to be more careful as you set down upon it. It can convey spin, but if your velocity is not aligned with its, there is a vector coupling, a torque—

"Shut up!" He did not want to set down on the golden surface again, the ghostly curtain that could clutch and break him like a stick.

But the velocity he was picking up from the thing flung him sidewise, not up. Only his rebounding kept him above the flickering radiance. If he slipped, tumbled, went shooting across the damned thing as he spun out of control—

The flickering golden sheet rushed at him.

He struck solidly. This time his left leg shrieked with distress and he barely managed to kick free. The strobing glow seemed all around him. He was going to hit again.

He windmilled. This time the shock was not as great but the muscles of his left leg seized up in an agonizing spasm.

Blinking away sweat, a weakness came over him. His ears rang. He wearily spun himself again, slower this time because the motion hurt his leg.

He expected to hit quicker but the jolt did not come. He looked down and could not judge the distance. The glow had dimmed. It took a long moment before he realized that the sheet was curving farther away from him, wrapping down to follow the arc of the planet.

He was free. Out. In the clean and silent spaces.

We are on a highly elliptical orbit, I gather. It should take us at a significant angle with respect to this hoop-plain. I cannot calculate the details, so it may be that we will return within its volume.

"Never mind," he said, panting.

We will need the information in due time, however, and—

"I doubt it. Look up."

Obsessed with its own mathematics, the Aspect piped with surprise as it responded to what Killeen saw.

Above them floated the sleek metallic body of the cyborg.

SIX

Quath made her way cautiously through murky warrens.

After the buoyant vault of space, these tunnels and cramped corridors weighed heavily on her, their air clotted and musky. Around her surged the endless parade of working podia, bound on their relentless missions, clattering and banging against one another in their haste. Lesser beings of russet scabrous shells scampered underfoot, bound on their menial tasks. They had been hatched in the bodies of native animals, to save the Hive's resources. Genetically programmed, they worked with fanatic purpose, as though they knew their own short lifespans.

Quath, though, went slowly. The presence inside her throbbed. The Nought kicked and fought, its puny jabs an irritant impossible to ignore. Her ceramic sensors saw it as a burning tangle of infrared deep in her guts.

But it was not this small nettling that bothered Quath. She knew what lay ahead of her, and so dawdled, picking at her cilia as though grooming herself. Some tiny hatchlings approached and Quath let them police her carapace. They caught microparasites, which were the inevitable inconvenience of strange worlds: native mites who had already learned to feast on the leaky joint sleeves and porous sheaths of the podia.

Soon, too soon, the great glowing cavern of the Tukar'ramin opened before her. Its murky mouth seemed to swallow all the certainties of her life.

You have done well, the Tukar'ramin greeted her from high in the glistening webs.

Quath preened at this ruby-flavored compliment, until she saw that Beq'qdahl had entered simultaneously from another of the innumerable tunnels that gave onto the Tukar'ramin's underbowl. Beq'qdahl did an artful dance with her many legs, accepting the Tukar'ramin's words as if they were directed at her alone.

<We did little more than your wiseness instructed,> Quath

154

said, using the collective noun first for formality. Then, to irritate Beq'qdahl, she shifted to first person. <And *I* have captured one of the pernicious Noughts who infested the station.>

What breed of Nought is this?

<A soft-skinned, bilegged thing. Crafty for its size.>

Doubtless so, for it engaged that station and co-opted the mechs there. I had understood that we had total control there. Yet these Noughts infested with humiliating ease.

There was no doubt, from the grammatically past-imperative hormonal inflections, that Quath and Beq'qdahl were among those humiliated.

Quath suppressed the impulse to cock her pods into a gesture of total apology and mercy-plead. Instead, she quickly transmitted a set of images and sensory details of the thing. These were taken after she had stripped it of its suit and weapons, back inside their ship.

<Observe, please, from your lofty perspective,> Quath said reverently. <This thing displays obvious signs of recent evolution. Note the hair—atop its head and at the genitals only. The former for protection from sunlight, I believe. The latter—perhaps some primitive way of gathering attractive musk about the area it would most like to have revered by others?>

Doubtless some such business. Absence of a pelt does suggest a highly sensory life, serving as it does to expose the surface nerves optimally.

<Filthy creatures!> Beq'qdahl hissed severely.

<But effective.> Quath seized the chance to appear more shrewd. <I believe it had taken the shuttle ship to the vicinity of the Syphon in order to study it.>

<Nonsense!> Beq'qdahl jeered. <I directed that shuttle to leave the station, as soon as its inboard systems showed presence of Noughts. To harvest a sample.>

We cannot be too careful here, the Tukar'ramin said slowly. *This Nought may have intelligence and mastery beyond its apparent mawkishness.*

<I agree.> Quath ventured to release a scent of confidence, edged with dangling, frayed filigrees of mature concern. She was about to add that she had kept the sample Nought for further study, when the Tukar'ramin continued thoughtfully, plainly without registering Quath's words.

Well that you disposed of them all, then. They are oddly able. Even one might cause hindrance to us.

Both Quath and Beq'qdahl fell silent. Quath struggled to find a way to agree and yet not divulge the truth, so she was glad when Beq'qdahl said, <They scattered before us like grains of dust! We chased them relentlessly into the upper atmosphere, where they flamed into oblivion.>

The fierceness of this declaration could not cover the underlying sweet cut of self-doubt that Beq'qdahl leaked from her unruly hind glands.

Reentry fires, you mean?

<Most, yes. I could not count them all.>

Quath bristled at Beq'qdahl's use of *I* when they had both done the searching. She quickly felt better, though, when the Tukar'ramin said forcefully, *You should have savaged them all!*

Beq'qdahl choked with mortification and farted a foul cloud of orange fear. She managed to get out, <I, that is, we—>

You were senior, Beq'qdahl. Can you assure me that these Noughts, who may even have the power to voyage between stars, are vanquished?

<Such assurances are surely impossible, savant of my life.>

This was a deft diplomatic sally, mingled with pious fogs of humble oil, Quath thought. But it brought Beq'qdahl no credit.

Then set about making sure of your task.

<Of course. Is this to be *our* task or mine alone?>

You are senior in experience. You both now sport six legs. Quath seems to be gathering her wits quite ably. I suppose you may call upon her for assistance. She acquitted herself well— perhaps better than you.

Burnt-yellow splashes of barely suppressed anger/anxiety shot up and down Beq'qdahl's thorax, but her voice remained crustily formal. Pleased, Quath glimpsed a tinge of bluegreen envy betraying Beq'qdahl in her milky proboscis hairs.

<I assume I may continue my fruitful mining explorations, while seeing to this minor problem?> Beq'qdahl asked.

What? What?

Quath saw at once that Beq'qdahl had miscalculated. Waves of an unknown emotion jetted down from the Tukar'ramin. *Pursue these Noughts! Drop your mining. I have received word that the Illuminates themselves have taken notice of these events.*

The very mention of these august entities stilled the chilly air of the great rock cavern.

Beq'qdahl, do not seek to vainly augment yourself when a vital mission awaits.

<I assure you, revered one, I did not—>

You can begin with a task of some risk, since your errors have precipitated this trouble. Witness—

Into Quath came a picture of the station. Beside it, now clamped firmly by crosshatched stays, was the Nought ship.

Beq'qdahl began, <We can—>

Chords of vexed concern sounded through the unfilled spaces of the image, sucking Quath along with the Tukar'ramin's mood.

This little vessel is their conveyance. You ignored it. Perhaps some still cower within. Your task is to cleanse this craft. Inspect, analyze! Find its inner minds. Flay them open for my inspection.

Startled beneath this torrent of stench-commands and acrid air-cuts, Beq'qdahl tried to protest. <I, we, cannot master all the craft necessary to—>

Go! Now!

The sudden spitting-green anger of the Tukar'ramin startled Quath. She was grateful that Beq'qdahl caught the force of it, a yellow-white jet that scoured through Quath's sensorium. Beq'qdahl, in the full stream, backed away with trembling legs.

The Tukar'ramin did not dismiss them, in fact took no further notice of the two scurrying forms. They scrambled away as the Tukar'ramin's bulk tugged itself up glistening damp strands into lofty darkness.

Quath felt Beq'qdahl's jittery, addled state as the two scuttled away. On a subchannel Beq'qdahl sent her preliminary thoughts about logistics, search patterns, weapons—assembled impressively quickly, considering the blistering she had received.

Quath's thoughts submerged beneath a rising distress. She broke away from Beq'qdahl and fled down a narrow shaft, letting herself fall in the hushed cool air until the depths of the warren rushed past. Somehow her petrifying fear of heights did not occur in the cramped chute. Heights in the open—or, far worse, flying— terrified her race. Beq'qdahl had overcome this, another reason to despise her.

Her magnetic brakes pulsed. A passing food-cloud brought stinging encrustations to her eyes—yet it was as though she ambled in a dream.

She registered nothing, consumed by the unspoken lie that she now carried within. The Tukar'ramin and Beq'qdahl and all the podia assumed that she had snuffed out the Nought after taking samples from it. They would expect immediate scrapes of skin and nuggets of brain, to better understand the pests.

But the Nought rapped against her inner steel partitions. It thrashed and jerked and emitted foul odors. Perhaps the thing had even excreted inside Quath. What a risk to incur, all for Nought!

Quath's levered arms began to pry open her innermost carrypouch to pluck out the Nought—but she slowed, tugged by flickering doubt . . . and stopped.

This puny thing was indeed the same breed of Nought which she had slaughtered with valor in defense of Beq'qdahl. In the moments after her victory she had studied the carcass of such a Nought. That had helped her to cast off her fear of death.

So for this one last Nought she felt an odd sense of connection. She had told herself at first, on the way down from orbit, that keeping the Nought alive was simply a way to be sure her samples were fresh. But once in the smoky, constricted warrens, she had begun to feel vague musings, strange lacings of sensation, canted views of her world.

It was the Nought. At this intimate range, her probings of it had overlapped the Nought's own surprisingly complex sensorium— which felt to Quath like a spherical coil of brightly colored threads, writhing like languid serpents.

Try as she might, she could not penetrate the knot. A small, oily pocket of exotic zest now seeped into Quath's mind. She could not give it up. Not yet.

The thing inside interlaced with Quath's electro-aura, giving forth images and undefinable tangs. They led her down into a labyrinth of airless corridors, lit by scattershot, smoky fogs, brooding silences, lurid accelerations down unseen gradients. This small creature dwelled in a slanted universe blurred by currents, hormones, scents.

Something in this tilted world caught in Quath. Blunt wedges of pinched obstruction bloomed bony-hard inside her. Her pale certainties splintered. The already shifty terrain of her oblique interior landscape warped and canted.

But she had no choice, Quath thought. She *must*. The Tukar'ramin would banish Quath forever if she knew, cast her into a starved life of ragged foraging in the ruined lands beyond the Hive. . . .

Worse, she could not merely yield it forth, no—too late for that. Quath had to slaughter the unfolding thing within her. Hide it. Mash the body into paste, pack it into porous walls where it could never be found, or recognized, or understood.

Could she? Quath teetered on the brink.

SEVEN

Killeen could barely breathe.

He swam in a cloying fluid, but when he opened his mouth to gasp it did not fill with the syrupy acid-tinged gelatinous stuff that surrounded him, buoyed him, made his every movement sluggish and impotent.

Dreamlike, he thrashed. Swam. Punched angrily at torpid air that caught his fists in cobwebbed resistant softness, blunting every movement.

Like a baby in an awful ambient pouch, he thought. Helpless and fearing birth.

His skin was a stretched, livid thing. The burning he had suffered now returned doubly. A searing, itching sheet covered him, tight, a livid seethe. He ran numbed hands over his chest and thighs, and each touch brought an angry, prickly dart that launched small storms of heat across him.

Something scratched at his mind.

A clawing itch that worked its way inward. A stuttering run down his spine.

Cool liquid pain. He braced himself against this sudden brute invasion.

A tentative, telescoped presence slid by him in murky shadow.

Tiny warm breezes licked him, feathering his hair.

Something massive and deliberate circled. It moved in tides of light, filigreed by dancing shadows that flittered like small mad birds against the windowpanes of his mind.

Abruptly he was not in the tight, rubbery air. Before him welled a streaming aura. Red and pink scraped and rustled. Shifting blobs drifted, eclipsing each other like sluggish planets. Their shadows played among blue traceries.

He squinted, or thought he did. His arms and legs still swam in the gurgling, patient fluid that forgave all movement, but he smelled an acrid wind. Heard harsh clacks and clatters. Tasted blood and a biting, cool jelly. Glimpsed a foggy tunnel projecting away from him in ruddy, smoldering splendor.

He realized that the cyborg had tapped into his sensorium. It was sampling him—he could feel a blunt, chilly, awkward rummaging. Astringent light played along rumpled walls nearby. Slithery harmonics played somewhere, lurking just beyond clear hearing.

And he had gained symmetric access to its warped world. A ledge studded with ornately shaped protrusions swept by. Without something he knew for comparison he could not tell how quick this motion was, but a sickening tug in his stomach told him of lurching acceleration, wrenching turns around corners, abrupt surges up seemingly impossible wall slopes.

Gobbets brown and sticky rained down everywhere. They were languid, oscillating spheres that blew on a warm wind, voluptuous and fat. Killeen realized that a dim echo of the cyborg's hunger had leaked through to him, making his mouth water. A savory drop struck the wall and bounced, wobbly and fat and beckoning.

The cyborg ate it. A rasping tang shot through him, not in his mouth but somehow up and down his chest, striking hard into his cock, squeezing his ass tight in an exquisite, ungovernable reflex. Killeen felt a stretched sense of something plunging through him, blundering.

The cyborg accelerated. Killeen felt himself rushing with a rolling yaw toward a snub-nosed cylinder of white and orange. The cyborg did not slow and Killeen instinctively braced himself for a collision—which did not come.

Instead, the cylinder swallowed them. What had appeared to be a protruding point was instead an opening. As they sped through hexagonal tunnels, banking up onto the side faces with centrifugal ease, Killeen began to get a sense of the place outside. Arthur said:

> Your eyes saw the cylinder as pointing toward us, because of the cast of shadows. Grey points out that the human eye has evolved to see by light from the sky, remember, and reads shadows with that bias. Here the glow comes from the floor, and more weakly from the walls. The shadows are therefore reversed, and mean the opposite of what your automatic reactions assume.

"Can you change that?"

No—such matters are buried deep in the brain. The cyborg sees by infrared, I gather. On a perpetually cloudy planet, the ground would often be warmer than the sky, and thus more luminous in the infrared. Such an evolutionary aspect would explain why these tunnels are floor-illuminated. Since we are receiving this cyborg's raw data, we process it with our bias and get exactly the upside-down result. To see as it does we would have to invert your accustomed perception patterns.

"Look, how can I get quit of this?"

Consider—such an ability probably implies that the original species, which has now cyborged itself, often lived underground. It no doubt foraged above ground, but infrared vision would allow it to see from the warmed walls of its burrows. Once occupied, their own body heat would allow them some dim wall radiance. Such ecological niches stress skills at construction and three-dimensional spatial abilities. Perhaps this explains why they are building the huge things in orbit.

"Guttin' this planet, just so they can build bigger anthills?"

Perhaps so; evolution is destiny, I've always believed. But there are other implications.

"Somethin' we can use?" Killeen had listened to enough empty talk.

My first conclusion is that we're underground, doubtless. If we leave this pouch we're in, we'll wander quite blindly through a maze of tunnels. Hopeless to escape, I fear.

Killeen grunted sourly.

I advise caution.

"Don't see it much matters what I do."

Until we know why it brought you here we should remain flexible.

Killeen tried to distance himself from the sensations that washed through him, tried to think. Despairing, he wondered what had happened to the Family. He had gotten a distant impression, as the cyborg ship reeled him in, of other craft moving swiftly in the sky. His comm had squawked twice with human voices, faint and unintelligible.

Has anyone survived? It was one thing for a Cap'n to die in a chance encounter with a mech, or with a thing like this huge assembly of living and mechlike parts, and quite another to be cut off from your command, still alive while everyone you loved and honored was dead, killed by your own incompetence.

He made himself envision possibilities. The cyborgs might not have bothered to get Jocelyn from the Flitter. But unless she got to the surface, the Cap'ncy would go to Cermo automatically. He wasn't quick to lead in a crisis. The man would try, of course, but Shibo would probably have to make the hard decisions. She and Cermo could hold the Family together on alien soil.

If any of them still lived . . .

PART FOUR

SUCH MEN ARE DANGEROUS

ONE

The pouch clenched and split and spewed him out.

Killeen gasped for breath, as though he had been holding a single lungful the entire time—days? weeks?—he was enclosed. The featherlight emulsifying fluid that had held him somehow managed to bring air and food in through his lungs, for he felt no hunger.

He got to his knees, expecting to see tunnels in the cyborg warren. Instead a fresh, sharp breeze brought him smells of fragrant mold and dusty hills. His eyes cleared. Fuzzy patterns telescoped into crisp images, the world seeming to stretch and draw closer to him.

He stood in a field of crumpled stone, weaving unsteadily. His ankles ached with the memory of slamming into the cosmic string's sheen of magnetic pressures.

The cyborg rose like an unlikely natural encrustation behind him. Its double-jointed arms smoothed a fast-healing seam.

Useless to run, he thought. He shook himself dry—though the moisture he felt seemed to be beneath his skin, not on it—while the cyborg clicked and hummed and watched him. They were alone together in a blasted landscape. In the distance Killeen could see what appeared to be a malformed hill but he instantly knew it was an entrance to some mech structure. Craters pocked it. It had the empty, defeated look of a skull.

He felt a tickling throughout his body, like cold wires drawn slickly out of him, letting his arms and legs relax into smooth sausages of muscle. He wobbled.

Images cascaded in his mind—silent, meditative, embroidered. Section views of *Argo*. A striking picture of something large and sticky-white, attached to descending, puffy-pale strands.

163

Then, like a swift slap in the face out of nowhere, it let him go. His mind lost its pervasive, leaden fog. He felt a grimy wind stir his hair.

The cyborg's massive bulk moved away. It had a long, lizardy tail that ended in an antenna, like the bulb of a leathery flower.

The cyborg simply walked away, moving with surprising speed. Its many legs clacked and hummed.

Killeen limped away across the broken land, sore and tired. Slanting sunlight brought a twilight glow to a far rumpled ridgeline of tawny hills.

He stopped and leaned over to shake his head. Some milky stuff oozed from his ear and his hearing sharpened. Slime dripped from his suit.

The cutting yet spongy-sweet smell of the cyborg's interior spaces clung to him. He began trotting. Soon his own sweat washed away the alien scent.

For hours he made his way down a crushed valley. The cosmic string hung just above the horizon, its dull ruby-hued curve cutting across the shimmering of a frayed molecular cloud. Killeen remembered the perceptions he had gotten (accidentally?) from the cyborg—something about a temporary halt, stilling the cosmic string, to allow construction to catch up with the supply of vacuum-formed nickel-iron. Now magnetic fingers held the loop steady, a smoldering cut in the sky.

Without its bright golden glow the slow coming of sunset allowed the far reaches around Abraham's Star to display their fitful life. Faint flashes wriggled deep within the glowering banks that hung beyond this cramped solar system. Quick bursts of saffron yellow seethed against a slowly gathering wash of blue. Vibrant pink discharged energies within a cloak of sullen brown dust. Spidery scarlet filaments formed and died and swelled again, as though beads of blood caught the setting sun and glinted with evil beauty.

Killeen wondered if these momentary effervescences that washed through dark sinews of dust were mechworks, or natural storms and tossings brought forth by the constant whirl of matter in the Galactic Center. Or could unimaginable tools like the cosmic string be at work there?

He moved cautiously, using natural cover. There was plenty of it among the upturned stone slabs and jutting hummocks. The cyborg had returned to him all his equipment, even his shortarm rifle. His shanks were fully fueled. His Arthur Aspect commented:

Indeed, they have far greater capacity. Your suit reading
says there is more than one hundred kiloJoules stored in
each fuel gram—far higher than anything Snowglade tech
achieved. The cyborg has outfitted us well.

Killeen moved cautiously, ignoring the tiny pleadings of his
Aspects. In this strange world he relied on the instincts of his youth.
His hunting senses were still tuned to the subtle graces of
Snowglade. Here each detail was slightly skewed. He automatically searched each gully for a trap, sniffed the breeze for oily
clues. A distant cone-shaped mountain gave the air an acidic tinge
with a long, charcoal plume.

The land needed rest. Everywhere once-proud cliffs had
slumped. Layers of rock splayed out like decks of cards tossed
aside by a bored gargantuan. Dust covered every ledge and narrow, and fat dirty clouds of it drifted lazily on the horizon.

Yet here and there tinkling springs leaped into the air, frivo-
lous fountains among ancient upturned strata. He stopped by one
and let the stream play over his hands. Scooping some into his
face, he tasted a distant, rusty echo of waters he had drunk on
Snowglade so long ago.

The internal heat liberated from the infall has worked outward from the core. I suspect deep-buried ice deposits are
melting, providing this water.

"Uh-huh."

Killeen was not in a mood for techtalk from Arthur. Still less
welcome was the piping voice of Ling. He needed to flee the
clogged, solemn pockets of his mind; the cyborg had left a damp,
musty smell there.

It was time also to let go the control he had sustained for so
long, while the cyborg rummaged through him.

All that while he had run his mind from the top down, keeping
consciousness in the foreground, a hard layer which his lower
minds could not penetrate. Now he let his inner self emerge and
relax, beginning to digest his wrenching experience and make his
mind's peace with them. The simple fact of living, of survival, was
a continuous miracle. He gave himself over to it. From Snowglade's
raw battles he knew the sensation well, and relished it. Pain,
grief, fear, rage—all had to flourish and ebb and find their places.

Bemused, he released his Aspects—Ling, Grey, Arthur, even
the lesser Faces like Bud—and allowed them to play joyfully in a

cloistered pocket of him, but without letting their squeaky voices snag his attention. They frolicked as they tasted the chilling air of New Bishop, caught the dusty fragrances. They talked to and through one another, minute presences strumming through his sensory net, streaming by integrating nodes and causative factor points.

So much had happened to him! To avoid crippling disorder, he had to enlist his Aspects and Faces in at least a partial integration of his torments. Without the Family he was an odd scrap wandering this smashed world . . . but he did not know if the Family lived. He had to keep himself together until he knew, even if that meant years of questing.

So he focused on the crushed forests that he picked his way through, on the gutted plains and ruptured ridgelines that swept beneath his fast-flying boots. The limp was gone, his servos responded again, and now he was gnawingly hungry.

Family Bishop had always been deft foragers, and he called up an old woman's Face to help him locate edible berries and leaves. She was a cranky sort, full of curt advice. Much of her lore did not apply to this strange world. She found tasty roots but squawked with alarm at the acidic leaves and ellipsoidal fruit he found. Tentative bites told him they were suitable.

He prowled the wrecked forest. Trees had been slapped and mangled by a vastly casual malice. They slanted crazily, exposing their bowls of snaky roots. Leaves of exact, pale green circles piled high in streambeds, and small things skittered deep in them. Damp flats were covered with tracks: three-toed, seven-toed, split-wedged, with some broad smooth pads. Killeen had never seen traces of such large creatures, and they filled him with respect for the past wealth of this place. His Arthur Aspect put in:

> All the cyborgs' work, of course. They emptied the tube we fell through. That kilometer-wide shaft caused the land to fall only the length of a finger here.

"Huh? Take that much rock and metal out, seems like there'd be a big drop here, too."

> Not at all; it is a property of simple geometry. The loss is spread over the much larger surface area of the planet. Watch—

The three-color diagram that sprung into Killeen's right eye made sense, once he studied it, but even so— "Droppin' a finger's length did all *this?*"

All layers felt it. Seismic adjustments occur unevenly.

"I'll say."
Killeen was crossing a clearing. Suddenly a tan fountain sprayed up, showering water and sand on him.

Ah yes. Hydrostatic forces still being released. The vibrations have made the soil here more like a slurry.

Rolling, sea-swell tremors drove Killeen to make for more solid ground, drowning out the Aspect voice in his own panting. He found edible leaves and chewed them down with relish. The ground continued shaking and bucking, as if trying to throw off the scum of persistent life.

Filled for the first time in what seemed like days, he began to feel better once he broke into a steady, loping trot. Over the next line of hills lay a mech city. It had been torn to pieces. Explosions had ripped apart immense factories. Much of the destruction seemed to have come from charges planted inside, as though someone had smuggled in bombs.

Brown mech carapaces lay strewn everywhere. Something had scavenged the bodies for parts. Cyborgs, he guessed.

He wandered in the hush of the ruined streets. No mechs labored to put this right. Nothing moved. At some intersections towers of ornately worked alloys rose. Killeen remembered the art of the Mantis and could not tell if these spindly things had some function or were intended to ornament the city.

He felt uneasy in the mechworks and did not try to find food among the ruins. At sundown he still had not crossed the sprawling mechplex. That night he hid in a parts shed and slept. He awoke several times, pursued by fevered dreams. His time inside the alien returned and he strangled in jellied air, vainly swimming upward, his lungs scalded. Each awakening left his arms and legs clenched tight as though he had been fighting in his sleep. And then he would doze off and again the dream would come.

Before dawn something moved nearby. He carefully peered out. A large animal was creeping closer. The largest creature he had ever seen was an old orange chicken back at the Citadel. This thing could easily eat the chicken in one gulp. Something about its large teeth told Killeen that this idea might be pleasing to the animal.

Plainly it had scented him. After all his years of hunting mechs and being hunted by them, he had no idea how to deal with the animal. It came nearer. Its ears flattened. Killeen held his rifle at the ready. Silently he stepped from the door of the shed and stood watching. The animal froze. They remained that way for a long time. A strange sense of communion stole over Killeen. Its yellow eyes were clear and deep.

Pale dawn seeped around them. The animal finally licked its lips with bored unconcern and walked away. It stopped at the corner of a storage bin nearby and looked back at him once and then went on.

As Killeen set out walking again he realized his rifle was set for an electromag pulse. It would have had no effect whatever on the animal.

Without thinking about much of anything, he felt conflicts within him flare and simmer and die. Beneath this world's calm, the natural clasp of life pealed forth its own silent message.

TWO

The day was sharp and clear. He found berries and edible leaves and kept going. Faint sounds from a second destroyed mech city made him skirt around it until he could find another route.

From a distance the buckled ramparts reminded him of his last sight of the Citadel, at the Calamity. Innumerable times he had replayed that day in his dreams. The very air had seemed to roil and stretch, he remembered. Rippling radiances had washed the clouds even before the mech attack on Citadel Bishop began, giving them some warning. Not enough, though, for the mechs had thrown immense resources into their assault. His father had been at the center of the Citadel's defense. Despite the desperation that crept over them all as the first reports came in, all bad, Abraham had kept a calm, unhurried manner. Killeen had been nearby when the mechs breached a Citadel wall. Abraham had directed an effective flanking attack on the intrusion. Killeen had not even comprehended the mech purpose until his father's deft sally cut off the head of the mech advance and chopped the remnants to pieces.

But then he had lost sight of his father in the hammering chaos of multiple assaults. Mech aircraft had bombed the central Citadel and the ramparts fell.

Killeen had helped carry ammunition to the air-defense guns as strange lights filled the sky. They all had sensed unseen presences above the battle.

When Killeen's wife, Veronica, died he had ceased to register very much. He had felt her death in his sensorium, since they were linked. But it had taken a long chaotic time to find her, to be sure.

He stood on a far hill, looking back meditatively at the mech city. Part of him relished the sight of the mighty mechs brought low. Another remembered the Citadel, and not only because of the city. The sky far beyond began to move with washes of pale luminescence in a way that reminded him of the Calamity. The luminosity was in the air itself, not the fainter play of colors in molecular clouds. The sight chilled him.

Yet it also recalled his encounters on Snowglade with an entity which had somehow spoken through the magnetic fields of the planet itself. The thing had talked incomprehensibly of Abraham, and of issues Killeen could not follow. Recalling that, he wondered if the magnetic being had been at the Calamity, had lit the sky with its witnessing. Why should such a vast thing care for the doings of a small, inconsequential race? There were no answers.

Killeen finally shook off the mood and moved on. The quiet of the natural world enfolded him.

But then a biting sulfuric tinge filled his nose. A hollow bass note caught at the outer edge of his sensorium. A mech trace?

It carried a strange sugary aftertaste, though, unlike any mech signature he knew. His sensorium translated its electromag-tags into smells because that was the human sense directly linked to memory centers; a brief whiff of an old odor brought long-buried memories welling up, often of use.

Killeen slipped between the slumped trunks of trees that somehow still showed fresh green growth. The land had collapsed, but root systems seemed resistant even to the implosion of the planet. He flitted quickly among the tangled growth and peered ahead.

Siiiggg!—something fast cut the air near him. He dropped into a dry streambed and strained to feel his way forward through his sensorium. Hot smells rang through him.

He angled along a ridgeline and three more times the quick, thin wail sliced the silence. Something was shooting at him, but not well. A fourth bolt caught him slightly and he smelled a cutting microwave pulse. It had the pungency to blow out the inner structures he knew by the name Diode, but whose function he did not fathom. He felt his own Diodes clamp down, sheltering themselves.

Silence. Cautiously they popped open. His sensorium filled with regained color and perspectives. He carefully edged up to the ridge rim and used a lightpipe to steal a glance over it.

A lone mech was struggling up the opposite face of the ridge. Deep scars marked its thick shell. Bolts had crisped away the steel. Its angular design was unlike anything Killeen had seen on Snowglade.

Without thinking he aimed at the mech and caught it full in

the forward antenna complex. It stopped for an instant. Killeen could see no damage and he fired again. This time the mech clearly blocked the shot. His electrobolt ricocheted off into a ruby flare that momentarily lit the scene against the encroaching gloom of twilight.

His Ling Aspect cried:

This is a totally unnecessary risk! Run while you can.

"Run long enough," Killeen grunted.

He dimly saw that he needed to strike out at something, anything. Suddenly meeting a mech had brought out all his suppressed anger.

He had seen sophisticated defenses like this before. Nothing in Family Bishop's weaponry could penetrate it. The chunky mech's treads caught on an outcropping. It swiveled, bringing projectors on its side around to have a full field of fire at him.

Killeen ducked, knowing the fringing fields of a broadband microwave burst could catch him even well below the ridgeline. He hunkered down, gritting his teeth hard to tell his subsystems to button up.

But nothing came. Not even a whisper.

He risked a glimpse. The mech had flipped over and was burning. Through the curling black pyre he saw a cyborg approaching, its body a complex set of coupled, interlocking hexagonal blocks. Thick brown skin wrinkled and stretched as it made its way up from a broken valley below. A shot had blown open the mech. Its lateral carbosteel housing puckered outward into twisted fingers, a clear sign that the cyborg had somehow triggered an internal energy supply.

Killeen decided to lie low. This cyborg was probably part of a team assigned to clear out any remaining pockets of mechs or humans. If he ran it could easily catch him. His only hope lay in the possibility that the cyborg had not registered his own small, ineffectual fire.

He shut down all his systems again and moved to his right, downslope, seeking more shelter from the rocky ridge. The burning mech was so near that without acoustic amping he could easily hear the crackling and then a loud bang as some vat exploded. Standing still, panting, he thought he could hear the quiet approach of the cyborg: a rustling, clicking cadence as carbosteel limbs articulated.

The cyborg's noise grew against the pop and snarl of the flames. It should have reached the mech by now. But the sounds did not stop. Instead the steady rhythm seemed to move to his left, skirting around the mech's pyre.

And slowing. It was coming around on him from above.

Killeen carefully backed farther downslope. The cyborg might not know what was over here; it would be cautious.

Stealth was his only ally. He might be able to slip back over the ridgeline as the cyborg crossed, keeping low so that his opponent missed him. Then he would have a few moments to run. He strained to hear the whispery sound of the cyborg's flexing leathery hide.

There—it was clambering up over the last shelf of rock which crowned the ridge. Softly he backed away. Time contracted for him and he heard each cyborg step, each swivel and adjustment of pads as they sought purchase on the steeply sloped stones.

The alien was near the top now. Killeen could not tell how far away it was. In the enormous silence, punctuated only by the snapping of the mech's oily fire, his natural hearing seemed to amplify each small sound into deep significance. Somewhere upslope on the ridge a pebble rattled down. Killeen heard it before he saw it bounce off a boulder and scatter fragments into the soil.

His eyes followed the pebble's probable trajectory back into a saddleback where a shelf petered out. It had been a natural wash once and he guessed that a steep streambed led down from there, spreading out onto the other face of the ridge. Which implied that the cyborg had paused at the top, maybe resting but more likely just waiting, cautious, probing throughout the spectrum before it exposed itself on the other side.

The saddleback was not far away. If he was right, the cyborg was reconning the far slope. But he did not dare power up any of his sensory net to check.

Killeen set himself and in one quick rush was up and over the nearest jagged shelf. He rolled over the peak and down into a wash of gravel. He came up on his feet, feeling bulky and awkward without any of his inboard systems running. Sluggishly he ran downhill, his joints aching, looking for shelter.

A glance back. The cyborg's tail antenna was disappearing beyond the saddleback as it headed down the other side. But the alien wouldn't take long to figure matters out.

Killeen ran pell-mell, stumbling on stones and nearly sprawl-ing more than once. There was no place to hide. The planetary convulsions had brushed this slope free of large boulders and the gullies were folded in, shallow. He searched for any minor cranny in the ridgeline, but the few small caves had fallen in. He ran completely past the burning mech before the idea struck him.

The mech lay blistered and broken now, shattered by internal explosions. Flames began to gutter out. Thick, greasy smoke licked the rocky slope.

Killeen chose a crimp in the hull just above the heavy tread assembly. He looked back at the ridgeline. Something moved there and he did not take the time to see what the cyborg was doing. He flung himself into the stove-in section of the burning mech carcass. He was caught immediately in a tangle of parts and smelly goo.

Still no sign that the cyborg had seen him. Without his sensorium, the usual mech attack modes—microwave, infrared saturation, hyper-fléchettes—would give him no sign unless they struck him square on.

Cowering in the stinking jumble of the ruined mech, he felt a slow rage building. He had been chased and hurt and mistreated and he was damned if he was going to go out this way. He could wait for the cyborg to go away—assuming it did not return to harvest the mech for parts or scrap. But something made him peer out, wanting the big thing to lumber into view, wanting at least one clear shot at it. Ling barked in incredulous anger. Killeen instantly slapped the Aspect down.

He listened intently but could pick up nothing this close to the smoldering fires. He would have to expose himself to see what was going on.

Now that he looked closely at the mech body, he recognized housings and struts and assemblies like those he had yanked out of destroyed mechs back on Snowglade. The outer skin had looked odd, but apparently the same principles of basic design ruled among all mechs at Galactic Center.

Carefully he inched out. Most mechs had visual detectors that registered rapid movement, and the cyborg seemed at least as sophisticated. He saw movement on the ridgeline. Coils of acrid smoke stung his eyes, blurring his vision. He began to wonder if it had been such a brilliant idea after all to hide here. All the cyborg had to do was amble up and overturn the mech body and—

Without any warning the cyborg appeared in his field of view, a watery image refracting through the pall of sour smoke. It articulated deftly over the broken ground, antennae swiveling.

But it was not coming toward him. Instead it surged with startling speed across the broad wash of the streambed. A parabolic dish turned and Killeen felt a faint buzzing in his neck. Even with his sensorium deadened, the chips he carried along his spine had picked up the cyborg's burst.

Such a powerful pulse could not have been simply a comm signal. The cyborg was firing at something. Something that worried it considerably, for it now scrambled forward, its double-jointed limbs clashing with haste, its pads sometimes slipping on the loosened topsoil.

Killeen bit his lip to try to restrain himself, but it was hopeless. Long years of training, the recent humbling capture—these combined to make him seize his narrow-bore rifle, the one inherited from his father and his grandfather before that, and jack a precious shell into it. He leaned against an aluminum strut and aimed with luxuriously deliberate care at the forward comm housing of the cyborg. He squeezed off the round. It struck the base of a big spherical web antenna, shattering it. The cyborg lurched visibly.

Killeen knew that ordinarily he would never have gotten such an easy, unopposed shot. The cyborg must have been in serious trouble before it lumbered into view. Which meant that something was coming after it. More mechs. This cyborg had been unlucky enough to meet overwhelming strength when it was alone.

Killeen made himself tuck the rifle back into his side sling. He had vented his rage, and already he felt a tug of regret. He had felt odd moments of connection with the cyborg which had carried him down from orbit and finally set him free. He owed that single cyborg some gratitude, perhaps. But the outrage perpetrated upon him had needed vengeance, by a law as old as humanity, and now that need had been met.

He settled back into his cranny, hoping nothing had seen where his one shot had come from. The cyborg scrambled on, downslope. It was nearly out of sight before a ringing shot burst beside it, spewing brown soil into the air. Killeen blinked. Mechs seldom used ballistic weapons. They preferred cleaner, lighter, more precise electromagnetic means.

Then a second shell struck the cyborg in its middle. That apparently cut a prime mental function, for the long chunky body convulsed, jerking in spasms of almost sexual frenzy.

The cyborg turned on its pursuers. There was a desperate,

abandoned look to the maneuver. Killeen sensed stubborn, fatalistic defiance in the cyborg's movements. Its arms came up in a clenched gesture, like six fists shaking in rage at once.

It fired everything it had at something out of view. But its cause was hopeless. It lurched to the side and took another massive blow. Smoke poured from it. Small rattling bursts struck its natural, organic body, leaving shallow red craters in the rough hide.

Without pleasure Killeen watched the thing die. The cyborgs were, for all their uncaring brutality and deep strangeness, based on natural beings, organically derived from the world. He had felt some strange respect for the one which had spared him, cast him onto this maimed planet. He was not happy to see one brought down by mechs, even though he himself had been among the killers.

The faint calling came to him as he thought this, and at first he did not register it. Only when the small human figures came running into view, waving their puny weapons in triumph, did he understand.

THREE

The tent was worn and frayed and stained. Killeen wondered if this was for camouflage, since it blended well into the jumbled terrain.

All during the walk here his escort had said nothing beyond curt orders. He had not been surprised that their thickly accented speech was in his language; it had never occurred to him that humans spoke more than one way.

They had led him through rambling encampments of tattered tents and lean-tos of scrap and brush, past more people than he had ever seen assembled. Even the Citadel had held fewer Bishops than this. Flapping pennants with unfamiliar symbols suggested that this was a full Tribe. No such grand meeting had occurred on Snowglade within living memory.

A woman in gray coveralls pulled back a tent flap and someone poked Killeen in the buttocks. He walked in, taking long quick strides to avoid another poke, and to maintain some shred of dignity.

The tent seemed larger from inside, with a high peak lit by a phosphorescent ivory ball. Oil lamps glowed along the tent's four oblique diagonals, casting blades of yellow down onto the heads of dozens of people. They were gathered at an orderly, respectful distance from the man at the very center of the tent.

A black desk of polybind ceramic dominated the room. Killeen wondered if these people had carried that heavy mass around with them. It looked mechmade, smoothly curved and sculpted so that its sharp arc focused the eye on the small man behind it, lounging in a light metal chair.

The figure did not seem impressive enough to merit the fixed, hushed attention of everyone else in the tent. He was short, stocky, with hair as black as the ebony desk. A long gash of sullen red ran from above his right temple down across the swarthy skin

176

to the hinge of his jaw. Something had nearly struck his eye, for the mark burrowed into his heavy eyebrows.

About a dozen men and women flanked the desk like guards. No one said anything. They were all watching the man eat a large piece of green fruit. Juice ran down his chin and dripped onto a white cloth set on his chest. The man's uniform was made of a cool-blue, light, comfortable-looking fabric unlike any Killeen had seen before. He smacked his lips. He was giving all his attention to his eating and everyone else seemed to be, too.

The long silence continued. Killeen wondered if this show was for his benefit and dismissed the thought when he saw the rapt look on the faces around him. This was some sort of privileged, special audience, unlike any meeting of a Cap'n and his Family that Killeen knew. The man eating wore no signifying patch. The people nearby had makeshift uniforms of rough cloth, with insignia vaguely similar to the house emblems of Snowglade. Their faces, though seeming dazed, bore a certain intense look of authority. Some wore small medals of tarnished, ropelike silver. Could these be the Cap'ns of the legions he had seen outside?

Finally the small man sucked on his snaggly teeth, smacked his lips, and tossed the remnant core of the fruit over his shoulder.

As someone moved to pick it up the man leaned back and stretched, yawning, still not looking at anyone in particular. Then he seemed to notice Killeen and regarded him with unreadable blank eyes. "Well?" the man said.

"I, my name is—"

"Knees!" the man shouted.

Killeen blinked. "What? I—"

Someone hit Killeen hard yet neatly across the backs of his knees, knocking his support away so he dropped forward and hit the floor, barely managing to stay on his knees.

"Signify!" a voice whispered near him.

"I come from Family Bishop. I honor these lands of, of . . ." Killeen had begun the old greeting in hopes that some idea would come to him, but now he needed to insert the name of this Family.

"Treys!" the whisper said.

". . . Treys, seeking help in a time of dire need, against the depredations and torments inflicted by our mutual—"

"Bindings!" the man behind the desk shouted.

Instantly hands grabbed Killeen's arms and swiftly tied them behind him. He let them without protest, because of something he glimpsed in the man's eyes as the orders were given. The empty eyes had suddenly jerked with animated fire, a spasm of wrenching pleasure.

The man stood up. Honorific pendants swayed from a broad scarlet belt that neatly bisected his blue suit. "He is disarmed?"

A whisper answered, "Aye, Your Supremacy."

"He understands his position in our cause?"

The whisperer near Killeen hesitated, then said, "He is a Cap'n, Your Supremacy, so we did not feel qualified to instruct him."

Evidently this transparent attempt to shift responsibility worked, for the swarthy man nodded calmly and spread his hands toward Killeen, as if addressing a problem. "I must attend to this myself, then." Abruptly he frowned at Killeen. "Your Family?"

"Bishop."

"No such."

"We're not from this planet."

"Never heard such."

"We came here searching for refuge from the mechs."

"Ha! You chose well. Here we have vanquished them."

"So I see."

"You see only that which I determine," the short man said reasonably. "You will understand that."

"I, ah—"

"It is the devil Cybers we fight now. They too shall yield to our bravery and ardor and spirits of fire."

"Cybers?"

His Supremacy nodded, eyes empty again. Lips pursed, expression expectant, he seemed to be listening to some distant voice. Then his attention returned and the muscles of his face stretched his olive skin so that it gleamed beneath the cone of phosphorescent radiance that cascaded around him. The brilliant ball directly above cast a pearly circle on the floor, with the swarthy man as its center. The crowd kept its distance, venturing only as far as the softer glow of the oil lamps intruded into the hard, white circle.

He continued abruptly, as though there had been no pause. "They cut the lands with their great sword. Just as victory came to us, as the mechs fled before our assaults, these giant things fell upon us from the sky. Our triumph was denied. But we shall conquer!"

This provoked loud shouts of agreement from everyone in the tent.

The man looked expectantly at Killeen. "This action is, of course, a tribute to my immortal nature. They send against me the very worst that the evil-hinged skies can muster."

His eyes left Killeen and shot around the room, moving intently from face to face beneath the oily yellow glow. His lips bulged out as if barely containing a vast pressure.

"They compliment us! By sending their most awful and powerful, now that the mechs are rabble scurrying to escape our bootheels. They do us honor! And they shall die."

Abruptly he deflected his glowering, building rage down to where Killeen knelt, and in a long sigh the rage evaporated. In a blink his eyes regained their neutral emptiness.

He said mildly, "And I am glad that you have come to aid in my time of need."

Killeen said carefully, "I am alone now, sir. My—"

"Supremacy!" a hard whisper in his ear urged.

"I am alone, Supremacy, my Family—"

"The Bishops, you called them?" the short man said judicially.

"Yeasay, they—"

"I had thought they were lying. I had never heard of any such Family, and fancied them wastrel renegade Deuces or Trumps."

Killeen asked excitedly, "Bishops? Here?"

"You understand, a mind focused on the defense of our race cannot but leave details to others. I reserve my time for communion with the spirit that moves over and within and through us."

"They're here, Supremacy?"

The heavy, dark eyebrows arched in an expression of bemused interest. "We found them wandering. They had a story about landing in mech craft and escaping the Cyber air raids that we had seen the day before. I thought this a mere fashioned lie. Now that you appear—a Cap'n, I judge from your insignia—this explains it."

"How many?"

The man's face froze and Killeen realized that he had made some error. What could it be? Was his question too direct? The complete silence of everyone around him suggested that he could amend his mistake. . . .

"Your Supremacy, I beg you—yield to me the number who have lived."

His Supremacy's mouth lost some of its tightness and he flicked a glance at a woman to his left.

"Over a hundred," came the reply.

Killeen's breath caught. Most of the Bishops had gotten out.

"I shall cause them to be released," His Supremacy said grandly, his arms making a sweeping gesture. Everyone in the tent cheered, as though this were some unique act, as though this man who called himself by a ridiculous title had somehow saved the Bishops' lives.

The swarthy man's face knitted into a reflective cast, his eyes wandering up to the peak of the tent. "I had judged them as scabrous cowards, laggards from destroyed Suits in the Families. As such, they were unworthy of any role in our grand assaults to come, and so would be used for labor. Fighting within our invincible Tribe is an honor not lightly dispensed. You understand, I am sure."

"Uh, yeasay."

The eyebrows met in a scowl.

"Yeasay, Your Supremacy."

The eyebrows parted and the face relaxed, the eyes again sliding into blankness. "Now they may take part in the heroic struggles to come. I expect you to assume command of them again, as Cap'n."

"Yeasay, Supremacy, as soon—"

"And sacrifices will be exacted."

Killeen looked at the man but could not read his meaning.

His Supremacy gestured and someone unbound Killeen's arms. Should he get up? Something in the way the short man stood, hands on hips and legs stiff, told him to remain kneeling.

His Supremacy pursed his lips, eyes wandering again. He said distantly, "I understand, in my all-reaching facets, your confusion. You have voyaged here from some other sphere of human action, and that was as I wished. You moved in response to my injunctions, though ignorant and in darkness. *I* was the unseen force which drew you across the night canyons that separate the worlds. *I* desired it and sent my emanations to guide you."

A murmur greeted this speech. Hushed exclamations of awe filled the tent.

"Now you enter onto the full stage of human destiny."

This speech had the ringing quality of a set piece. "Ah, yeasay . . . Supremacy."

"I am the given. You have in this conversation verged on disrespect toward me." The eyebrows knotted. "Mayhappen this arises from ignorance. If so, now it is just and proper that I reveal to you my deepest nature."

Killeen said guardedly, "Yeasay." The tent rustled with anticipation. Someone damped the lamps and shadows crowded the tent further. A hushed expectation rustled among the men and women like a sudden wind.

"Witness!"

The short man extended his arms and abruptly his entire body shimmered and glowed. Against the blue fabric a yellow skeleton appeared, like a second entity that lived inside the man. It moved with him, bones and ribs and pelvic girdle performing their rubs and rotations as His Supremacy stepped first to one side, then to another. Atop the curved spine a death's-head grinned, turning proudly. The bones worked smoothly, suggesting that a creature made of the pure, radiating hardness could walk and know the world, encased in its enduring strengths. It oozed ample light into the tent, cutting a blackness as deep as that in the unblemished spaces between stars. In these dim working shadows, with breezes flapping the tent like far-off thunderclaps, the intricate lattice of crisp light implied an interior race of invulnerable beings, harder than human.

Its burnt-yellow jaw pulsed on an unseen hinge as His Supremacy said, "I am the essence of humanity itself, come to avenge and save. Through me human destiny will be made manifest. The mechs and Cybers shall be vanquished alike."

In the thick, shadowy air his skeleton vibrated with life. Vagrant hues shot through the bones as they articulated, knotty joints swooping with artful animation in the framing dark.

"Mortal?" he cried. "No. Mortality lies within me and yet I am not mortal. I am the manifestation! God Himself!"

Killeen gathered that this techtrick was supposed to impress him. He let an expression of amazement settle onto his face while he tried to see how the moving rib cage and legs were imaged on the blue.

"I am the immanent spirit of humanity, as given by Divine God! In this most dire and yet pregnant hour of mankind, the glorious truth is that *I* have been endowed with godliness entire. No longer does God act through me. He has become me. I *am* God! *This* is why the Tribe will follow me to its certain destiny. *This* is why you, Cap'n of the lost Bishops, will give your final effort to my cause, the cause of humanity's true God!"

FOUR

The human sprawl down the valley was broad and impressive. Two women escorted Killeen through the knots of Family gatherings. They were both Cap'ns but Killeen asked them nothing.

He had allowed himself to be led into this massive encampment because the men and women who had found him insisted. But every sense in him shouted *Caution!* These people were grim, silent, and the interview with His Supremacy had unsettled Killeen considerably. He remembered his father's wry advice: *"Thing about aliens is, they're alien."* That might apply to this distant vestige of humanity, too.

Twilight cast slanted sulfurous rays across the wracked land, picking out details for fleeting amber moments.

A wheezing old man passed, dragging a carryframe that dug deep ruts in the soil. Young couples held hands around smoky campfires, squatting together with their small babies. Beside a spitting orange lamp, a dumpy matron made an outraged face as she haggled with a trader over a plastic sack of grain. Children scampered among lean-tos, aiming and firing at one another with sticks and calling Family battlecries in hoarse, excited voices. Men sat solemnly checking and oiling weapons, the shiny parts carefully arranged on worn dropcloths, their scarred stocks held between bulging, augmented knees. A young woman leaned against a commandeered mech transporter, idly playing a lightly liquid tune on a small harp. She kept her boots and calf sheaths on, pneumatic collars gleaming and tight at her ankles, plainly still on ready-guard. But the music lilted on the tumbling breeze, promising a lightness nowhere to be seen.

Here and there were rickety huts and stalls made of poles and canvas. Greasy fires inside them splashed ruddy light against the thin walls, amplifying every inner movement into pantomime shadow dramas. Crowds clustered around the brimming flames and in their faces Killeen read not the exhaustion he had expected, but a firm, silent, unassuming strength. They worked at their techcrafts, using the last glow of available light.

Gangs unloaded mech carriers. There was a whole fleet of mech autotrucks as well. He was impressed at their high level of scavenging; this surpassed anything he had seen on Snowglade. Everywhere there were mech implements and a wealth of spare parts.

Killeen asked for Family names and his escorts called them out as they passed campsites: Treys, Deuces, Double-Noughts, Niners, Septs, Five-ohs, Jacks, Aces. As they approached each group a guard hailed and they replied with code words.

There was a plan to the camps, which he at first had thought just a random conglomeration. Each Family was deployed in a pie-shaped wedge, its long-range weapons facing outward to command a fraction of the perimeter. He passed a wide wedge of Family Niner, clustered beneath an array that poked long-snouted rods skyward.

"Skybolts," one of his escorts replied to his question. She sniffled with a cold and her eyes were swollen. "Can knock down mechs."

"How?"

"Electromagnetic."

"What band? Microwave? IR?"

Her sunburned face tightened with suspicion. "Family business." "You a Niner?"

"Naysay. Families keep their tech stuff to selves, though."

"Your Family does?"

"Sure. I'm Cap'n of the Sebens. Believe me, we got reasons."

"Like?" Killeen persisted.

"Old ways, from back in the days when the Families didn't have so much trouble from mechs."

"I thought we were all united under the Supremacy."

"*His* Supremacy."

"Yeasay, yeasay. Look, how the Sebens fit in w'all the other Families? I can't follow all the Family names and—"

"Old sayin', Seben Come Elebben. Only there aren't many Elebbens left now. Mechs cut 'em up somethin' awful. What was left the Cybers pretty well mashed."

The woman's voice was like gravel poured down a pipe. Killeen could hear the edge of authority in it that Fanny had possessed. He said carefully, "Still, we united, why not share tech?"

"Won't be secret then."

"It'd help if we knew each other's weapons."

"Howcome?"

"Things get tight, more'n one Family can use 'em."

The woman shook her head. "You don't keep a craft to yourself, you lose it."

"But—" The woman's exasperated shake of her head told Killeen this was useless territory to explore. He changed tack and said casually, "Must be hard, carryin' 'quipment big as all that 'round on your backs."

"Seen worse."

"Okay for holdin' someplace, like a Citadel, but—"

"Your people had a Citadel?"

This was the first sign of interest in his origins anyone had shown. Killeen wondered how concerned he would have been when he was running from mechs on Snowglade; probably not much. "Yeasay, a great one. Good air defenses."

"We kept some our big weapons. Held off the mechs long enough, so's we could break 'em down, pack out the parts on carryslings."

Killeen could guess the price paid in such a holding action, caught in the wild, unreckonable swirl of battle, crossed by deviant slants of deadly fortune. He said respectfully, "That stuff must slow you down when you hit and move, though."

"That's true 'gainst mechs. Up 'gainst Cybers, though, you better have the heavy stuff or they'll squash you. Cybers're harder."

"Howcome?"

"They can read your tech straight out. Feel a ticklin' in your head and then it's gone."

"You mean invade your sensorium, take your knowhow? But that'd kill you."

"Don't hafta." She hawked roughly and spat a brown wad a hand's length in front of her right boot, all without breaking stride.

Killeen said, "Where I come from, mech bothers to do all that much, it just kills you suredead long as it's taken the trouble."

She nodded and coughed. Fifteen men came struggling up the path carrying a piece of mechtech that Killeen could not identify and the three of them stepped aside to let the party pass.

She said, "I 'member when mechs did that. But they stopped when we started gettin' the better of 'em."

"His Supremacy says you had 'em beat."

Grudgingly she said, "For a while."

"How?"

"We cooperated a li'l with some mech cities. Helped 'em take out their competition."

Killeen was puzzled. "Other mechs?"

"Yeasay. His Supremacy worked it out with 'em."

"Where I come from, we had some Families try that. Dangerous, though. The deals never lasted long."

"Ours did. We'd smuggle stuff onto mech carriers. See, one mech city would give us fake supplies. Made up so looked like real thing. We'd slip in, get it onto a convoy headed from the outside fact'ries into the big cities."

"Impressive," Killeen said respectfully. "How?"

"Wear no metal. Crawl through the convoy's detectors real slow."

"Sounds pretty slick."

"Was. Kept us alive."

Killeen said, "His Supremacy did all that?"

"Yeasay. Started out cuttin' a deal for just his Family. Mechs they'd work for would give 'em protection. Once we seen how it went, whole Tribe was his for the askin'."

"I saw some mech cities pretty well done in."

"We did that. We'd smuggle in bombs, plant 'em."

"Dangerous work."

"With mech help we could get through the traps."

"We never learned that," Killeen said, hoping to keep drawing her out.

"Easy, once you know. We'd grab fancy stuff, 'quipment. Wish it'd gone on like that."

"What happened?"

"All sudden, no mechs aroun'. Least not many. Seemed like most were up in orbit. We'd see 'em at night. . . ."

"Maybe they had more important business. Cybers."

"We figured."

"When was that?"

"A while back, maybe two seasons—not that we had a decent summer, not with the clouds coverin' the sun most times."

"And you skragged the mechs good," Killeen prompted her. She kept looking alertly around, a habit Killeen knew never left you after you had spent years running in the open.

"His Supremacy, he said this was our big chance. We raided mech cities ourselves. Knew the tricks, see."

"Ah," Killeen said appreciatively.

"Hit 'em hard. Just when we're seein' our way clear, there comes five nights when there's big lightballs goin' off up there"— she gestured with a gnarled hand skyward—"and thunder comes down sometimes. All over the sky, loud as you please."

They were passing a large roaring bonfire with hundreds of people packed around it. Killeen could feel the heat snapping off the flames. A low moaning song rose in the surrounding murk as the last traces of twilight ebbed. It was unfamiliar and yet carried a mournful bass solemnity that reminded him of the Citadel, long ago, and Family songs unheard for many years.

The Sebens' Cap'n walking beside him made a gesture, crossing from shoulder to hip, through the belly and back to the opposite shoulder, evidently a sign of respect. The crowd blocked the path and they stopped.

She whispered, "So then after that we don't see mechs much anymore. But Cybers we get plenty."

"You ever see Cybers before these times?"

"Naysay. Family Jack say they fought some Cybers long 'fore this, but my man Alpher says Jacks, they're always yarnin' on 'bout things they dunno ass-up 'bout. And he's right." A closed look came into her face. "Not that I'm sayin' anything 'gainst another Family united under the Supremacy, you understand."

Killeen nodded. "So the Cybers beat the mechs, you figure?"

"Looks like."

Killeen considered telling her about his experience in the Cyber nest and decided he hadn't sorted it out enough himself to make good sense. Instead he started working his way around the close-packed crowd. They were singing their slow song more rhythmically now, punctuating it with unnerving shrill wails that made his scalp prickle. All faces turned toward the crackling flames, eyes unfocused and tear-filled. Killeen sensed the gravity of this Family ritual but it was unlike any he knew. A large red insignia on a man's shoulder told him they were Eight of Hearts.

The three of them circled around and reached the rutted path just as a small cart emerged from the gathering amber dusk, drawn by six women. Killeen stepped aside for them to pass and at that moment the crows saw the cart and a collective sigh rose. Twisted, anguished cries filled the gloom.

An honor guard flanked the cart, weapons at port arms. People swarmed around, pressing Killeen against the cart. He saw three bodies arranged formally on the flatbed, their arms at their sides. Each stared open-eyed at the night above, faces unlined and dispassionate above bodies that belied their calm. Two were women—scrawny, their skins puckered and lacerated. And each bore a massive bruise that spread down from her prominent collarbone to her belly.

But it was not truly a bruise, he saw. The purpling had spread up into the women's breasts, pushing up ridges of yellowing flesh. The edge of the wound was crinkled and warped, as though something inside had tried to escape by prying off the chest of each woman, and finally had failed, and so was still lurking within them, the pressure of it forcing the ribs apart and making of their bellies and lungs a great swollen blister that peaked in a watery, transparent sac.

The male corpse between them lay face down, ragged hair covering his head entirely. A bulge split the back of his uniform. Another glossy, stretched dome. His was ringed by a crusted brown scab like dried mud.

The three were laid close together, just fitting into the width of the cart, so that the bodies could not roll and burst the tight, shiny, grotesquely bloated wounds.

Killeen felt his mouth water with incipient nausea. He turned away, sucking the air through his teeth to take away the sudden foul taste that came through the air like a slap. Pushing out against the press of bodies, looking directly into the eyes that stared past him without seeing, he made his way back to the path. The two women were waiting. He whispered, "What . . . what caused . . ."

"Cybers," the talkative woman said. "They do that sometimes, when they can get in close."

"But . . . what . . ."

"Infested, that's what those people are. His Supremacy says they must be cleaned, purified. Dealt with right."

"Let's . . . let's go."

She shook her head, the coils of her black hair wrestling like living ropes. "We leave now, it'd be disrespec'ful."

Bodies pressed against him, their mute momentum carrying him toward the bonfire. In the wake of the cart the slow grave swell of the Eight of Hearts' mourning song rose. He watched as gloved hands drew the dirty, stiffening bodies from the cart. The corpses were laid out gently, the man still in the center and face down, and a single red heart made of cloth laid upon the head of each. Then a tall woman wearing a Cap'n's signifiers spoke, her voice well modulated and practiced and strong.

Killeen did not follow the words. He was watching the bodies.

As the corpses stiffened further their legs and arms jerked and trembled slightly, as though the rhythms that defined a Family's way—running, the endless succession of nomad flight—carried on remorselessly across the divide of death.

Then the Cap'n approached the first woman, made a ritual pass with a long knife, and plunged it hard and sure into the glassy blister. The shiny dome broke with an audible pop. Milky fluids gushed all down it, over the corpse's face, running into the open rictus, covering the still-staring eyes, trickling down over the legs. There seemed an impossible quantity of the stuff and when it drained away the yawning husk of the blister cracked and broke under the Cap'n's repeated thrusts.

She probed deeper. The point of the knife burrowed in and abruptly the body shook within, shuddering with a wet sucking noise. Something struggled inside, rocking the body from side to side, jerking, pushing the broken ribs farther out. A spasm, a last convulsion, and then the body went completely still. Snapped ribs collapsed inward.

The dead woman looked shrunken, emptied. In final rest her face now resembled those of her Family hemming in the spectacle, a blade of a nose between prominent cheekbones. Her eyes seemed to sink beneath the darkened lids. A tiny insect crawled out of one nostril and lingered on a bloodless lip.

The Cap'n pulled out her blade. Pinned on its sharp point was a thing hard and brown and chitinous that still wriggled with frantic energy. It was tough but somehow unformed, as though legs and head had still to push their way out of the moist, interlocking brown segments. It fought the knife, twisting. Then suddenly the life drained out of it and the thing went limp.

The crowd backed away. The Cap'n threw the brown mass to the ground. Instantly a woman leaped forward and crushed it with both boots. She cried out something Killeen could not understand, a shout of anger and sorrow and despair. Then she backed into the crowd again. Men and women nearby clasped her, passing her among them, hugging and sheltering her with soft murmurings.

The Cap'n did the second woman the same way. Killeen watched numbly. This time a man crushed the brown thing. It snapped like the joints of a hand being crushed. The man sobbed as he did it and stamped the thing again and again before going back into the crowd.

The blister on the man's back was larger than the women's.

The bulge was thinning, growing translucent. In tiny movements the skin pulsed—a convexity here, a concavity there, until the whole back and chest of the man was alive with purpose. The trunk of the body was unrecognizable now, save for the parentheses of ribs that yawned aside to frame the quaking fleshy hill that rose and throbbed.

The Cap'n of the Eight of Hearts quickly brought her blade up, calling out some ritual words. Before she could plunge it into the man's back the blister began to split. Milky ooze gushed out. Dark cracks ran down from the summit.

Something crabbed and small pushed itself out into the flickering firelight. It scuttled away. The Cap'n did not hesitate. She slammed the knife into the thing as it ran down the corpse's leg. Small legs fought and scraped their way up the blade. But the knife made its point.

A collective sigh rose from the crowd. The three bodies were flaccid and spent now. Their nearest relatives—for all present were related, however distantly—came forward to accept the honor of burial.

Killeen made his way on wooden legs away from the roaring, snapping bonfire. Regaining the path, he said hoarsely to the Sebens' Cap'n, "That's what the Cybers do? Plant their, their seeds in us? They don't even let us die straight and clean?"

The sunburned woman answered, "Yeasay. Only those li'l things, they're not Cybers."

"What, then?"

"Some kinda li'l scrabblers. I seen 'em doin' small jobs, followin' Cybers. Sometimes climb up on Cybers, pick at their joints 'n' stuff."

"Like fleas?"

"I'd guess."

Killeen said disbelievingly, "Just use us for hatching out fleas."

"They leave us lyin', few hours later out comes those things. Or they'll kill clean from the distance, if they ain't got the time."

"What they use mechs for?"

"Dunno. Parts, maybe."

Killeen sucked at his lip to hide his queasiness. The woman said, "Cybers're worse 'n mechs, plenty worse."

The woman who had said nothing until now put in bitterly, "Damn sure, but we'll triumph. 'S God's way, givin' us a trial."

They moved on through gathering murk lit by oily fires. Above them the sky yawned and flexed.

FIVE

To Killeen the look on Jocelyn's face was abruptly, immensely funny. She gaped, eyes and mouth making big round *O*s.

They embraced, then, and the other Bishops squatting near a small sheltered fire leaped up loudly and were all around him.

Cermo slapped him on the rear and hugged him and the rest went by in a heady, quick, intense blur. Faces and laughter released into the cooling night air a fervent joy as word spread and shouts went up and answering calls sounded among the converging forms that sprang up from nearby campfires and came running, voices raised in excited and disbelieving celebration. Then Toby was there, his face haggard and gray even in the warming glow of the crackling flames—which someone had already augmented, summoning forth a welcoming rush of heat and crisp radiance—and Killeen lifted his son into the air, swinging him around in a sudden hard blossom of feeling, finding the boy's hefty weight surprising.

"What, why, how—?" the voices asked, but Killeen shook his head, his throat filled and his world blurred. Toby needed no explanations, just yelped and laughed the way he had in years past, before the protracting processes of coming to age had caught him up. Killeen laughed wildly and turned to see more—glorious clumps of Bishops, a flood where he had only hoped for a trickle— all rushing in, crossing the last faint blades of dusk. His throat hurt, to feel himself again at the center of all he truly cared about—centrifugally spun out into the Family that in turn came streaming inward from the darkness to enclose him. Questions bombarded him and seemed to be not separate ideas but merely the means that the Family used to draw him again back into itself. And then in the brimming firelight, cutting through the mad talk and shouts, he saw her. Hanging back, hands clasped behind her so that they could not betray her emotions, eyes batting furiously as she reflexively contained herself, mouth warped by inner anguish, eyes moist and plaintively wide, Shibo.

190

*   *   *

She did not plague him with questions, as the others did. Shibo invoked a time-honored Bishop custom, whereby a woman may withdraw her man from Family matters if he is wounded or distraught. Never had Killeen heard of such privilege used for a Cap'n, but he raised no objections. He let Shibo guide him to a boxy tent of odd design, and there seemed to fall into a musky warm pit.

He ached everywhere. The fear and anguish he had suppressed were lodged in tight muscle complexes, gnarled deposits in his sensorium like granite nuggets in a bed of sand. Each stored increment awaited only a release of control in order to speak its pain. Shibo said little, simply began singing a high, drifting song of ancient deeds, as his clothes slid from him and a tracery of warmth crept across his filthy skin. She applied the heavy scented oils and scraped them away with a honed stone blade. His skin shrieked at the cleansing and then simmered into a tingling glow.

She moved over him, gauzy and ghostly and light, and seemed to pluck words out of his throat, so that the story seeped from him involuntarily, oozing through his skin as it answered her hands. His sensorium trembled and snagged on her moist breath, on the quickness of her. He could feel her own despair and bleak days, lacing the air between them and merging with their desire. They were together in a new place, a zone they had never penetrated before because for years now life between them had been mild and calm and incapable of reaching deeply in. They pressed, pressed. Sank into each other, bone into bone. Killeen felt angered by the stubborn flesh that resisted with its mulish weight their blending; he wrestled with the sheer lazy obdurance of their bodies. Shibo bit and pulled and strained and they became thin wedges driven into each other. Their bodies were left behind. Together they glided in sailing, recessional spaces.

There was a long interval without a tick of time.

Then, casually, Killeen heard a distant muttered conversation. The ringing clatter of someone fumbling with metal. Crackling of fires. Children's weary giggles.

The world had started up again.

"Ah," Shibo said, eyes heavy-lidded. "Here."

They lay together in each other's arms and laughed. Killeen felt a whisper of ache in his lower back and knew he had not banished all the past, never would.

They had come back from the silent spaces. A blank and yet expectant pressure came upon him.

Facts, facts, yes. Always the blunt mass of facts.

They were stranded in a ruined land, besieged by two breeds of hostility. The Family dwelled in the close embrace of a strange strain of humanity.

His plans for New Bishop were dashed forever. Escape seemed the only solution, yet—if he understood the mottled, warping time he had spent in the bowels of the alien—the *Argo* was captured, lost.

Killeen curled up against Shibo and let himself seep into the musk of her, seeking a moment more of forgetting.

SIX

Plips and plops of rain dampened his spirits. Pale morning cut through a mass of purple cloud. Killeen huddled under a lean-to, sheltered by a tarp that flapped in a cold wind that seemed to be racing to catch the storm front.

"Looks like clearing," he said to Jocelyn, who squatted nearby.

She surveyed the low, jumbled valley where dozens of breakfast fires sent threads of smoke slanting up the sky, blown by the wind. "Hope so. I'd hate running in this mud."

"I been thinkin' the same. How come they camp like this, a whole Tribe rubbin' elbows?"

"His Supremacy says so." Her face was blank, eyes giving nothing away.

He bit into a grain bar. There were weevils in it. Well, there had been weevils in the *Argo*, too; pests were eternal. But here humans themselves were pests.

"Mechs'd smash this place," he said, "if they knew they'd catch so many."

"Near as I can tell, mechs don't matter. They've got 'nuff trouble with Cybers," Jocelyn said.

"Okay, how 'bout the Cybers? Those campfires last night give us away. Howcome they don't hit a big crowd like this?"

"Not their style."

"Who says?"

"His Supremacy."

"And what's *he*? He put on a show last night, was all I could manage keepin' a straight face."

Jocelyn's brow creased with a disapproving frown. "Don't make even small fun."

"Everybody crazy as he is?"

"Come look."

Killeen didn't feel like creaking over the muddy terrain but something in Jocelyn's voice made him follow. He felt every joint

193

and servo like heavy damp wedges moving in his legs. He had run a fair distance yesterday, and hiked some of the night with the party that brought him in. Along with the crew he had exercised in the g-decks of *Argo* to keep muscle fiber. Optimistically, he had expected that the lesser gravity of this world would help. Not so. The rain brought a special dull ache into his calves and lower back, making him hobble around all tight and gimpy, hunching over the way old men did. He was mulling this over as he grunted up a steep hogback ridge behind Jocelyn, and wasn't ready for what he saw on the other side.

A large steel girder was stuck into the ground so that it stood nearly upright. A woman was tied to it, head down. Her purple tongue stuck out between clenched teeth and her eyes protruded. "Ah, ah, pl-please . . ." she croaked.

Killeen stepped toward her, unsheathing his knife.

"No." Jocelyn put a restraining hand on his shoulder. "Touch her and you'll be in trouble. We'll all be."

"Ah, please . . . hands . . . God . . ."

Killeen saw that the woman's hands were swollen and blue where wire tied them to the girder. At her ankles wire cut into grossly large feet, dark with congested blood. "I can't let—"

"We've all kept clear. His Supremacy says anyone who helps them gets the same." Jocelyn's voice was careful, controlled.

"Why's she up there?"

"She's an 'unbeliever,' as they put it around here."

"An unbeliever in *what?*"

"In His Supremacy. And their inevitable victory, I guess."

"This is . . ." Killeen's voice trailed off as he looked beyond the woman's pleading, reddened face. In the narrow gully three more girders had been jammed into the soil and kept nearly upright with stones. Each held an upside-down body. He remembered suddenly the "art" that the Mantis had displayed years ago. Human artworks. These crude monuments to human evil had a strangely similar quality.

He took a few steps toward them before he saw the cloud of insects that whispered and buzzed around each. He approached the nearest on wooden legs, scarcely believing the sight of hundreds of mites swarming over the inverted body. They buzzed angrily as he came near and stooped to see the congested, blood-black face.

"This is Anedlos!" Killeen cried.

Jocelyn tugged him away. "Don't look. They put him up days ago. Yes'day he died. Other two are Tribe—from Card Suit."

Stunned, Killeen stammered, "Anedlos—Anedlos was a good crafter. He . . . he . . ."

"He wouldn't take part in their religious service. He argued with His Supremacy."

"And for that—" Killeen made himself stop, try to think. "What did you do?"

"His Supremacy? I pleaded, but—"

"Pleaded? That's all?"

"What could I do?" Jocelyn asked defiantly.

"Tell that maniac that *nobody* hands out justice in Family Bishop 'cept Family Bishop."

"That's . . . that's not the way things work here."

"No decision by the Tribe can set aside a Family's justice, you know that."

Jocelyn spread her hands in a gesture of futility. "Old rules don't work here. His Supremacy says he's God's embodiment and what he says is law."

"He's crazy."

"Yeasay, but he has many, many Families who think he's God."

"Killing mechs doesn't make you God."

Jocelyn shrugged. "These Families, they always had Gods and stuff. His Supremacy pulled it all together some way."

Killeen remembered the Nialdi Aspect he had carried years before, an ardently religious man. Nialdi was never any real use, though the Aspect had given guidance to Cap'ns down through the ages. As soon as he became Cap'n, with power over Aspect assignments, he had put Nialdi in chipstore.

Religious fervor . . . typically arises in times . . . of unsettling change. End of the Chandelier Epoch saw . . . much ardor . . . Nialdi . . . came from . . . shortly after . . . seems likely His Supremacy carries . . . several such personalities . . . and may give him . . . charismatic power . . . over the Tribe . . .

His Grey Aspect whispered weakly. Killeen saw her point. Nialdi applied the apparent truths of that time to the present. His Supremacy was doing the same. Maybe the trick of hiring his people out to mech cities had given the man enough power to let the underlying powerful Aspects come into play.

Killeen said, "Still, we can't let—"

"Look," she said heatedly, "I been tryin' *ever*'thing. His Supremacy put me in charge since we thought you were dead. It's all I can do, just getting food. We were pretty bad off when we landed. These people took us in. We're lucky—"

"Crazy man will do you in bad, you follow him," Killeen said, exasperated.

He stalked back to the woman, unsheathing a tool to unwind the wires. They were hard to free because the wire had cut deeply into her wrists. Before he was through he saw that blood was running out of her mouth, spattering the gray mud and mingling with the spitting rain that came blowing into the gully. She was dead.

Back in the Bishops' camp he assembled Cermo and Jocelyn and Shibo and questioned them closely. He started with the escape.

Shibo had led the flight from the station. She had even reactivated the Flitter where Jocelyn was hiding. The Cybers who captured Killeen had ignored the craft. As soon as they moved away and lifted their control of it, Shibo had commanded it to join the dispersed Flitter fleet that carried the Family.

They had been very lucky. When the cosmic string stopped spinning Shibo saw their chance. Her deft handling of the shuttles' microminds had brought them on a steep dive into the atmosphere. One shuttlecraft had come apart with four Bishops aboard. She guided them to a rough landing a day's hardmarch from here. They had come down at night. The watch here had sent a runner to see who they were.

"Thing is, who're *they?*" Killeen asked.

"Tribe of Cards. They've got pasteboards they play games with, got their Family names on 'em," Cermo said. His face was drawn and crusted with beard.

"Um. Seems funny, makin' Family from some game," Killeen said. "But they're all we got here."

Shibo said, "A Niner told me *our* Families come from a game."

Killeen snorted in disbelief. "Bishops 'n' Kings 'n' Rooks?"

Shibo shrugged. Cermo said, "I bet they made that up. Just 'cause we thought was funny they're named for li'l cards."

Killeen said thoughtfully, "We got lot in common though. Tribes, Families, even same rules."

Shibo said, "Must've come from same place."

Jocelyn nodded. "His Supremacy says we're all from same Chandelier."

Cermo asked, "How's he know?"

"His Aspects," Jocelyn said. "I bet Aspects kept us all 'bout the same. Rules and such—Aspects're big on those."

"And talk," Killeen said. "Aspects always nag about speakin'."

Shibo said, "That might explain why we can still understand these Cards."

"Makes sense," Jocelyn said. "Our language changes, we couldn't understand our Aspects. Or trade 'em with these Cards."

Killeen said carefully, "Who says we'd do that?"

"His Supremacy," she answered.

"Why?"

"Pool our tech."

Killeen said, "The Sebens' Cap'n didn't seem interested in that."

"Well, His Supremacy says he wants to check out the Aspects the Bishop officers use."

They looked at each other.

Shibo said, "Maybe he thinks we don't have enough God-loving Aspects?"

Jocelyn said, "All I know is what His Supremacy tells me."

"Which sure's not much," Cermo said.

"I can deal with him," Jocelyn said proudly. "I got us food and tents."

Killeen remembered how, years before they left Snowglade, the Family had been surprised at night and had to leave behind all their bedding and tents and a lot of cooking gear. Though they had fallen far from the wonderful, hypnotically exotic comforts of *Argo*, he was glad to see that the Family had adjusted quickly to the hardships of the land.

Nearby a metal-crafter was fashioning a carryrack from some wrecked mech tubing. The Bishop camp stirred with effort as old talents came into play again, and Killeen could see on faces a reborn confidence that came from finding the old methods still good and true.

He covered the arrangements Jocelyn had made with the Tribe, details of supplies and food. He dispatched fifty bishops to help with the day's foraging, which was conducted as a coordinated effort ranging far from the Tribesite. There were many matters of Family business to straighten out. Killeen had to decide how to reconfigure the Family's elaborate sequence of order-giving, since they had lost the four in the shuttlecraft and, of course, Anedlos. That matter Killeen dealt with, speaking between clenched teeth. "We won't take such treatment. But we'd better look sharp till we understand things better."

His lieutenants nodded. Even as he went on to discuss other issues he knew that there was really nothing he could say that would inspire much confidence among them. The plain bare facts of their predicament spoke in the barren plain. Here they squatted in the ancient manner, ready to jump up and move at the slightest alarm. They had lost everything, the *Argo* and their dreams as well, in the span of a few days.

It was Shibo who made their thoughts plain. "Comes a chance, I say we get back aboard *Argo*."

"Wish you could've gotten control of it," Killeen said gently. "Could've gotten away then."

"Naysay," Shibo countered. "That Cyber ship that got you—it moved lot faster than *Argo*. Could've caught us easy."

"It took off after me, though. Caught me on the other side the whole damn planet."

"Only after we'd left in the Flitters," Shibo countered.

"Guess they wanted me," Killeen said lightly, trying to slip by the moment.

"For what?" Jocelyn asked.

"Gave me a lookover, let me go."

"Sure that's all?" Jocelyn eyed Killeen.

Was she trying to raise suspicions? "Can't explain it. Just lived through it."

Jocelyn picked at her coveralls and said nothing. Killeen felt some uneasiness seep out of his officers. The simple presence of a clear leader helped.

He had learned from Fanny the value of putting past errors and disputes behind the Family. Abraham had been a genius at that. Killeen knew he lacked his father's lightness of touch at moments like this.

To break the mood he slurped from a cup of warm brown fluid—and then abruptly spat it out. "Send out a small party, the five with the best noses," he said. "See if there are any jodharran bushes in this godforsaken place. We could brew a decent drink, at least."

Cermo gulped his. "This stuff's not so bad."

Killeen wrinkled his nose. "Tastes like mechpiss."

"Yeasay," he agreed. "Got some good features, though."

"Like what?"

"Well, it's not addictive."

They all stared blankly at one another for a long moment, and then from Cermo came a mild chuckle, and a guffaw from Jocelyn, and then they were all laughing, the yelps and rattling coughs issuing from them as though from deep internal pressures, bursting forth into the rain and chilly air like small cannon shots, explosive assertions, little gestures against bleak fortune.

SEVEN

Dawn of the next day brought a howling flurry of dust that sleeted through the stinging air. It came as work started on breakfast. The Family Niner campfire got out of control. A moaning wind swept it in angry gusts. The flames blew into tents and across the spare dry grass. A pall of smoke rolled through Family Bishop's grounds and Killeen hurried to pull a team together.

Nobody wanted to come, of course. The wind snatched his orders away and that made a good excuse to not hear them. The fire was the Niners' fault but that wouldn't matter much when it reached them. He had to haul more than a dozen men and women out by the scruffs of their necks.

They advanced into the teeth of the gale, clawing away the grass before the tongues of orange that leaped forward with blurring speed. They couldn't get control of it. They linked up with a brigade of Niners who were devoting most of their effort to getting tents and equipment out of the way.

Killeen argued with their lieutenant and got nowhere. He didn't dare leave his own team and search out the Niner Cap'n, or he might well return to find that most of the Bishops had gone back to protect their own valuables. The biting dust made it easy to slip away into the billowing banks of grit that skirted along the ground like huge dirty brown animals. There was no good solution so Killeen sent a runner back with orders to muster the whole Family, and set to work.

With trenching tools they cut a broad gap before the leaping flames. It was impossible to face into the storm, with its smarting flame and stinging sand. They stopped the fire just before it reached a stand of dead trees, uprooted and dried out, that would have gone up in a rush, spreading cinders everywhere.

The wind trickled away as suddenly as it had come. They stomped out the remaining flames and went back to their camp and found dust everywhere. Every tiny crack in a tent let in powdery drifts of the stuff. Killeen and Shibo were sweeping out their little tent when Toby came ambling along, hands stuffed into his side pockets.

"Knew I'd be glad I pitched in the open," he said happily.

"Yeasay, I saw you hunkered down under somebody else's shelter yes'day, when it rained." Killeen grinned.

"All dried out now."

"You just sleep in a bag?"

"Got no bag, don't need one. Suit keeps me warm." Toby had on his full running gear—aluminum pelvic cradle and shin servos and heavy carbosteel shank shocks.

"Must get tired, haulin' all that around," Killeen said.

"I like 'em," Toby said, sitting down and adjusting a compressor lock. "Traded some my 'quipment for 'em."

"What'd you give?"

"Some backup chips I had in my shoulder."

"Those're Family chips."

Toby looked edgy. "Well . . ."

"They ask for any old religious Aspects?"

"Huh? No, no, nothin' like that."

Killeen felt relieved. He was sure His Supremacy would eventually try to get chips away from the Bishops simply because knowledge was power. On the other hand, he shouldn't mistake every minor incident as a vast portent.

"What'd you give?" he repeated.

"C'mon, Dad, I'm carryin' tech chips nobody'll ever use again."

Killeen kept his voice flat. "Like what?"

"Buildin' stuff. Puttin' up walls usin' mech parts, like that."

"We might need that."

"When? Can't build anything here."

His voice finally got away from him, turning sharp. "We'll find someplace. Build a Citadel, one bigger'n the last. Better, too— only we won't know *how*, 'cause you gave away the knowhow."

Toby said sarcastically, "That time comes, I'll just trade 'em back. If I'm gonna settle down, won't need trekkin' gear."

"You'll find whoever you gave the chips—"

"Two Niner guys, it was. And I traded 'em square, didn't *give* 'em—"

"—and trade whatever you must. Just get those chips back."

"Dad!" Toby sprang slightly into the air, driven by his compressors. "I can't just go—"

"You *will*. Family property stays in the Family."

"Look, other people're tradin'. It's natural."

"Who?"

"How you expect we got runnin' gear, tents, cookin'—"

"Make it, same's on Snowglade. Who?"

"There's not enough mechwreck around. And shapin' it would take—"

"I saw parts over at the Niner camp. Scrounge some, set down, 'n' start usin' the craft you got stored in you. Now who else?"

When Toby had told him the names of four others, he called Jocelyn and gave her the job of finding them and getting back the gear they'd bartered. He could see from the stiff set of Jocelyn's mouth that she didn't like the job but she went off to do it without a word.

Killeen stood watching Toby making toward the Niner camp. He was vaguely aware that he could have handled matters better. Shibo came over and slipped an arm around him, nuzzling his cheek wordlessly.

He grunted with frustration. "Hard to switch back to father after bein' Cap'n."

She nodded. "Toby's scared, like us all. Needs something that gives him a lift."

"I can see that. But . . ."

"We're all recovering. Lost *Argo*, need some direction."

"Toby seems pretty steady."

"He and Besen have helped each other."

"You mean . . .?"

She nodded, making a sign that meant love, romance, courting.

"Oh." Killeen blinked. "I hadn't noticed."

"Parents often don't." She smiled.

"Well, I . . ."

Killeen struggled to say something wise and firm, and gave up—his inner world was a muddle. He knew he was being absurd, but his first reaction to this news was a piercing sense of loss. To acknowledge that seemed to slight Shibo—he still had her, after all. And Toby's growing up was inevitable.

He told himself that maybe this crisis had made him vulnerable, and the sudden pang he felt was a side effect of the greater concerns that weighed upon him. While he tried to sort this out he saw Shibo's mouth tilt with compressed merriment, and realized that she could read his consternation. Finally, he gave a resigned chuckle and threw up his hands.

"Got to happen sometime. Damnfine girl, too."

"Glad you finally woke up," Shibo said happily. He kissed her.

His Ling Aspect said sternly:

I still advise against public displays of affection. You face grave difficulties, and every lessening of the command structure—

Killeen shoved the Aspect back into its cramped space, relishing the sensation. Now that they were back on solid ground, he could trust his instincts more.

He left Shibo and moved among the Bishop camp, wondering what measures he could take to ease his increasing sense of danger. Besen was sitting on a natural ledge as she flux-shaped some mechmetal into carrygear.

"Toby's nose's li'l bent," she said as he sat down.

"So's everybody's," he countered.

He had always been able to speak naturally to Besen. Now that he thought about her it gradually dawned that this "girl" was in fact a woman with easy self-assurance. Her angular face had a quality of shrewd reserve.

"Some say we're worse off than we were on Snowglade," she said.

"Could be."

"They figure that string's up there ready to move any minute. We'll never get back through it."

"Unless we can figure when it'll move," Killeen countered.

"How?" she asked.

Killeen grinned. "No idea."

Besen laughed. "Well, least with you back everybody's not so glum."

Killeen blinked. "Huh?"

"I'd given up on us. We just sat around starin' at the ground till you showed up."

He was genuinely startled. "Why?"

"Jocelyn tried to pull us together. It just didn't work."

Killeen said nothing and she went on, "We followed you 'cause you had a dream we believed in. That's the only reason to leave home, ever."

"Dream's gone."

"Yeasay, we know that. We're not dumb." She gave him a stern look, mouth pursed.

"And Cybers're worse than mechs."

"You got more than one dream in you though."

Killeen was startled again. "What?"

"You'll think of some way. We know that."

He did not know what to say and covered this by standing up. "C'mon, you can show me the area."

Her wide mouth seemed to hold some suppressed mirth at his awkwardness. She said solemnly, "Yessir."

By all the precepts he had learned, to idle in a huge camp like this, clearly conspicuous from the air or even from orbit, was foolhardy. Bonfires at night, smoke plumes by day, regular arrays of tents—all these mechs knew well. Cybers, too, presumably.

He walked by the Bishop slit trenches, already fragrant, and tested the grab-pole running along one side for strength. More than once, when a boy, he had squatted beside a trench without one and lost his balance. This pole was a long alum-ceramic arm from some mechtech, caught in Y-sticks at the ends. It took his full weight as he squatted and did his daily ritual, always performed after breakfast. The Bishops had long since lost their shyness about such matters and did not erect any shelter around the trench; even in the longlost Citadel, privacy had been a minor concern. He walked over the spur of the next low ridge and saw that this Tribe felt differently. Some had fold-up shields, one even with a roof. But farther down the valley he saw a rivulet, gorged with the recent rain, serving first as drinking water and then, downstream, as a sewer.

"Plain dumb," Besen said at his elbow.

"The river?" he asked.

"Yeasay. Already got dysentery in some the Families. Big camp like this, you get a worse sickness, it'll jump aroun' pretty quick."

"Any signs yet?"

"I heard rumors," she said.

"Let me know if you hear more."

"Hard gettin' much from 'em."

"Howcome?"

"They're full of talk 'bout righteousness and how if they follow the true path everything'll turn out right and so on."

"Could be some their Aspects ridin' them a little hard."

Besen surveyed the valley as she said, "Yeasay. From the High Arcology time seems like."

Killeen felt oddly pleased. "Most young people don't care enough about history to remember stuff like that."

She turned to study his face. "How can you not? Only way we can make sense of all this."

"Sure—if you've got time. We'll be hustlin' pretty hard now."

Her eyebrows narrowed. "Forget who we are, what's the point goin' on?"

"Right." Killeen was obscurely proud of her quiet vehemence. This Tribe might succumb to His Supremacy, but he was quite sure the Bishops would not.

"Besen . . . I'm glad you're with Toby. He and I aren't getting on well right now."

She smiled. "Rough times for us all."

"The time when a boy breaks away and makes his own path, well . . ."

"I know."

"I . . . I appreciate the help," he finished lamely.

"You're not doing so bad," she said, and went back to her labors. Killeen stood regarding the valley and wrestling with his thoughts. In principle he was in a simple situation. A Cap'n followed Tribal orders. But he sensed something deeply dangerous in all this.

"Reportin', Cap'n," Jocelyn said formally. He had not heard her approach.

"You take care those chips?"

"Kicked a li'l ass, looks like it'll be okay."

"Good. How're our reserves?"

"Not much." She punched her wrist and a graphic-display inventory of edible supplies appeared in Killeen's right eye, available on blink-access.

He studied the hills. There had been thick woods in the arroyos. Many were clogged by mudslides. Swaths of trees were already gray and dead. "Bet we'll scavenge the territory around here fast, too. Pick it clean."

"I'll see if the Families got any food stores."

Killeen gestured toward the creek that snaked its way down the dusty valley. "Water'll be no problem for a while. If something samples that creek downstream, though, it'll know we're here."

"Cybers?"

Killeen scowled, looking at the sprawl of Families open and

careless in the valley. "Likely. Point is, what we get from fightin' Cybers?"

Jocelyn studied his face. Did she suspect anything? he wondered.

He had told Shibo as much as he could about his time inside the Cyber. She had agreed that until he understood it better, it was probably a bad idea to relate the story in full to others.

To the Family's questions he had let on, without actually lying, that he had somehow stowed away on the body of a Cyber and then escaped from the subterranean nest when a chance came. He could scarcely explain the colliding sensations that had assaulted him inside the Cyber's body. Those memories now provoked shudders of disgust in him. Images from them shot through his sleep. He had intentionally worked hard the day before in hopes that fatigue would grant him oblivion in sleep. But the brooding, shifting dreams had troubled him again. This morning's fire had roused him from a terrifying sensation of suffocating in spongy air that swarmed into his lungs whenever he tried to draw a clean breath. To be yanked into the real world, even one with a raging fire to be put out, had been a relief.

"We have any choice?" Jocelyn asked, her eyes concerned. Killeen wondered if he seemed odd to the Family; certainly Jocelyn was acting a little awkward and formal with him. Shibo, too, had been careful with him since his return, as if he were both fragile and unreliable. Well, Killeen reflected, maybe he was.

"Prob'ly not. Looks like Cybers're mostly interested in guttin' this planet, though, not usin' its surface."

He gestured above, where a thin skirt of clouds partly obscured a distant gray mottling. Patches of Cyber construction arced in polar orbits low on the horizon. The long arc of the cosmic string was a faint, pale yellow scratch across the sky. Something turned at the limits of his vision. He focused on it but saw only a thin trace image moving in equatorial orbit. Cybers owned space but for some reason did not use sky assault against them. Why?

Jocelyn said, "They suck the core dry, take all its metal, we'll have nothin' but scrap left. That'll kill all the plants, and prob'ly us, too."

Killeen listened to Arthur a quick moment and said, "My Aspects say there won't be any big change in temperature for a while. Quakes are the big problem."

"His Supremacy says—"

"Look, a man who thinks he's God can't be trusted much."

"I think we should believe in him."

"Believe him, or *in* him?"

Jocelyn said warily, "I've watched him several more days than you have. He was most gracious. After all, we were people who suddenly dropped from the sky and placed demands on his Families—food, shelter. He helped us get away from the shuttles, before the Cybers tracked them. He is a natural commander!"

"Look, 'member how Fanny was? *That's* leadership. This guy—"

"He is using new methods," Jocelyn said adamantly. "These are terrible times, the old ways don't work."

"They're all we've got."

"Well then, by our mutual laws, as Elder he should have appointed a new Cap'n. You were gone, prob'ly dead. So if he'd stuck by the laws, you wouldn't be Cap'n now."

Ah, he thought. "Who would?"

She hesitated, then said, "His Supremacy asked me and I took on settling into camp. Negotiated with other Families."

"You're to be commended. That's all for now," Killeen said, giving her a clipped salute. He pointedly turned his back to survey the valley again.

His Ling Aspect broke in on his thoughts:

That officer likes the taste of command. My experience is that even dangerous times do not slake that thirst.

Killeen kicked a stone, enjoying the satisfying *thunk* as it bounded down the slope.

EIGHT

His Supremacy's tent was sultry with sweet incense and tangy sweat. The fifteen Cap'ns arrayed in a crescent before the broad black desk stood stiffly at attention, as ordered. A layer of blue smoke hung over their heads. The cloying smell caught in Killeen's throat, making him cough. His Supremacy frowned at the sound and repeated his command.

"All Families will commit the same strength in this attack. We strike simultaneously. We all risk, we all triumph."

Killeen thought, *And if we lose, nobody'll be positioned for rear guard, nobody'll cover our ass.* But he did not dare say it.

"We shall follow our same, victorious tactics—the way of right action that has brought us so far. Following the assault, we must destroy as many of the Cyber buildings as we can."

Killeen said, before caution could intervene, "I am most sorry, but I do not know the proper tactic."

His Supremacy turned almost lazily to gaze directly into Killeen's eyes. Until now the swarthy, compact man had delivered his speech with his eyes fixed on the blue haze, as though secrets lurked high in the tent.

"I had imagined that you would have learned the revolutionary developments in battle I have brought about."

"I've seen your weapons. Quite extensive, some I've never heard about, but—"

"Cap'n of the Bishops—a Suit unfamiliar to me as yet, but one I am willing to allow into my company of the devout—I understand your ignorance. When I foretold the arrival of your Family, I said the help which would fall from heaven would demand shaping. I and my officers are willing to fashion you to my higher ends, rest assured."

"Well, sir, I appreciate that. My Family will need—"

"Perhaps you have not noticed that no one, in addressing me, uses the slight and paltry honorific 'sir.' "

Killeen made the gesture he had seen the other Cap'ns use—a bow, while stepping back and casting his hands down at the floor. It seemed to imply total acceptance.

His Supremacy nodded, looking almost bored. "You practiced the frontal assault, on whatever world sent you?"

"On Snowglade, yeasay—but hardly ever, 'cause mechplexes got their perimeters bracketed. Pick you off fast . . ." It took an effort to conclude, "Your Supremacy."

"I devised a devastating new way to use the frontal attack. It involves designating one Family as prime warriors, those who expose themselves early, to draw fire. A second party then surprises the enemy by springing forth from concealment. Then the main body assaults the nest."

"That second party—how do they stay hidden . . . Supremacy?"

"By slipping into the tunnels of the vile Cyber nests."

Killeen frowned and said nothing. But the short man in his brilliant uniform looked reproachfully at him and said, "You have much to learn here, Cap'n. My revelation, which yielded this splendid method, assured me of our victories. It is not as though we proceed forward in shadow and uncertainty."

Killeen nodded, not knowing what he could say.

"I foresee our triumph, carried on the wings of God, and my shoulders. You see, Cap'n of the Bishops, I have ascended to the panoply of Gods. As the representative of the Essential Will of nature, I am necessarily Divine in my own right."

His Supremacy explained this as if he were talking to a bright but ignorant child. Killeen had questions to ask but something in the curiously blank eyes of His Supremacy kept him silent.

His Supremacy nodded as if satisfied and then shouted suddenly, "Sound the convocation! I must prepare the Families for the next step in their destiny!"

Cap'ns and underofficers scurried to alert their Families. A rank of armed men and women fell to, their full running gear gleaming from a fresh polish. They clanked and wheezed as they escorted His Supremacy outside, dwarfing him in their sheathed shock boots.

Killeen sent a quick summons to Jocelyn, Shibo, and Cermo. The assembly was already nearly complete in the valley outside, their Bishops positioned in rectangular ranks to the right flank of the formation. The brief address by His Supremacy to his Cap'ns had barely followed what Killeen knew of Tribal forms. Most of it he had found incomprehensible. Now His Supremacy would address the entire Tribe.

The Tribe comprised all the surviving Families of this portion of New Bishop. No one spoke of the other Tribes which had lived on this world. Apparently mech cities had lately begun using humans in their conflicts. Though there had been incidents of that on Snowglade, Killeen's Family lore held that competition among mechs was more like pruning unwanted branches from a fruitful plant. Here, though, mechs warred with one another. Had the Cybers timed their invasion to take advantage of that?

Killeen walked down onto the valley floor beside the Cap'n of the Treys. Afternoon sunlight broke in patches through the cloud cover. He searched for the cosmic string but it was invisible. If it began spinning and preparing to suck again from the core, Killeen intended to get his Family to flat ground, no matter what the Tribe did.

It seemed like a long time since the Treys' Cap'n had led him away from His Supremacy's tent, past the transfixing burial ceremony. Killeen mentioned that to her and the Cap'n replied, "Had a few more since. Cybers're operatin' over the next mountain range—what's left of it. Couple Cybers nailed some Sebens, left the bodies with those mite eggs buried in their guts."

"Cybers could plant somethin' more in the bodies, too," Killeen said delicately.

Lines furrowed the Cap'n's already weathered, resigned face. "Like what?"

"Tracers. Find us, usin' 'em."

She shook her head. "They don't care enough. Just shoot our people when they get in the way. Not like mechs—least not yet."

"You worked for mechs."

"Sure—only way we'd survive."

"Where I came from couldn't trust mechs that much."

"They got crazy. Started bustin' up each other."

Killeen said cautiously, "That question I asked back there . . . I didn't understand all he said."

"Just integrate your people's electromag-tags, hailing codes, stuff like that."

"But look, there's planning—"

"We go in separately, once the team's penetrated into the tunnels."

"What about supporting fire?"

"Manage it yourself. Each Family backs up its own."

Killeen said skeptically, "Seems it'd be better if—"

The Cap'n of the Treys gave him a tired, sardonic look. "I kinda like it this way. His Supremacy says do it this way, fine. That way I can pull my Family out fast, if things go bad."

"But coordination—"

"Look, this plan's the word of God."

The Cap'n said this in a voice that was suddenly flat, factual. Killeen opened his mouth to reply with a cutting jibe and saw that behind them walked three officers. When he glanced over his shoulder they seemed to be taking an interest in what he would say. He shut his mouth and nodded woodenly.

He reached the Bishop formation just before His Supremacy began speaking. The words came to them over general comm, broadcast by linked capacities of a triangle of officers assembled just below His Supremacy on a small knoll.

Even though Killeen had been told that the Tribe numbered well over two thousand, the sight of so many people turned out in ranks, nearly crossing the valley with their columns, was impressive. He had not seen so many since a grand holiday at the Citadel, when he had been a boy younger than Toby was now. Then the occasion had been festive; now a solemn, grim air pervaded the comm. Hoisted Family flags fluttered and snapped in the wind, patched and sunbleached.

His Supremacy began with a convoluted history of their valiant battles, so filled with names and honorifics that Killeen could make no sense of it. Certainly it told him nothing of how the Families had fought, and Killeen began to suspect that His Supremacy in fact cared little for the essential details of maneuver and command. This emerged soon, as the man waved his hands wildly and described the evils of their enemies, his face congested with rage. The Cybers did not accidentally resemble demons from the pit, no—and soon they would return there, banished.

"Rebuke and scorn, do they face! Defeat and castigation!"

His Supremacy drew himself up and, even though Killeen kept a cool and skeptical part of himself withdrawn, the force of the man's ardor began to penetrate.

"Death comes to us all! But it cannot sting. The grave has no victory! It is where we are rewarded."

The vast crowd stirred as more long, rolling sentences washed over them. Killeen felt himself moved by the rhythmic, chantlike sweep. For the first time he understood how His Supremacy had held together a Tribe that had suffered shattering defeats and now faced an incomprehensible enemy of casual viciousness.

"—at whose coming, to judge the All that Is, I shall stand upon the right hand—"

The very air seemed to flicker with new intensity, hot filaments running on the breeze.

"—*render* the things of metal and flesh into base matter! *Shatter* these minions of history's last battle against us! For we arise from the natural substances of the universe, and are at one with it, and enjoyeth its fruits without artifice or corruption of spirit. *We* are the product of God's own evolution. Monsters shall not fall from the sky and have these holy rewards, not if we hallow the ancients' names."

Distant rumblings, as if mountains rubbed a coarse sky.

"—for after the final liberating battle we shall go faring forth. We shall call to the most holy and majestic Skysower and be fed and brought forth!"

Illuminations shot through the clouds. Something silvery stirred high up.

"—to deliver us from the evil of this place. These devourers of worlds will fall, as the mechs fell before them. Believe in me—"

A cyclonic churn parted the banks of mottled clouds. Killeen felt the crowd begin to notice.

"—on Earth . . . as it is . . . in heaven!"

Striations of blue descended, curving along long arcs. Traceries frenzied the air. A rush of heat beat down from a sky that seemed emptied. Yet Killeen's sensorium quivered with pale, swift intricacy.

"Thy kingdom come. Thy will be done. Malevolence focused by supreme will, we entreat you—"

A gathering presence loomed in Killeen's sensorium—yet the air showed only translucent, skittering feelers of luminescence. Killeen remembered suddenly seeing such immense flickerings before. They had lit the distant skies the night after the cyborg released him.

"What—what?" His Supremacy croaked. His rhythm broken, he gaped at the display above.

And a voice Killeen knew came fluttering, at first almost lost in wind-whisperings:

I seek a particular human. Give sign if you can perceive this. I speak on magnetic wings, and bring tidings from the very center of this realm.

His Supremacy's voice boomed, full of undisguised surprise and joy. "I am here! I have brought your word by sword and daring—"

No, you are not the one. I am enjoined to convey this only to the target human. My feet are mired in plasma, while these arms extend even unto your bitter-cold zones. Find me the one named Killeen. I speak for his father.

NINE

A tide of rustling disquiet swept across the valley. The ranks of the assembled Families wavered. Feet shuffled nervously, stirring dust that rose like a visible answer. Heads leaned back, trying to make out the shadowed filigree that danced featherlight across the sky.

"What?" His Supremacy's voice was weak and strained, compared with the full, resonant power that came hammering down from the fretted air. "It is . . . God? God speaks in this manner?"

I seek a being of the class I perceive is gathered here. I have searched this world far beyond my obligation to do so, and found fair few of you small things. Such low forms are usually numerous, but you are rare among these sheltered enclaves I have examined—these rude, chilly planets of uninteresting, slow matter.

"*I* speak for all humanity here," His Supremacy cried.

In Killeen's sensorium the human voice seemed awash in a lapping fretwork of smoothed waves. The massive swells were gridworks that bulged and slid. He remembered the mathematically generated ocean he had sailed in the grip of the Mantis's mind.

Are you the one I seek? You emit a pungent reek, similar to his, I see. But your essence is shaped with less angularity, and colored in the deeper hues of frying gases. No, you are not that one. Be gone.

His Supremacy's mouth twisted with dark rage. "You are not God! You come from the Cybers. You must! Say it! Be gone with *you*, foul demon!"

Killeen held himself back, unsure. This was the very voice that had called to him years before, on Snowglade. It had advised him

214

to not rebuild the Bishop Citadel, and to seek the *Argo*. After the Bishops had found *Argo* buried under a weathered hillside, Killeen had expected further contact with the voice, more orders— but nothing had come in the two years of *Argo*'s voyaging. He longed to answer it.

But here? The voice would be heard by all, and might reveal what Killeen should do next.

He tried to guess what His Supremacy would make of it, especially since the man's red face had already knotted with frustration. The act of receiving the message might in turn make it impossible for Killeen to act upon it, if His Supremacy could somehow turn the information to his own ends.

So many of you small things, each with a different aroma and shape. Vexing! Creation is diverse, but trivially so— what need can there be for this variety, these endlessly multiplied shadings and nuances? It is not as though you mites are works of true craft, after all. It simply makes my task more difficult.

"Flee, foul agent!—or we will crush you!" His Supremacy put all his considerable throaty power into the jeering shout.

You venture to clash with me? To crush a being made of the most tenacious fields? My magnetic skirts could sweep you to dust, little worrisome grub. The discharge of my merest idle thought would wreak charring violence through a thousand such as you. But no matter—I cannot be bothered to fathom the mire of vile scents and squashed angles that make up your fledgling race. I cannot rummage through a legion of such, all to deliver a message of muddled meanings. I go.

The roiling seethe began to ebb from the heavens. The pressure in Killeen's sensorium trickled away.

"No! Wait!"

He leaped in the air, arms flung up as if to grab the retracting lines of blue flux high above them. "I'm Killeen! Here!"

The lacy pattern of radiance paused and rippled. Killeen watched it shoot fresh feelers downward, following the arcing magnetic field lines of the planet.

So you are. I sense your flat odor and slanted self. Good—I tire of this pursuit, this obligation. I received

this injunction from a power which sits farther in toward the Eater than do even I. Though my head can reach up into the realm of cool, sluggish worlds such as this, my many feet stand upon a crisply ordered plane of storm-cut plasma, the accretion disk that hotly feeds the appetite of the Eater. From far inside my tossed realm comes this frame of questions which I now ask.

Killeen watched His Supremacy as these words poured down. The man's anger seemed bottled up, making his eyes bulge and lips protrude. His jaw waggled to the side, back and forth. But he gave no orders. Killeen stepped clear of his Family so his sensorium would be as clean as he could make it.

"Tell me—last time, you said somethin' calling itself my father was there. What—"

The first is a question. *How is Toby?*

Any doubts Killeen had harbored about the meaning of that strange sentence, years before, now vanished. Who but Abraham would ask first about his grandson?

"He's fine—growin' like a weed. Standin' right here beside me. See if you can pick up his—"

I perceive a weaker aura, yes, somewhat similar to yours. I shall relay it backward, down magnetic lines which spiral into the Center. It shall be refracted into the tangle of geometries where something darkly awaits. There is a spray of antimatter near my footpoint, arising from some artificial means, and thus I cannot guarantee precise transmissions of such flimsy data as your minute auras.

"My father's there with you? Tell him we need—"

Not here with me, no; all I ken is the assertion that he lived farther in, whirling somewhere in time-racked eddies.

"*Lived?* Does he live still now?" Killeen's voice tightened.

Forms such as yourself seem to lurk there, for purposes not revealed to me. I cannot tell if that particular unit persists. The presence there of such inconsequential, prim-

itive entities is a greater mystery than anything in your
messages, little mind, but I shall not trouble you with
issues you cannot comprehend. Attend you, then: The
next message is *Apply the* Argo *ship's codes to the Legacies.*

Killeen shouted, "Legacies? But we've lost—"

Silence, small mind.

"Our ship is gone!"
Unconcerned, the electromagnetic entity above stirred as
though restless. It cast auroras of shimmering green into the nearby
clouds, pressing them back so that the whole vault of the sky
opened. The high cirrus banks yawned, as if to bite the somber
sky beyond.

**The messages I am enjoined to deliver are not simple
statements, but rather microscopic intelligences—fragments
of the mind that sent them. Thus I must wait for this
speck to conjure up some reply to you. It now says,** *Then
you are lost.*

"But that's—"
His Supremacy shouted, "Cap'n of the Bishops! I command
you to desist. Converse with this agent of corruption will confuse
all our Tribe and bring error to us all."
Killeen glanced at His Supremacy and waved him away, trying
to think. His father—
"I warn you!" His Supremacy's voice gained menace. "Dealing
with—"
"Cermo! Perimeter star!"
The Bishops broke rank and reformed into a well-spaced,
outer-directed phalanx. The air sang as their sensoria focused
outward, crisping the tangled fields of the other Families.
Killeen said levelly, "I'll brook no interference. This is no devil
or God-killer. Leave us be!"
"I command—" But His Supremacy broke off the sentence as
he felt the impact of the massed, merged Bishop field.
Weapons came down from shoulders, clicked on, pointed at
primary targets—beginning with His Supremacy.
"We Bishops require a moment. Hear me! I invoke the ancient
rules, the first and most revered among them being Family privacy."

The valley buzzed with unease. The other Families made no move. His Supremacy clenched his fists but only watched as Killeen turned his sensorium back skyward.

I was not to deliver these portents until you were free of the grasp of mechanical intelligences. That was why I did not speak to you on your ship. It is inhabited by mechanical forms which should not receive the key to the Legacies.

"*Argo*'s got mechs aboard?" Killeen had known some small forms still evaded capture after the successful human mutiny on Snowglade, but he had thought they were powerless and insignificant.

Mechanicals are pervasive. They are the dust that hangs between the suns.

There was almost a note of sympathy in the brooding voice that pressed through Killeen's sensorium.
"Look, is there any way my father can help us? We're trapped here. Some other lifeform's ripping the whole planet apart. No way we can get free, unless somethin' powerful as you aids us."

I am a messenger, not a savior.

"Tell my father, if he's still alive. Send us help!"

The small mind I can interrogate sends wails of remorse, if that is any comfort to you. But nothing else. My powers are not at its disposal, in any case.

The colorful traceries began to fade.
"Don't leave us here!"

Farewell.

"No!"
But it was gone.
Killeen slumped to the ground with sudden fatigue. A heavy depression settled into him like a cloud and he panted as if he had been running. Color seeped from the world.
Shibo tugged him up. Hands supported him. Toby put an arm

around his shoulders and brought Killeen forward. The Bishops still held their defensive star formation. The air was tense as the other Families studied them, hands hovering not far from weapons.

Shibo said, "It will return. Don't give up."

Killeen gazed around at the bleak, dusty plain and the ranks of ragged humanity that filled it. "Right. Right," he said automatically, without believing the words.

His Supremacy's voice boomed, "We have frightened it, be sure of that. The being fled our show of solidarity before it!"

Killeen shook his head and said nothing. He expected instant retribution from His Supremacy but the swarthy man merely glared. An empty, glazed look came into his eyes.

His Supremacy turned from the Bishops and began intoning more of the ancient litany. Killeen made a sign and the Bishops relaxed from the star formation, making straight ranks again. But the edgy tension on the plain, though muted, did not go away.

Beside Killeen, Toby whispered, "That guy won't forget."

Besen added, "Maybe that sky thing scared him. Sure did me."

"Hard, scarin' a man who's already God," Shibo said wryly.

Killeen listened to the rest of the service numbly, the words passing like raindrops sliding on a windowpane.

When the ceremony was finished he led the Bishops from the plain. They stepped smartly, though their eyes were hollow and distracted. He registered the bitter whisperings from the other Families. Some called taunts and threats. He let it all slip by. He was remembering his father's face.

As they passed the clump of officers around His Supremacy, the man gave Killeen a pinched, assessing look, eyes narrow and dark. "We will speak to you later, Cap'n," was all he said. Then he turned away sharply and stalked off.

Killeen's Grey Aspect said:

Yon Supremacy . . . has a lean and hungry look. Such men are dangerous . . . as the ancients said.

Killeen nodded, but compared to what the Bishops had just lost, the opinions of mere men seemed quite trivial.

PART FIVE

SKYSOWER

ONE

Twilight seeped through grimy clouds, casting pale blades along the hillside where Family Bishop retreated. Killeen stopped and looked back. The tail guard had just reached the foothills of this slumped ridge and would stop there to defend their rear.

"Hold till we clear the summit," he sent to Cermo.

—Yeasay,— Cermo replied at minimal comm level. They were keeping their transmissions few and weak, to avoid detection by Cybers in pursuit. —Running low on ammo.—

Killeen did not answer because there was nothing he could do. There was no more ammunition with the main body of the Family, where he was. Given the Cybers' ability to attack from any direction, there was no point in reinforcing either the advance guard or the rear party.

Cermo had been forced to use arms and energy-store to pick off the small, tubular things that were trailing the Family. These dog-sized creatures seemed to be miniature Cybers, with reddish carapaces and aluminum-sheathed legs. Unarmed, they had followed the Family ever since the disaster at the magnetic generating stations. And they had proved smart, too; they hung back and scattered when Cermo sent people to pick them off, delaying the Family still further.

Even one of the cyborged insects could give away their position, and there were thousands of hiding spots in the jumble of the valley they had just left.

He walked up the steep hillside. His feet were blistered and he favored his left, hobbling slightly. Some water had gotten into his thigh sleeves and had dribbled down into his webbing socks. All the boot- and compressor-shock tech in the

221

world could not keep pressure off the sore, inflamed tissue of his heels.

The water had come from geysers bursting suddenly from a sandy canyon. They had been crossing it at full speed after the battle. There had been no time to stop and check, and now dozens of Family limped along with the same ailment.

—I've found Jocelyn's beeper,— Shibo sent. She was already over the summit, leading the advance guard. Killeen sent a quick trill note as acknowledgment, hoping that would be less a telltale than a human voice if the Cybers picked up the transmission.

The message brought a glimmer of cheer. Jocelyn led the Family's other party, cut off during the battle. Their fallback plan of retreat was working, then; she had found a way along parallel ridgelines and passed through the low canyons beyond, leaving a signifier, as planned. That meant they hadn't been forced to skirt around any Cybers, which in turn implied that perhaps the aliens were not following the Bishops at all. Slim evidence, but Killeen grimly allowed himself that hope. At this point, hope was a vital as energy.

But then Shibo sent, —More dead,— and Killeen's mood darkened.

He cut in his reserves of power and bounded up the last long shelf of shattered rock before the summit. A red sunset cut momentarily through the smoky cloud deck, casting stark shadows in the rutted arroyos beyond. He reached the top, panting. He expanded his sensorium momentarily and picked up Shibo's green tracer. Closeupped he saw her dispersing her party to the flanks, where they took up defensive positions.

Killeen boosted off on full power and made his way down the steep slope in a series of jumps. His compressors wheezed and he let his calves take most of the shock, but his feet howled in pain.

Strangely filigreed foliage cloaked the arroyos. He slowed to get through it. Spindly trees formed a green canopy over him as he passed Family members in the shadows. The tough, warped trunks still clung to the ruptured soil and already had begun to correct their slant, turning to seek the sky along new verticals. Though there were wide swaths cut in the willowy, silent forest by hillslides and fresh, carving streams, life seemed able to hang on tenaciously. Sharp paw prints testified to the survival of large animals, though Killeen seldom saw these except at great distances. They were wary of mechs and Cybers and men alike.

He found Shibo sitting at the base of a rise, staring upward.

He followed her gaze and saw a body hanging from a large, gnarled tree. "Any of ours?"

"Naysay," she answered. "Looks like a Jack."

Several Family members followed them as they approached the tree. The woman's gaunt body swayed on fiberweave ropes, expertly trussed. Her entire chest and stomach bulged with one of the glassy, opaque blisters Killeen had seen before. This one was oozing milky fluid from its peak.

"Looks 'bout ready. It'll pop soon," Shibo said.

"Right. How long ago did Jocelyn come by here?" Killeen asked.

"I figure couple hours. Her beeper was pretty played out."

"Where was it?"

"Down where I was sitting."

"So either she left it here so we'd see this . . ."

"Or somethin' left this by the beeper."

"Yeasay—after she'd gone on."

Shibo peered at him, the blades of bone beneath her cheeks seeming to stretch her browned skin taut and shiny. "Which?" she asked uncertainly.

Killeen tried to figure how a Cyber might think. "Why'd Jocelyn point out this? More likely she'd steer us away."

Shibo nodded. "So some Cyber found her beeper and left this."

Killeen stood back and watched ants swarming over the face of the body as it turned slowly in the wind. "Wonder if it's s'posed to scare us."

"See that?" Shibo pointed.

The hands and feet were pierced. From the bloody wounds protruded green stalks ending in fully opened yellow blossoms. The flowers seemed to grow out of the woman.

Killeen felt a sick chill spread through him, remembering the grotesque sculptures of the Mantis. The same horribly rendered theme. "Why'd a Cyber do that?"

"Combined plant and animal," Shibo said.

"Some kind of message?"

"Why'd it do that?"

"Thing 'bout aliens is, they're alien." He spat on the ground in exasperation. Why did both Mantis and Cyber make this "art" warping humans and plants?

A man nearby moved toward the body and extended his knife to cut the ropes.

"No!" Killeen knocked down the man's hand.

"I's just fixin'—"

"Don't touch it."

"—get it down, poke the thing that's livin' inside it."

"It's prob'ly tagged. You cut it down, alarms go off, Cybers come running."

The man looked outraged. "You let it grow in there, come out, it'll be one more Cyber!"

Shibo said, "Naysay. They grow their li'l helpers in us, not themselves."

The man blinked and then a pale, washed-out expression stole over him and he turned away. Killeen looked down the rise to the forest, where Bishops were straggling in from the long retreat. They slumped down, not even bothering to lean against trees, and lay with their heads resting on their carrypacks.

"We're 'bout played out," he said reflectively.

"Can't stop here," Shibo said. "Cybers know this place."

Killeen nodded. "Might come back."

He wondered if Cybers found it any more difficult to move and seek at night. Probably not, since he remembered their natural optical senses worked best in the infrared. Which meant that the gathering gloom gave Family Bishop no advantage here.

He walked to the middle of the gathering crowd and sat, his legs gratefully ceasing their aches. The quakes had shaken most of the odd, triangular leaves to the floor of the forest, providing a deliciously soft loam for rest. Approaching Bishops' bootsteps made no noise whatever, and the ebbing twilight suffused the scene in a soothing, serene light.

His feet screamed for release, but he did not dare take off his boots for fear that he would not be able to get them back on when his feet swelled. He was tempted to expand his sensorium and get a quick head count, but the hanging body had made him wary of even the slightest electromagnetic tracer.

And in any case, he knew the rough dimensions of their loss. Family Bishop had been the outer flanking element in the assault, a relatively less dangerous position affording a clear escape route. They had gone in after the forward units sprang from their concealment in the Cyber tunnels. The battle had played out on the plain beneath the magnetic generator buildings. Those units had appeared directly among the Cybers.

Killeen had witnessed the fate of those brave Families. The assault ratio must have been at least one Family per Cyber. The first rush had brought down two Cybers and things had looked good. Then men and women began to fall on the plain as though blown over by a sudden soundless wind. Killeen had not been able to pick up any signatures of microwave or optical or even kinetic-kill weapons. People fell in midstride, as though picked up and slammed into the ground by an invisible giant.

The rush came to a sudden halt. Families regrouped behind the fallen, smoking Cybers. Even there some weapon picked them off one at a time. They tried a rush toward the magnetic generators that loomed above like mud-colored, rectangular hills—and fell by the dozens, their strangled cries twisting through the comm.

The Bishops answered the blaring attack signal of His Supremacy. More Families poured over the distant hills. They spread out and moved in jerky dashes between the covering shelter of arroyos and clumps of trees and boulders. The battlefield was a gray scabland left by some recent magma-spewing vent which had obliterated the life there. Whether this was by accident or design Killeen could not tell. The Cybers had already bored tunnels in the barely cooled lake of lava. Cracks in the crusty scab gave some shelter as the Tribe descended and brought withering fire to bear on the four remaining Cybers.

Had they been mechs, the directed bursts would have sheared away legs and burned out antennae. Here, nothing happened. The Cybers paused, as though reassessing the situation, and then went on picking off the darting human targets, as if nothing more bothersome than a summer's rain fell upon them.

Killeen had been running at the middle of the Family. He saw the first Family members fall and ordered everyone down. They had poured a torrent of fire on the nearest Cyber, and succeeded in blowing away several appendages. But even the natural, warty skin repelled all shots.

This Killeen could not believe until he tried three successive bolts straight into the exposed midsection of the thing. Only after all three failed, fading away to mere luminous blue traceries in the air, did he notice the slight shimmer that hung over the Cyber, and hear the crackle of ionizing air in his sensorium.

That was when he called retreat. His Supremacy had immediately broken into Killeen's comm line and cursed him, demanding another full assault. Killeen had hesitated for a long moment, while Bishops died all around him. The chaos of the rest of the battlefield had stormed against his sensorium, blinding him with its agonized calls and screamed pleas.

He had to resist the press of centuries of Family tradition, the absolute rule that said an Elder of the Tribe must be obeyed, especially in the split-second tumult of battle. Killeen had paused, agonizing, and that was the moment when he saw Loren, a boy Toby's age, blown apart. The boy simply went to pieces. Something had struck him in the chest and made a bloody flower of him. Even though Loren was down in the apparent shelter of a lava crack, the burnished rock failed to stop whatever the Cybers used.

He called retreat then. Similar orders seemed to echo faintly in his comm, coming from other Cap'ns, but he could not be sure. He had provided some covering fire for the main body of Bishops, but harshly commanded that no one try to recover any fallen bodies. They had lost eleven getting off the plain, and still more working their way through the arroyos and over the ridgeline. He had barely stopped the retreat from turning into a rout. And all the while, he had ignored the mad, rattling curses of His Supremacy.

The only blessing in all this was that the children, pregnant women, and older Family members were all with the supply train. That was an improvement over their clashes with mechs on Snowglade. The abilities of the Cybers more than made up for that, though.

Killeen let himself wonder for a moment about the next time he saw His Supremacy. Would the man order him hoisted up on a spit, like the suffering remnants of people he had seen at the Tribal camp? There was a fair chance of it. Nonetheless, Family Bishop had to make for the designated rendezvous point. Without the Tribe the Family would fare badly in the open countryside; they simply knew too little about this world to survive for long.

For a moment Killeen weighed his own personal fate against the needs of the Family. He had seen quite enough of His Supremacy's tactics already. They were ruinous used against Cybers, and probably not highly effective against mechs, either. His Supremacy's victories had come with mech allies, after all. And after Killeen's insubordination on the battlefield, His Supremacy would certainly put the Bishops in the thick of things in the future, where he could keep better control of them—whether or not Killeen still lived to lead them.

He sighed, and Shibo lying beside him cast a wise, pensive

look. She knew what he was stewing about, yet said nothing. He took out a chaw and bit into its dense, sugary grains. Cermo came in with the rear guard. Killeen scowled at him, his usual signal that he was not in the mood to talk. He needed to think.

On balance, he had to lead them to the rendezvous. It was to be at a mountaintop, apparently a site having to do with one of the locals' revered religious symbols. There they could meet the supply train. Then, if they decided to leave the crazed leadership of His Supremacy, they could slip away with full packs and bellies. That was worth risking his personal fate; in the end, no true Cap'n could decide otherwise.

His Arthur Aspect observed:

> One should expect religious fervor, even rabid fundamentalism, in the face of such calamity as these people have endured. Be mindful that their ardor reflects an underlying fear they can barely contain. They have been rooted from their homes—

"So were we," Killeen muttered.

> Yes, but we have dwelled for years in the comfort of *Argo*.

"We didn't turn crazy, not even in the worse times on Snowglade."

> What about Hatchet? Wasn't he unbalanced?

Killeen remembered the closed, tight look to Hatchet's face. "Naysay—just plain mean. Thought he could strike a deal with mechs, when all the time they were usin' him, planning a zoo for us all."

> I won't belabor such distinctions. But do notice that the Tribe also experienced apparent victories over the mechs when the intercity conflicts gave them an advantage. The crushing advent of the Cybers followed, however. Plus the disemboweling of their planet. Their strong reaction, their need for a perfect leader who embodies their hopes, who tells them that he speaks for God—such an effect is quite within the bounds of human responses.

"You makin' excuses? This guy says he's *God*."

I merely point out that the Tribe can still be effective, and it may not be best for the Family to leave it.

Irritably Killeen called up his Ling Aspect and asked, "What you say?"

A smart Captain plays to his superiors' foibles. I—

"Foibles?"

A slight frailty in character. Staff discipline is essential, and I cannot fault a commander who disciplines a Captain—

Killeen jammed the small voice back into its recess and stood up. They should move on before the light gave out completely. The rest had made his feet more sensitive. He would have to march awhile before some numbness returned to them.

Lined faces watched him with interest. One in particular, that of the woman Telamud, seemed to blaze with energy. She got up and walked stiffly, legs straight. Eyes open wide and blinking, she looked around. Experimentally she rocked to the side and then flexed her knees, as if trying out her calf-shocks. She walked again, tongue flicking out to taste the air, breathing rapidly. Some others had noticed by this time. A man stood and asked her if she felt all right. Killeen wondered if she had a sudden fever. Telamud looked around as if she had never seen any of them before. She began to shake. Killeen feared she was going into Aspect storm, her riding intelligences overwhelming her. She shook harder, a low gurgling coming out of her open mouth. Then she fell, completely limp.

Telamud's friends examined her, slapped her, tried to bring her around. The woman came back slowly, groggy and ashen. She could say nothing, but she seemed able to walk all right.

As Killeen looked around, drops began to patter through the decks of leaves and branches above. It was a pale green rain, alien and cold, curtains of it moving like filmy lace among the trees.

The Family lay sprawled as though dead. Some had already taken food from their packs, as though settling down for the night.

"Heysay, rain," someone said drowsily.

Another answered, "Never thought I'd hate rain. Never got enough on Snowglade. But now . . ."

"Water above, water below," Killeen said. "More in my blisters than's comin' out that sky."

A man called, "It'll keep the Cybers in, I'll bet."

Killeen shook his head. This futile logic had no basis, but the fatigue in the man's voice was deep. He called up his inventory of old tales and said, "You 'member Jesus? The Great Cap'n? Well, I'm greater, 'cause I'm walkin' on more water than he did."

The small joke got a laugh, and he cajoled a few to their feet. They were too tired to resist very much, but Killeen knew he could not get much more out of them before their reserves would be gone. Then he would face real rebellion.

"C'mon," he called. "Step proud! Double rations t'night."

Their mood lightened a little and the column moved off slowly into the gathering murk.

TWO

Quath pursued the Noughts with a strangely mixed glee.

She enjoyed the mad dashes she could perform, racing from one fleeing band of panicked Noughts to the next, chopping and blasting and cutting them. It was a consummation of her plan, and a great joy.

Yet vagrant impulses shot through her. She felt glancing pain as the Noughts died. She suffered a momentary trembling fever as they fled in fear.

This unsettled her, slowed her arms fractionally, veered her aim. So Beq'qdahl cried, <You're overshooting! Correct!>

<Yes, yes,> Quath replied, hoping none of the podia noticed how shaken she was.

<Pursue them!> came the joint cry of the armed podia. Quath joined their rush.

Up ragged ridgelines, through gray mech ruins and gutted green forests, and down onto the smashed steppes of this fractured place, they harried the stupid, witless Noughts.

Quath's adroit plan had worked. Her captured Nought, when released in the area where the largest packs of Noughts were thought to prowl, immediately sought out its fellows. A tiny device attached to the Nought gave a locating signal several times a day. Quath had tracked them and had guessed their intention of again attacking some of the magnetic field stations which controlled the movements of the Cosmic Circle.

And now the trap she had laid for them had sprung, catching thousands of the mites. As Quath made haste through a mech factory, searching for hiding Noughts, the Tukar'ramin's voice sprang fullblown into her aura.

You are a true fierce and canny sort, she said. *I have observed your admirable scheme unfolding. Be careful that you do not risk yourself in these brute encounters, however.*

230

<We are weapons-augmented, vast one. Fear not,> Quath replied.

I can bring you glad news, too. The second of the encoded slabs, which you extracted from the Nought ship, is now decoded as well as can be done. It is truly valuable.

Quath felt Beq'qdahl, who was clambering up a nearby slope, seethe with amber-shot jealousy. She pretended not to notice. <Oh? I am made twofold happy. But . . . who translated them?>

The Illuminates.

Quath's subminds babbled in a crossfire of astonishment.

They have deftly picked their way through the thicket of compressed meaning in those slabs.

<The *Illuminates* delve here?>

These two slabs bear directly upon large matters.

<You speak directly to them . . . now?>

Yes, across the span of suns. I have received instructions from all those Illuminates within light-travel time of this system. Two are here, overseeing our orbital constructions. Even now they debate among themselves.

<Do the Illuminates know the answers that vex and try me so much?> Quath blurted.

Quath—

<What of death? Is there meaning to what we do, meaning beyond our final endings? What of—>

*The answers we all believe—the Summation—the Illuminates themselves formulated. That wisdom is ancient indeed. Now they do not delve into such matters. They ponder how to *accomplish* our grand purpose. Remember what I revealed to you before, about your own nature?*

Puzzled, Quath paused to reflect. At the same time she plowed through a stand of twisted trees, their bark stripped (eaten by Noughts? she wondered). She searched for targets. But Beq'qdahl had already bagged the two Noughts Quath had been trailing, and now loudly trumpeted her puny victory out of ego-need. Quath turned and raced down a talus slope. <Of course, I recall all that the Tukar'ramin has given unto me. I am a Philosoph, you say.>

You approach this subject with hesitation?

<Yes . . . I wonder, why am I singled out?>

The fateful cast of genes. We incorporated facets of that ancient race; they surface perpetually in us.

<I would rather be a pure and rage-filled fighter!>

You cannot be purely anything, Quath. That is the legacy of that lost species—to see each aspect of life as mitigated.

<But I do not like it so!>

No matter. Your pain, your indecision, your questing after higher answers—that is your trial and labor and destiny.

<I would rather be sure!>

Certainty is the lot of those who do not ask questions. Such are nearly all the podia. We have mastered the material world, we ken its workings. But we do not puzzle at the questions you do, Quath.

<Would that I were like you!> Quath shouted in a strange lonely anger.

As a Philosoph you should now know that the traits long ago genetically implanted will manifest themselves in you in ways that are unpredictable and disturbing. Further, they shall increase with age. You may display the inborn traits of ancient beings, or a combination of podia nature and theirs.

<I see no way to *answer* my questions.>

There are other, perhaps even grander issues, Quath. Of such matters I bring news. The slabs you brought to me contain enough information for the Illuminates to contemplate a daring adventure, something the podia have never dared brave: a voyage to the very center of the galaxy.

<But all the texts say that is *impossible*—you remarked so yourself. The mechs muster enormous forces there.> Quath clambered through a mire of muck and ripped soil. Great quakes had torn these mountains savagely.

The slabs tell of a time when organic beings—the ones who wedded their genes to ours, perhaps—ventured close to the black hole at the very center. There may be a way in, free of mech interference. It will require all our resources, however.

Quath stopped beside a ravine. In the forest beyond were the humans she was tracking. The telltale she had planted flashed for a microsecond; her own Nought was among this company. But she could not think of the hunt now.

<I volunteer my sinew and soul to such an enterprise.>

That may indeed be necessary.

Something in the Tukar'ramin's tone made Quath inquire, <We . . . could learn much at Galactic Center?>

One hopes. The mechs disguise their activities in the inner few light-years. For millennia the Illuminates have wondered at their incessant collecting of pulsars, their veiled experiments. We can scarcely hope to extinguish such beings if we do not know their deepest, perhaps most dangerous abilities.

<I have only meager abilities. I know of nothing of—>

You have something we must possess.

<What? How is that possible?>

Your Nought.

<I . . . I do not . . .>

I sensed your small passenger while you were still in the Hive.

<I . . . I intended to . . .>

Know that I fathom your crosscurrents and dark broodings, Quath. We have not had a Philosoph in the Hive for a great while. I decided to let you follow your inner compass.

<My Nought . . .>

Perhaps you kept it as a pet; podia have done such before. It is no crime. Indeed, your secret keeping of this mite is ample evidence of the mysterious wisdom that comes, often unbidden, to a Philosoph. Care for your pet well.

<No, I . . .>

Yes?

<I do not have it.>

What?

<I am using it to track the other Noughts.>

Alarm shot through the Tukar'ramin's projected aura. *The Illuminates themselves now need it! It was a principal on the ship that brought them here—a vessel we must have.*

<But I—>

Find it!

With that command the Tukar'ramin's aura blew away as though a breeze had taken it. Quath had the sense of the Tukar'ramin's hurrying to convey this information to some distant place.

She should have felt some elation at this sudden turn. The slabs she and Beq'qdahl had found now proved more important than any fabulous dream. Her Nought was somehow a key because of its ship. Quath's transgression—hiding the Nought and lying by omission to the Tukar'ramin—had been lightly passed over.

Yet she felt somber and vexed as she quick-stepped toward the forest ahead. If the Illuminates did not know how to answer Quath's questions, what authority in all the podia could? Was it possible that the terrible vision of an utterly empty and meaningless universe was unquestioned, even at the highest levels?

Restless, Quath cast forward with her aura, hoping to pick up some pinprick taste of her Nought. Finding it would not be easy if she relied on the few quick flashes its telltale emitted in a day. She had slipped it into the crude equipment it wore, elemental augmentations like a crude parody of the podia's sleek lags.

She had never thought that she would need to find that particular Nought again, only the pack it joined. What an irritant!

She caught an electro-savor of Noughts spread through the dense, leafy mass ahead. Here in the open it was difficult to taste whether one of them was hers. She amped the signals—and gasped.

Ugly horizontals and verticals everywhere. Unchanging, muted light. And mixed in with these blunt perceptions came a torrent of strong surges.

Silent colorations of fatigue and pain. Bitter red smells of fear. Yellows of shame.

Rasping pride. Banging, loud confusion. Acrid envy, livid malice, and incomprehensible muddy longings.

All seething, unknown, under an oily smear of senses. It was difficult to believe that these Noughts were so unconscious!

Cryptic semisentience floated through these minds. They suffered continually from forking senses. Their entire thought-train was constantly interrupted for messages detailing their surroundings, their hungers, their incessant sexual signaling (even when exhausted!)—their tumbled, vivid, small worlds.

Quath gingerly focused her aura down to a needlepoint and thrust it toward one particular Nought who lay several hills ahead. Was this hers?

She could not tell, awash in the scattershot jostling of quick, coarse perceptions. In this sticky swamp she could not even separate its subminds. Carefully she held its muscles rigid, made it stand up from where it crouched. Did this feel familiar?

One of its upper limbs was pressing a soft thing against its face. No, into the face. An awful salty burst told her that this was a mouth, perhaps its principal one. Certainly it enjoyed an enormously augmented tasting system, for the food cast piercing rivulets of lava-hot bile all over the interior of the mouth-pouch.

Its fellows were staring at the Nought. She perceived that they would find alarming the act of spitting the food out onto the ground, where it could perhaps burn the foliage. These Noughts were gaunt; wasting of food would arouse suspicion. She must not frighten them before she found her own Nought, or they might all flee in a panic. Quath forced the thing to swallow the stuff, just to get the taste away.

What could this primitive form do? She had not entered her own Nought in this way; she was getting better at it. Curiosity egged her on.

She made it stand on one foot, then another. The sensation of bipedal instability was strangely exhilarating. She made a pod take a step, caught the body as it began to fall, and then brought the other leg up to join the first. This sensation of courting disaster, falling and catching oneself, carried a delicious excitement.

She stepped again, and again. The legs carried the impacts of walking upward and she quickly learned to absorb these with the cumbersome knees. A single knobby columnar spine felt as though it rode on a cushioned pediment of hips and buttocks.

Worse, it ached at the lower back. The muscles there were firmly knotted, as though this was a constant condition. What poor design! And they were so unimaginative that they simply tolerated such irksome pains!

She rotated the head and saw a surprising proportion of what she knew had to lie outside the Nought—but missing the fine-grained texture Quath knew, and overlaid with freightings of emotion.

This Nought could scarcely see anything without immediately reacting to it. Passing a low bush with tiny red berries brought gushing forth a hard hunger. The shaded sky above demanded to be searched for threats. A moist breeze crept into its primary nostrils and visions of rain sounded warnings. A nearby face excited memories of happier times, laughter, a warm fire—

But Quath saw that this approaching face emitted sounds which disturbed this host-Nought. The face gave quick signals of alarm. A wrinkling just below the top hairline. Its single mouth parted and lips slightly reddened, bringing teeth further into view. A narrowing of the space between the hair-hedges above the eyes.

Apparently Quath was not managing this Nought well, despite her exciting discovery of two-podded walking. She thought she had done that quite expertly. How well could such a rudimentary construction perambulate, after all?

This nearing Nought said something incomprehensible. Its primary message lay in the timbre of the speech, rising higher as the crude acoustic stutterings came faster. Quath did not want to frighten away this pack before she had a chance to explore it. And there was some deeper element about them that she could not fathom. Even clotted subminds should have appeared by now. They must be oddly integrated.

She put aside the matter and decided to leave the Nought. No need to alarm its fellows, after all. She disconnected smoothly. In an instant she was back inside her own electro-aura.

Now rain came sweeping toward her, warming and oddly pleasurable. It reminded her of the tantalizing food-streams of the Hive. She basked in the soft caress of wind and air. Then she wearily crept forward. This business of finding her particular Nought might prove difficult. She regretted not giving it a steady, bright telltale. She had feared that even a dull-witted being would eventually notice. Very well; she crept on through the splashing torrent.

THREE

It was sunset again before they scaled the last foothills and straggled across the breast of the mountain.

Killeen watched a ruddy sun sink beyond the next peak in the chain that marched up from the south. He had been slow to adjust his senses to this planet and to realize that it had milder seasons than Snowglade. Its lesser gravity and shorter days threw off his rhythms. The effect told on them all, he thought, as he watched the Bishop rear guard struggle up the slope of dark granite. A chilly wind had come up after the rainstorm of the night before, making marching harder. Once water got into their leggings, nothing worked quite right until they had a chance to stop and work on metal-shaping. But there had been no time for that. Killeen had cajoled and ordered and joshed, keeping the Bishops moving across silted mud and wrecked forests.

He looked back now, searching for Cyber pursuit. His feet yearned to be set free of his boots, and he compromised by sitting on a boulder and releasing the pressure-catches of his shocks. The relief would have made him sigh, but Cermo was passing nearby and Killeen's sense of discipline kept his lips closed.

The land had been ribbed and ridged anew by the quakes. A river below was busily digging a fresh channel, having been tossed from its old one. Geology seemed to have hastened its pace, as if in fear of more disasters. The rain had clogged innumerable new streams with mud, and they spread like hands with snaky fingers across the plains, feeding brown lakes. Drowned stands of spindly trees poked from the waters, the slanted sun catching their doomed topknots.

We are near the equator, so at least we have not suffered the cooling effects occasioned by the cosmic string. It seems to have stripped away some of the atmosphere, so there is less insulation against the cold of space.

237

"Thought the land fallin' would heat things up," he answered his Arthur Aspect.

The loss of air has a larger immediate effect. Deep heat must diffuse out from the interior. However, we can soon expect another excavation from the core. Note how the string pulses with more energy.

Killeen peered up into the darkening sky and saw the razor-sharp curve against the mottled colors of the interstellar clouds. It had not moved in the sky all day, which meant that the Cybers were rotating it with the planet. If it began to spin they would have to prepare for quakes or worse.

Only for dwellers in cities or Citadels are quakes a threat. In the open your greatest risk would be landslides, and I expect most loose soil has already been shaken free.

"Maybe, 'less this whole mountain decides it's better off in the valley."

He heard gravel scattering down the slope nearby, as if in forewarning, and turned to find Shibo coming from the advance party.

"Tribe pickets up ahead," she reported. They had been keeping comm silence since emerging onto the mountain face, because line-of-sight receivers could pick them up at a great distance. It meant greatly slower information flow, but Killeen felt too conspicuous here already. Every pebble could be a Cyber telltale, waiting for a foot to step on it or merely set down nearby.

"Police up the column," he ordered. "Let 'em see us march in all formed up, gear in place."

He was proud of the Bishops as they passed through the Tribal lines, headed for the crown of the mountain. The Families were spread out on the jutting slabs of silver-flecked granite below the summit, but Killeen did not stop to pitch camp. He marched the Bishops straight into the center, where the large tent was already erected and billowing in the cold winds. Killeen gestured to his lieutenants to flank him and did not slow their step until they reached the broad clearing at the very peak of the mountain, where the tent flapped loudly.

His Supremacy emerged to meet them. Standing beside his officers, he gazed stony-faced with empty, expressionless eyes as Killeen gave him the traditional salute.

"You withdrew without my order," the man said abruptly, without returning the salute

"I felt my Family would be overrun," Killeen said formally.

"Who could outrun those who turn tail so quickly?"

"We took large losses. Eight—"

"*All* Families sustained such casualties," His Supremacy said. Then he repeated it loudly, tolling out each word. People heard and came running.

Killeen watched as the Bishops were engulfed by the Tribe's greater numbers. There was going to be a show.

"*That* is the way . . . we *must* follow . . . *if* we are to de*feat* these monsters." His Supremacy boomed out the long sentence with relish, a clarion call. An exalted expression transfixed his face with passion as he turned to Killeen. "Other Families have not bellyached about their dead. They simply bury their heroes and carry on, obeying."

"We buried no one," Killeen said cautiously. "They were left on the field."

"Ha! The Niners brought out over a dozen dead."

"How many'd they lose doing it?"

A rustle from the gathering crowd. His Supremacy scowled.

"We do not count those losses as different. All fell in the noble cause."

"I'd rather get hit on the attack, not haulin' bodies around."

"So I'm sure you would, Cap'n. I have noticed that you have little respect for our time-honored methods. Nor do you have any sense of your transgressions."

Killeen started to reply and held back. This was to be a public humiliation. Or worse. He tried to see a way to mollify the short man whose face had a transfixed, glassy quality.

"Further, I have noticed that you have verged on disrespect toward My Holiness. I have until this moment been kind enough to ascribe this lapse to your origins around a foreign star."

Killeen could not resist agreeing. "Yeasay, that might be it."

His Supremacy's eyes lost their odd blankness. A dark look narrowed them to menacing slits. "Perhaps you think that God's rules do not apply to foreign Families?"

Killeen's effort to catch his tart reply made his jaw go tense. Then he said slowly, "Of course not. Your tongue is different from ours. I have trouble speaking in it, maybe my meaning gets garbled. We humans been separated a long time, 'member. How . . ." He clenched his jaw again, then went on. "How could anybody possibly imagine that I lack respect for His Supremacy? For the greatest mind in the history of our race?"

The short, swarthy man nodded as though this last lavish compliment were simple fact. Killeen was relieved to see that flatout flattery did not bring forth the slightest suspicion. Such talk was probably a steady daily diet for this man who thought he was God Himself.

"You have a strange manner of showing your reverence, Cap'n. The battle was going well."

"They swatted us like flies."

"*Every* battle costs us—that is the glory of it! Only by great sacrifice can we win great victories. *That* is the point which eluded the shortsighted Elders and Cap'ns before me, and which only Divine intervention, in the form of myself, has countered."

"I see, Your Supremacy."

"It is our fierceness, our sacred rage, our Divine fearlessness of mortal wounds and even of death, that places us above the monsters and demons which curse our motherworld!"

This brought a shout of agreement from the Tribe. Hoteyed, grinning, the mob was mesmerized. Their nostrils flared with anticipation. Killeen joined in their cheering tardily and so did his lieutenants. But His Supremacy noticed this and abruptly held his hands up, silencing the crowd.

"I see a slowness in you, Cap'n. A reluctance to follow the commandments of My Holy Self."

"Naysay, I—"

His Supremacy's eyes flashed. "Naysay?"

"Well, I—"

"The God of Sacred Rage does not like this word *naysay*. Especially from a Cap'n who runs. I think you speak it far too much. Knees!"

Officers instantly and expertly struck the back of Killeen's knees so that he dropped forward to the ground. Someone pinned his hands behind his back, lifting them so that he bowed involuntarily. He looked up at the pendants that swayed from His Supremacy's broad, scarlet belt. One was a tiny carved human head, grinning. Another seemed to be a fragment of a mech carapace fashioned to resemble a long stalk from which a large seed sprouted.

"You realize that bodies left on the field are used by Cybers?"

"Yeasay." Killeen could not trust himself to say more; sarcasm crept in too easily.

"They infest our heroic dead with eggs. Demon eggs!"

"Yeasay."

"Yet, knowing this foul fact, you chose to disobey."

"Ah, I thought only 'bout my Family's safety."

"And how will you feel when you see demons crawling the hills, demons born of your abandoned dead?"

Killeen could think of nothing to say to this, so he simply bowed his head.

"A portion of my godliness urges that you be erased from our cause. I could order you to the spit, to abide there until the corrupt fluids have drained from you."

The crowd murmured with animal anticipation. Killeen saw Toby begin to edge a hand closer to his rifle. Killeen shook his head slightly. His son reluctantly let his hand drop. Killeen caught Shibo's eye and saw there something he could not deflect. She stood still and compressed in a way he knew well.

"We Bishops," he said hurriedly, "we hunger for your cause."

"Fiercely? Despite the sky demon we all witnessed?"

"A deep hunger. Yeasay, yeasay." He made himself shout, "Show us the righteousness."

Catcalls and jeers came from the crowd.

A puzzled expression swept over His Supremacy as his eyes went blank. His lips trembled and he gazed up as though seeking celestial advice. The mob rustled. A chilly wind swept across the mountaintop.

Finally His Supremacy said, "Yet generosity is sometimes wise. Mercy can flow from me as well as punishment, Cap'n."

The crowd groaned with disappointment.

"Still, I cannot allow a Family to suffer the guidance of such a Cap'n."

Killeen opened his mouth, closed it. The man's moods flickered so fast Killeen could not keep up.

"So! I shall appoint a new Cap'n of the Bishops. In time of trial—and this is surely such—I retain that right. You"—he pointed at Jocelyn—"you will be the new Cap'n. Step forward!"

Jocelyn took a pace forward and saluted smartly.

Hands released Killeen and helped him to his feet.

"I expect *instant* obedience in all things."

"Yessir!"

"We begin planning immediately for our next battle, a great struggle which shall turn the tide against the legions of monsters. And this time the Bishops shall lead."

"Very good, Your Supremacy," Jocelyn said. "We are honored."

"Prepare, Bishops!" His Supremacy called. "And tonight, cele-brate with your holy exalted Tribal fellows the victories to come!"

He waved her away. She stepped back, bowing. The crowd yelled halfheartedly and began to break up. Bishops glanced at one another uneasily.

Jocelyn came to where Killeen stood, still unmoving. Only when she came to attention next to him did he realize that he should return to the ranks. Mutely he swiveled and went. Behind him His Supremacy went on, announcing the celebration of some religious event. The idea of carrying on a festival that evening, after the withering losses every Family had taken, gave Killeen a bitter taste. Family members, shocked by the abrupt change in Cap'ns, stared at him as he passed their sharply squared-out squads. Some in the formation gave him hidden signs of salute and others nodded in respect. The world seemed crisp and fresh to him as he just kept walking on blistered feet.

FOUR

Quath hurried up a steep raw cliff. She should not expose herself so, but she needed to search these mountain passes quickly for her Nought. She had thought she was following it closely, but then she had come upon a large pack and had to slip away to avoid detection.

The Tukar'ramin agreed that she should avoid alarming the Nought packs until she was sure of snaring the right Nought, the one who knew the workings of the Nought ship from antiquity. To be certain her Nought was not caught in the ambushes that her fellow podia were springing on the fleeing stragglers, the Tukar'ramin had called off all attacks. Now all attention turned to Quath's search.

But where *was* the Nought? Its telltale had not reported on time. Probably it was damaged.

This complication irritated Quath. She cast her electro-aura outward and caught fragrances of Nought lacing the senso-air of the mountains. They were congregating here, yes. What an opportunity! The podia could annihilate these pests by the thousands, once Quath had her catch safely encased.

This vantage, scrabbling up the rough face of canted rock, gave her an umbrella coverage of the jumbled, sharp peaks of the entire range. She quelled the simmering panic among her subminds that height brought on. Only her sure grip saved her from succumbing to her deep fear of heights.

Strangely, here at the planet's equator the effect of the Syphoning had thrust tortured crust still higher. It had compressed the basaltic underpinnings, splitting great seams and poking them into the underbelly rock of the range. Far away she saw a cone spitting sooty gouts into air already laden with churned dust. Calamity had cut broad swaths through the forests and plateau brambles. Mech mines had caved in. Their railways were smashed and buried.

243

All good, but the rubble gave pests myriad hiding places. Quath clambered with six legs onto a high notch in the mountain. The main gathering of Noughts was one peak farther away, and she hoped they were as dull-sensed as they had appeared to be in the battle, or else they might detect her here.

Quath! came the Tukar'ramin's call. *I bring grave word.*

<My Nought?> Quath broke her communications silence in alarm. <Has someone killed it?>

No, far worse. There is conflict among the Illuminates.

<What . . .? How . . .?> Chaos reigned in Quath. <But they hold the supreme wisdom of our kind!>

Yes.

<How can they disagree?>

I cannot fathom it myself, young podder, and I am far more skilled than you. This is the first time I have ever been privy to any Illuminate proceedings. To tap into a small fraction of the flow is to sense vast, sliding conjectures as tides in one's very soul. Do not ask me to describe it, for I cannot. Conflict rages among them like the smashing of suns in my mind's sky. I—I am still recovering my teetering equilibrium.

<I understand,> Quath said, though she did not. The Tukar'ramin's signals carried a sucking undercurrent of doubt and gray fear.

Some Illuminates do not want any foray into Galactic Center. They wax fiercely.

<But . . . why . . .?> Quath trembled at her audacity to question as great a being as the Tukar'ramin about the far grander majesties of the Illuminates.

They sense a larger design behind this. A mech artifice, perhaps, to draw us into the Center.

<But that is our historic aim, you once said.> Quath was careful to couch her objection in terms of the Tukar'ramin's own dictates.

I had been so told, and until this moment I had never doubted. You are a Philosoph, Quath—you cannot know the wonderful shelter that we unmitigated intelligences know. . . .

Quath had a thin glimmering of what the Tukar'ramin felt. To have that certainty shattered by the spectacle of the Illuminates' differing among themselves must be a terrifying experience. Quath felt sympathy for the Tukar'ramin—and abruptly felt how far she had come from the Quath of her simple Hive days. To feel anything but unblemished awe for the Tukar'ramin would have been incomprehensible only days ago.

Other Illuminates think it is our true historic destiny to use these trifling Noughts, who by pernicious accident carry a key to the inner region. The Tukar'ramin's muted carrier frequencies ran somber, muddled, tossed with flecks of pale doubt.

<What design do the Illuminates see in all this?>

They differ. They have studied all these events and some feel that the Noughts were sent here as part of a larger work.

<What kind?>

A concept we do not fully understand. Some mechs do things for inexplicable reasons. They term it "art." Such works seemingly have no use.

<Then we need not worry about them,> Quath said practically.

Not necessarily. Some Illuminates feel the Noughts came in the ancient craft as an aid in stabilizing the mech city conflicts.

<So they are our enemies, then.>

Perhaps. Like us, the mechs use a hierarchical system of command. The entities controlling this world before our arrival were low on the mech ladder of being. This was a mere tendril, an operation at the periphery of mech interest.

Quath suppressed her momentary shock at this news. All along she had supposed their efforts here were of great import, driving terror into mechs everywhere.

In such cases, control must be delegated to the local level, and liberal use must be made of the stimulus of competition among subunits.

<Clarify, please.> Quath sent undertones of confusion.

Efficiencies arise out of carefully regulated conflict. Note how much more diligent were your own strivings, small one, when you were stimulated by your rivalry with your sister, Beq'qdahl.

How little had escaped Tukar'ramin's attention! Had she engineered every detail of Quath's life?

This use of inter-unit striving is nearly universal. The mechs had a unified design for this world. But individual mech cities and complexes here were allowed—even encouraged—to compete for resources, for challenging roles. Even the cells of all living things act in such a manner, jostling each other, seeking nutrients and higher tasks. Delicate chemical balances keep the process under control. When it goes well, the whole organism flourishes.

<The mechs were weak on this planet. Are you saying this process broke down here?> Quath recalled the plentiful, livid

signs of inter-city battle on the planet's surface. Such scars did not
look at all "well-regulated."

*Indeed. With mechs, as living things, there is a danger to
such a process. These tensions can spill over into greedy excess. It
is known as cancer. A wild burgeoning of ego—of blind aggression
by a part against the greater whole. The mid-level mech minds on
this world began striving in deadly earnest. They employed new,
vicious weapons against each other.*

Quath experienced a leap of understanding. <The Noughts!>

She detected a rumble of satisfaction coming from Tukar'ramin,
accompanied by something else . . . a hint, perhaps, of respect?

*Indeed, young one. Your nimbleness of mind is pleasing.
Noughts had long infested the interstices of mech culture as no
more than irritants, occasionally employed for small purposes by
lesser mech entities—more often, seen as pests to be squashed
underfoot. Until the cancer began. Then they proved powerfully
useful to one of the warring sides. The result was catastrophic.
Their alliance weakened mech power in this system.*

<A weakness we exploited.>

*Just so. It is why the Illuminates risked sending our expedi-
tion, with the precious Great String, to this place so near the
fringes of mech power.*

Quath felt she was beginning to sense some of the scope of this
tale. It was vast, intimidating.

<Have not the greater mech minds, farther into the Core,
noticed this setback?>

*Certainly. But the cancer spread so rapidly, and our might
descended upon this system so quickly, that we were able to
establish ourselves before they could act to eradicate the cancer.
With the string at our disposal, we defeated all expeditions sent to
"cure" this wayward mech colony. And the Illuminates estimated
that economics would prevent any truly massive counterstrike.
This outpost was too unimportant to merit any such major
undertaking.*

<The Illuminates are vastly wise.>

*Nevertheless. Mechs elsewhere may have sought to send aid
to their brothers here in more subtle forms, using sneaky tactics to
slip medicine under our cordon of guard.*

Quath felt a burst of insight. <The *other* Noughts! The ones
who arrived in the little ship. They were sent as *medicine*? . . . To
interfere with the cancer?>

*That is what is believed by some of the Illuminates—those

who see the vessel as a deadly missile, sent by our enemies, carrying agents harmful to our cause. It is why I received orders to sear them. It is why, at first, I sent you and your sister after them, to destroy them one and all.*

Tukar'ramin paused, then resumed in lower tones.

*But now *other* Illuminates contend that these strange new Noughts are special in yet another way. That theirs is a destiny linked somehow with ours. It is all so very confusing. Evidence on their ship points in both directions at once. There is a clear sign of mech design in their flight profile and in shipboard traces. Yet those ancient slabs you found have caused many Illuminates to believe that there is much more involved.*

Quath's subminds whirled with the complexity of the choices. It reminded her of the queer conflicting emotions she had felt while hunting the Noughts out on the hardscrabble planet surface. <I . . . what is it we are to do, then?>

She detected an echo of her own confusion resonating openly from Tukar'ramin, and found that more disturbing than anything else.

This is a crisis unlike any in my long life, little Quath. I obey a majority of those Illuminates who are within range to hear and judge on these matters. Since this mission itself was a venturesome one, that majority consists of several who believe in daring, in doing, in taking swift advantage of the opportunities hinted at in the ancient slabs.

<But why . . .?>

Tukar'ramin shook her great form, rejecting the question before it was spoken.

*What I know is *how*. The rude laws of matter and light, of blunt mechanics and silky thermodynamic flows.*

<Yes, of course. And deeply do you know them.>

*I do not know *why*. That is not the strength of our race, as you must realize by now, little Philosoph.*

<You fear the whipping winds of indecision?>

Of course. You did too, once. But I have observed the genes of the old, dead race emerge in you, gathering, reaching out. You will know better what to do in this grave whirl of chaos.

<In conflict lies defeat. If the podia reflect the division among the Illuminates—>

Yes. Then we are doomed. Only our single-minded ferocity has given us sway over this world and others.

<Without that we fall to the mechs,> Quath said with abso-
lute certainty.

*Then let us decide this matter before the howling storm of
doubt besets us! Find your Nought and let us be done with it.*

Quath trumpeted a brave song-answer, clarion-clear and sharp.
The blaring sound was ceremonial. Yet it was oddly gripping—
even now, when she knew the falsity of all such gestures before
the immense questions surrounding the podia, encircling all life.

Newly resolute, she lumbered up a fissured scarp. She found a
crevice near the brow of the peak, as close as she could approach
the Nought gathering without revealing herself.

Deftly she probed the night. She brushed against a faint reek
of mechthought. It was clotted with pain and mired in agonized
confusion. Probably, she thought, the last of its kind in this area.
It seemed to be nearby, perhaps watching the Noughts as well. Its
typical jangling and zigzag patterns were somehow immersed in
Nought caterwauling, making it hard to find. Deal with it later,
then.

She probed again. Voices, pale hungers, timid musics—and
abruptly her electro-aura drew her into the field of a Nought. Its
essence resembled that of her own Nought, but Quath was unsure
if it was identical. A tender-skinned thing this was, excitable, with
spotty aches distributed through its body. It had the same stubby
but clever hands, knobby spine, the surprisingly long legs with
impossibly small pods to balance them on. It radiated feeling-
tones that rattled the air with their timbre, and Quath suddenly
understood.

This one had the same flavor as her own Nought, because it
had the same sex. How shockingly strange, to render the sexes so
differently. Why? This one was taller, heavier, with 1.8 times the
ratio of muscle mass to body mass than the last Nought she had
entered. Was that the intention—specialization of function through
altered bodies?

No, she sensed immediately that these differences descended
from the natural origins of the Nought. What selection pressure
would force such divergences among the sexes? What advantage
could it possibly have? On the contrary, Quath could see immediate conflicts in such an arrangement. She had simply never suspected that the strong Nought flavors meant sexual differences
—indeed, seemed to salt the very air between them.

So she had mistaken this Nought for her own because it, too,
was muskily male.

She held its muscles semirigid, as it seemed to want to do. With some effort she made the unnecessarily complicated apparatus of bones and interlocked muscles contract and stretch, successfully bringing a tool toward the face. Smells wafted up into cavities in the head, where recognition-flares called warm welcoming cries.

She let the semiautomatic systems of the Nought bring the food into the primary mouth. She allowed it to chew. Sensesounds exploded in Quath's electro-aura, which she understood were the sensations of taste that this creature enjoyed. The savor of masticating food swam through it, building notes upon submelodies, making a small symphony of gratifying song.

Three others of its kind were gathered near. A primitive naked oxidation bristled yellow-hot at the center of their little group. The Nought basked in its infrared emissions.

Acoustic patterns played through the Nought's head. Quath saw that this was their only means of communicating at short range. Had they kept this as a nostalgic tribute to their early forms? Or— startling thought—were they still this elemental?

Quath tried to sample the subminds of this Nought but found a mire. Where were the kernels of subsidiary intelligence? The interior bramble was too confusing to sort out now. She turned to more practical matters.

The Nought could say nothing without Quath's taking more control. What was discourse like in this ancient acoustic mode?

Gingerly she released the mouth. Curved the lips. Curled the fat, soft tongue that—now that Quath concentrated on controlling it—seemed to swell to fill the entire mouth.

"Food good," the Nought said.

Quath made sure the words carried a simple meaning. Less chance of error that way. The two words had bloomed naturally in the Nought's mind, streaming up from the concept-swamp. Quath had inspected them carefully as the Nought's nervous system began to transmit the instructions to the mouth to emit the sounds.

Two words, very nearly the simplest possible message. A good start. They complied with the language's rudimentary grammatical rules, which were astonishingly one-dimensional, with hardly any methods of adding shadings of meaning in parallel dimensions of discourse. It was almost like speaking to a grooming mite in the Hive.

But this experiment seemed to bring disturbed features blooming in the faces of the other Noughts. She decided to cover this mistake, whatever it was.

"Mouth feels wrong," the Nought's mind reported saying. Was something wrong with Quath's control? The other Noughts displayed widened eyes, slightly opened mouths, and more of their curious, archaic white teeth.

"Fire is good," she made the Nought say. Perhaps slightly complicating the sentence would settle the problem. She took special care to make the lips and tongue do their appointed jobs well.

Among its companions Quath saw more sliding of muscles and tendons beneath the sallow skin. These simple signals conveyed tension but she did not know how to read them accurately. Small furrowings deepened near the eyes. Mouth muscles struck lopsided positions. Yes, a lack of symmetry was probably supposed to communicate concern. Or anger, possibly including threats? It was all so confusing.

And they babbled at her, the acoustics coming in such a mixture of modes that Quath could not tell if they were speaking the same language as this Nought she had entered.

"I do not feel so good," Quath made the Nought say.

She elevated it to its precarious two feet and walked it away. The others did not follow immediately. Good. Quath did not want to provoke these simple beings into suspecting what was happening.

The rattle of acoustic complexity that pursued her confirmed Quath's suspicions. Each of these things spoke a kind of idiosyncratic self-language. Their mouths were so inelegantly and inexpertly made that each minor slide and hitch of muscle and cartilage rendered words differently.

How inefficient! Each word would have to be separately filed and tagged in the quick-mind, associated with a remembered word from some individual, and then in turn integrated with the *other* words in their primitive linear sequences—all in order to catch the meaning.

That would tie up enormous submind space. No wonder they had never advanced beyond a one-dimensional model of language!

They started at the beginning of a word sequence and had to march helplessly past every single sound group, before comprehending the whole. Yet that was essential, given the endless trouble they would have to go to in order to filter out and translate the infinite variety of pronunciation that came flooding into their knobby little ears. What conceivable purpose could there be to allowing this unending variation?

Whatever the reason, the Noughts were still concerned. One of them rose and called after Quath's possessed Nought. Quath decided to vacate this being rather than try to repair the situation.

But when she tried to let go of the small mind, her connections would not sever.

She yanked. Nothing.

Harder. Still she could not free herself!

Some dim perception was trying to leak up from her subminds into foreground consciousness. No time for that. She had to get free before the Noughts understood. They might then damage this Nought in their tiny anger. If Quath was still present, the trauma might surge back along her own electro-aura and do her injury.

She needed something to jar herself loose from the curiously sticky, hampering aura of the Nought. She made the hands slide over the body, seeking some useful tool. Ah, there.

Then she had a very good idea. She swiftly carried it out.

FIVE

As a simple Family member Killeen immediately joined in the jobs essential to setting up camp. The Tribal supply train had brought meager provisions partway up the granite slopes and each Family had to haul their portion to their campground. The wind was coming up stronger and colder with nightfall. His Supremacy's tent dominated the broad stone crown of the mountain and his staff was erecting some sort of altar in front of it.

Killeen and Shibo pitched their small tent in a narrow athwart the gathering wind. Toby and Besen were nearby. They all divided the skimpy food supply and figured how to cook the strangely spiced ingredients.

Much of the Tribal supply had been stolen from mech stores. The stuff was gooey and lime green; Killeen guessed that it had been foodstuff that fed and lubricated the partly organic mech components. Spices had been added to make it barely edible. A thin reward for a day of hard marching. When Bishops protested, Tribal officers said mysteriously that there would be more to eat later that night. Small fires already dotted the mountainside with flickering orange dabs. Killeen didn't like this and started telling his people to stop.

"What're you doing?" Jocelyn asked at his elbow.

Without thinking Killeen said, "This high up, anything can get an IR on these fires from down below. They'll stand out against the sky."

"His Supremacy's allowed fires tonight. Celebration coming."

"I still think—"

"You're not Cap'n anymore," Jocelyn said sternly.

"I—well, look, we both know namin' Cap'n is a Family affair. That lunatic doesn't have power over—"

"He's Elder. You heard him, he invoked emergency power. And you'll do as you're told." Jocelyn folded her arms and smiled coldly.

From her look, Killeen suspected that Jocelyn had already willingly accepted some of the special "priestly" Aspect chips His Supremacy had offered him upon his arrival. They were to be in exchange for what the leader had termed "irrelevant" Aspects from more recent times. The carrying of Aspects was so personal, by ancient tradition, that even the messianic Elder could do no more than "strongly advise" this swap. Killeen had managed to politely decline. Conversations with other Cap'ns had convinced him that those chips reinforced the fanaticism of His Supremacy's followers.

Was Jocelyn even now hearing new, forceful voices, urging her to zeal and obedience? If so, how long before such Aspects were installed into every member of Family Bishop? How many, then, would have the force of will to retain independent thought? It was rare, by all appearances, among the locals.

When he simply looked at her Jocelyn said angrily, "And I'll thank you to deliver up the tactical systems chips."

This was at least reasonable. A Cap'n carried those into battle. "You want 'em now?"

"I'll send a techtype to pop 'em."

Killeen watched her go, feeling a churning in his gut.

A demotion from command can have serious psychological consequences. . . .

He savagely suppressed Ling, before the ancient starship captain could pronounce eulogy over his unsatisfactory tenure in command. Killeen had other ghosts to do that for him.

Sitting on a rock, waiting for the tech-boy to arrive and strip him of his last prerogatives, Killeen moodily recalled the other Bishop Cap'ns he had known. Fanny—so sure and capable—who died in his arms. Old Sal—who retired in honor and grace to make way for one apparently born for leadership . . . Abraham.

Yes, Abraham himself. Whose smile was relaxed. Whose laughter was earthy and infectious. Whose confidence was unshakable. Who led Family Bishop through times of grit and grinding poverty, skillfully foiling the tricks of the mech exterminators, showing them how to hold back the encroaching desert, guiding the Family's labors until their Citadel was the flower of Snowglade.

Abraham had drawn little notice from mech civilization, leading precise, efficient raids which took from the mechs no more than needed. He had taken just enough to maintain a level which—if

inestimably lower even than the High Citadels of Arthur's time—
nevertheless afforded dignity and grace. One in which even luxury
was not unknown. Killeen recalled never missing a full, aromatic
bath on his birthday. Not while his father was alive.

Unfair. The Calamity had been such an unfair end to Abraham
and all he built. For they had done *nothing*, nothing unusual, to
draw such overpowering attention from the mechs! And yet titanic
forces came down to crush them.

Why? Why? The question had tortured Killeen for years.
Things happened on that day which Killeen still did not understand. Sensations . . . bizarre colors in the sky. Swift clouds and
flickerings he had never seen before or since. It had been as if all
nature had joined with the mechs in their assault.

Yet Abraham had fought on. Never flagging. Resonating encouragement. No one lost confidence in him, even at the last, as
he held the rear guard firm, allowing Lieutenant Fanny a narrow
chance to guide survivors away into scabrous exile.

No one ever lost confidence in father. The words echoed inside
him. *Even in defeat, he was all a man should be.*

Miserable, Killeen allowed his head to slump down into his
hands. He smelled acrid smoke, and knew that it was not from
today's struggles. Rather, it was from that day long ago. The day
when he should have died at his father's side. His sensorium had
inadvertently called up the scent association.

Why . . . do you persist . . . in thinking that he died?

Killeen's head snapped up, partly in surprise that his Grey
Aspect would rise up, unsummoned, to make a personal observation. He blinked.

. . . The magnetic entity said . . .

He shook his head. "I believe what I saw. I saw a bolt *take
away* what was left of the Citadel. A flash, an' it was gone.
Abraham is dead. An' soon so will we be."

Killeen realized he had muttered aloud. He glanced around
and saw Toby looking at him across the way. For his son's sake he
made an effort to straighten his posture. He tried to wear an
expression more serene than he felt, and had partly succeeded by
the time a skinny boy with instruments and cold hands came to
take away his command chips. He sat still, making no motion as

the tech snapped open the back of his neck and removed bits of sensoria that had become as familiar as the nerves of his hands. A numbness settled in where each had been.

He was in a good position to watch when Jocelyn came up the hill with a punishment detail and a Bishop man, Ahmed. They bound the man's hands and Jocelyn flogged him. From the techtype Killeen learned that Ahmed had made some disparaging remark to a member of the Sebens and His Supremacy had overheard.

Normally such a thing would be passed over. Matters were not going to go easily for Bishops, that was clear.

Killeen watched silently as Jocelyn whipped Ahmed. He recalled how agonizing he had found such matters on *Argo*. It was no easier to watch now, but at least he did not have to feel responsible.

He had been vaguely planning to strike some deal with Jocelyn, since he knew she would have trouble leading a Family which had already suffered so much. Changing Cap'ns was unwise amid disaster, and their situation transcended any difficulty he could remember, even the worst days on Snowglade.

He now saw in her glinting eyes and set mouth a woman who had waited for just such a moment, and would not be talked into sharing the smallest speck of authority. He wondered for an instant whether he would have done the same if their situations were reversed. It didn't matter.

In that moment he felt the weight of the Cap'ncy lift from him, cutting through the shock and sorrow of loss. He could be just another Bishop again. He could pay more attention to Toby and Shibo and perhaps escape the catastrophe he felt closer and closer now, a dark presence lying in wait in this blighted place.

The cold-handed boy was finished. With genuine relief Killeen got up and walked away.

Shibo and Toby cooked the green stuff over a crackling fire. It tasted far better than it had any right to, a sign of how tired and hungry they all were. Killeen let his feet soak in a warm, briny bath, hoping to drain his blisters. The pleasure of it alone was worth the trouble. This water-rich world had its compensations. His years aboard *Argo* had softened more than merely his feet. He thought wistfully of the comforts of the ship, the rich and exotic foods, the simple but crucial matters of warmth and light. He studied the haggard faces around the fire. How quickly they all had been cast down from the skies, forced back to the desperate existence they had known on Snowglade. Shibo had kept them together, but their dreams were shattered forever.

There was no way to avoid discussing the battle and at first they kept their tones almost dispassionate. Their voices were low, somber, carrying the accumulated gravity of memories too fresh to be digested.

First they analyzed the Cyber defense, a relatively neutral subject. Besen said, "If they know where main attack's comin' from, they can block shots."

Toby said, "Then let's fire from different directions at the same time."

"Hard," Shibo said. "Their screens move fast."

"Still, we can try it," Besen said.

Killeen was glad to see that Toby and Besen had figured their way through the lessons to be learned without prompting. They were growing up fast. Besen particularly would make a good lieutenant in a while. She was decisive. And Toby was improving under her influence. Killeen remembered how a boy was first entranced with sex, and then somehow started to learn from it. He felt a quiet satisfaction that Toby was coming out of the awkward teenage muddle. Both he and Besen had shrugged off the horror of the battle well.

But then Toby said quietly, "Who started the runnin'?" and Shibo looked at Killeen.

"Like most times, panic started in the rear," he said evenly.

"Howcome?" Besen asked.

"People back there got a better view, can see what's happenin'."

She said pensively, "You'd think it'd come in the front."

Shibo said, "The rear units think nobody's watching them."

"Nobody at the front broke," Killeen said.

Toby blinked. "You mean Loren wasn't turnin' tail?"

"Naysay," Killeen said softly. "He was cuttin' left, tryin' for a better angle on a Cyber."

Relief washed over Toby's face. "Good. Rumor was he'd dropped his beam-shooter, cut, and run."

"Naysay. Cyber killed him outright while he was in what looked like good cover."

Besen and Toby both sighed, their faces losing some of their pinched sorrow. Killeen understood then that the seemingly small issue of Loren's behavior in the moments before he died had loomed as large for them as his death itself. The curious and yet utterly human morality of the battlefield shielded them from the full brunt of their grief; they clung to the hope that good conduct meant a good death. He envied them that common defense of the young. It would not last long.

Killeen sat immersed in his own gray thoughts until Toby abruptly said, "Fudd gud."

Killeen glanced at him, thinking that the boy had his mouth full.

"Mauf fills rung."

Killeen gave him a quizzical glance, suspecting a joke. Shibo and Besen seemed more concerned.

"Fir hiss gud." Spasms flitted across Toby's face like storm clouds scudding.

Toby got up unsteadily, eyes veering around. "Ah donut fill so gud."

On ramrod-straight legs the boy took awkward steps away from the fire. Killeen called, "You better lie down. This chow—"

Toby fished forth his belt knife. It was a prized possession, the blade of worn but flexible blue steel, fully as long as the boy's foot. Toby's mouth worked as he peered down at the blade as though he was studying his reflection. Then he took two stiff steps to a thick tree with rough bark that slanted out from the ravine wall. Without a pause Toby drew back the knife with his right hand and placed his left hand on the tree, palm down.

Killeen saw what was going to happen a long, slowmotion instant before it did. He leaped forward, a shout beginning in his throat.

Toby slammed the blade down into his hand, pinning it to the hilt in the tree.

By the time Killeen reached him Toby was screaming with all the force of his lungs. When the air ran out the boy gasped and then started screaming again. Blood flecked his cheeks and hair. A thin red trickle began running down the tree, following the crevices in the crusty bark.

Toby's right hand now yanked back on the handle of the knife but without effect. He screamed hoarsely and gasped, gulping in air, and screamed again—forlornly, this time, hopelessly.

"Let go!" Killeen shouted. He grabbed Toby's right hand, which was trying to wrench the knife out. The blade was driven halfway into the bark.

"Let me take it, son. I'll get it."

Through a glazed, crazy sheen in his eyes Toby seemed to

recognize his father. He opened his mouth to gasp and began screaming again.

"You're twisting it!" Killeen shouted. Toby's yanking at the handle had rotated it, cutting the hand more.

The trickle of crimson thickened. It reached the ground and began to spread into a pool.

Killeen cried to Shibo, "Hold him."

She and Besen quickly slipped arms around Toby, who had started to rock back and forth on his feet, screaming and gasping. The wail roughened and Killeen could hear his son rasping his throat raw.

He carefully pried Toby's fingers from the handle.

"Grief! Grief!" Shibo cried, an ancient mournful curse.

"Toby—how, what—" Besen began, then burst into frightened tears.

Sobs escaped from Toby's strained throat. His mouth contorted but he could not speak.

Killeen braced himself. He concentrated and with one movement pulled the knife cleanly from the tree.

Toby collapsed. The women lowered him to the dusty gravel nearby, avoiding the puddle of brown-crusted blood.

Killeen threw the knife aside and found his carrypack a short distance away. He found some organiform cloth tucked in a pocket and cut it into slices with his own knife. Toby was thrashing under the women's hands, moaning, gulping, shouting incoherently. Other Bishops came running.

Killeen made a tourniquet and bound up the hand while the women continued to hold Toby down. Then Shibo untied it and did the job again, better.

Toby gasped fast and shallowly, face ashen.

"Son—son," Killeen said. The boy stared up at the night, where ruddy light seeped from distant molecular clouds between the stars. "Son, what . . .?"

Besen had stopped crying while the three of them worked on the hand and now she started again, sobbing softly. Killeen's mouth was dry and he could not get the coppery tang of blood out of his nostrils.

"I . . . Somethin' . . . Had an idea. Do that." Toby got the words out between chapped, white lips.

"Your idea?" Shibo asked.

"I . . . dunno."

"What was it like?"

"A big . . . Slick. Shiny, almost."

"What did it *look* like?" Besen asked, choking back her tears.

"I . . . Big, pressin' in on me. Look . . .?" Toby frowned, staring into space.

"Oh, why, why—" Besen began.

Killeen held up a hand to cut her off. He nodded to Toby. "Yeasay, son. What did it look like?"

"Looked so . . . so shiny. And . . . no face. No face at all."

SIX

The jut and tumble of these ragged mountains snagged Quath as she fled. Sharp stone teeth nipped at her. She stumbled several times, barely catching herself. Fresh outcroppings had flowered into spreading black fans, liberated by the last quake. They rasped on her undercarriage. Her minds rattled with percussive confusion and her only reaction was to move, run, escape.

It had been a near thing. She had almost been caught and pinned, drawn into the Nought mind she had invaded.

Yet that was *impossible*. Hers was a well-ordered, multiple mind, capable of calling up enormous volumes of knowledge, of marshaling mental resources in a microsecond, of overwhelming with layered mass any simple, linear Nought mind. When she had carried her own Nought inside herself she had merely verged on its mind. Preoccupied, she had made only glancing contact. Occupying her second Nought had been equally simple. And, she now saw, each time some unsuspected barrier had fallen.

All her wrenchings and lacerating blows had not gained her freedom from this latest, apparently minor intelligence. Trying to extricate herself, she had found her self-aura immersed in a swampy, sucking underlayer. It was cloying and thick, a muddy sludge of clotted, unconscious impulses, memories, gnarled subsystems.

Here was where this Nought truly lived. Quath had sensed its raw, sticky pull in a jolting instant of profound surprise. The mind's upper layers were mild and obliging, like cool, smooth corridors beneath the linear engagements of the conscious—while far below, in chambers walled and ramified with bony purpose, lurked a complex, ropy labyrinth of strange power.

Or minds. Quath was not even sure the Nought *was* a single intelligence.

Its highest echelons had seemed to be more like a passive stage than a directing entity. There, on a broad, level area above

260

the syrupy seethe, factions of the undermind warred. An abyss yawned.

Instincts spoke quietly, effectively, never falling silent. Emotions flared prickly hot—heckling, yearning, always calling the higher intelligence away from its deliberations.

Zesty hormones surged—not to carry wedges of information or holistic images, as in Quath, but to flood the bloodstream with urgent demands.

Organs far from the brain answered these chemical heralds, pumping other hormones into the thumping flow, adding alkaline voices to the babble.

Ideas rose like crystalline towers from this swamp, glimmering coolly—but soon were spattered with the aromatic chemical murk, blood on glass.

These elements merged and wrestled, struggling armies rushing together in flurries, fermenting, spinning away into wild skirmishes. Lurid splashes festooned the brittle ramparts of analytical thought. A churning mire lapped hungrily at the stern bulwarks of reason, eroding worn salients even as fresh ones were built.

Yet somehow this interior battle did not yield mere confusion and scattered indecision. Somehow a single coherent view emerged, holding the vital, fervent factions in check. Its actions sampled of all the myriad influences, letting none dominate for long.

Quath marveled at the sheer energy behind the incessant clashings, and at the same time felt a mixture of recognition laced by repulsion.

This Nought's inner landscape was far more complex than it should be. No wonder it had not attained the technological sophistication of the podia!—it labored forward in a howling storm, its every sharp perception blunted by fraying winds of passion.

But by the same stroke, it had a curious way of skating on the surface of these choppy, alchemical crosscurrents. Some balance and uncanny steadiness came from that. It was much like the way they walked—falling forward, then rescuing themselves by catching the plunge with the other leg. This yielded a rocking cadence that echoed the precarious nature of the being itself.

Not a single mind . . . and not multiple, interlocking intelligences, such as Quath.

She should inform the Tukar'ramin, she knew. This discovery came as a complete surprise, with implications Quath could not fathom. But for now she was unable to think clearly. Her smaller minds urged different courses, yelping and squirming. She silenced them and imposed a stony resolve: keep far enough away from the Noughts to escape detection. She had to learn more of what they were.

Cobwebs of the Nought mind still clung to Quath. They brushed across her field of vision, shimmering traceries of doubt. The very air clamored with skeptic winds.

In rattled confusion Quath stumbled on.

SEVEN

Killeen was sleeping deeply when the first hard jolt rolled through the mountain. He came awake at once and rolled out of the tent, coming to his feet as Shibo followed him out. A second shock knocked him down.

Jarred, his opticals took a moment to adjust. His eyes automatically cycled through to their most sensitive mode, because he had left them set for night vision. But this made the landscape glare as if under a noonday sun.

Brilliance cascaded down, bleaching out colors and shadows. The entire bowl of the sky glowed with rich gold.

The Syphon. The cosmic string was again revolving, sucking the rich ore from the planet's center. Imploding rock far below sent immense waves. He felt through his feet the slow, rippling surge of colossal movements thousands of kilometers below.

"Out!" he called on comm. "Leave the ravines. Get into the open!"

He and Shibo had slept in their full boot rigs. They swept up their packs and were headed out of the arroyo when he saw that Toby and Besen were sitting, pulling on their boots.

"Belay that!" he called. The ground wavered beneath him, making it hard to stand. "Run barefoot."

Toby looked up at his father vaguely, still half-asleep. They had given him what pitifully few medical measures the Family still had against the pain and infection of his wound.

Killeen scooped up Toby's pack and Shibo got Besen's. "Come on!" she yelled.

A rock as big as a man came thundering down the ravine. It rolled straight through two tents above them. It thumped hollowly and rushed by. Edges smashed off, showering them with shards as it lumbered past. It took their tents with it.

They ran up the slope until they reached the scree. Killeen helped Toby stumble along the parts where recently settled dust made slippery going. The boy was still groggy and cradled his left hand. Killeen kept an eye out for the stones clattering down and steered Toby away from them.

The sky's steady glow made it easy to dodge the debris and boulders that rumbled past them. Not everyone was as quick or as lucky; surprised cries of pain came from the ravine below.

They stopped when they got onto a flat, open slab of rock. The tall granite buttress and angular crest above seemed already scoured of loose stone. "Rally here!" Killeen called on comm.

—Shut up!— Jocelyn shouted furiously. —Bishops! Home on my point!—

"Jocelyn, it's clear over this way," Killeen said.

—Bear on me! Don't rally to Killeen!—

The ground shook and rolled and trembled endlessly. Bishops crawled and ran up the flanks of the saddleback, fleeing the ravines which funneled rockslides. Killeen said no more on comm.

Jocelyn was clinging to a chimney slope nearby. It looked safe as long as the shoulder range above didn't slide. Few Bishops joined her. Most made their way to the ground below Killeen. The quakes eased slowly. Jocelyn's area held. After a while she inched down the slope and led her small party across the saddleback. She came onto the open slab where by now over a hundred Bishops had spread out so they could easily dodge the tumbling rocks.

"You're undermining my Cap'ncy," Jocelyn said, panting, as she approached.

Killeen shook his head, not trusting himself to say anything. From downslope came crashes and shouts. A deep, slow rumbling swept up the mountain, as though the whole planet were breathing in painful gasps.

—Assemble! Assemble!— came the harsh call of His Supremacy.

"Let's go!" Jocelyn cried to the Bishops.

"Safer stay here," Killeen said.

"You'll do as His Supremacy orders!" Jocelyn snapped.

Toby and Besen had gotten their boots and packs in shape. The four of them set off across a granite plain scarred by rockslides. The tremors muted somewhat, as though the gnawing at the center of this world had ceased. Killeen studied the shimmering curtain of gold overhead but could see no sign of the extruded core metal. Something dark moved high up, a mere scratch against the glow, but nothing more.

When they arrived at the next broad rock shoulder His Supremacy was already speaking to the Families that were raggedly assembling before him. "This is yet another attempt by the demons and devils released upon us, a *failed* attempt to make us disperse, to miss our conjunction with our sole remaining thread of hope. The Skysower shall arrive soon, my Aspects calculate. Prepare!"

The other Families began to gather gnarled branches and bushes for a large fire. They stumbled and fell as the ground shook, but they kept on. Killeen and the others stared in disbelief.

Then His Supremacy cried, "Behold! The moment is upon us!"

Killeen looked up. A thin band hung above the mountain, visible only as a black segment against the glow. It moved. The nearly straight line slowly shortened and grew wider.

Killeen had the sense that he was looking along the length of something far larger than it appeared. The band curved slightly with an almost languid grace. The gossamer glow behind it added to the perception that the band was moving rapidly, sweeping across the sky like a black finger that turned adroitly, serenely. Killeen thought that it looked absurdly like a stick thrown so high that, twirl as it might, it would never come down.

Then the sound of it came. At first Killeen thought he was hearing a deep bass note that came up through the soles of his boots, but then he realized that the slow, gravid sound came pressing down from the sky. It boomed, a single note that frayed into a chorus of shifting overtones, plunging deeper and deeper into frequencies that he felt rather than heard, wavelengths resonant with the entire length of him, so that he listened with his whole body. It was like the beating of great waves from space itself, driven by tides of light to hammer against the small pebbles of planets and stars, washing over them in rivulets.

Something came climbing down the sky.

The slow, rolling notes brought long-reverberating fears. The rock below them had betrayed its ageold promise of solidity and now the strange dark ribbon above opened its own chasm of doubt. Killeen wondered if the thing could be some Cyber device, like the cosmic string. If so, there was no escape. Clearly it was headed down toward them here on the bald, exposed crown of the mountain. He sensed the immensity of the thing without being able to see any detail in it.

Then he began to hear strumming notes that hung in the air. They rose like the sound of wind streaming through tall trees, as though a gale swept the huge thing above, as though it were made of wood and leaf.

His Supremacy was shouting something, religious phrases that ran together and made little sense to Killeen.

"Behold, a sower went forth to sow. And to those chosen it was given to know the mysteries of the kingdom of heaven, brought by the sower. And to all things mechanical it was *not* given!"

He saw suddenly that the ribbon above, expanding gradually, was slowly curving down to point its long, tapered end directly at the ground. At them.

Now that it drew closer, Killeen could make out details lit by the skyglow. Great sinews like cables stretched down, interrupted by knobby bulges, like the vertebrae of an immense spine. It groaned. The thing rushed down the sky at them, emitting vast twangings. Taut strands split the air with great hard cracks. A symphony of snappings and protracted pops sounded, building to a torrent of noise—

—and something smacked into the rock near them. It smashed open, showering Killeen with aromatic juice that caught in his beard. He jerked back, but the smell was pleasant, sweet, cloying.

Another slammed into the mountain, then another. They pelted the whole mountainside. Families shouted with glee, not terror, as more of the big, oblong shapes rained down on them.

Killeen dimly realized that he had not felt fear as the band rushed toward them. Somehow he had quickly sensed that this was not a Cyber machine, not a threat.

Pops and cracks still rained down, but ebbing now, as he saw the long thin line, slightly curved, drawing away again. It had seemed to come nearly straight down, spearing through the sky as though to point a finger of accusation—or beckoning?—at the huddled humanity upon the mountaintop.

Wonderingly, he walked over to the nearest fallen object. The egg shape had split, spattering moisture everywhere. Small gray spheres were mixed in with the juice. Killeen scooped some up and smelled a light sweetness. Without thinking, his normal caution swept away, he bit into one. A pleasant, oily taste flooded his mouth.

"No! No!" A Trey rushed up to him. "Save—for the cooking."

Killeen watched as the man gathered up the split pod and staggered off with it, scarcely able to carry the weight. Everywhere on the mountainside people ran to collect them. Others stoked the growing fires. Some already spitted the pods on sticks and began roasting them over dancing flames.

Killeen let himself be caught up in the jubilation. The Tribe, worn down by its long retreat and short of food, needed a celebration. Without questioning why, he knew that this manna brought literally from heaven was good, healthy. The thick, heady aroma of the roast promised delights to the nose and mouth. Even the continuing shocks that surged through the mountain did not bother him.

He watched the dark blade that had cut the sky recede farther, making the sky shudder, curving slightly as it rose. It had spent only a long moment at its farthest stretch, hovering over the mountain summit as though to deliver a benediction—which it had.

EIGHT

Through the cold mountain night Quath felt a massive presence descending.

She had taken shelter in a fissure beyond where the Noughts lurked. From this vantage she could pick up their effusions and leakage radiation. They plainly thought their small bubbles of electric perception, damped to the minimum, could elude the podia. Quath penetrated the tiny, wan spheres with ease, inspecting the fitful firefly radiances that simmered there.

But she could extract little of use to her this way. Certainly she learned nothing that went beyond her scorching revelations while actually encased in the Nought. Rivulets of Nought thought slipped through the chilly air and snagged in Quath's electro-aura, flapping like tiny flags in the perception-breeze. And the telltale she had planted on her Nought was silent.

Still she was reluctant to approach the mountaintop. Another incident might alert them fully, scattering them and making Quath's quest harder.

Then she had felt the first high, tenuous note sounding down from far to the west. The high treble skated on the air, pursued by booming bass notes. They rolled like steady thunder. The source came down and forward at a speed that Quath thought at first must be an illusion. Stuttered Doppler images came too fast for her. Old fears welled up.

The podia had come from ground-grubbing origins. Heights brought acute, squeezing panic to them. That was why they did not hunt for enemies from the air, no matter how efficient such searching could be. It had taken millennia for the podia to be able to tolerate the keening sense of falling that came in orbit. Only genetic alterations had made space travel possible for them . . . though it did not erase the persistent terror that flight over the nearby landscape brought, with its gripping images of precipitous possible falls. Quath and the others managed to loft for short distances only by turning control over to a submind, reducing the task to distant mechanical motions.

But this thing!—it plunged as though oblivious to the ram pressure of air. A ship?

No—the dark line spanned a quadrant of the sky. A falling chunk of the podia's construction? Impossible—its browns and greens were unlike the enormous gray labyrinths they built.

Down it came. Quath broke her aura-silence and called to the Tukar'ramin.

The swelling intelligence came at once, flickering in the crisp air.

I understand your panic. Had I not been concerned with more grave and pressing matters, I would have warned you.

<Will it fall on me?> Quath asked, trying to seem composed.

No. It will not touch the ground at all.

<Mechwork? Is it mechwork? I shall shoot it—>

Attempt no such foolishness. Here.

In Quath's aura burst a flowering electrical kernel of knowledge, fat and sputtering. Data impacted, data rampant.

She swallowed it, converting the spinning ball of inductive currents into readable hormones. Scents and aromas bloomed, packed with stunning detail.

<This is so rich!>

It comes unfiltered from the Illuminates.

The honor of receiving such a holy kernel stunned Quath. She tentatively tasted. An astonishing central fact swept over her like an icy stream: The thing above was alive.

Its history had been buried in a musty vault of supposedly minor knowledge, Quath was shocked to find. Certainly none of the podia had spoken much of this thing. Yet, as she unpeeled the layers of hormonal implications, the crux became ever more impressive.

<Why were we not told this?> Quath cried, as the history of the thing poured through her, her subminds dissecting the myriad nuances.

We did not consider it vital, the Tukar'ramin replied. *It is a curious object, granted. It may be of use to us in the future.*

<Of use—!> Quath felt dismayed shock at the Tukar'ramin's bland unconcern. Then her characterological submind took hold and reminded her that she was, after all, only a recently augmented member of the Hive. Her great advancement, the revelations about her Philosoph components—these still did not mean she

could blithely question the Tukar'ramin's judgment. She savored
the strangely cool presence—the very voice of the Illuminates.

Above, the thing came down through thunderclaps and vortex
night.

It had started as a seedbeast, far out at the rim of this solar
system.

It was then a thin bar of slow life struggling in bitter cold.
Threads trailed from it, holding a gossamer mirror far larger than
the bar. Wan sunlight reflected from the mica mirror, focusing on
the living nucleus, warming it enough to keep a tepid, persistent
flow of fluids.

In hovering dark far beyond the target star the bar waited and
watched. Passing molecular clouds brushed it with dust, and this
grimy meal was enough—barely—to help repair the occasional
damage from cosmic rays.

Filigrees of muscle fiber kept its mirror aligned and formed
the rigging for later growth. Even so far from the star, sunlight's
pressure inflated the large but flimsy structure. A slight spin
supplied aligning tension, through crisscrossing spars.

The wan but focused starlight fell upon photoreceptors, which
converted the energy into chemical forms. The seedbeast did not
need to move quickly, so this feeble flow of power was enough to
send it on its hunt.

No mind sailed in this bitterly cold, black chunk. None was
needed . . . yet.

The filmy mirror played another role. As the bed of photoreceptors grew through the decades, the image formed by the
mirror broadened. Occasionally contractile fibers twitched. Weightless, the mirror canted to the side and curved into an artfully
skewed paraboloid. Slow oscillations marched across the field of
sewn mica. Leisurely, undulating images of the star rippled away
to the edges, sending long waves through the rigging. The shimmering surfaces cupped dim radiance, compressed it. Momentarily this gave the receptors a sweeping image of the space near the
approaching sun.

For a very long time there was little of note in the expanded
image—only the background mottling and lazy luminescent splashes
in the molecular clouds. Against this wash of light the prey of the
seedbeast would be pale indeed.

But at least the beast found a suspect pinprick of light. Was it a
ball of ice? Ancient instincts came sluggishly into play.

Specialized photoreceptors grew, able to analyze narrow slivers of the spectrum that came from the far, dim dot. One sensed the ionized fragments of hydrogen and oxygen. Another patrolled the thicket of spectral spikes, searching for carbon dioxide, ammonia, traces of even more complex though fragile forms.

Success would not come on the first try, nor even on the tenth. Not only did the seedbeast demand of the distant prey a filmy, evaporating hint of ices; the precometary head had to move in an orbit which the seedbeast could reach.

At last one target daub of light fulfilled all the ancient genetically programmed demands, and the seedbeast set forth. A long stern chase began. Celestial mechanics, ballistics, decision-making—all these complex interactions occurred at the gravid pace allowed by sunlight's constant pressure. Great sails grew and unfurled from the beast. Snagging the photon wind, the thing tacked and warped.

Centuries passed. The tiny image of the prey waxed and waned as the elliptical pursuit followed the smooth demands of gravity. The prey swelled ahead, became a tumbling, irregular chunk of dust and ice.

Now came a critical juncture: contact. Data accumulated in cells and fibers designed for just this one special task. Angular momentum, torques, vectors—all abstractions reduced finally to molecular templates, groupings of ions and membranes. Achingly slow, the beast made calculations that are second nature to any being which negotiates movement. But it could expend its limitless time to minimize even the most tiny of risks.

Slender fibers extended. They found purchase on the slowly revolving ice mountain, each grappler seizing its chosen point at the same moment. The beast swung into a gravid gavotte, spooling out stays and guy threads. The slight centripetal acceleration activated long-dormant chemical and biological processes.

Something akin to hunger stirred in the cold bar.

Its sail, mirrored by countless mica-thin cells, reflected the distant star's glow onto the prey. This patient lance of sunlight blew away a fog of sublimed ice. The beast tugged at its shrouds to avoid being thrust askew by the gas, but kept the precise focus.

A shaft deepened. At random spots inside, residual radioactivity had melted the water ice, forming small pockets of liquid. The seedbeast extended down a hollow tendril.

The first suck of delicious liquid into the reed-thin stalk brought to the seedbeast a heady joy—if a conglomerate of reproducing but insensate cells can know so complex a response.

More tendrils bridged the gap. They moored the beast to the iceball and provided ribbed support for further growth of the sail. The glinting, silvery foil sent lancing sunlight into the bore-hole, exploding the chemical wealth into fog.

Food! Riches! Many centuries of waiting were rewarded.

Thin, transparent films captured the billowing gas. Eager cells absorbed it. Nutrients flowed out to the seedbeast's core body. Spring came after a winter unimaginably long.

Finally the conical hole was deep enough into the ice to ensure protection from meteorites and even most cosmic rays. The bar tugged at new contractile fibers. Its nest was safely bored. Gingerly, it migrated. Care informed every move. Painfully tentative tugs at its contractile strands brought the dense, dark axial bar safely down into the pit. Here it would reside forever.

The descent of the central axis, now swelling enormously, inaugurated fresh responses. The beast grew crusty nodules that sprouted into pale, slender roots. Deep molecular configurations came into play. Though it had nothing resembling true intention, the beast began preparing for its next great adventure: the fall sunward.

No intelligence guided it yet. The rough bark and dark browns of the body sheltered complex genetic blueprints, but no mind.

Roots poked and pried through the ice. Complex membranes wriggled, the waste heat of their exploring melting a path. Then they sucked out the thin liquid—building more tissue, forcing open crevices. A fraction of the slow wealth worked back to the central body, where more minute blueprints unrolled in their molecular majesty.

Mining roots sought rare elements to build more complex structures. Ever-larger sails grew. The iceball that might have become a mere comet felt patient, cautious probings. The beast could take unhurried care, lest it find some unexpected danger.

Fans of emerald green crept over the grimy surface ice. In a century the tumbling ice mountain resembled a barnacled ship, overgrown with mottled, crusty plants that knew no constraint of gravity. Sap flowed easily in wide cellulose channels. Contractions brought warming fluid to stalks that fell into shadow.

This spreading, leathery forest occasionally heaved and rocked with sluggish energy. It extended great trunks high into the blackness above. Trees of thick brown butted against one another in competition for the sun. Leaves sprouted, wrinkled and lime green.

Only the ever-swelling sails could stop the woody spears' outward thrust. When a trunk shadowed the sails, a signal worked its way down through the tendrils. In the offending tree sap ebbed, growth stopped.

The trunks were not simply made. Inside the ice, mining roots sought lodes of carbon. Though the plants above displayed impossibly ornate convolutions and flowerings, this was a minor curlicue compared with the sophisticated complexity that went on at the molecular level of the mining roots.

They harvested carbon atoms and towed them into exact alignment, forming its crystal: graphite. Slight imperfections in the match were negotiated by a jostling crowd of donor or acceptor molecules. Great graphite fibers grew with cautious deliberation, flawlessly smooth.

Countless other laboring molecules ferried the graphite strands beneath the tree bark. Years passed as they merged, providing structural support far beyond what the gravity-free plant needed. The fibers waited in reserve, for the overgrown ice world was steadily swinging inward, toward the sun.

By now the forest had swelled to many times the size of the parent iceball. The star ahead was no longer merely a fierce point of light. Millennia of tacking in the soft breath of photons had brought the comet-beast within range of the planets.

The pace quickened aboard. Small, spindly creatures appeared, concocted from freshly activated genetic blueprints. They scampered among the foliage, performing myriad tasks of construction and repair.

Some resembled vacuumproof spiders, clambering across great leathery leaves with sticky-padded feet. They could find errors in growth, or damage from piercing meteoroids, beneath the pale light of the distant sun. Following instructions carried in only a few thousand cells, these black-carapaced beasts poked thin fingers into problems.

If a puzzle arose beyond their intricately programmed routines, they found the nearest of the coppery seams that laced around the great trunks. These were superconducting threads. Making contact, the spiders could communicate crudely but without signal loss to the core-beast.

Electrical energy also flowed through the threads steadily, charging the spiders' internal capacitors and batteries. Though biologically hardwired for their tasks, the spiders could receive and store more complex instructions for temporary problems. The greater core-beast was simply a larger example of such methods; complex and resourceful, it was nonetheless not yet an autonomous intelligence.

The moment came for more powerful maneuvers. This registered in the core-beast and brought forth a response that a witness might have found to be evidence of high originality. Silicates began to collect on the one surface spot left bare by the plants. Spiders and crusty fungus together fashioned ceramic nozzles and tanks, linked by clay-lined tubing. Carefully hoarded oxygen and hydrogen combined in the combustion chamber. An electrolytic spark began a steady contained explosion. The comet-beast moved sunward again.

Still, its destination was not the fiery inner realm. Its hoard of ice would have sublimed there, disemboweling the beast. The sun could never be a close friend.

Instead, it followed a gradual inward spiral. In time the heat generated in the crude rocket engine threatened to warm the comet too much. When melting began, the beast switched to smaller pulpy bulbs, grown like parasitic sacs far up the towering trees. These combined hydrogen peroxide and the enzyme catalase, venting their caustic steam safely away from the precious ice reserve.

It pursued a particularly rich asteroid which the solar mirrors had picked out. Cellulose bags grew near the photoreceptors and filled with water. These thick lenses gave sharp images which the comet-beast used to dock itself adroitly alongside its newest prey.

Breaking up the tumbling, carbon-rich mountain took more than a century of unflagging labor. Larger spiders came forth, summoned by deeper instructions. They ripped minerals from the asteroid with jackhammer ferocity. Crawling mites urged on the slow, steady manufacture of immense graphite threads.

From silvery silicates the myriad spider swarms made a reflecting screen. Swung on contractile fibers, this fended off the occasional solar storms of high-energy protons that came sleeting into the comet-forest. The beast continued to spiral inward. Protecting the more delicate growths and preventing ice losses became its primary concern.

The beast grew now by combination. Graphite threads entwined with living tissue along a single axis. What had begun as a thin bar now replicated that form on a huge scale.

The skinny, iron-gray thing grew slowly as meticulous spiders helped the weaving. Gradually the asteroid dwindled. The bar became immense. It was thickest at its middle, where the core-beast now lived inside. Even cosmic rays could not reach through the protective ice and iron to damage the genetic master code.

Then chemical vapors poured again from low-thrust ceramic chambers. And a new trick was turned: electromagnetic drive. Induction coils surged with currents, propelling iron slugs out through a barrel. This mass-driver shed matter that the beast did not need, banging away like a sluggish machine gun.

The assembly began another voyage, this one much less costly in energy. Still, it needed many orbits to complete the efficient loop to the next asteroid.

Centuries passed as the ever-lengthening bar consumed more of the stony little worlds. Solar furnaces made of the silvery reflecting films smelted, alloyed, and vacuum-formed exotic, strong girders for the bar. But the central art was the incessant spooling out of graphite threads to join those already lying along the great bar.

Many thousands of years passed before the final stage in the great beast's growth to maturity began. The last, most complex gene sites deep within the original biological substrate began to replicate themselves.

Intelligence is, finally, in the eye of the beholder. The actions which followed would have seemed to observers to be obvious evidence of problem-solving and creativity on a scale, and at such speed, as to completely prove the guidance of a considerable mind.

Perhaps the cells that directed the vast bar-beast still farther sunward *were*, by now, a mind. Here distinctions turn on definitions, not data.

The beast had decided on its final destination long before: a planet with abundant liquid water.

The beast was immensely long by now, grown to a third of the target planet's radius. To the eye of an inhabitant of the planet, though, it was very nearly invisible—because the vast brown-black construction was only slightly thicker than the original comet-beast. Indeed, a dab of ice still clung to the exact center of the immense cable. Caution dictated that the beast always have a reserve.

Still, as the planet swelled from a dot to a disk, more mirrors deployed behind it—a precaution against defense by possible inhabitants. None rose to meet the beast. Mechs had not yet come to the world, and the lesser life which dwelled there probably did not give even passing attention to the slim, dark line in the night sky.

Still, a few small asteroids did pass momentarily across the face of the planet. Ever cautious, the beast focused its great mirrors. The offending motes fused into slag.

The beast always erred on the side of prudence. Still, its greatest risk now yawned.

With grave deliberation, mass-drivers began to fire all along its length. They slowly flung away the last reserves of useless slag, subtracting orbital angular momentum. This planet did not have a moon, so the beast could not undergo repeated flyby encounters to lose its momentum. Instead, decades of careful navigation brought it closer to the world.

The grand moment came at last. The nub end of the bar-beast swept up the first atoms of the atmosphere. This sent complex signals through the superconducting threads that wrapped the bar. Something like elation triggered more rapid molecular transitions.

It tasted the tenuous air. This was wealth of a new sort: mild gases, water vapor, ozone. Especially broad leaves captured minute amounts and pooled them in great veins. Samples reached the core-beast and were judged good.

The land below lay ripe with life. This was the long-ordained paradise the beast sought. Now it began on the full task of its maturity.

The great bar began to spin.

As you witness, the Tukar'ramin interrupted Quath's meditation, *the Illuminates know much of such objects.*

Quath had absorbed the yawning history of the beast in a glimmering fragment of a moment, faster than an eyeblink. The massive thing still plunged down the sky, framed against the glow of the revolving Cosmic Circle.

<It is safe? The Cosmic Circle will not kill it?>

No, the Circle orbits much farther out. Your signal carries overcurrents of alarm, Quath. Why?

<I fear for it!>

Fear?

<It . . . it is *huge*. Yet living! To fly so . . .>

*Do not concern yourself. This object was here when we came.

The mechs had made no use of this odd, rotating thing. Perhaps they did not realize that it is alive—else they would have killed it.*

<Who made it?>

This self-replicating form spreads naturally among the stars of Galactic Center. We do not know its origins.

<So immense! What purpose has it?>

None that we can see. What does brute life know of purpose, Quath?

<Life always moves forward, if only to propagate itself.>

This presumably does so. They have been seen near other planets. We have not taken the time to study them in detail.

<But we must! They are grand beyond anything I have ever seen!>

Surely you err. The Tukar'ramin's tone was suddenly cool.

Quath said diplomatically, <I meant, other than yourself.>

Do not neglect the Illuminates, the Tukar'ramin said formally.

<No, of course not. But still . . .>

Their conversation had proceeded through several microseconds as Quath peered upward in awe. <It is . . . wonderful.>

Not at all, the Tukar'ramin said condescendingly. *Such structures are a minor element in the greater equation of this world. I have news for you—*

<No! You see only *size* in this thing. I see . . . *majesty.*>

A torrent of emotion burst upon Quath. The terror and wonder she had felt so much lately now swelled to become a toppling wave, drowning her in sudden, wrenching currents. She felt, at last, what separated her from all the rest of the podia. Awe— simple and yet unendurably vast. It swept through her, cleansing and divine.

Come, Quath, pay attention. There is grave, deep division between the Illuminates. Some Illuminates have seized podia here.

<Seized? But so august a presence would merely need to make its will known, and any of the podia would gladly kneel in abject gratitude, to serve.> Quath repeated this timeworn homily while her overmind swirled with smoldering, long-suppressed impulses.

The Tukar'ramin's acousto-magnetic profile took on tints and flavors Quath had never felt before. *There is holy conflict. Even the Illuminates are divided, and struggle against one another.*

Mordant hues conveyed the gravity of this revelation. <And they . . . war?>

I do not understand what is happening. Some of the podia of our own Hive do not respond to my commands. They are carrying out purposes I do not know.

Quath said sharply, <To what end?>

Some of the Illuminates feel we should not pursue this aim, should not venture toward Galactic Center as yet. Certainly, they say, we should not do so using the unreliable knowledge gained from a lowly Nought craft.

<And these Illuminates act against us?>

Yes, I gather so. Sadness and disbelief resonated through the Tukar'ramin's rich spectrum.

<Who? Where?>

Many, and everywhere.

<Here? I am about to capture the Nought we seek, if I can merely sort it out from the swarms of them nearby. Give me time—>

That we do not have. Find it! But beware others of your Hive—they act now for agencies I do not fathom.

<I shall!> Quath said sternly.

But her bravado was a cover for her own churning inner world. She stared upward at the massive presence and murmured to herself, <All this talk of Illuminates, beings I have never seen— and now they fight one another! By what measure are they greater than this whirling thing I can barely comprehend?—whose majesty I sense with my every pore and membrane? No, there is error here. They see mere size, and that is the fulcrum of their world. What I seek is *meaning*. That I hunger for—far more than I need the pesky Nought.>

The fragile air filled with glorious notes.

NINE

Killeen woke in a puffy languor. He rolled over and found himself beside Shibo. She snuggled spoon fashion against him and he let the moment of lazy pleasure take him. It was a while before the restive minds of his Aspects nibbled at his sweet indolence, bringing forward the questions which he had put aside the night before.

The seed-fruit, that was it. Its aromatic wealth had swarmed up into him, canceling all the vexing voices, smothering his long-trained instincts of vigilance and nervous caution.

Partway through the celebration Shibo had said to him, "Good for you. For us all." When he had only mildly agreed, she had laughed merrily and pushed his face down into a moist husk of seed-fruit.

The rogue banquet had spun on for hours. The fruit baked and fumed over the Families' fires. Songs had rolled over the mountainside. Spontaneous, mournful dirges for the newfallen dead had risen from the firesides. The chants roiled with rage and then swerved into bursts of bawdy energy. As the bountiful seed-fruit had its effects, the songs turned to soft, low ballads of the old-times. These Families had their former great ages, their sites made sacred by work and sacrifice, their Citadels and lush fields now lost and smashed. Yet they carried on singing into the teeth of fresh defeats.

There had been alcohol, too. The precious small flasks that some carried were much like those the Families of Snowglade had so lovingly fashioned and ornamented. Killeen had made himself pass the fruit-flavored brandy each time it came by him, even though his mouth watered at the heady smell of it. That way lay a steep slope.

His Supremacy had gathered the Families finally, as the general celebration-and-wake subsided into addled fatigue and drunk-

279

enness. Killeen had half-listened to the man's shouted words, hoping they would explain what had happened this night. His Supremacy spoke of the Skysower, and such it was: The seeds came down on each descent.

Religious jargon obscured His Supremacy's rhythmic incantations. Rolling phrases described the Skysower as the source of humanity's connection to all natural forces. The Tribe felt itself somehow part of Skysower's life cycle. The small but commanding man spoke of returning the bountiful gifts with the ripeness of the infinitely fertile soil. The signature of life was its webbed unions, threading All into One. There was much loud, vague talk of the Skysower as the Tribe's living link to the time of the Chandeliers, as God's sovereign messenger, as the one living being no mech could destroy. Eating its seeds was a religious act, a holy communion with the high sources of life's dominion.

"The blood and body of vaster realms was here delivered unto us," His Supremacy had yelled, his eyes rolling and face streaming with glistening sweat. "Take! Eat! And prepare!—for tomorrow's march. For victories to come!"

This news of more planned battles had quieted the Families, damped their aimless celebration. His Supremacy again used the device of lighting up his own skeleton. In the cloudy night the effect was more eerie than in a tent. Killeen had wondered why anyone would keep electrical tech which had so little everyday use. Maybe it came along with some larger craft.

Still, Killeen had seen no such human abilities on Snowglade. The Mantis had displayed similar skills when Killeen was embedded temporarily in its sensorium. Humanity here must have used such craft in the past, perhaps as a tradition to augment leadership. He had to admit that the articulating, luminous bones had a strangely commanding presence. Other Tribes, he reminded himself, were sometimes as distant as true aliens.

Killeen also had great respect for their way of dealing with the unending funereal air that enveloped their retreat. His Supremacy's closing, gravelly chant:

> Sower, sorrower,
> Giver, griever

spoke of a long and mournful history that incorporated the Skysower into the fortunes of humanity.

These Families had their casualties in order, including the men and women who simply stared into the distance and had to be told what to do next. They kept the wounded in the care of the old and the young, all those who could not fight cloistered at the center of the Family formation. All this, too, resembled the tactics handed down through time-honored practice on Snowglade, habits that ran marrow-dark, blood-deep.

He lay in the morning's sharp, chilly air and stared up into the scudding, dusty clouds raised by the quakes. The cosmic string had stopped during the celebration. The mountain still creaked and rumbled, as though trying to shrug off the human mites upon its brow. Between gusting, grimy clouds he caught glimpses of the pale blue above and searched for a thin, swift line. Nothing. The puzzle of the Skysower vexed him still.

He summoned his Grey Aspect and the scratchy voice took a long while in replying.

I believe . . . must be . . . pinwheels, they were called . . . by our historians. Living cables . . . grown in interplanetary space . . . even between the stars . . . or in molecular clouds.

"How they live in space?"

The ancient woman's voice carried a quality of wonder and regret.

Legend . . . all lost . . . do not know why were made. Some partial texts . . . appear to imply . . . evolved from asteroid harvesters . . . or some say from . . . comet-steering craft . . . must then date from . . . at least . . . Age of the Chandeliers . . . or even before.

"What's it doin' *here?*"

Forages for planet surface . . . lays seeds . . . this is its reproducing phase . . . must have access to biowealth . . . not enough in comets . . . or so was believed by historians. This was long before . . . era of my . . . foremothers . . .

Abruptly there bloomed in Killeen's left eye a chart of the Skysower's orbit. He tasted Arthur's skill in this, but the voice remained Grey's.

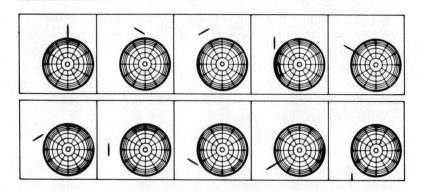

"Comes clean down through the whole atmosphere?" Killeen could scarcely believe these frames from a stopmotion simulation.

I must say I find this information more than a bit doubtful. Grey must be addled. Consider the engineering difficulties of such a project! The strength of materials required! Further, no planet is a perfect sphere. Bulges would attract any such orbiting cable, causing it to drift in longitude and latitude. Moreover, there must be severe torsional vibrations induced by its passage through the atmosphere. And how can such a dynamical system overcome the drag of the atmosphere? No—it would crash to the ground in short order.

"How you explain what we saw, then?"

I am formulating a model at this moment. It will require work, of course.

"Look, just do the calc'lations, yeasay?"
After a pause Arthur's nettled voice said:

I cannot *dis*prove these vague memories, of course, but I feel called upon to point out that the speed of such a thing would be more than a kilometer per second when it entered the atmosphere. Such—

"Yeasay, that'd make those booms we heard."

You miss my point. How could a *plant* withstand such forces? I find it impossible to believe—

Killeen let the faint, often garbled and heavily accented voice of Grey come through.

*Many historians . . . even those of the Chandeliers . . .
thought the same. But we knew that . . . starfarers spoke of
them . . . pinwheeling over worlds of grass and forest . . .
beneath far suns . . .*

"What for?"

*Concept of motivation . . . in biology . . . complex. Life
seeks to reproduce . . . to fill as much . . . of its environ-
ment . . . as it can.*

"But this thing, it lives in *space*."

Could fill . . . whole galaxy . . . in time . . .

"Seems like mechs'd be better at that. They can take vacuum
and cold."

*True . . . and perhaps in reply to that . . . somehow . . .
someone . . . made biological materials . . . could survive
cosmic rays . . . drift among stars . . . spread.*

"Who?"

*Historians of . . . Chandeliers . . . spoke of earliest humans
at Galactic Center . . . of the Great Times. Thought . . .
perhaps . . . pinwheels made then . . .*

"They could do *that* . . . I mean, *humanity?*"

*We were . . . so grand . . . not like my own age . . . of
pitiful . . . crude . . . Arcologies . . . that were no larger
than this mountain . . . mere tiny things . . . compared with
the Chandeliers. . . .*

"Uh . . . I suppose." Killeen tried to imagine a city as big as
the great slabs of rock that spread so far around him. If *those* were
what Grey considered small, trivial constructions . . . "The Chandeliers, sure, they were the best we ever did, so—"

*Oh no, never . . . there were grander works . . . far grander
. . . before . . . in the Great Times . . .*

Killeen wondered whether he should believe the disconnected
rememberings of the little Aspect. Maybe Grey was just repeating

old stories. Humanity had subsisted for a long time now on little more than scavenged food and glorious lies.

He shook his head and started to get up, his joints protesting. Time to look after his duties. Then the singular fact hit him once more—that he was no longer Cap'n. Simultaneously he felt elation at the burden lifted and depression at his reduced role in the Family. In all, he decided, they came out even.

Which meant he could forget Family business for a moment. He got up without waking Shibo and went to see how Toby's wounded hand was doing.

TEN

Quath lay in wait for the approaching podia. They came up through a long, rumpled valley in which dust haze settled like a dull gray blanket. Stands of the curious spindly trees obscured their approach, but Quath could see them plainly by the pulsing, pale electro-auras they could not help but emit as they communicated.

Here on the lower flanks of the mountain the land was turned and crumpled. All the humans had retreated to higher ground. An ominous quiet prevailed all down the range of tossed rock. The shards of broken hills gave countless hiding places for enemies.

Were there already podia out there, sent by the Illuminate factions? The Tukar'ramin had warned that some were coming. Then her signal had fallen behind the curtain of static.

<Hail and stand!> she called sharply. The party was still at a great distance, but she was cautious.

<What? Who's that?>

Quath tasted spiked emissions and recognized their familiar signature. <Beq'qdahl! The Tukar'ramin sent you?>

<Yes. She implied that you were in a tangle, monopody.>

<I have pursued a particular Nought, and very nearly have it in my grasp.> Quath brought her high-resolution sensors to bear. <And you?>

<I have come to aid you.>

<And the others?>

<They march under my direction.>

<Your fiery blue ossicles can command such a company?>

<I have risen far, remember. As have you.>

<Far enough to directly carry out the Tukar'ramin's orders?>

<Indeed. We can bring needed firepower to bear.>

Quath felt sudden tightness as her subminds understood the implications of Beq'qdahl's seemingly innocuous words. The Tukar'ramin was out of contact. A wall of hot static had descended between Quath and the great Hive to the south.

Quath said joshingly, <Firepower? Ground-groveler, I do not need to kill.>

<You hunt, do you not? Such work is always dangerous.>

<I hunt to capture.>

Beq'qdahl's shimmering voice-tastes took on a hedged air. <So you do. We can rout the Nought packs and drive them toward you.>

<That is too full of risk,> Quath said stiffly.

Beq'qdahl made a flavor of dry mirth. <For such as we, old burrower?>

<No—for the Noughts. They will stand and die before they retreat much farther. They are already cornered.>

<Noughts flee before us, that is an eternal rule.>

Beq'qdahl was either boasting for the benefit of the podia around her or being crafty beneath her air of idle arrogance.

Quath said, <These will hammer at us.>

<Let them!>

<Recall an earlier battle we had?> Quath said pointedly.

<We were unprepared then.>

<And the Noughts were less desperate,> Quath countered.

Beq'qdahl sent a spike of wry amusement. <Noughts are by definition always desperate. And you only need one, correct? The rest we shall slaughter.>

Quath made her decision. <Come forward, Beq'qdahl. I am losing your signal. There is some static.>

<Yes, I smell it here also. Some difficulty back toward the Hive, I believe.>

The squat outlines of the podia moved quickly. They seemed to flow around the outcroppings and faults that marred the valley floor. Quath had a good vantage to see them. She found Beq'qdahl and sighted in on her old friend and rival.

<Hold there!> Quath cried. Try as she might, she could not keep wavering tones from undercutting her stern carrier wave.

<What?> Did Beq'qdahl's hormone-tinge carry irritation, or the darker musk of crafty guile?

<You should move westward if you seek Noughts.> Quath hoped this ruse would deflect them.

<We register Noughts at the crest of the mountain, not down here.>

<I have those trapped. Another evening of study and I shall snare my Nought.>

This was only a partial lie. Quath felt her Nought's faint,

strumming flavor atop the mountain even now. In truth, she could
not get the heady, enticing scent of it to leave her now—a disturbing fact. But she needed time to locate the Nought precisely.
Then she had to devise a way to capture it without provoking a
struggle that might kill the Nought instead.

<We are sure it is up there,> Beq'qdahl said mildly.

One of Beq'qdahl's companions cut in, <Pap-gorger, let us by!
We come to forage, not to jabber.>

Quath's proboscis clacked angrily at this insult, and found the
offending one in her target array. <Careful, quadpod.>

<Let us drive them toward you, venerated and tired one,>
the companion added.

Quath gave them back quick, raucous contempt. <I can outrun you all, dung-shapers. And you shall not pass.>

Beq'qdahl suddenly sent a sharp, bile-laced taunt: <Out of the
way, cyst-sucker!>

<No.> Quath aimed at Beq'qdahl, began to charge her capac-
itors . . . and found a curious reluctance steal over her.

<You have always stolen the fruits of my labor!>

Quath said simply, <Come no further.>

<Or tripped me from behind!>

<No more warnings.>

The podia spread into an attacking fan formation. <Now!>
Beq'qdahl called wildly.

Quath tried to fire at Beq'qdahl's approaching image . . . and
could not.

She swiveled her antennae. The companion who had shouted
welled up in her sights. She sent a crisp bolt into the target. Its
upper carapace blew to tumbling fragments.

Beq'qdahl did not even cry out in dismay. She ducked into a
hollow, as though she had expected conflict all along. Quath lost
sight of all the podia as they dodged and ran and threw out
conflicting aura-clues.

She resisted the desire to fire at momentarily exposed targets.
They could triangulate her that way. If she kept her silence,
though, she could hold them off. They could not reach her here,
she knew, across so much exposed ground.

Taunts came to her as they realized their predicament: *Sphincter-
sharer! Orifice for all!*

Their insulting warblings dwindled as she relegated them to a
submind. If they slipped and said anything revealing, this smaller
facet would alert the full Quath-self.

Now she had one great goal. The urgency of it surged through her like the sudden, biting, inexplicable sandstorms of the ancient podia homeworld. Something primordial seized her imagination, a fevered desire that went far beyond her duty to the Tukar'ramin or even to the distant, mysterious Illuminates. Quath had to seek the Nought.

ELEVEN

"Family Bishop will carry out the flank attack," His Supremacy said dramatically.

The morning sun seemed to press against the tattered walls of the large tent. There would be heat in this day down the slopes of the mountain, but up here the tent still held the cold of the night. The Cap'ns and underofficers of the assembled Tribal Families stood at parade rest before His Supremacy, who paced back and forth.

Killeen remembered the huge desk which His Supremacy had lounged behind the first time Killeen saw him. No doubt it had been abandoned by the baggage train. Even the commandeered mech transports had trouble getting up the mountainside, and no team of men could have pushed the desk so far uphill. Still less likely was the possibility that anyone could be induced to try.

"I shall direct the main body, of course. After the Bishops have diverted the enemy, I shall strike the final, mortal blow." The man stopped, stamped his feet, and looked searchingly at his officers. "Understood?"

Jocelyn, standing beside Killeen, said, "We Bishops are honored at being given first chance at the enemy."

His Supremacy's face, which had been compressed with concentration, smoothed. "You are being accorded an opportunity to make up for your regrettable performance in the most recent action."

"Rest assured we'll do well," Jocelyn answered, bowing her head slightly.

His Supremacy's eyes showed pleasure at this. Then the eyes went blank as a rapt look came over him. "This is the opportunity we have awaited. The foul Cyber demons are concentrated in the broad valley to the east, as our scouts have shown. With their attention directed down the valley, they will certainly bunch up as they move to attack the Bishops. At that moment we can mass our fire. Once we make a breach, all the Tribe can flow through it.

The Bishops can then disengage and join us in the next valley, beyond the eastern ridge."

The Cap'n of the Sebens said, "How we know we can hit 'em hard enough? Could be plenty Cybers there, and we'd—"

"The more the better," His Supremacy said vehemently. "They will be dense on the ground and vulnerable to directed fire. We can hit them even more easily from the mountain as we come down."

"Yeasay!" another Cap'n called. "More we hit them, fewer we have to fight through later."

The entire tent rocked with the shouted assent of the other officers. His Supremacy nodded, rewarding them with a thin smile. "We do not know their numbers, but we know our cause is holy. We shall win through!"

Killeen could not stop himself from saying, "There're twenty-eight."

Complete silence. His Supremacy's eyebrows arched. "Oh? You have patrolled the valley?"

"Naysay. But I . . . I can tell how many there are."

"You see through Divine revelation?" His Supremacy seemed to be asking a genuine question, as though this was a plausible source of knowledge.

Killeen caught a significant look from the sharp-nosed woman who was Cap'n of the Sebens. She shook her head very slightly.

"No, I've gotten a good count by watchin' the valley."

Killeen saw now the fixed look in His Supremacy's eyes and guessed its cause. Of course—the man believed himself God, and so any other person who claimed a direct line to the infinite would be a rival. Killeen thought of the men and women spitted and left in the sun. Perhaps some of them had claimed a special role, to their misfortune.

"Very good. But I should think that even a person of your little experience and lack of battlefield skills could see the error in your statement. You count only the enemy who reveal themselves. We know that the demons often burrow below ground, as doctrine says they must, since they are agents of the underworld. Therefore, you have counted only a fraction of them."

"Ah, yeasay, Your Supremacy," Killeen said.

"I apologize for this officer's outburst," Jocelyn put in.

"We understand," His Supremacy said grandly.

"Be assured, Supremacy, that we Bishops shall carry the fight hard and sure," Jocelyn added firmly.

"Very good. There is no need to stay here, caged in by these demons. Skysower will not soon return to this mountaintop, my computational Aspects tell me. It spreads its sacred wealth around the girdle of our globe, a hundred descents in a single day. Our nourishment complete, we now fulfill *our* exalted mission."

The man lectured as though speaking to children, his eyes focused up into the tent top.

"Supremacy, we wish your battle benediction," the Cap'n of the Niners said in a closing ritual.

Killeen kneeled with the rest and received the windy, sing-song speech. It contained references to battles lost and cities fallen long ago, all meaningless to him but somehow ringing with the same sad truth that he had heard in the orations at Citadel Bishop as a boy. No matter that this Tribe had clutched at this queer little man in their desperation—their pain was perhaps even greater than those on Snowglade had suffered. Here humanity had enjoyed what it thought was a kind of victory over the mechs, actually destroying cities—only to have the more deadly Cybers arrive and finish the job. To be lifted and then dashed again did double damage. Perhaps this finding refuge in religion, and in one tyrannical Elder, was understandable.

As Killeen left the tent he caught the sidelong glances of others and understood what a close call he had survived. His Supremacy brooked no competition.

He had felt the urge to tell them of the odd perceptions that shot through him incessantly now. It was like being swallowed whole, gripped in a moist mucous cloud. In lacy filaments he saw shifting dun-colored terrain. Huge Cybers ran quickly through it, their shiny skins sprouting projections. Snatches of percussive talk came in a hollow, staccato language.

Killeen knew the valley they would try to cross, knew it in a deep, skin-tingling sense. He could close his eyes even now and feel the taste of Cybers moving through it. But how?

He thought he knew. What the answer implied, though, he could not guess.

No doubt if he had spoken of this in the tent the proper interpretation would have been quite clear to His Supremacy. Divine revelation, yes. And by now Killeen would have been groaning out his last on a stake atop this barren mountain.

TWELVE

Quath knew she should remain fixed in the present, moored in the reality of craggy reaches and massive buttresses. She had to keep watch on the podia Beq'qdahl led in the plains below. They kept slipping nearer. Only Quath's ranging shots kept them at bay.

But the tangled world within beckoned. . . .

She had found the one Nought, she was sure of that now. Edging closer, lightly touching the tiny pale spheres of their separate selfhoods, Quath had finally pressed against one who had the tang and bite she recognized. The earlier Nought that she had invaded, yes, she saw the resemblance—but not the same. This property in itself was intriguing, but she had no time to inspect the myriad rivulets of meaning in these sublattices.

Quath now saw that with each close encounter she was learning a different pathway into Noughts. Each entrance brought fresh perspectives. And pitfalls. The portals of her own Nought had ushered Quath into a miasma.

At first it had been like dusky radiance descending through murky memories, creaky with age. Yellowed filigrees rotted and fell away, lace parted, cobwebs lifted from glinting, brass-hard facts . . . which themselves dissolved like singing dust beneath the rub of remorseless time.

Inside the Nought, yes . . . But where?

Quath had felt herself walking through a broad courtyard like that which gave onto the Hive's great hall of worship. The walls cast an embroidery of shadow on stones—only the floor was not rock at all, but bones, white skulls, worn red carapaces, skeletal cages of ribs and abdomens. They snapped as she clumped over them, making her way back into a wide, gloomy past. Empty eyesockets seemed to follow her wobbly progress. Whispers and words bubbled from the street of bones. Some were sharp and bitter, ripped from throats which still longed and yearned. She could not understand these twisted, clangorous sounds. Abruptly she saw that they came from the podia past, stitching blood and marrow and desire and history into a tight sound-knot.

Her solid footing grew flesh-soft. Quath plunged forward help-lessly, each frightened step taking her up to the knee in the cloying, mossy past. Suddenly she was falling, falling—and petri-fying fear shot through her like red pain.

No! her subminds cried. She landed in soft feathers.

Here beneath the street of the dead lay a labyrinth of sultry darks. Its angled corridors fanned like fingers into webbed de-signs. Quath tried to follow. She was running hard now.

Though she knew that in some sense she was merely im-mersed in the falsity of another's electro-aura, she could not extricate herself. It was like the time before, with the Nought who had held her, but far worse. She was not pinned to the sliding experiences of one Nought now, but caught in some swamp of deep desire, some collective mystery.

The shambling things came to her, finally. She had heard their feet slapping on the worn, ebony floors, not pursuing but still coming. They loomed up in the dank darkness that seemed to come streaming out of the walls. Pervading and consuming shad-ows, exhaled by far antiquity.

Quath lurched away from them. Whacked hard against a brit-tle corner. Stumbled on.

Though they had only two legs these Noughts were quicker than she expected. They drew closer in the alloyed silence and then she saw their faces and knew it all.

<Tukar'ramin!> she called.

The talus slope she slid down sent boulders crashing before her, like heralds announcing the coming of a queen. <Tukar'ramin!>

Her experience had jarred her deeply, but now the world was not muddled as it had been before. A hard-edged clarity pressed toward her out of the congealing, sharp air.

I feel you weakly.

<Here! Here I am! Narrow your spectrum and we can cut through the electroblizzard.>

I tried to send reinforcements but they were blocked and ambushed. Beq'qdahl and others have isolated your area. They serve an unwise faction of the Illuminates. They seek—

<I know, I know. Forget them—I have made a discovery!>

Do not dismiss their threat—

<I know the source of the Philosoph genes.>

What? How could—

<It is these Noughts!>

Impossible. Little Noughts could not have—

<They were not Noughts then. They have been so trampled by the mechs that they muster few resources now. But long ago they knew our Elders. The Philosoph elements entered us then.>

You delved into them?

<Deeply! And found my origins!>

I . . . I see. This is even stranger than I had imagined.

<Imagined? You suspected these Noughts?>

From the beginning I sensed complex elements beneath the surface chatter of their minds. I was curious. That fact, and the arrival of more Noughts in a ship—it all aroused my slumbering suspicions.

Quath had thought that there could be no more surprises in this day, but a lancing thought came to her. <The station! You sent Beq'qdahl and myself there. You knew me for a Philosoph and—>

Yes. If there were any uncovered aspects of these supposed Noughts, I knew you were the best of the podia to seek it out.

<You should have told me the true nature of my task!>

No. Your ability lies in the formulating of questions—and those cannot be assigned.

<But, but—some hint! It would have saved me much soulful worry.>

Anxiety is your lot.

<*That* is what it means to be a Philosoph?>

*This *you* must discover. The genes express themselves in many ways.*

Quath felt empty, adrift. <To be so related to such Noughts . . . many of them I have already killed. . . .>

*Quath, I master great weighty arrays of information, and have a bounty of technical skills far transcending yours—but I do not and *can*not have the queer talent you manifest.*

<But . . . what does it *mean*, to be related to these mites?>

I can venture no answer.

<Who can?>

You.

<No, there are others,> Quath said with sudden conviction. <The Noughts.>

THIRTEEN

It was at this moment, Killeen thought, when he could see the fight but was not yet in the middle of it, that fear rushed up into his throat and clamped it shut.

No matter that he had flung himself into a hundred conflicts before—all the old sensations returned. Fear of injury. Of death. Here, to be hurt badly was the same as dying, but slower— carried in the baggage train, suffering lurches and slow bleeds.

More acutely, Killeen felt the piercing fear of failure. To falter now would render pointless everything they had attempted. If they lost, their long pursuit of a shelter for humanity, *any* shelter, was vanquished and would never return.

He knew how to loosen the tight grip that choked his breathing. Once engaged, training and instinct would take over. But as his eyes searched the dry broken plain, flickering through the spectrum, there was still some trifling chance to back out. The rational side of him plead for a reason, any reason, to halt, to reconsider. After all, he had been left here by Cap'n Jocelyn, in charge of the reserves. Yesterday she had rightly claimed the overlay chips which gave a Cap'n a complete view of all Family movements.

And a few moments before she had taken the reserves under her own direct command. Cermo's advance was stalled below. Jocelyn evidently wanted to break the impasse by quickly throwing more into the head of the attack. She had led them off to the right, down a narrow ravine which afforded good cover from the prickly, long-range shots of the Cybers.

She had pointedly left Killeen nothing to do. Very well. He could join in the attack as the Family plunged down the long slopes of the mountain, into the confusing welter of foothills.

Or he could simply stay here. So said the thin, hoarse cry of judgment. If he fell back he could provide cover for the Bishops in the Tribal baggage train. That, too, was a vital role. . . .

He had not felt this way in years. It was momentarily, darkly delicious to skirt responsibility, take the easy way. Safer, too.

He sighed. He was a different man now. Not wiser, maybe, but aware of how he would feel if he carried out such a fantasy.

Wistfully he aimed downslope. He could never hang back while those he loved fought.

He found a fleeting Cyber target and fired. No sign of a hit, but that did not matter. His training carried him forward, running and dodging now, and he let it.

Family Bishop was spread over the entire belly of the mountain. They moved down through the forests of spindly trees that thronged the slopes. Slanted afternoon sunlight cast confusing shadows. His Supremacy had insisted on launching the action even though not many daylight hours remained; his Divine judgment had, of course, prevailed over his officers' advice.

Killeen had watched the valley beyond from a group of fat boulders above the tree line. As he entered the woods he glanced up through the curious umbrellalike arches of the trees and searched the sky. No sign of any craft. That was a relief. Cybers seemed never to copy the mech advantage in the air.

"Cermo! Bear left. You can bring enfilading fire down through that notch in the hill."

—Yeasay,— Cermo answered on comm. —Taking some IR bursts here. Nobody hurt.—

"No point getting blinded. Damp down."

—Already have,— Cermo replied primly.

Killeen reminded himself to let the officers have free rein. Jocelyn was Cap'n, even though Cermo and Shibo gave her only grudging acceptance. In the heat of the fight, the officers would probably still react to his suggestions as though they were commands.

He ran through the thick forest with a long, loping stride. Rich loam absorbed his footfalls. The dense woods seemed to listen for the battle with a hushed expectancy. Fresh power reserves for his leggings gave him a buoyancy that carried him downslope quickly, not even bothering to seek cover. The only useful information they had learned from the previous, disastrous battle was that Cybers still devoted a lot of their energies to microwave pulses. Mechs saw the world principally in the microwave and perhaps the Cybers thought humans did, too. Or else, he reminded himself, they thought so little of their human opponents that they did not bother to refit their weaponry.

He broke from cover above the foothills as hoarse calls resounded through the comm. Jocelyn cried, —Form the star!— to the main body. He saw her moving quickly across a barren scarp. The reserves were mere scampering dots at this range.

Turning to his left, he watched Cermo's party firing steadily through the notch in a steep hillside. Landslides had opened jagged opportunities in this terrain and Cermo was skilled at making use of them.

But Cybers could do the same, he noted, as a distant figure crumpled. Killeen blinked three times and into his left eye jumped an electromag amplification. A crackling blue swarm was fading around the fallen Family member, signature of a microwave halo strike.

—Dad!—

The shrill quality in Toby's voice forked sudden fear into Killeen. Could the fallen figure be—but no, Toby's signifier flickered in an arroyo farther east. "Yeasay," Killeen answered.

—Shibo's cut off downslope.—

"Where?"

—Can't tell. Cybers've thrown up some static screen.—

Killeen scanned for Shibo and found no answering color-coded trace. The center of his expanded sensorium was a gray sheet. "Hold still."

He set off at full tilt, damping his sensorium to the absolute minimum as he plunged downslope. Amid the brush and stubby trees insects sang merrily, oblivious to the stinging death that arced through the air.

Toby was crouched at the rim of a narrow gully. As Killeen landed on loose gravel, a microwave burst reached down toward them, then dissipated into a hiss.

"Down there." Toby pointed. "See? Heat waves."

But the rippling images on the next hillside had a fuzzy quality unlike the effect of refracting air. "False image," Killeen said.

"Hard tellin' where the Cyber is."

"Wish we knew more 'bout their tricks." Killeen looked at Toby's bandaged hand. Jocelyn had decided the boy could stay back from the skirmish line, carrying reserve ammunition in his pack. "How's it feel?"

"Not bad. Glad it wasn't my right hand. Couldn't shoot then."

"Keep back, you won't need shoot today."

Toby bit his lip soberly. "You think so?"

On Snowglade Killeen would have given his son an optimistic, offhand remark. Here . . . "We're point party for the whole Tribe on this one. Be hard to pull back, once the Cybers are on us."

"I figured the same."

"One good thing 'bout not bein' Cap'n, I can move around less."

Toby grinned. "Almost as good as a bum hand."

"Bum Cap'n, yeasay." Killeen put his hand on Toby's shoulder. "Look, stick close. We'll cover for each other."

Toby nodded silently, his eyes always following the scan-plane of his own sensorium. "Wish I knew where that Cyber is."

"Let's circle 'round."

They used standard fire-and-maneuver. One loosed a quick, gaudy infrared pulse while the other sprinted in the cover provided by the afterimage effect. They covered ground rapidly this way, leaving the last stands of umbrella-topped trees. Tangled scrub in the foothills beyond offered a thousand pockets for human concealment, but few spots big enough to hide a Cyber. Toby went dashing freely from cranny to cranny, Killeen noted, far faster than his father could. There was also a certain unthinking bravado in his son's manner, despite the Snowglade years Toby had spent on the run.

"Getting somethin' over left," Toby called.

Killeen cut through some brambles and reached his son, puffing hard. Through a swampy clearing he saw a large form moving in the trees beyond. "Don't shoot yet."

"You figure one Cyber's puttin' out this whole screen?"

"Could be." But the creature seemed to be staying as well camouflaged as it could. It did not fire, even when a distant Bishop momentarily appeared in the open, charging downhill.

"What's it doin'? Listenin'?"

Killeen whispered, "Or looking for somethin'."

"What?"

"Maybe wants His Supremacy for supper."

Toby laughed. Killeen settled down and watched the Cyber clamber up a far rock shelf. The gray slice in Killeen's sensorium narrowed and thinned.

He watched telltale Bishop spikes work their way through the surrounding hills, headed for the valley. It was a plausible-looking excursion, designed to draw the Cybers in force. But how long could they go without being cut off and systematically hunted down? He handed Toby a sugar-rich lump saved from breakfast and got up. "Let's go left from here. Keep low—no high jumps."

"Yeasay. Besen's with Shibo, y'know."

A crisp buzz snapped by Killeen. Both of them dropped flat.

"Damn!" Killeen spat out dirt. "Somethin' close by."

Toby fired a burst toward the last place they had seen the Cyber. "Looks like we do it the hard way," Toby said.

They crawled away, banging into rocks with their heavy leggings and shank shields.

Killeen stopped and examined his shoulder padding. With a small thrill he found a neat brown burn-hole through it. The laser pulse had not severed any important control systems. To his surprise he felt no fear, only exhilaration.

"Squeeze down your sensorium," Killeen said tightly.

They cut through a draw half-filled with fresh slumped soil and pebbles, evidence of the latest quakes. The Cyber was on the far side. It was a tubular sheath of glistening, moist skin that seemed to be sweating. Insets of brushed metal and tan ceramic made a patchwork across the crusty brown hide.

Toby shot it first, burning its hind antenna. Killeen knew they had only an instant before retaliation. Into his mind flashed a sudden understanding of the Cyber's underlayers, a picture sharp and sure and unbidden. He snatched at a projectile from his precious hoard and clicked it into place on its stubby launch rod. He aimed at a middle bulge in the shiny carapace and snapped off the shot without thinking. The small, birdlike cylinder blew away a small hatch—seemingly insignificant, but Killeen knew the master controls for its transmitters ran close to the skin there. Abruptly the gray screen vanished from his sensorium.

"Come on," Killeen said, not waiting to see what the Cyber would do. As they slipped away it went into what looked like spasms, effervescing a yellow electrostain. Killeen sensed the thing was immobilized and did not question how he knew.

Shibo's telltale winked, not far away. They scrambled through two patches of scrub and rushed up a fractured face of dark strata. Besen was guarding her party's flank and could have tripped Toby as he came charging forward. Shibo was approaching from the other direction, calling orders as she ran. Killeen found himself panting so hard he could not speak, and just gazed inquiringly at her.

"Starting take hits," she said calmly, but Killeen could see the small signs of worry in her thin, drawn lips.

"We knocked out two already!" Besen said cheerily.

"Great, great," Toby said, gazing cautiously around. "We got one."

"Cybers don't stay down, though," Shibo said.

"Repair themselves?" Killeen asked, though somehow he already knew the answer.

"Yeasay, and quick," Shibo said.

Toby said, "Mechs did that sometimes. Mantis—"

"Not this fast," Shibo said.

"Makin' ground?" Killeen asked.

"Some."

"This's all too easy," Killeen said.

Shibo studied his face. "You mean howcome we're hitting them this time."

"And they miss us, too."

"Something's here."

"Yeasay."

"Your Cyber?"

"Feels like. Can't say how."

She shook her head. "Don't understand."

"Me either."

They all peered between two boulders at the valley floor below. Cermo's party was pouring down through the last rank of foothills before the dusty plain. Jocelyn was maneuvering the reserves through a maze of arroyos that gave good shelter. The star formation was ragged but moving. Her tack would take the reserves into the vanguard once they emerged from the thick scrub. Killeen could just barely recognize the distant figures with his highest telescope setting.

"We got Cybers in among us now," Toby said, and told the women about the screen-thrower they had hit.

Shibo nodded. An IR burst crackled nearby. "Won't be long before Jocelyn hits the plain."

"See any Cybers comin'?" Besen asked. Her round face held a slight grin that occasionally, for no visible reason, broadened into a sunny smile.

No one answered for a long moment as they surveyed the valley's dun-colored jumble sprawling to the horizon. Runoff from the mountain range was cutting a broad new river down the center, fed by several white-water tributaries.

Shattered mech factories covered the once-flat valley floor. Broken walls stood like snaggled teeth, casting pointed shadows in the late afternoon sun. Evidently Cybers had fought a large battle here before, because mech carapaces littered the ground. Burnt-out mech carcasses of every class were beginning to rust. Killeen reflected uneasily that the Cybers probably knew this terrain quite well.

Killeen found himself uneasy also at the eager way Besen longed for combat. The years aboard *Argo* had perhaps given him a sentimental coating that would take a while to wear off. Family Bishop was again a grimly practical band of foragers. He would have to get used to that.

"Spotted two," Shibo said. She sent the image into the arrays of the others. Fuzzy forms rippled and danced among the fractured terrain near the broad, muddy river. "They're messing with our sensoria some way."

Toby said, "I get just darts and splashes."

"Where?" Killeen asked.

"Spread all 'cross the valley. Movin' slow but I can't get a fix on 'em." Toby fiddled irritably with the controls on his collar tab.

Killeen saw the same fitful hints. If each momentary flicker was a Cyber, and not some ruse, the enemy was closing in and there were a lot of them.

"Let's get down there," Shibo said. She sent a call to her party, which was spread across the nearby hills.

Faint calls over comm told Killeen how matters were going below, even without expanding his sensorium. Halfhearted shouts and the ragged *pang-pang-pang* of Family microwave volleys implied uncertainty, confusion. As he moved and searched for targets Killeen automatically kept the running tally that anyone, once a commander, never neglected. How many casualties so far? Were their skirmishing lines moving uniformly? Was a salient vulnerable to a flanking attack? Was the star formation closed up, distances between parties short enough for mutual support? Did tactical alignments fit the terrain? Did the constantly shifting fields of fire leave any opening to the enemy?

The elusive Cybers were harder to judge. How steady was their fire? Were they holding off? Clearly the flitting forms were advancing down the valley, trying to cut off the salient under Cermo's command.

For some reason, a firm and unhurried approach was far more intimidating than attackers at a run. But the Cybers' pace was furtive, odd, seemingly running at angles to what Killeen expected. Still, the Bishops were drawing the main force away from the Tribal attack point for the breakout.

Up from the fractured valley crisp bolts came echoing. Jocelyn's vanguard was spilling down onto the plain. A fault line ran straight through the floor of the valley and already streams had converged on the cleft. Waterfalls crashed down from steep jutting ramparts, cutting at the freshly exposed strata. The newly formed river was a muddy finger pointing at the horizon. Against this image Killeen saw the ghostly, wavering dabs of momentary fog-thin light that might be Cybers.

"Time for the Tribe to make their run," he said.

Shibo nodded. "Cybers comin' fast."

Their comms suddenly sprang to life: general call. Jocelyn cried, —Shibo! I've hailed His Supremacy three times. I get no answer.—

"Sure you're getting through?" Shibo said.

—Must be. I can pick up his carrier.—

"You give 'em the start-down code?"

—Course. Cybers closing in.—

Killeen said worriedly, "She's pretty exposed down there."

"Let's go," Shibo said.

"We're serving as flank guard here," Killeen said, trying to keep his voice neutral.

Shibo licked her lips. "Won't need flank enfilade if they're overrun."

"We can provide covering fire when they pull back."

Shibo's mouth compressed. "Let's go."

They all followed her down through the remaining foothills. Killeen agreed with Shibo's decision when he saw the fire that raked the Bishop skirmish line. The Cybers used few projectiles, so the battle appeared mostly as lancing signatures in the IR or UV or microwave. The bursts struck Bishops and knocked out their systems, sometimes flooding inside powerfully enough to kill. Cermo was taking a lot of hits and Jocelyn had bogged down already. For the first time Killeen was genuinely glad he did not wear the Cap'n's emblem.

—Can you hear anything from the Tribe?— Jocelyn sent again.

"No," Shibo replied.

Killeen swore softly. "Combat without comm's always a mess."

Shibo popped the release on her comm. "Supremacy! Hear me?"

To Killeen's surprise the man's calm voice immediately replied, —Yes. I have been following the situation.—

"Then why in hell aren't your Families breaking into the valley?" she demanded.

—The Cyber demons are far stronger than I believed. I think

it unwise to commit my main body until their full strength is known.—

"Full—!" Shibo gaped in astonishment. "We're getting cut up down here!"

—Regrettable, yes. But I must know more.—

"We can't hold 'em long," she said.

—Dusk is falling. I think I shall move only under sufficient cover of darkness.—

Shibo shot a glance at Killeen. "Pull back," he said.

"Jocelyn!" Shibo called. "You hear that?"

—I, I caught some. I can't believe . . .—

"Better believe it. He'll make his move when he wants, never mind what we planned." Shibo's face was a glazed mask of anger.

—What . . . what can we do?— Jocelyn's voice was ragged with fatigue.

Toby broke in, "Dad? Three Cybers."

Killeen followed Toby's indices in his sensorium. Three flickering images were hardening into substantial forms. The pale ghosts descended the hills just behind their position. "Damn," Killeen said.

Shibo took this in instantly and said, "They've got the high ground here. Closing fast."

Jocelyn sent, —If we retreat we'll have to fight uphill in the dark.—

Cybers saw best in the infrared. As the land cooled, human body heat would stand out against the background. They had planned to be across the valley by nightfall, holding positions on the far mountain range. Then the Cybers would have no convenient moving targets. Instead, they would have had to attack upslope against a closely ordered line.

—Let's make a stand in the valley,— Jocelyn sent sharply.

Shibo frowned and looked at Killeen. "Why?"

—His Supremacy must make his break soon. We will be in a good position, can link up.—

Killeen said, "Assuming he means that."

—Why shouldn't he?— Jocelyn demanded hotly.

"Could be 'cause he's sacrificin' us. We're foreign. We've already given him trouble. Killin' us off'll take the Cybers time."

Shibo nodded slowly. Besen and Toby looked stiff and grim.

—I, I don't know if I agree with that.— Jocelyn's clear, commanding tone had slipped into hesitation.

Toby said, "Dad, looks like two more Cybers've worked 'round behind us."

Killeen checked and saw the trap closing. "Jocelyn better be right. We got no choice now."

"Not much time," Besen said. Her face was drawn, her eyes large.

Shibo threw Killeen a despairing glance. He replied. "Start thinkin'. Must be some way out."

Without a word they all began running toward the main body. Ahead, Bishops fired and fled and fell.

FOURTEEN

Quath knew only one imperative in the clangor of combat: the Nought. *Her* Nought.

The Nought excursion had come down the mountainside at a considerable distance from Quath, surprising her with their speed. Beq'qdahl and her gang had moved to intersect them. Quath had watched them speeding up the broad, jumbled valley below.

Her own progress across the high, broken strata was slower. She called out to the Tukar'ramin for help.

Chaos reigns here, Quath'jutt'kkal'thon. Insurrection infests our Hive. The Tukar'ramin's heavy, somber musks shot powerfully through Quath's electro-aura.

<I need help!>

Know that I understand. But I am besieged here in what was once my grand province.

<Send only a few, then.> Quath sent desperate lacings of need.

I can spare no more. I sent help twice but both groups were ambushed. The renegade podia who jump to the command of the divisive faction of the Illuminates—they clog the passages nearby. Such heresy! Such treason!

Quath clambered across gutted mech carcasses, crunching them without taking notice. She did not doubt that the Tukar'ramin was in the right, but prudence alone should be her guide now. <What shall we do?>

Remain loyal to our injunction! The glorious Illuminates, the leaders of the true Path—they still say the Noughts of the ancient ship must be found.

<I can reach the principal Nought,> Quath replied. <What then?>

You must escape with it. Return to their aged vessel.

<Send a shuttle. I can rendezvous—>

The shuttle landing fields are captured by the renegade podia. They are everywhere!

Quath saw that her view of events had been hopelessly narrow. She had fretted over issues of fate and death, while all around her, no doubt, podia had conspired and schemed. Insurrection against the Tukar'ramin! Worse, the revolt was fueled by division among the Illuminates. The idea still dizzied her.

<You cannot seize a shuttle?>

I barely hold my fastness in the Hive. This admission rode on a gravid undercurrent of black dismay.

<Beq'qdahl has many. I cannot hold them for long!>

You are better equipped than they. Remember, they outfitted hastily for their slimy task.

<Even if I can capture my Nought in the racked play of battle, surely they shall dog me to exhaustion.>

I can render no help, Quath.

This somber hormone-tinged message sobered Quath as she struggled down the mountainside. Noughts already sprang and dashed among the lower foothills. Their agility made them difficult targets. These were swifter and more crafty than the packs she had slain so long ago, in defense of betrayer Beq'qdahl.

She saw Beq'qdahl now, a pale fog seeping among some smashed mech buildings. Her defenses were good, then. To delay them Quath would need guile and craft abounding.

She stretched a cone of electrointerrogation down among the Noughts. Now that their own small auras pulsed readily, she could enter them more deeply. She did—and recoiled.

How could she have missed this? The many flavors of Nought separated into two groups. Not a crude set, like digital/analog or acoustic/magnetic, but an ancient distinction: sex.

She had known these Noughts still kept the rudimentary mechanism laid down by simple evolution. She had experienced it earlier, when she entered the male Nought. Now she saw why she had been unable to extricate herself readily from its swampy clutch. To them, sex was an absolute bedrock. It defined them powerfully. Quath's inability to untie these primordial knots in the Nought mind had nearly trapped her.

Had they not learned to banish such primitive and blinding forces in the personality? The podia had long ago seen the male as irrelevant, easily supplanted by genetic tailoring. Some were kept in preserves on the homeworld, but only for historical interest.

Among the Noughts, though, the sharp tang of sex clouded

every perception, every judgment. How could they *think* in such a howling storm?

She sifted through the scattershot scents and harmonies of the Nought pack as it went into battle. So many conflicting emotions! And not delegated to subminds, either. Instead, myriad impulses fought and scurried across the open stage of the sole mind. Factions shouted and clashed inside each Nought. Instinct, reason, the whole motley company of hormone-steeped emotions—each breathed in the veils of sex that spiced every fervent moment.

What impossible complexity! No wonder they seemed so antic. Their inner worlds were scenes of endless combats.

This further clouded her search. Just as she despaired, though, she sniffed her own Nought. Here it was—safe! Her antennae picked up tangs of it below, moving fast.

Its aura mingled with another's—the Nought Quath had briefly occupied before. The two of them were circling one of the podia. Quath clattered downhill. If she could get within range—

The two Noughts were clearly planning on assaulting the hexpodder. Quath was too far away to be sure she could hit the podder without striking the Noughts. Instead, she pried up the musky layers of her own Nought's mind, searching for some inlet.

There. Quickly she injected a lump of knowledge about the hexpodder. It would be jarring to the Nought, but perhaps it could assimilate the data.

Yes—she watched as the Noughts struck the podder cleanly with disabling shots.

Good. She could help them somewhat. But would she be smarter to simply collect it and scurry away?

No, there was something else. As she settled into the back recesses of her Nought's electro-aura she felt springy threads of connection. It was linked to others here. The web vibrated and undulated with a curious song of thick emotion and feral, emerald instinct.

As the Noughts scampered downslope Quath struggled to understand this new facet. Though each Nought imagined itself quite individual, beneath their consciousness lay thick, sinewy connections. They operated proudly alone yet yearned for union. That was why sex had such heft for them. To disconnect the Nought from the others would do it severe injury. While her orders from the Tukar'ramin were clearly to excise this one Nought, she saw now that this would not work. Noughts did not live by head alone.

She had scarcely sensed any of the depth of this Nought when she had carried it down from orbit. She had ignored its pain of separation from its kind. Now she saw that Nought links, if severed, damaged all.

The two Noughts met others. One produced a sharp, eager spike throughout her own Nought's buzzing self. Here was true resonance. Her Nought felt a symphony of urgings heavily laced with the complex musk of sex.

No, she could not yank it from these strange moorings. She would have to devise some better way.

Meanwhile, booming shots and rattling near-misses caromed through the foothills. Quath ran desperately toward the valley floor, where a battle was beginning. One of Beq'qdahl's gang sighted in on her Nought below. Quath sent a crackling blast into the podder. It tumbled over and began to smoke.

Good. This podder was a stranger to Quath, and she was able to brush away the stigma that came welling up from her subminds. But in the valley was Beq'qdahl, and Quath did not know what she could do there. She felt a hard, sinewy knot of conflict arise in her. She tried to force it down into her subminds but they would not accept the bulked fibers. It churned in her like a bleeding pink cyst. Could she truly kill her own kind in defense of a Nought?

Quath could not unravel the bristly knot. She ran on.

FIFTEEN

As Killeen approached Jocelyn's small command party he checked his pace. It was a bad idea to display haste or anxiety. That would unsteady others.

Then it occurred to him that he was thinking like a Cap'n. At the beginning of the battle he had relished his freedom; now it seemed a hollow pleasure.

"Reporting," he said simply as he reached Jocelyn. She crouched behind a broken mech-factory wall, listening intently to her comm. Her face was drawn and smudged with dirt, but her eyes danced with nervous energy. She had ordered him down from Shibo's position commanding the hill.

Jocelyn gave him a look of harried relief. "Killeen—good." She seemed to have to dredge her words out of some inner struggle. Breathing heavily, she sat down on an overturned mech carapace. Factory debris littered everywhere. "I . . . I'm afraid His Supremacy has decided against the breakout."

Killeen said nothing, just nodded.

Surprised, Jocelyn asked, "You think it's because we pulled out last time?"

"That guy's crazy. Pointless, tryin' figure him out."

Jocelyn pursed her lips, obviously gathering her resources. A microwave burst hissed past nearby. Killeen saw that Cybers had moved closer in from the hills, cutting off the cover of undulating terrain. Family Bishop had formed a skirmish line along the river. They maneuvered now among the shattered rock that bordered the deep fault line. Twilight cast long blue fingers from each protrusion now. As Family members fell back from the gullies and dry washes their shadows made them even more prominent targets.

He watched a running woman retreat under covering fire from the Family. A UV bolt struck her in the lower back, bathing her in crisp darting fireflies. Dying blue sparks glowed in the gloom. She fell. It was Lanaui, an old friend. Too far away for him to do

309

anything. He strained forward, watching, hoping that the shot had not damaged her major systems. Twangs and booms came as Family hammered away at Cyber targets. Lanaui moved. She rolled over and hobbled to the shelter of a burntout mech transporter. From her gait Killeen could tell her power systems were dead. Now she would have to flee using only normal human strength. A Cyber could run her down easily.

"What"—Jocelyn bit her lip—"can we do?"

He said carefully, "Can't make the hills, not without cover from the Tribe."

"I agree." From her stiffness he saw that she was having trouble yielding enough even to ask advice from him.

"Can't keep goin' either."

"No."

Microwaves rattled through Killeen's sensorium. Nearby Family members ducked, but he just leaned against the smashed factory wall. He was afraid that if he sat down his legs would refuse to get up.

"Night comes, we'll stand out by our body IR." Killeen felt an idea percolating somewhere and the only way he knew to get it out was to keep talking, let his subconscious send it floating free.

Jocelyn's eyes kept darting as she surveyed the combat grids in her eyes. She was having trouble keeping up with the situation as parties of Bishops fell back toward the rough, gullied terrain opened by the recent quakes. "Right. Think maybe we should send the fastest out? Leave the rest, have 'em provide cover?"

This violated all Family combat doctrine and she knew it. Her eyes fixed on him for an imploring moment.

"They'd just hound us down," Killeen said curtly. No reason to let her know how much this proposal disgusted him.

"I . . . I guess we're stuck here. If we can hold our lines through the night—"

"Never happen. We don't even know if Cybers sleep. Once they got us pinned, they can call in whatever they want."

"Then . . . then . . ."

Since there was no point in making matters worse, he hid his irritation by flicking his sensorium to infrared. It might give him an idea of how Cybers saw their situation. He remembered the time in their Hive, how they automatically interpreted objects as though illumination came from the floor. Yet obviously they had adapted well to the surface.

As night thickened, the ground shone more fully, brighter

than the mottled molecular clouds above. This resembled the Hive lighting and probably gave them some further advantage. The cool, splashing streams were darker than the land now. The forested hills were holding their heat well and glowed like soft green carpets. He turned toward the fault line and saw a slight brightening where apparently lava coursed beneath. As if to confirm his guess, the ground trembled slightly, like a beast shaking off a fly. Beyond the fault cleft he could see the black ribbon that was the new river. It frothed as if excited to be cutting a fresh bed through the valley, running dark and swift.

"Wait," he said. "Wait just a minute."

He watched the night cautiously. A Cyber had been moving to their left and now it was gone. Was it beyond view, or had it simply tuned to his sensorium so well that he now missed it entirely?

He fired a short microwave pulse toward where he thought it might be and then crawled around the shelf of broken rock that sheltered him. Shibo was already moving back to the next line. Killeen ran heavily along the shelf and then angled in toward a gully. Something sang past him as he sprawled down the slope. Dirt jammed in his shin shocks and he had to stop to work it out. By the time he looked up, Shibo had ordered another fallback.

—New drill! Toby!— Shibo called.

Killeen saw his son's signifier move back toward the river. The boy was running fast.

—Carmen!— Shibo sent.

The woman broke from cover and dashed. She had to leap over the fallen body of a Bishop man who had been hit only minutes before. The man's suit gave no life signs so nobody had tried to retrieve his body. They were leaving everything now, even supplies and ammo. This was the rear guard and it had to stay light and quick.

Killeen called to Jocelyn, "We're comin' in soon."

—Give us a li'l bit time,— she answered.

"Damn little left," he said.

Nearly all of Family Bishop was evacuated. But among the factory walls and gullied land many bodies lay, too many.

—Killeen!— Shibo ordered.

He heaved himself up on weary legs and plunged across the dry wash. It was a hard run to the next skirmish line and his eyes began to cloud with the exertion. Blue dots danced at the edges. The cool air cut in his throat.

He tumbled over an outcropping of sharp stones and rolled into the dry wash beyond. He fetched up against a pile of mechmess. In the rolling his vision had clicked back to normal human and he lay for a long moment, gasping in total darkness. He switched back to IR. Shibo crouched nearby but she did not even look at him.

—Besen!— she sent.

Killeen got up on his knees, his shocks wheezing as loudly as he did. The gritty soil got into everything and he had to clear his suit collar in order to turn his head and watch Besen angling in from a factory ruin. She came into the dry wash at a dead run and was nearly under its edge when something orange struck her helmet. She seemed to fly forward and hit the ground solidly. She did not move.

—Toby!— Shibo sent as though nothing had happened.

Killeen reached Besen and tapped in the codes at the back of her neck. Her running numbers all read zero.

Toby loped into the gully, moving easily. A microwave bolt hummed harmlessly over his head.

He saw Besen. "What—what—"

"She's . . ." Killeen could not make himself say it.

Shibo sent, —Harper!—

Toby knelt beside Besen's body and lifted her arm. She was face down and when he rolled her over they could see a fine web of cracks in her faceplate. They were electrostatic fractures. Through them they saw her eyes, still open. She gazed at them as if about to ask a question, one Killeen knew he could not answer.

Harper came running into the dry wash, panting. She squatted down and immediately let loose a UV shot back the way she had come.

Shibo sent, —Jocelyn! All in.—

—Hold there,— Jocelyn replied. —Nearly got your rig ready.—

Shibo duck-walked over. Toby said numbly, "She can't be. She can't just . . ."

"Hit her clean," Killeen said, and instantly regretted his bluntness.

"No. No." Toby fumbled with her helmet.

"Leave her," Shibo said.

Toby unlocked the collar ring. He gave it a one-quarter turn and lifted the helmet free. The trailing connectors into Besen's neck popped free of their sockets but there was no answering jerk from the body. Her eyes were still open.

Toby touched her face. "Besen, listen. Wake up. Come on. Wake up. Besen—"

"Take it easy, Toby," Killeen said numbly. People hardly ever came back from a system attack like this.

"She's just out, that's all. Just out. We give her a stim, she'll be okay." Toby started rubbing Besen's cheeks.

Shibo said, "Check her indices."

"Just out, is all." With fumbling fingers Toby reached around and rotated Besen's head. He and Killeen had to take off her backpack to get a clear look at her internal monitors. The digital circle at the top of her spine was uniformly blue. Numbers slid through each window, cycling meaninglessly.

Shibo glanced at them and then looked back at the hills where the Cybers were. "Looks bad," she said.

"No. No." Toby rubbed her face harder, faster. "She's overloaded, sure. That's all though."

"Could give her a stim," Killeen said, reaching for his pack. He had to make the gesture even though it was the last bulb he had.

"Chancy, doing it right away," Shibo said. "Systems need reflex time."

"I'll bring her back," Toby said. "She just needs blood in the head—"

"Here." Killeen helped Toby screw the stim bulb to Besen's head.

Toby stared into Besen's unblinking eyes. "You *got* wake up."

A microwave bolt whooshed overhead. Shibo said gently, "We have to try her now."

Toby licked his lips. His mouth wrenched jaggedly. "If her systems overstim . . ."

Killeen put his hand on his boy's shoulder but he could think of nothing to say.

Toby's hands trembled over the bulb. "How . . . how can I? If . . ."

"She's yours. You must decide."

Toby's face was white. He looked at Killeen for a long moment. Then he took the stim bulb and asked, "What—what setting?"

Killeen said, "Better try full. She's pretty far gone." He thought Besen was almost certainly dead but the next moment would make that plain enough. He would have to get Toby away fast, though, no matter how much the boy wanted to linger over the body.

"Okay." Toby clicked the setting all the way over.

"Son, I—"

Toby triggered the tab. It made a small percussive thump.

Besen jerked. Her lips opened. She coughed. Toby lifted her to a sitting position and they all saw the indices stop rolling on her neck. She blinked furiously.

They looked at her speechlessly. She coughed again and said, "I . . . what . . ."

Toby embraced her and began crying.

Two quick IR pulses raked the air.

"Get her walking," Shibo said.

Toby and Killeen helped Besen to her feet. She stared at them blankly.

—Shibo! Start falling back!— Jocelyn sent.

Shibo called, "Harper! Cover! Carmen—go!"

Toby massaged Besen's neck. "Got to go now. Just a step, that's all. Here, lean on me."

Shibo said gently, "Toby, Besen—we have to go now."

"What?" His head snapped up. "No, she—"

"Rest the flanks're folded in," Shibo said.

Killeen took Besen's other shoulder. "Come on, we'll get cut off."

"Her pack," Toby said.

"Leave it."

"No, wait—" Toby reached into the pack. He fiddled with an unseen catch for a moment and then jerked something free. "I gave her this," he said, holding up a chain with a small yellow pendant on it. "Don't . . . don't want damn Cybers get it."

"Yes, take it." Shibo looked at Killeen. "Cover."

Killeen lay against the wall of the steep dry wash and fired a quick burst into the night. Shibo and Toby fell back with Besen. Killeen slid back down to Besen's pack and found her weapon. He expended it noisily, throwing several high-energy pulses at every flickering target in his sensorium. Return fire chipped and burned the brow of the wash. He ducked under it and fled, running with a sudden fevered spike of fear. All the way to the riverside he was acutely aware of how big and tempting a target his back was.

He slid down the narrow sand embankment of the river and crashed into Jocelyn. An IR pulse whispered close by.

"How many more?" she gasped.

Three Bishops were manhandling a big mech part down the slope. Killeen looked around and saw Toby and Shibo getting Besen into an awkward assembly of mech sheetmetal that floated in the water.

"None," he said, and started toward the water.

"Three's the most for that. No room for you."

"You sure?"

"Get down that way."

"Look, I want—"

"Shut up and move."

"I—" Killeen shut up.

"You're the last, then. Help us with this."

Jocelyn was crisp and efficient again. She worked well when following a plan. But there was more to being Cap'n than that.

Three large men rolled something forward on its edge. In the infrared it looked to Killeen like a big shell. He grabbed it and helped splash it into the shallows. The water was cuttingly cold at his ankles. He smelled the tint of Cybers nearby. Microwaves spat from the embankment above.

Big chunks of rock caught at his feet as he held on to the shell. It bucked and tossed in the frothing current.

"Get in," Jocelyn said.

Killeen hesitated. Already the team was bringing down another piece of sheetmetal that some crafter had quickly bent into a crude cup shape. The metal had already lost most of its day heat and was so dim he could barely see it.

"How many to go?" he asked.

"Just us," Jocelyn said.

"I'll stay till—"

"Go." Jocelyn looked at him squarely, her features blotched by the infrared glow of her face. "I'm Cap'n, I stay till the last."

"Yeasay." No point in arguing.

Killeen stepped into the shell as Jocelyn held it steady. He lay down awkwardly. The shallow bowl rode only a hand's height above the black water. Jocelyn pushed him off. The river snatched him to itself as though he were a valued bauble. It swept him along, jostling the shell and throwing bitterly cold spray into his face. He tossed over hidden ridges and banged down hard.

He stayed as low as he could. His infrared image would be submerged in the cold water. Cybers on the shore could easily miss him. Or so went the reasoning.

He waited and clung to the smooth inner shell as the rush and roar of the water rose around him. No shots sang through the air nearby. He wondered how far the torrent would take him. It had not occurred to him until this moment that the Family should have been told how long to stay in their makeshift boats. Now they might disembark anywhere and end up spread far down this unknown river.

He lay worrying for a while before he recognized the faint odor of the shell he was riding. It was the used carapace of a mech. He rode down the raging rapids in the hardened skin of his oldest enemy.

SIXTEEN

Quath crawled carefully forward. She had nearly exhausted her armaments now. It was time to use care and guile, else the day was lost.

The Noughts continued to fall. Against Beq'qdahl's band they would have been squashed long before. But Quath had maneuvered in the gashed landscape and caught the attacking podia from behind. Like an ephemeral gauzy cloud she had danced upon the slopes. The extra outfitting the Tukar'ramin had provided worked and purred and salted the very air with deceptions. When podia fired at her the shots went wide, baking the already tortured soil.

But the game was narrowing. The Noughts were backed to the river now and there was little Quath could do for them.

She heard Beq'qdahl bray excitedly, <The main pack of Noughts is moving! See them?>

Quath tuned to the far mountain, where tiny Nought auras flickered. She had wondered why these distant Noughts did not give battle.

One of Beq'qdahl's podders asked, <Shall we pursue them?>

Hope leaped in Quath. But Beq'qdahl answered, <No. Finish the mites here first. Otherwise we shall never be sure.>

Of course. Quath had forgotten that Beq'qdahl did not know which Nought was crucial. Still less did she suspect that in the end, they might all be necessary, how interdependent these seemingly autonomous beings were.

<Get them all!> Beq'qdahl cried.

Quath caught a distant podder with a quick burst of ultraviolet. It lurched, disoriented, and rolled down a hillside, snapping two legs. Good.

As she drew closer to her own Nought she caught a tremor of the scorching outrage it—no, *he*—felt. Not toward the attacking podia, but toward the distant main body of Noughts.

These nearby Noughts were webbed together by the gossamer

strands Quath could now feel ever more strongly. Their curious tension between self and other gave forth a binding energy. There was true sinew in them. She felt the translucent threads gradually cloaking her own minds. Their touch was cool and oddly comforting.

And their smoldering rage arced among them. A marrow-dark anger at their own kind, fueled by betrayal. Quath realized with a start that the bitter scents were akin to the core-hot ire she felt toward Beq'qdahl and the other traitors.

Quath's mood rose alkaline in her dry throats. She slipped down a yawning gap freshly torn in the hills. Her Nought was ahead, his mood urgent. Those close to him fought on, wrapped in a haze of burning fatigue. Despair laced bile-yellow through them.

Quath saw Beq'qdahl clambering forward in short rushes, using the shelter of the shattered rock and broken mech factories. Gloom descended. Orange flames crept up the cowling of a dead hexpodder nearby.

Quath switched to her full normal vision. The soil simmered in crisp pinks. The far mountains cooled faster, fading blue redoubts sinking into the night. A purple-black streamer marked the great fault line.

She articulated softly forward. A multipodder appeared briefly and she quickly numbed its microwave dishes with a stinging shot.

As she turned, she saw a Nought retreating. Before she could even judge which of the podia might catch the little fleeing form, a sharp bark split the night.

Too late. Another Nought wounded or lost.

And the web among all the little creatures wrenched and tore violently. This was what they felt in the face of death—if anything, even stronger than Quath's stunned recoiling from the flat facts of the universe. A deeper sadness, laced with somber mortality. It was worse, she saw, to be small and fragile and still face the great night. Yet these things did.

Too late. Too late.

SEVENTEEN

Killeen had tried to sleep in the makeshift boat, but the shallow mech carapace spun and slewed and rocked endlessly. Once he had dozed off, but only because the current had swept him into a slow vortex inlet. He did not know how long he had circled there.

At the merest hint of dawn he paddled the bobbing carapace ashore. He waded onto a rocky beach, cold and sore and dizzy with fatigue.

Carefully expanding his sensorium, he caught the hazy fog-dots of Cybers. They were far behind him. Spread out, combing the riverbank. But coming fast.

He got back into the carapace boat. The current was weaker here. It took him in a jouncing path over boulders that swelled up from the muddy waters like enormous speckled white fish.

He went through two rough rapids before he heard the dull bass roar up ahead. It sounded like no battle he had ever heard before. When he asked his Arthur Aspect, the small mind said:

> I had forgotten that Snowglade had dried out so in your lifetime. I remember that sound from pleasant days of sport on the rivers that once blessed the valley of the great Citadel. It is a waterfall—probably a high one, judging from the amplitude.

Arthur drew him a quick sketch. Killeen had always visualized water as a glorious, rare, placid entity. That it could rage and kill seemed a violation of some implicit promise. He quickly stroked against the suddenly gathering current. The shore was near but he swept by like a leaf in a gale.

The water numbed his hands. He leaned far out of the awkward boat and stroked with furious energy. The shore inched closer. A roaring was all around him now. Spray hovered just ahead. He looked in that direction but the river seemed to vanish.

319

It was hopeless. The carapace was speeding faster toward the brink.

Killeen rolled out of the carapace. The water stung as he sank. His head went under just as he sucked in a breath. His boots struck something solid. He stroked against the current to keep upright. Already he wanted to breathe.

The water was a brown wall. Where was shore? Currents had turned him around so much he could not tell. He stepped heavily and found that the riverbottom was steep. He headed upward. Knowing little about water, he saw that his only hope was that the mass of his equipment would keep him from being swept away.

He slipped. For an agonizing moment he tumbled. He got his boot on a rock but it rolled out from under. The water was bitterly cold. He pulled himself forward with his arms and then got enough purchase to stand up. The burning in his lungs was worse. He surged forward, hoping he was going the right way. His boot slipped but he fanned his arms against the current and kept upright. Three more steps—and his head broke water. He struggled up the slope and fell on gravel.

He sat letting the cold seep away and watched the plume of spray towering nearby. Glassy-smooth water shot by into empty space. Trees and bushes bobbed in the slick, brown surface—and then lurched into oblivion.

He walked through the roaring and watched the great white column crash down with dazed fascination. The water had such a quixotic spirit, going from placid muddy flow to harsh, beautiful froth in the space of a heartbeat. He wondered if in some sense it was truly alive, as much entitled to the sovereignty owed to all life as were the plants and small creatures and humanity.

Then something pricked at his weak, collapsed sensorium. He started, suddenly afraid that the Cybers had caught up to him already.

But no—it was a faint voice. A gathering call on Bishop comm.

It fell silent but he had gotten a fix. He followed it for a while toward a range of slumped, ruined hills. The jagged stones of shattered strata seemed to snatch at his boots. He stumbled and nearly fell.

—This way,— Shibo sent.

He could not use his searching sensorium for fear that Cybers would detect him—if they hadn't already.

—Dad!— Toby's quick spike was enough to give him a fresh directional.

He ran down a crumpled hill into the seeming shelter of a thick forest. The same umbrella trees stood stately and serene in the faint promise of dawn. Beneath them he felt safer, cloaked in the remnants of life in this battered place.

His power reserves ebbed. He slumped against a tree. The woods were silent and brooding, and then without transition Shibo was walking steadily toward him and the weight of the night lifted away, insubstantial.

"You . . . you . . ." He could not shape any words that expressed what he felt. Then Toby was there and it was like his return to camp before, the Family enclosing him in an unspoken clasp.

He simply let go, sinking to the ground. Time meant nothing. The world was immediate, without past or future. Every tree and bristly bush attained a sharp, stark clarity. Faces loomed, split by immense grins. Crisp light poured through them all, illuminating everything with an even, eternal glow. A mouthful of water drenched his throat in pure coolness. The snap and bite of rations burst in his mouth like explosions of unendurable pleasure. His muscles sang with release. The brush of Shibo's hand, Toby's arm about his neck—these framed each moment, lending a halo of incandescent immediacy.

He had no idea how long he spent like that, but the moment came when the ordinary world snapped back solidly.

"On your feet," Jocelyn called. She stood among the scattered party of Bishops, looking tired, her jaw set stiffly. "I located His Supremacy. They're headed down, followin' that ridgeline up there."

"What about Cybers?" Toby asked.

"We'll deal with 'em better if we got the Tribe with us," Jocelyn said.

"Besen can't make good time," Toby insisted.

Besen leaned against a tree. Her eyes were hollow and her face was drawn.

Jocelyn nodded. "We'll take turns helpin' with the wounded."

"Not good for 'em," Toby said. "Wear 'em out."

"We got no choice."

"Howcome we should hook up again with those sonbitches?" Toby demanded.

" 'Cause when the Cybers run us down, I want help."

There was no good answer to that. Killeen was proud of the

way Toby had stood up for Besen but he knew Jocelyn had to keep them moving.

Nobody said anything as they got up and wearily made ready to march. There was no time for the Family to gather and count the dead or to mourn them. Desperation hung in the dry silence.

Killeen discovered that his feet were sore. His boots had kept their water seal intact but his leggings were still damp from the night. It was a simple fact of life in the field that such a discovery quickly banishes whatever joy or pain the previous day brought. Every fresh pain demands its own audience. Every joint protested. As he got up Killeen swore he could hear himself creak.

He helped Toby reset the bandage around the boy's hand. They said little. Toby spent all his time caring for Besen, who was dazed and weak. The boy seemed far more energetic and focused than he had been before.

Killeen moved down the line cajoling a few Bishops who were simply staring into space. There were always those who could not forget the losses of one battle and carried them into the next. Years on the run had taught Killeen that people would put aside emotional weight when action came first. Their resilience was surprising, even noble. But if they had time to brood, or if someone belabored them about it, they could crack completely. He chided a few onto their feet and got them started. It helped him forget how many faces he did not see in the marching column and never would again.

Everyone was low on power now. Some had a little more and they started out strongly, taking long strides and getting out in front. Killeen smiled at that. It was stupid to waste your reserves when you were still fresh. Jocelyn barked at this vanguard and made them take flank and point positions.

Sunrise sent yellow blades cutting through the upper cloud decks. Killeen thought of all the activity above the misty overcast— the huge warrens abuilding, the cosmic ring orbiting as it waited to be used again, the Skysower that churned on, planting its seeds. For what? All these immense structures seemed without human implication, as natural and inevitable as the weather—and equally beyond human hope of changing.

The Family line straggled out along the slopes as they worked up into the hills. Cermo had taken a tech hit in the waist; no bodily wound, and he could still walk. He fussed with his equipment and got most of his upper shocks working again. Then he went up and down the line, joshing and giving sympathy and pulling together Family elements that seemed most discouraged. Jocelyn did the same toward the front of the column.

Killeen watched all this with approval, curiously calm. Up ahead lay the Tribe and the supply train. Behind came the Cybers. If they were to survive this day the Family would have to be swift and lucky.

Having turned the matter over in his mind for a while, he put it aside. There was nothing more to do but enjoy what was probably his last glimpse of morning. He walked with his arm across Shibo's shoulders, resting on her exoskeleton. It was charging from her solar panels and helped her up the steepening slope. Its catlike purr seemed to waft on the warming air. The slow, lazy sound floated through his mind. It was a long while before he realized it was not sound at all.

A dry cool weight rested in the space just behind the nape of his neck. That was the way it felt when he had just taken on a new Aspect—a lumpy wedge tugging at the back of his brain. But this was stronger, as though air had twisted and condensed into a hanging dark syrup. Traceries of half-sensed ideas flapped through the ball of blotchy air. Killeen labored up the gravelly slopes, keeping march speed with the others, saying nothing, his attention sucked toward the presence that seemed to hover like buttery heat. He felt his arms and legs moving as though in thick oil. His lungs contained a patient, gurgling fluid. Air tasted like metallic blood.

"It's here," he whispered.

Shibo looked at him quizzically. He stumbled, caught himself.

The massive, deliberate movements were unmistakable. It was the Cyber who had captured him. And it was behind them.

No wonder the Cybers had stuck to them so well, he thought. They undoubtedly had a tracer of some kind planted on him. Nothing complex, just a transponder which could reflect a keyed signal. It could be no thicker than a thumbnail.

At the next rest break Killeen inspected his equipment. It would have been put somewhere he was unlikely to see it. . . .

In only a few moments he found the small circle stuck to the inside of his left upper shocks. But it was cracked and pitted, probably from the spills he had taken. When he tried some sounding signals it failed to respond.

He tossed it aside and stared off into the rumpled hills. Morning mist rose from the great stands of barrel-trunked trees. Their topmost limbs arced evenly out in the characteristic umbrella formation. Birds circled and dove among the pale emerald reaches. And the sluggish presence still sat at his neck.

The circular transponder had probably failed some time ago. Now the Cyber was following him by sniffing out his sensorium.

The thought sent hollow dread through him. But another memory tugged. In the fighting yesterday he had also felt something like this tenuous weight. And it had made clear things that had helped disable and elude Cybers.

The blunt presence did not seem hostile. Still, Killeen became more uneasy as he felt the ponderous wedge waiting, expectant. Images like frescoes of the real world slid through his mind, filigree-thin. They dimly recalled his past voyages in the mind of the Mantis. There had been huge caverns of separate experience, volumes that dwarfed Killeen.

Now he felt himself on the verge of another plunging gray abyss. The sensation made his heart race but gradually fear left him. He got up wearily, leaning on Shibo, and started into the next stand of trees.

Some Family were foraging for food. Small shoots on the bushes were edible, his Ann Aspect told him. The big trees had fungus of deep turquoise circling their lower trunks. A Bishop woman was scraping it off with a laser cutter in one hand, eating with the other. As they went by she gave them some and it was sharp but meaty.

Toby and Besen were too far behind. Besen could walk steadily now though there were still dark circles under her eyes and she moved with rickety care.

They had gone a few steps when the woman behind cried out. The tree was smoking. She stepped back, cutting off the laser pulses, and the tree trunk began jetting a thin, whitehot flame. Blowtorch intensity threw a sudden, welcome heat. The fierce gout of smokeless flame grew rapidly.

The woman stared dumbfounded at the glowing lance. Toby pulled her away. "Run!" he shouted.

Killeen tugged Besen uphill. The Bishops took a moment to register the danger. Then they started off at a determined trot, laboring uphill as the flame grew behind them. Cermo was shouting orders.

"What . . . what you think . . . was?" Shibo asked beside him. The best they could manage uphill was a ragged trot.

"Some kind energy resource, maybe," Killeen answered. "Mechs must've grown 'em."

"Mechs use biotech?"

"Did on Snowglade, some."

"Just fact'ry stuff. Replacement parts for their own innards."

"Far as we know, yeasay. Here they did better."

They stopped at the first shoulder above the broad forest. Toby and Besen struggled up the slope with a wall of billowing smoke behind them. The woman had started a ferocious forest fire.

At least it might slow the Cybers, Killeen thought. He tried to see a way to use the flame trees against them when they came up through the forest. The thought gave him a spurt of energy and he overtook the point party, led by Cermo. He was still mulling over the possibilities when they saw a squad of people on the far ridgeline.

"Tribe!" Cermo called ahead. "Bishops approach."

—That fire'll show us up good,— a distant voice answered sardonically.

"You bastards left us back there!" Cermo called.

—Orders. His Supremacy said was only way.—

Cermo said, "Only way of savin' your asses you mean."

—Stuff that. His Supremacy says, you do. Lucky you got out.—

To Killeen the Tribe's attitude was bizarre. As the Bishops came up onto the stark ridgeline they found ranks formed in moving defensive perimeters. The Tribe was making good time toward a high, wooded knoll. Though the Tribe greeted the Bishops with some warmth, many showed no sign of guilt over having left their fellows on the battlefield. Bishops muttered angrily. Some of the Tribe were reticent and moved away. The bulk, though, looked at the struggling Bishop remnants with interest but obviously without for a moment considering that a gross breach of ordinary human morality had occurred.

"Don't give a damn 'bout us, do they?" Toby said.

"It's their faith," Besen said. "His Supremacy says we're expendable, so be it."

"None so blind as she who will not see," Shibo said, her voice soft with fatigue. She had helped Besen up the last rise and her power reserves were gone.

Killeen looked at her quizzically and she said, "One my Aspects fed me that. Old saying from Cap'n Jesus. Figure we need all the wisdom we can get."

The situation would have been far more tense if the Bishops

had not been so tired. They rested along the ridgeline as more
Families marched past in open-arrow formation, wedge flanks far
out to guard against Cybers.

Oily smoke came rolling up from the spreading fire below.
Killeen could see trees catch and spurt out their pencil-thin gouts.
Curiously, the trees burned only at regularly spaced points up the
trunk. He watched as a tall one caught. The first plume shot out
near the base. Then another started farther up the trunk and
directly above the first. Soon there were seven whitehot flames
evenly spaced along the trunk. The top of the tree began to rock
and then it went over, pushed by the thrust of the escaping
brilliant gas. He marveled at them in his exhaustion.

The forest fire guttered out into sour smoke as the stand of trees
was exhausted. Killeen felt in his mind the persistent weight of
what he now thought of as his Cyber, but he could not tell if it was
getting closer. Smoke layered the valley like smudged glass and
made it impossible to see approaching Cybers. He smelled their
fog-dabs at the edges of his sensorium, though.

They lay in the waxing morning sun and let it take some of the
ache out of them. Besen was throwing off her dizziness and even
made a joke. It was as if they had all agreed to set aside the press
of the world and evoke some vestige of earlier Family times.
Shibo contended with a riddle: "What's the best kind pain?"

Killeen murmured, "What's this, old Pawn Family saying?"

"Yeasay." Shibo was the only surviving Pawn member.

"No kind pain's good," Besen said reasonably.

"I give up," Toby said.

"Can't be real pain, right?" Shibo hinted with a slight smile.

"Fake pain?" Toby was puzzled.

"Right," Shibo said. "Champagne."

It was weak humor but they were weaker and everybody
laughed. Nobody had seen champagne since the Citadels and the
origin of the term was buried in antiquity. His Grey Aspect tried
to tell Killeen something about Family France but he lay back in
the warming sun and ignored her. Bishops repeated Shibo's joke
and he could hear the tired laughter work its way along the
ridgeline.

A rest can seem to last a long time when you need it and so
Killeen came back from a place far away when the voice said
loudly nearby, "So you have rejoined us?"

His Supremacy stood with his marching escort talking to Jocelyn. Killeen had not registered any of the conversation until this point, but when he did sudden anger spiked through him.

"You left us out there," Jocelyn said flatly.

As Killeen got up, His Supremacy said grandly, "I determined that your feint was insufficient."

"We lost plenty people!"

His Supremacy coughed slightly as a wreath of greasy smoke drifted up from the valley. "In our heroic struggle there are martyrs, of course."

"You ran off!" Jocelyn's fists were clenched.

"I used your diversion to effect an escape—"

"You turned tail!"

"—from our untenable situation. And I expect you to keep a respectful tongue while addressing myself."

"We could have withdrawn if you'd told us. Before we reached the valley floor."

"As I said—"

"I couldn't even raise you on deep comm. You wouldn't—"

"That is *enough!*" His Supremacy's eyes flickered with a strange pale cast.

"I demand that you—"

"*No* one demands of *God.* You will now—"

"Some God! You're just a—"

His Supremacy made a small gesture with his hand. One of his guards stepped smartly forward and clipped Jocelyn expertly on the side of her head with a pistol, as if he had done the same thing many times. She went down heavily and lay still.

"Stake her," His Supremacy said. "She is obviously ridden by the demons she has battled."

He gazed out over the ridgeline where Bishops were gathering. A knot of them had formed behind Killeen, who stood absolutely still.

"And as well, I see there are *others* among the Bishops who seem to neglect the holy nature of my office." This was plainly calculated to throw fear into the Bishops.

A Bishop man shouted, "You're bunch cowards!"

"You turn 'n' run pretty quick, for a God," a woman called sarcastically.

Some Bishops' hands began to creep toward their weapons but His Supremacy's escort leveled theirs immediately, catching them by surprise. His Supremacy said hotly, "I believe I see demons dancing in the eyes of many here. Careful of your wild talk."

"Keep your damn hands off Jocelyn," a voice yelled from the knot behind Killeen.

"Yeasay!"

"Gutless bastard!"

"Yellowbellies!"

"Fatass poltroon!"

His Supremacy gestured slightly and two men in his escort started toward the knot. They trotted forward, trying to see who had yelled.

Killeen said, "Stop them or you'll have a fight."

His Supremacy gazed at him as though looking down at an insect. "You would threaten the deputy of All Living Holiness?"

"Just predicting," Killeen said evenly.

—and as he finished saying it he clenched his jaw solidly shut against a sudden boiling turmoil inside. The wedge at the back of his mind was a swelling sore. Pressure bulged through him. His vision narrowed down to a tight blue cone centered on the swarthy face of the strutting little man.

His Supremacy raised a hand and his guard stopped. He licked his lips and assessed the gathering crowd of Bishops. Killeen wondered if the man had the stomach for a shootout at close quarters. If so, a lot of people would die very quickly.

But then the curious vacant look came into His Supremacy's eyes and Killeen saw that the man would try to talk himself out of this.

Talk. Endless empty talk. All Killeen's buried anger and sorrow rushed into his throat. Bile stung his mouth. A storm swept from the jellied presence at the back of his mind, blowing through him.

His Supremacy went on, "We are marching to meet again the bountiful grace of God as it descends from heaven. I say to all you brethren, turn *away* from these decriers of the immaculate path. Your Cap'n Jocelyn has erred gravely. She caused you many, many tragic losses upon the exalted battlefield. Be *rid* of her. Let—"

— and compressed rage ripped the air like a scalding release. Killeen felt a squeezing pulse of electromagnetic energy hum past his shoulder. It refracted the air with its wake and struck His Supremacy solidly in the head.

Killeen dove sidewise and hit the ground. The Cyber pulse had come from above and his first thought was to find the source. But as he rolled to his left he felt a sudden sweet dwindling of the heavy wedge behind his head. He realized in a rush that it was his Cyber who had fired the bolt. He sat up amid cries and shouts.

The little man who called himself His Supremacy was down. Killeen somehow knew there was no more danger. He stood up and walked to the crumpled form.

Tribe members gaped at their fallen leader. Confusion swept them. They looked for the source of this assassination and saw nothing.

The madman seemed even smaller in death. In repose Killeen could see that the face had carried its expression of dignity and power through sheer effort of will. Relaxed, it was an ordinary, bland face. But that was not what caught his eye. The pulse had fried away a big section of His Supremacy's temples where the comm gear and sensorium were lodged. The violence of the overheating had blown the entire molding material out of the head, revealing something beneath.

All along the skull lining lay an elaborately gridded inset. The heavy mesh was embedded below the ordinary gear.

Killeen knelt and plucked at it. Through his enhanced nerves he felt a repellent strumming sensation. The reek struck solidly at his memories.

"Mechtech," he said. He peeled back more skin.

Shibo squatted next to him. Her eyes widened when she saw the intricate sheath all around the crown of the head. It tapped into the brain directly with myriad connections. "Micro'tronics."

"No scars on the scalp. Been in here awhile, I'd judge," Killeen said tightly.

"What . . . what could it . . ." Shibo said.

"They must've got him before the Cybers ever came here. He was leadin' the Tribe by then and this must've been how he got that high."

"They could give orders directly this way."

"Yeasay. And be sure they were followed." Killeen looked cautiously at the Tribe members nearby but they all seemed in shock. They stared at the shattered head in confusion. He wondered what this would do to their precious faith.

Shibo said, "I guess when the Cybers came, mechs turned him against them."

"Yeasay. That's why he wouldn't allow anything but attack, never mind the cost."

"This . . ." She seemed unable to say the words. "Humans run by mechs . . ."

"We're just pawns here."

"It must have been awful. He was trapped inside there."

"Poor bastard. He wasn't just crazy after all."

EIGHTEEN

Quath squeezed her shot cleanly between the Noughts. The narrow spike struck soundly against the strange mech-ridden Nought. She felt the inner mech presence disintegrate, fragments and figments whirling off into emptiness. Good.

Her plan, hatched all through the smoldering night, hung only moments from completion. Until minutes ago, the Noughts had been perfectly arranged. She had only to act.

But then had come this squabble among the Noughts. And far worse, the arrival of Beq'qdahl nearby. Quath could feel her elegant plan slipping away.

Time slowed for her. Her subminds sorted and arrayed the flashflood of implications.

The mech parasite had been cleverly concealed. Quath had fleetingly felt it before, on the mountaintop. But the muggy Nought minds had obscured the steel-edged intelligence that scurried shadow-thin whenever Quath probed.

In the instant of killing, the mech lurker splashed open. Quath caught the maggot essence of it, the delicate, mosaic power. It had cleverly fastened upon a Nought weakness. Quath stretched and snared the scent of that Nought flaw: a black, festering need, heavy and clogged with bloodknot pain.

Yes! With monumental irony, this poisoning soft spot hinged upon the Noughts' great strength. Their wisdom, she knew, flowered forth from their keening sense of mortality. That gave them the sure grasp of each passing moment as unique and, if one peered remorselessly into it, luminescent.

Yet from that bedrock strength many Noughts fled. Their dewy fever drew them to fantasies of being not Noughts at all, but instead the most powerful of agencies, somehow linked with the embodiment of all nature itself. Madness! Surely wisdom meant accepting your station in a hierarchy of life and intelligence. To claim grotesquely huge powers belied all that life taught.

331

But in grasping this Nought facet Quath saw that her own podia were equally foolish. The Verities, the Synthesis—were they any different? To claim a connectedness between self and inert matter. To intone beliefs in unseen powers.

Clever mechs, to see this Nought vulnerability. A bitter chill ran through Quath as she realized that the mechs must then fathom the deepest motivations of the podia, as well.

After such knowledge, the mechs must have enormous advantage over the podia. Why, then, had they allowed podia to seize this planet so easily?

Quath felt the very ground slipping away beneath her, all in the fractional instant that her minds knitted together thin threads of suspicion that had been waiting for so long.

Yes!—there was more to the mechs than the podia had ever guessed. Her subminds rattled off long-smoldering riddles:

Their introduction of these Noughts and the ancient ship into the struggle with the podia.

The strange mech experiments near pulsars, never explained.

Their defense of Galactic Center against all lifeforms, for unknown purposes.

Of course, one of Quath's subminds argued, energy densities were great here. Mechs were supreme at harnessing the raw flux of currents and photons. Life was more vulnerable to such hard energies. In the natural scheme of matters, organic life would not naturally be drawn to dwell near the all-gnawing appetite of the black hole. Even the podia, encrusted with ceramics and tough alloys, suffered from the ripping hail of protons in deep space. The soft Noughts were far more threatened by the endless sleeting effusions of the hole.

Yet they came. Why? Quath had never pondered this mystery to its depths—indeed, until this moment, had not seen it as a profound puzzle.

All life, whether swaddled in bone or carapace or filmy flesh, seemed to feel that Galactic Center held a goal, a secret. A clue, perhaps, to the meaning of their brief passage.

But what did they seek? Why?

Did the Illuminates know? The simple fact that those lordly beings had split over the destiny and use of a mere Nought argued otherwise.

Could the Noughts hold some crucial tidbit of the puzzle? Suddenly the notion did not seem entirely mad.

Quath reeled for the smallest fragment of an instant. Then the ageold lessons asserted themselves. She focused outward, beyond the raucous clamor of her subminds.

For the worst had come. Beq'qdahl's gang now moved to attack.

Quath had lain hidden among the broken strata above where the Noughts clustered. Their rear guard had already passed and their destination lay not far beyond.

Here the faults were like fracture planes snapped off in midair. Shelves of stone jutted at a platinum sky. Beq'qdahl and his podia had crept among these to within easy range of the Noughts, who milled in confusion.

Quath caught the ready signal from Beq'qdahl. They would wreak havoc. She had to give the Noughts time and warning.

<Hold!> Quath called. She let the signal scatter through the spectrum. Her Nought was sure to sense it.

Beq'qdahl jerked with surprise. <Quath!>

<Yes, traitor.>

<You have dogged us, hurt us!>

<You disobey the Tukar'ramin. There was a time when you would have rather bitten off half your legs.>

<There was a time when you were not a fool.>

<Oh, was there? Perhaps it was when I helped your vain self.>

Beq'qdahl was cautious, striving to conceal her anger. <Ambition is no sin.>

<Nor loyalty.>

<I follow the Illuminates!>

<*Some* Illuminates.>

<Stand clear of these animals while we do our work. Then we shall deal with you.>

<No, you'll deal *now*—>

Quath sent a hard, prickly burst toward Beq'qdahl's voice. It scattered among the walls of rock.

The battle began. Quath ran and dodged. She had chosen her position well. Her superior equipment enabled her to block most shots. She disabled three podia with quick, stuttering pulses. But her armaments were wearing thin.

Beq'qdahl was the key. The others would flee if their leader fell. Quath reached out with a cone-shaped aura and touched Beq'qdahl.

Now she saw into Beq'qdahl's true self. Her goals were simple. Lounging in burr-rich strands. Sucking down sweetbreads and plotting meanness, guilty only of casual malice and ignorance, stuffed with a bland assurance of self.

Beq'qdahl would have been no worse than this, but for the distant conflict of Illuminates. For such a minor, accidental matter, should she die?

Quath could not reason the question. Had her Philosoph genes left her alone, she knew, these vexing issues would not even arise. Gathering herself, she rushed forward.

The moment came when Beq'qdahl was exposed—and Quath could not fire.

She clambered instead over the last upturned layers of fractured strata and ran pell-mell into the milling band of firing, fleeing Noughts.

Cries, shrieks, bangs. They brushed against her like passing motes. Her superior shields were up and their bolts were no more than pesky itches.

Her Nought! There! Shedding opalescent waves of heat. Helping another Nought to its—no, *her*—feet.

But Beq'qdahl had now seen which was Quath's Nought. Quath could see Beq'qdahl carefully aiming for the small figure.

Still Quath could not fire. This was Beq'qdahl, strandsharer. Beq'qdahl . . .

The simmering presence of her Nought abruptly broke through Quath with rainsquall momentum. It—no, he—comprehended the quicksilver essence of the moment. He turned and picked Beq'qdahl out from the jumbled landscape.

Aimed. Fired.

And Beq'qdahl burst open. Flames leaped from the holed bulk of her.

Quath felt a jolt of sudden pain. She heard dismayed anguish leak from Beq'qdahl. It spattered through the spectrum.

Her friend and rival was dying. The projectile weapon of the Nought had breached her main compartment. Fragments lodged in Beq'qdahl's subminds. Unless Quath hastened to salvage what scraps she could, Beq'qdahl would dwindle, ebb, die.

Leaden remorse filled Quath. But she kept on.

Toward her Nought. Ignoring the stings and arrows of the harrying crowd around her.

Toward the appointment she had made with the whirl and gyre of gravity and time.

NINETEEN

Shibo fell before the first volley.

The Cybers opened up from the shattered ridgeline above. Their timing was perfect. His Supremacy's escort was still startled, confused, scrambling for cover.

Killeen had just started to get up when he felt the stinging bolt go by his leggings and saw it strike Shibo a glancing hit. She toppled forward from her knees. No visible damage on her suit. A tech-disabling shot, then. He grasped her shoulder and rolled her over.

"Close . . . that time," she gasped.

"Can you feel your legs?"

"Yeasay."

"Arms?"

"Yea . . . yeasay."

"Move 'em."

The pulse had knocked out most of her exskell. It heaved and jerked in a dying spasm. The riblike frame wheezed, purred, and went dead. Without it she had less strength than even the simplest augmentation of leggings and shocks gave. She would not get far if they had to run.

And it looked like they would. The Cybers were cutting up the escort guard.

"Can you walk?" he asked.

"Don't know. Head's li'l wobbly. Here—"

She got up onto one elbow and grunted with the effort of rising to her knees. A pulse ripped by with a loud *whoooom*.

Killeen started to help her further and into his mind came a sharp, pointed imperative. Something was narrowing down on his back. He felt it as a circle of compressed heat. It rasped against his sensorium.

He spun away. A bolt frayed the air where he had been.

For the first time in their long battle with the Cybers Killeen

335

had a sudden, sure knowledge of where the fire came from. His sensorium Dopplered back along the bolt path and found among the rocks a smudge of greasy fog.

He knew immediately that this was his enemy. Unbidden, he felt its raw immensity. It was a mind that came from a place of shining movements, from moist dark spaces, from velocities bleak and hard. All this sudden, crisp certainty came streaming from the gravid wedge that rode in the back of his mind.

He rolled to his left. The enemy probed for him through the thickening haze of electrodeception that flurried across the rugged slope. A blizzard of flickering images cycloned by. It swirled through the milling mob of humans as they scattered.

He fumbled for his last projectile weapon. Clicked it into place. Sighted carefully—

—and felt intruding a feathery streamer of sorrow and hesitation. Not his.

The somber emotion washed through him, stilling his hand. Reasonless, it spoke only of regret.

Killeen sucked in air to break free of the heavy, choking mood.

Shibo gasped nearby, "Leave me. Get clear. I'll be—"

He fired. The bolt hit just where he had known to aim.

Instantly the air cleared. The snow-squall of flitting electrodeceptions was gone.

Through a compacted instant Killeen felt a sad spike of longing. Again it came as a flowing, many-streamered emission, from the shadow-blue weight behind his mind.

He saw Besen was well sheltered downslope. Toby—

His son was firing carefully from slight cover nearby. Killeen called to him, "Fall back!" Toby came running.

"Come on," he grunted, hauling Shibo to her feet. She wobbled weakly.

Hissing bolts refracted through the nearby air. Splashes of infrared strobed running figures into flash pictures of desperation. Microwaves rattled.

And something else boomed down from the vault above.

He and Toby got Shibo down the steepest slope. They were making for the shelter of a dry wash when Killeen felt rather than heard the hammering sound of pursuit. A massive thing bore down on them. He barely had time to turn and glimpse the crusted, warty hide.

It loomed even larger this time. The barrel-chested trunk had a glazed ceramic cast. Great shanks of carbo-alum worked noisily to carry the thing forward. He could not clearly see the head. Encrusted antennae and projectors sprouted like gleaming weeds on the wrinkled, fertile hide. A shimmering protection enveloped it. It moved to block shots coming toward them.

Then it was upon them.

A hurtling jolt. Scrabbling haste. Many-ribbed fingers snatching at them.

They slammed into resilient webbing. Jostling shadows heaved them roughly. *Oh no,* Killeen thought. *Again.*

They were inside the Cyber. A cutting reek swarmed in his nostrils. Again he felt the mucous-moist compartment close about him. Shibo's grasp eased and she lay back into the foamy stuff. A blur of mad acceleration took them away.

Killeen saw that Shibo was bleeding. It hadn't been only a tech hit, then. He cursed himself.

Her eyelids fluttered and her system indices rolled meaninglessly, so her internals were damaged as well. He ignored the thumping progress of the Cyber and slapped a quick patch on her belly where the rich blood oozed forth.

"Toby! Got a stim bulb?"

"No . . . no, I—"

"Damn!" He had used his last on Besen.

"You . . . hang on. I'll get . . ." He could not finish because he had no idea what he could do.

Shibo heard him and turned. She could not speak. Fresh light broke across her dazed features.

Killeen turned to find that the entire wall of the Cyber's body had gone transparent.

The Cyber covered ground with lurching strides. They were already beyond the frantic running forms of the battle. It carried them jolting down the ridgeline. He saw Tribe members fire at the Cyber but the shots had no impact. The Cyber reached the tree line and plunged into the cloaking shelter.

Killeen saw now that the apparently glassy wall was in fact a projection, an image. He watched the forest shoot by. His sensorium still functioned, though it was fuzzed by errant stripes and flecks. He reached out—and felt something high and massive.

"Damn," he said, disbelieving.

"What?" Toby asked. He held on to the moist webbing that enclosed them.

"Something above us. In the air. The Cyber's 'fraid."

"Mech?" Toby braced himself against the fast, rocking pace.

The Cyber's many legs came slamming down in a strong, rippling cadence.

"Naysay—" Killeen's throat tightened, squeezing off his breath.

He could speak no more. Swelling anxiety reached him, punching through all insulation between his mind and the other's.

The Cyber was terrified of what it had to do next. Yet a sense of duty propelled the thing swiftly forward.

They suddenly swerved. The wall scene of rushing emerald veered upward. The trees' symmetrically spreading limbs criss-crossed the blue above like cabling. And in that deep blue a dark spot grew.

The great long stripe came down the sky like a plunging rod. Out of the west the slim shape swept, poking at them like an enormous pointing finger. Now they could see that the Skysower had the color of ancient wood. Along its length carbon-dark veins laminated the deep mahogany. Vines wriggled over the great stretched slabs that gleamed like polished teak.

All this Killeen took in in an instant as his Aspects cried out. Grey said:

> *It moves . . . around the equator . . . so comes down . . .*
> *different spot each time . . . sowing . . .*

Killeen felt the Cyber gathering itself around them. He held Shibo and whispered to Toby, "Lie down." He worked himself flat on the spongy cushion.

> *So large . . . a third of the planet's radius . . . although is*
> *spinning . . . looks to us . . . as though . . . it falls straight*
> *down . . . and lifts off . . . nearly vertically . . .*

Killeen caught the tightwound anxiety that permeated the Cyber, its struggle to quell an ageold terror. The conflict seemed like a babble of separate voices at cross-purposes. Ancient alarms rang and reasoned tones urged caution, while others adamantly urged the Cyber to do what it knew it must. A cacophony beset it.

No, not it—she. He intuitively sensed that the thing was female. Yes—but in a strange, dry, mechanical sense of the term.

He sent blunt encouragement to her. She faced a challenge, he knew.

Go, he sent. *Do it.*

And in the quick-swimming thoughts of the Cyber he felt its

victory over its own primordial fears. One solemn, clear voice towered above the mad crosstalk.

Her triumph over herself was announced by a throaty roar that burst under their compartment. Thrust pressed them deep into the folds of foam. The Cyber was flying.

The wall showed a swooping view of trees as great thick trunks rushed past. The Cyber rose through them on its flaring jets. In a moment they banked and soared across a broad leafy plain that was the top of the forest. Killeen looked down on the huge platter of the world below, scarred and stained and cut. The treetops were bare. Their thick branches curled over to form the familiar umbrella effect.

The view tilted again, veering around to peer upward. The stubby nub end of the Skysower came rushing toward them.

But no seeds popped forth. Instead, long ropy vines curled out. They descended with blurring speed.

Killeen watched one flash past the Cyber. It was close enough for him to glimpse smaller black strands that coiled helically around each other, like the strong ropes he had known in the Citadel.

Dozens of these tendrils shot toward the forest below. The Skysower's downward speed flung them into the treetops. Some snagged in the bare branches there. Along these a reflexive tension ran. They suddenly tightened.

Killeen watched great undulations ripple down the snagged vines. He sucked in his breath as he saw what was about to happen—and before he could breathe again it was done.

Each caught vine heaved upward. Simultaneously, alongside the Cyber, the Skysower's tip reached its lowest point. For a prolonged instant of popping strain the great broad nub hung in the air, drifting eastward. Then it began to rise with gathering momentum.

At this instant the whiplash effect sent a surge along the extended vines. They yanked the trees upward. Some upper branches split and gave way. But others held. With a sudden lurch the trees came free of the soil.

They shot up from the forest, trailing their root systems. As if shaking themselves free of their planet, the trees lashed at the end of their tethers, spraying clods of dirt. Retracting vines brought the trees into a herd below the Skysower's blunt end.

As this happened Killeen felt a solid *thunk*. The wall screen veered again. They were attached to the side of the Skysower. The Cyber's legs extended grapplers and clung to the surface.

Killeen could see bushes and shrubs nearby. The Cyber grabbed these tufts. It also quickly bored shafts into the knotty surface.

He felt immediately the reason why. The air in their cramped compartment seemed to gain a weight of its own, pressing them down. His Arthur Aspect said:

> You should be prepared for substantial acceleration. Grey calculates that we must endure over two normal gravities within a few more seconds.

A vast hand mashed Killeen into the floor. It grasped his chest and would not let him breathe. Toby lay pale and drawn on the other side of the compartment. "Shibo . . ." he got out, but no more. She lay still and white.

Time slowed to a plodding succession of painful heart thuds. Killeen's sensorium seemed filled with wet sand.

Hollow, drawn-out thumps and pops reverberated through the compartment. He tried to reach for Shibo's hand. Even with his motored right arm his fingers could not crawl across the slight space between them.

> This acceleration is partly gravity and partly centripetal. As we rise, the gravitational component lessens as the inverse square. The centripetal fraction, however, is constant and—

Killeen moved his lips soundlessly. "How . . . long . . ."

> I estimate from observation (not that Grey is any use in this—she is really quite spotty in her recollections) that the object touches down into the atmosphere roughly every twenty minutes. We should experience less than two gravities for one-quarter of this period, as we swing up. That will occur in about five minutes. However, we face a worse problem before that. In fact, the effects are becoming apparent.

Killeen's ears popped.

> We are leaving the atmosphere.

It was hopeless. His arms were leaden logs. He could not reach his helmet to twist the screw-seal. And he did not know if the rugged treatment of the last few days had kept the O-rings intact.

Wind whistled through the compartment.

The shrill sound came from hair-thin seams in the wall.

For a long moment as the immense hand continued to squeeze him, Killeen could think of nothing. Then he marshaled his thoughts and let a pointed, simple message sit solidly in the forefront of his mind.

A strumming answer came. Cloudy, diffuse, as if it issued from several throats at once. The Cyber's voice.

Yes. We will try.

Something slapped against the outside skin of the Cyber. A sticky blue glob oozed out along the seam lines. The whistling died. An acrid smoke rose from the blue fluid. Killeen knew it was some internal pap the Cyber used. It gave off a foul odor. He fought an impulse to cough and retch. But the seams held. The screech of escaping air died away.

The immense weight now lessened. Killeen could turn his head a fraction and see the screen wall.

Outside, the Skysower stretched up into blueblack emptiness. He was looking along the great chestnut-colored length of it. Shrubs nearby were flattened against the rough bark. The wind's high howl tore fruitlessly at them.

Skysower was a great cable stretching into the steadily darkening sky. Ebony laminations reached along it. Ash-blond segments like cross-struts connected these into a grid. They hugged the woody curve of the bark and the fierce gale could find no edge to pry them up.

The solid, implacable roar made their compartment vibrate like a living thing. Its hammering ferocity rose. Killeen wondered how long even the Cyber's strength could hold it moored there.

Suddenly the noise muted as though someone had thrown a switch.

We are exceeding the speed of sound, I believe.

Along the towering length Killeen saw thin hickory-colored edges rise. They were like ailerons, sculpting the air. Long, strumming notes came through to Killeen.

It appears to be guiding itself like a giant flying wing. Net acceleration is lessening as we rise into the upper atmosphere. The structure is relaxing.

Pops and creaks rang out.

"I . . . what's . . ." Toby got out between clenched teeth.

"Hold on."

"Besen . . ."

"She's quick." Killeen tried to fill his voice with reassurance. "She'll get away from that fight."

Shibo's wound was worse. He tightened her bandage but working against the heavy acceleration made him clumsy. The systems damage worried him most. He wished he could tell Toby something to relieve the anxiety he read in the boy's face. He had no idea where they were going.

If the Cyber can cling to this for another fifteen minutes we may be able to leap off. Then we will be one-sixth of the way around the planet's equator and quite beyond the dangers of the other Cybers.

"Yeasay," Killeen managed to say. "And we'll slam into the ground."

True, our total acceleration downward will be considerable, about 2.4 gravities. But at the optimum moment, as the tip hovers over the surface, we can in principle simply step off, with only a net sidewise velocity. Then perhaps the Cyber can fly us to safety.

Such theoretical events seemed far away compared with the cycling of Shibo's indices. Her face was untroubled and chalk white.

Outside, the last haze of blue faded into hard black. Nearby stars bit brightly at his eyes. Molecular clouds gave their gauzy wash to the vault.

Killeen's thoughts came like thick syrup. The immense hand that pressed him to the floor had eased for a while. Now it leaned harder. His chest ached with the effort of breathing. He wondered distantly how long their air in the cramped compartment would last.

We shall be in high vacuum for about eight minutes more. I believe you can survive easily.

But Arthur did not feel the gathering ache that spread from his chest and into his arms and legs. Much more of this and Shibo would lose consciousness—which might not be a bad idea, except that Killeen did not know what they would have to do to survive. If the Cyber failed . . .

He could no longer afford the luxury of speculation. Living was labor enough. He turned his attention to the increasing effort of forcing breath into his lungs. His heart thudded in slow, tortured beats.

He grasped with leaden fingers for Shibo. A slight labored heave told him she still breathed.

Sluggishly he formulated a question and displayed it across his fevered and frayed consciousness.

We are Quath'jutt'kkal'thon. We carried you before.

"What . . . happens . . ."

We must cautiously adjust our dynamics.

Killeen could not understand. As he watched, the ivory curve of the planet rolled up in the wall screen. Farther away the cosmic string hung unmoving, a dull amber arc.

He felt the Cyber sway and rock in slow undulations. He could see great long swells racing toward them from the center of the Skysower. Waves excited by the air turbulence. As they reflected at the tip they gave it a sharp snap, like a whip cracking. The Cyber held on grimly.

Vibrations had moved his hand away from Shibo. He rolled to look at her and pain lanced into his shoulder. Her eyelids were sunken. He could not tell if she was still alive.

As they rose farther above the planet the whole disk became visible. Repeated sucking of the core metal had smashed the outlines of mountain ranges. Rivers now cut fresh paths. Lakes had spilled into new muddy reservoirs, leaving enormous bare brown plains.

He could see all of Skysower now. It curved like a slender snake that smoothly turned head over tail. The far end was just piercing the atmosphere. Undulations ran like waves in a long string, driven by the supersonic collision of this gargantuan living being with its blanket of air.

As he watched he slowly realized that some of the thicker vines nearby were throbbing. Bulges in them contracted rhythmically. It came to him that Skysower had to circulate its fluids, like any living thing. These coarse, chestnut-brown tubes were like vegetable hearts, working against the eternal outward thrust that came from Skysower's spin. Somewhere beneath the grainy bark something like muscles must be sliding and clenching, to righten displacements and masses and maintain the even turning of the huge whirling organism.

Suddenly, at the edge of his vision, he saw plumes of gas burst forth at the nearby teak-colored horizon. Luminous geysers caught the sun's rays. From the Cyber he caught a thread of understanding. To keep itself rotating, this huge thing breathed in air during its passage. Then it exhaled, perhaps burning the gases in some fashion to gain added thrust. This paid back the momentum stolen by the atmosphere's supersonic turbulence.

All this came to him as he fought the sure rise of pressure against his chest. He thought distantly now, barely able to hold on to consciousness against the worsening weight.

Then something rushed by them and caught his attention. A second tubular shape passed nearby and he saw that hot yellow balls burned at regular intervals along its length. He remembered the forest fire. These were the trees that the vines had snagged from the forest below.

Against blurring pressure he still managed to feel surprise. The forests of umbrella-topped trees—they must have grown from the Skysower's own seeds. Snatched up on the harvesting vines, they had now been carried aloft. Some deep biochemical command had activated their stores of fuel. Far from being a mech energy resource, as Killeen had guessed, these trees were now expending their stored chemical energy to launch themselves away from their mother plant.

Another tree shot past. Yellow plumes pushed it to high velocity. It hurtled after its fellows, which were already shrinking logs.

> After conferring with Grey (not an easy business, I assure you) I calculate that our speed exceeds thirteen kilometers per second. In your terms—

"Skip the techtalk," Killeen muttered. "What's it *mean?*"

> This creature—and I do not necessarily agree that it is simply a plant, given its many animallike functions, including an active circulation system—is spreading its progeny. They leave it here, at the top of its arc, with maximal velocity. They can easily reach the outer precincts of this solar system. From there they can drift to other stars. Seeding, pure and simple.

Killeen stared at Shibo and thought fruitlessly, rummaging for some way to repair her systems' failure. She grew whiter.

I am repeating the speculations of the Grey woman, of course. I have done the calculations and what she proposes is marginally within possibility.

"So . . . so in every one of those trees there's a seed for another Skysower?"

Killeen could barely breathe. He watched the trees jet away on their columns of flame. To swim the sea of stars. To grow into more Skysowers. Life persistent and undeniable. They hung within view over the still body of Shibo.

His bones seemed to stretch. He grasped for Shibo and could not reach her. Distant bass notes came strumming through the Cyber's body as waves made the woody surface thrash and twist.

Suddenly the Cyber freed its hold on the bark. All of its visible legs withdrew their steel grapplers and instead pushed against the brown surface. Instantly the oppressive weight lifted. Killeen floated in complete freedom.

"Are you—" He hugged Shibo. Did her eyes flutter?

In complete silence the Cyber rose away from Skysower's slim silhouette. The turning ribbon now pointed straight down into the wounded planet.

They shot out along a tangent to Skysower's whirling arc. Soon it had rotated below them. It was again a thin line cutting across the face of the ruined world.

We are properly pointed, the strangely liquid thoughts of the Cyber came. *My sisters have stilled the Cosmic Circle so it presents no obstacle. We are entering a rendezvous orbit.*

"Where?"

Close to the station. Your vessel lies there. There is a task awaiting your kind.

"Hurry! There're medical supplies on *Argo*—"

Killeen peered ahead and saw a glimmering that beckoned and promised.

But Shibo died long before they could reach it.

EPILOG

SAILING WITH THE TIDE

The Cap'n walked the hull again.

A long time seemed to have passed since he last was here. Only a few weeks, he knew. But time was not truly measured by the ticking of unseen arbiters. It made its lasting marks in the soul.

In that distant time he had watched the approach of the station, wondering what forces marshaled there. Problems of command had vexed him. He had fretted over whether to assault the huge, silvery construction. He could see the station now, too—a platinum-hard dab of light swimming near the brown crescent of New Bishop.

The name mocked him. The Bishops had found the same age-old trials here. This place had meant more struggle, not a peaceful destination. And losses. Huge, bitter losses.

"Shibo," he said. "Is this link working?"

The light voice came hesitantly. —I, I, yeasay.—

"Toby?"

—I'm here, Dad.—

Yes, Killeen thought, *we're all here. Together in the only way possible now.*

Toby lay in the control vault with complex apparatus enclosing his head. Close comm link brought his voice to Killeen. And Shibo . . . she was only an Aspect of Toby's now.

"You sure this won't do you harm?" Killeen asked.

—No, Dad. I trust her techcraft.—

Through Toby, Shibo had engineered this union. Normally an Aspect could never speak through its host. The term for that was "Aspect storm" and Family would take immediate measures to pull the offending Aspect chips from the host's neck.

347

But this was different. Killeen was tapped directly into Toby's sense of Shibo. The intricate meshing was Shibo's invention and, used cautiously, might extend the Family's abilities. She had modified techniques known to Family Pawn, she said. There had been no call for such a trick before, one that verged on Family taboos.

Now it was pure necessity. Only Shibo's deft command of *Argo* could save them.

"Any better fix on that Cyber ship?"

Shibo's wispy Aspect voice replied, —It has executed another dodging maneuver.—

"Damn! What's Quath say?"

Toby answered, —She's calibratin' somethin'. You want, I can tap her in here.—

"Naysay, let her work. Her last estimate said we still got a few minutes before they start firin'."

—*Argo* is ready,— Shibo sent reassuringly.

He still had trouble getting used to her voice. It was a fully incorporating Aspect and gave every appearance of a complete operating personality. He and Toby had managed to get Shibo's body into the recording room of *Argo* before there was significant damage from oxygen loss. The machines had spoken of potassium balances and digital matching matrices but it had all taken place someplace far from him, under glass.

He knew from sad experience that some people survived grotesquely bloody wounds while others seemed to die of a scratch. That had not helped when Shibo had slipped away from them, her systems simply tapering to zero.

Toby had taken the Aspect, of course. Not simply because Family rules were firmly against carrying a dead lover; that was inviting disaster. No, the overpowering reason had been that Killeen was too shaken to accept Shibo's Aspect. He had recovered only when her voice spoke to him through Toby. She had chided him and somehow dragged him back into the world. He had clung to her voice.

But it was only a voice. He would never see her again, never touch her silky skin, see the glinting mirth in her eyes—

He made himself stop. It was pointless. Stupid.

Killeen had told himself this a hundred times through the last few days. His emotions were held in check only by the necessity of command. Chaos would not wait for his grief to abate.

He looked back at the crescent of New Bishop. Explosions still flickered there on the nightside. Cyber conflict still raged. Quath's allies seemed to have the upper hand now, though.

The Family had been fortunate to take only a few dozen casualties there. Only because humans mattered so little had they been able to slip away.

Cermo and Jocelyn had been resourceful and brave in getting the Family off the planet. In the chaos that followed His Supremacy's death, they had held the Family together and slipped away from the Tribe.

The revelation that His Supremacy was a mech interloper had been enough to shatter the Tribal organization. The remaining Cybers had inflicted more casualties, but they, too, had seemed leaderless.

Jocelyn's dash and Cermo's confidence in the face of what seemed utter disaster had extracted Family Bishop with deft timing. Killeen knew well the difficulties of such a maneuver, the most intricate of all tactical feats. He had decorated both officers.

None of their work on the ground would have meant anything without Quath's help, of course. She had steered the sleek Flitter craft down to the surface, understanding that the Family had to be kept intact.

In the warfare between Cybers a mere band of fleeing humans was now irrelevant. The Flitters had managed to get off again with the Family aboard. No one fired at them.

Some members of the Tribe had rushed toward the shuttles when they saw the landings. They had gathered at the Bishop perimeter and begged to go, too.

Killeen had been adamant. He could not trust anyone from a Tribe already infiltrated by mech-ridden humans. They had taken most of Family Seben and some other ragtag elements of the Tribe. But once aboard, each was carefully inspected. Three proved to have mech inlay riders in their skulls.

They were killed. The decision had been a bitter one, but he had to make it. For a while he tortured himself with the admission that the decision was easier since he had not done the killing himself. But Jocelyn and Cermo had carried out his wishes without hesitation. In many ways, he reflected, they were tougher than he could ever be.

We have word which may reconcile you to the outcome, came Quath's diffuse message.

The bulky alien was inside the ship, but that did not impede communication between them. Killeen still did not know how this was done and expected he never would.

The alien did not speak in clear sentences. Killeen had to frame the filmy impressions he received into something resembling words before he could fully comprehend. It was like groping through a fog while fitful chill breezes struck you in the face. Each touch brought new comprehension. Equally, each brush left unanswerable questions in its wake. And the mist remained.

Killeen could not follow Quath's meaning. "How so?"

The Tukar'ramin now prevails in her struggle. Remnant elements flee. The Illuminates of good spirit shall emerge triumphant.

Much of this gave Killeen only a diffuse sense of the vast events playing out around New Bishop. He knew now, after only days of direct communication with Quath, that he would never fathom all the alien tried to convey. Much of Quath's explanations were unintelligible. The Illuminates were superior intelligences, apparently, but not above resolving disagreement by force. Killeen's task was to see that their conflicts did not casually and unthinkingly destroy his Family.

"How's that affect us?"

The Tukar'ramin will guarantee that those of your kind left behind shall be allowed to live.

Killeen sent Quath several questions before he was sure this was what the alien meant. When he finally believed it a weight rose from him. While Family Bishop owed the Tribe a debt for taking them in, that had been canceled by His Supremacy's betrayal. Still, he was glad that the vestiges of humanity left behind could survive.

"Send my thanks," Killeen said. The words were inadequate but he knew that Quath sensed his true feelings and would convey them to whatever the Tukar'ramin was.

Hope rose in him. "Does this mean whatever's followin' us'll stop?"

This time the answer was clear:

No. The renegade elements launched this attack ship after us as one of their final measures. It cannot be recalled. When it comes within range it will fire.

"You can deflect whatever it's got?"

Once, perhaps twice. Not for long.

Quath's answer came laced with somber forebodings. The alien hoped and feared, but other emotions which Killeen could not name flowed beneath the surface. They seemed more like quick bursts of separate lives, fragments of possibility. He was never sure which facet of Quath he spoke to. Sometimes the alien was extraordinarily patient. Other times he felt as though he were talking to a harried servant while the master of the house was preoccupied elsewhere.

But at least the alien's nature might slowly unfold. Other riddles would never be answered. Killeen amped his opticals and could just barely make out the rim of New Bishop. The Cyber warrens were huge now, a belt circling far out from the planet. Could such massive mazes truly clasp and tame the energy of a whole sun? The task seemed daunting even for creatures who could suck to cores from worlds.

A still deeper puzzle spun at the rim of New Bishop. Slow movement told him that Skysower churned on. More shadowy mystery.

He would never know if that entity was a natural consequence of life or an engineering construct made by beings of ancient and daunting ability. He could scarcely believe that it carried out such massive purpose while obeying the timeless commands of embedded chemistry and genetics. Such complexity seemed impossible without intelligence. Yet Killeen had to admit that he knew nothing of events on this scale. As a lower-order intelligence, he was surely no good judge of limits.

—That Cyber ship's fired somethin' at us,— Shibo's clipped voice came to him.

Killeen called, "Range and time?"

—Can't tell. Closing fast.— Her voice still sent a pang through him.

"What's . . . what's it doing?"

—More dodging, looks like.— The Shibo Aspect was crisp and efficient. He had to remember that she had not truly suffered her own death and its aftermath. This Shibo was the woman who last remembered being scooped up by Quath. She would be that person eternally.

"Crew ready at locks?" he asked.

—Yessir,— Jocelyn answered. —Suited up.—

"Check the seals again."

—Done that already.—

"I said *again*."

Jocelyn had been subdued since she and Cermo returned to *Argo*. Her leadership during the Family's escape from the Tribe had partly repaired the antagonism between her and Killeen.

Once aboard *Argo* she had mutely accepted Killeen as Cap'n, never asserting herself. Still, Killeen knew that Jocelyn's ambition had been damped but not destroyed.

A pause. "How's it going?" he prompted.

—Uh, we found a small problem.—

"What?" he demanded impatiently.

—Seal is broken. We're patching it again.—

The chagrined note in Jocelyn's voice gave Killeen a small, pleasurable smile. He had made all crew that could be spared from crucial ship operations work incessantly on the sewage-soaked corridors. The elements of Family Seben and other Tribal remnants had been rebellious, but he had sternly broken their resistance.

Someone had to do the job, after all. Quath had blundered through *Argo* while it was abandoned. She had found the Legacies but in the process had opened the deck where the plumbing had malfed. Now the mess covered three decks. They had sealed off the offending zone, using vacuum-worthy sealants.

The irksome task had consumed much labor which might have gone into erecting defenses . . . though it was unlikely that any puny human weapons would count much in the coming encounter. *Argo* had nothing beyond simple shields.

The approaching Cyber missiles might be fooled by Quath at first, but she was sure they were intelligent weapons. That meant each incoming missile learned from observing the one before it. If Quath failed . . .

Killeen tried to catch a glimpse of the approaching enemy. "Shibo! Let me have the grid."

Her quick response sent a crosshatched picture into his left eye. Three winking red dots trailed *Argo*, swelling visibly.

Killeen went back to normal sight. He had chosen to meet their fate while out here, where he could see and judge with his own eyes. Electronic helpers were all very fine, but some sense of human dignity demanded that he use his own capabilities now. A Cap'n should judge from his own experience.

And being outside might be safer if things went badly. He had officers posted at each lock to evacuate crew in pressure suits if *Argo*'s hull split. How they could survive for long without a functioning ship Killeen could not imagine, but at least such preparations gave them all something to do before the battle. Anything was better for the crew than agonized waiting.

Which was, he reminded himself, just what he was doing. He

stopped fretting and walked along the gently curving hull. *Argo* was headed out from the waning sun. Its lessened light made the ivory washes of molecular clouds seem nearby. They bore now toward the seething disk of the Eater itself.

—They're coming fast,— Shibo sent.

"Quath?"

We are acting.

Killeen held his breath. Suddenly the leading missile veered to the side. It wobbled and then streaked away.

We have deceived the first.

As Quath spoke, the missile burst silently into a crimson ball.

"Shibo?"

—Our shields are stopping the UV pulses.—

"Good."

But those were trivial threats. The main purpose of the missiles was simple: to crack *Argo's* hull.

The two remaining missiles had swollen to red disks in Shibo's grid.

We are tumbling the second.

One of the disks bobbed randomly. Killeen watched it explode into another soundless crimson globe.

We attempt the third.

"Are there others behind these?"

Not yet.

Then there was still a chance.

We are . . . difficulty . . . difficulty . . .

For the first time Quath's tone was streaked with warring impressions. Killeen had the sensation of watching multiple minds clamor and struggle to a single purpose. Before he could comprehend this he felt a heavy, drumroll urgency.

We . . . fail.

Death grew behind them. Killeen could see the sleek form now.

"Quath! Isn't there—"

No. It resists my deceptions.

Killeen stared at the rapidly growing dot. In the sharp clarity of vacuum he felt as though he could almost reach out and slap it away. Or throw something at it. In space even insubstantial things could—

The idea was so simple it startled him.

"Jocelyn! Cermo!"

—Yeasay!—

"Release! Open the locks!"

—Yessir!— they answered together.

Clouds spurted from three openings in *Argo*'s hull. On signal the maintenance locks had popped open in the polluted zone of the ship. Now the air rushed out, carrying foul fluids with it. Anything left within quickly boiled away into hard vacuum.

Sunlight caught the expanding clouds. Suddenly they became huge, spreading foils. Billowing yellow wings seemed to twist and fan, as though *Argo* glided forward by beating against utter vacuum. Expanding gossamer veils trailed behind as the ship steadily accelerated away.

Killeen stood uphull from the locks and so was spared the spray. For long moments the fluids burst into sunlight. Gusts came forth. Each added more radiance to the fluttering wake.

"Shibo! Side vector!"

Argo lurched. Shibo had fired the jets on one side. The ship coasted sidewise.

Now Killeen could not see the approaching enemy. The luminous fog obscured everything. He hoped that the missile saw the same wreathed confusion.

"Quath?"

Approaching hard. Accelerating.

"Fire main engine!"

To stay on the hull Killeen had to catch himself against a pipe. *Argo* accelerated strongly.

Glory burst behind them. The plasma drive struck the wake cloud. The agitated ions immediately provoked answering radiation from the gas. Like a searchlight playing through clotted fog, the exhaust brilliantly lit a huge irregular blob of mist.

Killeen held on against the rising thrust. He had done all he could. Now—

A fireball flared nearby. It lit the billowing fog further, casting shock waves of luminescence.

"Missed!" he cried.

—Hot damn!— Cermo shouted.

Shibo laughed. Her tinkling voice rang in his ears.

—Let 'em eat shit!— Cermo yelled.

"And so they have," Killeen said grimly. "Shibo?"

—No damage reports.—

"It went off where it thought we were. Couldn't find its way through all our crap."

Laughter pealed through the comm. Killeen could not help himself; he joined in.

"Quath?"

We detect no further missiles. Perhaps this deception of yours has worked. The radiant cloud is emitting signature frequencies typical of heated organic compounds.

"No surprise," Killeen said. "That's what it is."

However, the pursuing vessel will interpret such emissions as evidence of a ruptured hull. A clever ruse.

"Think they'll break off followin' us?"

It seems so.

"You sure these are the last enemy Cybers?"

We have been assured by the Tukar'ramin. Our victory is now complete. The rightful Illuminates now prevail.

"Damn glad to hear it." Killeen was still rankled to think that his Family had gone through so much because of a factional dispute among distant beings he would never know.

He let the spike of irritation pass. It was irrational to harbor resentments against beings whose motivations and meanings were so alien. He thought he caught glimpses of Quath, but he was sure the deeper essence eluded him. Who could have guessed, for example, that the Legacies aboard *Argo* would mean something to a Cyber—when simple spoken sentences often did not? The Illuminates had commanded that they be ferried up from New Bishop and returned to *Argo*. That had been done just as *Argo* cast off from the station. Cyber craft had tried to destroy the Flitter carrying the Legacies and the Illuminates had expended ship after ship defending it.

Why?

Killeen shook his head.

Standing beneath the roiling sky of incandescent majesty soothed his spirits. He walked the hull as their radiant wake dispersed. A few more moments out here would settle him and make the coming tasks of Cap'ncy easier.

Raucous laughter streamed through the comm. Let them celebrate. The Family needed some release. And they would still have to watch the pursuing craft carefully.

He allowed himself a grin. Maybe, just maybe, they were going to escape.

To what? He looked ahead at the yawning bluehot majesty of the disk that surrounded the Eater. It was a long voyage away. They would have to prepare for whatever lurked there.

The Family . . . So much had changed since Fanny had led a
scrap of Bishops away from Abraham's wrecked Citadel, into
Snowglade's bleakness. That remnant had joined with dregs of
Knights and Rooks. They had slipped free of their world and had
seen it as a speck in an ocean of night.

Now, here, the Family had been seared again . . . only to
cleave anew with new members who brought their own scarred
heritage. A new whole. A greater sum, perhaps.

He turned and walked back along the hull, boots thumping
down on magnetic anchors. The slowly expanding cloud thinned
and let in a little light. He could just make out the small golden
circle that lay far behind. It was more distant than the enemy, but
Quath said it was accelerating strongly. It would catch up with
Argo soon.

Killeen tried to imagine what vessels could transport the enormous mass of the cosmic string. Well, he would see. All in good
time.

That great scythe would follow them toward the Eater, Quath
said. So the Illuminates had decreed. They had stopped the
gutting of a world to send the ring along with *Argo*. Halted the
building of their gray warrens. Interrupted the labors of millions of
Cybers. For what, no one yet knew.

And after? There was still the enigma of the electromagnetic
being. Somewhere ahead it lurked, tied to the disk of the Eater.

His brushing contact with that mind, back on New Bishop, had
implied much while explaining nothing. It had spoken of his
father. Maybe Killeen had tempted fate by naming the star that
waned behind them for Abraham. But perhaps Abraham was a key
to all this. Yet how could his father, lost at the fall of the Citadel,
figure in the deliberations of a tenuous magnetic mind? Could
such a being revive those long dead?

His Grey Aspect droned for attention. Her voice came slowly,
as though working across the abyss of time that separated Killeen
from the High Arcology Era.

> *There were records . . . I once saw . . . incomplete . . .*
> *from a time long gone . . . Some said . . . before the*
> *Chandeliers . . . before even the First Comers . . . from . . .*
> *a culture of legendary origin . . . called Earth. That too was*
> *a time . . . when men lived . . . beneath the will . . . of*
> *beings vaster. Gods moved the heavens . . . determined . . .*
> *fate of men . . . and beasts . . . In those times . . . humanity*
> *scratched out its destiny . . . in soil . . . under tortured*

*skies . . . where huge things . . . in comfort . . . dwelled.
Some thought these superior beings . . . were gods. Yet
men lived lives of meaning still . . . despite their small
stature . . . in the scheme of things. So do not despair . . .
Humanity has found zest and verve . . . before . . . in the
shadows of vastness . . . in a place called Greece.*

Killeen nodded. So even this was not new. Humanity's most
heartfelt joys and crushing defeats had been mere sideshows,
small dramas acted out at the feet of greater entities.

It did not matter whether one termed these forces gods or the
products of further evolution. Enormity defied definitions. Skysower
was a living thing, but Killeen could not tell whether it even
thought. Perhaps the distinction itself did not make sense at that
level of grandeur.

He looked up into the colossal sky. Fingers of knotted fire
worked in molecular clouds. Storms frayed against the stars. Tides
of light ebbed and flowed with ponderous majesty. Amid it all,
Argo sailed on, a mote.

"Shibo," he whispered. "I love you."

It seemed as though the words were new, and that he said
them for the first time.

Chronology of Human Species
(Dreaming Vertebrates)
at Galactic Center

This summary was prepared at your request, in order to make intelligible the human point of view. I must confess that this is fundamentally impossible even to anthology-class minds such as myself, and probably to any entity which does not arise from an initial organic base. However, as much as is possible I shall take the cramped human version of their own history, however distorted or inadequate this may be.

These matters were of no concern to us until the strange events at the collapse of Citadel Bishop (see appendix 1). Some effort to understand that engagement led to my involvement with the humans who escaped our extermination.

I have made use of these survivors. They recently departed on an aged vessel of earlier human construction. They will arrive at World #1936B. The destructive intercity competition there may be muted by their efforts. I have arranged that they be met by our representatives, assuming the situation there has not deteriorated further by the time of their arrival.

However, as discussed in appendix 2, other purposes are served by their leaving Snowglade and going to World #1936B at this time. While these humans know nothing of the larger context, they may have methods of yielding further information of use to us. In light of our ignorance of these beings, higher entities have decided to allow their continued survival so long as they pose no serious irritant.

[Note: This entry is abstracted from larger files. Times refer to flat space-time measurements, though some important events have occurred in the curved geometries of pulsar magnetospheres and the black hole vicinity. Notes on one particular human refuge, planet Snowglade, are included.]

Existing manuscripts and datalogs allow some preliminary description of events leading up to the current epoch. The historical

scheme of humanity falls into periods which reflect stages in the
steady decline of humans at Galactic Center. Human terms are
used throughout, even where they are misleading or inadequate.

THE GREAT TIMES

This is a dimly remembered age spanning several thousand years.
Humans moved freely between the close-packed stars of the Center. Even then they had to stay out of the way of mech civilization.

Human legend holds that they arrived at Galactic Center in
several waves.

First was a small band which had captured a mech near-light
starship. Apparently they went undetected for a while because of
their conventional craft. This allowed stealthy investigation of
mech ways and purposes. By observing mech civilization and
learning from it, humans attained a level of ability rare among
organic forms. They apparently also formed alliances with other
organic forms nearby, though nothing is known of these.

The development of large pulsar configurations had begun
shortly before this time and occupied much mech energy. Creation of large electron-positron clouds contributed to the already
considerable gamma-ray background near pulsars. These gamma
rays heated molecular clouds and prevented human incursions
into several regions. The few remaining records suggest that the
first human expedition set about several pursuits involving organic
civilizations which lived near the Center. However, these humans
then vanished.

The second wave of exploration came directly from Earth. An
entire fleet of ramscoop vessels was launched within a century
after the mech-sponsored warfare, which had introduced alien sea
life into Earth's oceans.

Third came a larger expedition which sought the fabled Galactic Library which beacons had promised. Earth lies 8.63 kilopar-
secs from Galactic Center (see appendix 3 for Universal Standard
comparisons). This implies that the ramscoop vessels had begun
their voyage in an age when the Library was still announcing
itself. Well before their arrival the Library had disappeared, spir-
ited away by unknown parties. Efforts to find it failed. The Library apparently contained the records of many extinct organic
races. Searches for it tapered off when mechs finally took notice of
these intruders and set about opposing them.

THE CHANDELIER AGE

Here humans gathered into large cities in space for protection. Surviving logs from starfaring vessels show that mechs had begun to make interstellar travel dangerous. Also, radiation increased in the zone around the black hole at Absolute Center (sometimes "True Center"). This made conditions harder for organic forms everywhere nearby.

Scholars of this time studied the earliest humans known at Galactic Center and much of our knowledge of earlier ages descends from the detailed searches made then. Much art and literature survives from the centuries marking the transition into the Chandeliers, though most of this is abstract and useless for historical purposes.

HIGH ARCOLOGY ERA

This came after the "Hunker Down" (slang)—the exodus from the Chandeliers to planetary surfaces. Mech competition drove this desperate retreat. On most worlds, in the need for security humankind was forced into huge Arcologies, single-building cities which were still technically advanced and retained many facets of Chandelier life.

Planet Snowglade was a particularly fertile site and received extensive colonizing. Assignment of territories was made by Family structure, as elsewhere. The trauma of the "Hunker Down" drove religious fervor. This is best considered as a form of human art (appendix 4), though much must be interpolated here to render this mode of expression into rational terms.

LATE ARCOLOGY ERA

The last small Chandeliers and freighting ships were abandoned at the opening of this time. All starflight ceased. Even interplanetary travel and harvesting of resources became difficult because of the mechs. Moist, plant-bearing planets were previously thought to be uninteresting to the mechs. Even these now came under threat. Since such worlds were where the Arcologies flourished best, humanity was further circumscribed.

HIGH CITADEL AGE

The Arcologies became untenable under further mech pressure. Breakup of the mountain-sized Arcologies followed, primarily because of difficulties in maintaining the high techcraft. Many retreated into the less conspicuous Citadels.

Mech depredations were steady, but most damage was done by side effects of the expanding mech cities, which consumed resources and altered the biosphere. Many Arcologies were mined for materials and ores. Citadels the size of small towns survived. Mechs began to spread over most of Snowglade at this time, spurring climate-changing processes.

Many human-carried Aspects date from this time, apparently because the breakdown of the human infrastructure threatened the human database held in fixed computing sites. New skills arose as humanity began to supplement its dwindling agriculture with hunter-gatherer techniques and especially raids on mech storehouses. Humans began to lose their own technology and concentrated on reworking mechtech. No longer potential rivals, they became pests scratching at the edges.

THE CALAMITY (ON SNOWGLADE)

This opened the final chapter in the conquest of Snowglade. Though Family Citadels had been tolerated for some time, and humans had been used occasionally as pawns in mech intercity rivalry, their usefulness was marginal. Each Citadel was attacked in turn as mech resources allowed. Each Citadel of the human Families fell separately, banishing their survivors to the raw countryside.

It had become apparent by this time that Snowglade's star, Denix, was following an orbit designed to bring it close to the black hole region. Mech activities had brought this about through electrodynamic coupling to molecular clouds, using a magnetic grappling effect to convey momentum. This means that Snowglade will inevitably become uninhabitable by organic lifeforms. This orbit change appears to be unknown to humans. Generally their scholarly speculation concentrates upon the large scale activity at True Center.

Some humans still survive on Snowglade. The complex events

surrounding the Calamity at Citadel Bishop suggest that some humans should be kept intact in case they are somehow important to the events of that day. It is apparent that none of the principals, mech or human, understands more than a fraction of the continuing puzzle.

This report is most respectfully submitted. Appendices to follow.